THE VISUAL BRAIN IN ACTION

Second edition

OXFORD PSYCHOLOGY SERIES
Editors

Mark D'Esposito   Daniel Schacter
Jon Driver   Anne Treisman
Trevor Robbins   Lawrence Weiskrantz

The Visual Brain in Action

Second edition

A. David Milner
Professor of Cognitive Neuroscience,
University of Durham, UK

Melvyn A. Goodale
Canada Research Chair in Visual Neuroscience,
University of Western Ontario, Canada

OXFORD
UNIVERSITY PRESS

OXFORD
UNIVERSITY PRESS

Great Clarendon Street, Oxford OX2 6DP

Oxford University Press is a department of the University of Oxford.
It furthers the University's objective of excellence in research, scholarship,
and education by publishing worldwide in

Oxford New York

Auckland Cape Town Dar es Salaam Hong Kong Karachi
Kuala Lumpur Madrid Melbourne Mexico City Nairobi
New Delhi Shanghai Taipei Toronto

With offices in

Argentina Austria Brazil Chile Czech Republic France Greece
Guatemala Hungary Italy Japan Poland Portugal Singapore
South Korea Switzerland Thailand Turkey Ukraine Vietnam

Oxford is a registered trade mark of Oxford University Press
in the UK and in certain other countries

Published in the United States
by Oxford University Press Inc., New York

British Library Cataloguing in Publication Data

Data available

Library of Congress Cataloging in Publication Data

Milner, A. D. (A. David)
The Visual brain in action / A. David Milner, Melvyn A. Goodale.
  2nd ed. p. ; cm.   (Oxford psychology series; no 43)
Includes bibliographical references and index.
ISBN-13: 978–0–19–852472–4 (alk. paper)
ISBN-10: 0–19–852472–2 (alk. paper)
1. Visual cortex.   2. Visual pathways—Evolution.   I. Goodale Melvyn A.
II. Title.   III. Series.
[DNLM: 1. Visual Cortex.   2. Visual Pathways.   3. Visual Perception.
WL 307 M659v 2006]
QP383.15.M55 2006
612.8′255—dc22   2006022998

Typeset by Newgen Imaging Systems (P) Ltd., Chennai, India
Printed in Britain
on acid-free paper by
Biddles Ltd., King's Lynn, Norfolk

ISBN 10: 0–19–852472–2 (Pb)   0–19–852473–0 (HB)
ISBN 13: 978–0–19–852472–4 (Pb)   978–0–19–852473–1 (HB)

10 9 8 7 6 5 4 3 2 1

To Christine and Joan

The great end of life is not knowledge but action
T.H. Huxley, 1825–1895; from A Technical Education, 1877.

Preface to the Second Edition

Twelve years have passed since we wrote the first edition of *The Visual Brain in Action*. In the book, we put forward a model for an understanding of visual processing for perception and action that has provoked considerable interest and debate. In this new edition, we have made a deliberate decision not to change the body of the text, which we believe still stands as a coherent statement of our position. Instead, we have added an Epilogue at the end of the book, in which we review some of the key developments that support or challenge the views that we put forward in the first edition.

Research on the neural substrates of vision and visuomotor control continues to expand, although the methodologies have changed considerably. The biggest single area of development has been that of functional neuroimaging, allowing investigators for the first time to plot the patterns of activity within the brains of behaving and thinking humans. When we were writing the first edition of the book, in 1994, there were only a small number of relevant neuroimaging studies. These studies, several of which we cited, made use of positron emission tomography (PET) technology. Only a small number of laboratories were able to exploit this kind of methodology, and its limitations, including health risks and expense, have meant that it has never been very widely used. Functional magnetic resonance imaging (fMRI) was virtually unknown when we wrote the book, but has now left PET well behind in the number of published studies. FMRI has the advantages of better spatial and temporal resolution, as well as safety and relative cheapness. There are now literally thousands of fMRI studies of visual processing in the human cerebral cortex, and they are increasing rapidly all the time.

The development of fMRI, had it occurred 10 years earlier, would have dramatically affected the way we constructed our case in the book. In the absence of such data, we relied to a great extent on nonhuman primate evidence and therefore had to make a major (cross-species) theoretical leap. The demonstration that there were two cortical visual streams of processing was based entirely on work with monkeys, as was the physiological and behavioural evidence for how the two streams might operate. In contrast, virtually nothing was known about the organization of visual pathways in the human brain beyond primary visual cortex (V1). Although we were able to cite evidence from neurological patients to support our interpretations, these were necessarily highly conjectural in the absence of firm knowledge of the anatomy and function of human visual areas beyond V1.

The pioneering work of Tootell and his group provided the first major breakthrough. His use of fMRI showed for the first time that, in broad-brush terms at least, the visual areas in the human cerebral cortex were laid out in a remarkably similar fashion to those of the macaque monkey. As this work progressed it became clear that the notion of two visual streams of processing applies not only to the monkey but to the human brain as well. In other words fMRI has now confirmed the fundamental assumption in our book that the organization of the monkey visual system provides a good model for understanding the neural substrates of vision in humans. But more importantly, the advent of fMRI has allowed investigators to characterize differences in the patterns of brain activation during the performance of different kinds of visual tasks, including important differences in the processing of visual information by the dorsal and ventral streams. We attempt to integrate some of these new studies within the framework of our model in the Epilogue.

One particularly exciting new avenue of research is the use of fMRI in monkeys. This work allows investigators to go beyond the inferences that can be made from single neuronal responses alone towards an understanding of the whole pattern of brain activation involved in particular perceptual or behavioural tasks. It also allows a closer comparison to be made between monkey and human brain during similar perceptual processing tasks. We survey the current state of both human and nonhuman fMRI research in the Epilogue. We argue not only that they confirm the existence of human homologues of the ventral and dorsal visual streams, but that they also shed new light on the function of the various areas that comprise the two streams. Primate work has become more sophisticated in other ways as well, notably in the behavioural paradigms that have been developed to explore more fully the perceptual experience of the monkey during particular experimental tasks. This increased sophistication is well exemplified by the work of Cowey and colleagues in exploring 'blindsight' in monkeys and that of Logothetis and colleagues in the understanding of how neuronal activity in the ventral stream is correlated with the animal's awareness of the visual stimulus.

A major implication of our model is the counterintuitive idea that people's perception of the visual world does not always follow the same rules as their behavioural interactions with that world. One example of this dissociation, one which captured the attention of researchers in perception and psychophysics, was the surprising demonstration that a compelling illusion of visual size did not influence the way in which people picked up the misperceived stimulus. In other words, the grasping movements were calibrated to the real, not the perceived, size of the target object. Since we described this result in the first edition of the book, more than 100 studies, either supporting or challenging this finding, have appeared. Some investigators have concluded that our model must be wrong since in some situations actions *can* be affected by perceptual illusions. But, as we argue in the Epilogue, several factors have to be taken into account in interpreting the results of these various studies—and there are indeed some circumstances where our model would specifically predict an effect of perceptual illusions on action.

One of the most important developments in our own research since we first published *The Visual Brain in Action* has been a study in which we were able to examine the patterns of fMRI activation to be seen in the brain of patient D.F., whose visual abilities and disabilities formed much of the stimulus for writing the book in the first place. This study enabled us to make direct tests of our previously indirect inferences concerning the cortical mechanisms underlying her visual life. In the Epilogue, we review the main findings of the neuroimaging work on D.F. and relate those findings to the new data that are emerging about the functional organization of the dorsal and ventral streams in the normal brain. We use the Epilogue, however, not only to review the range of new empirical findings, but also to clarify and refine our ideas as set out in the unchanged main body of the book.

Our ideas have been sharpened over the intervening years thanks to the practical collaboration and intellectual stimulation provided by many colleagues, past and present, including Salvatore Aglioti, Steve Arnott, Liana Brown, Jonathan Cant, David Carey, Cristiana Cavina Pratesi, Erik Chang, Jason Connolly, Jody Culham, James Danckert, Chris Dijkerman, Richard Dyde, Susanne Ferber, Tzvi Ganel, Joe Gati, Herb Goltz, Claudia Gonzalez, Angela Haffenden, Monika Harvey, Charles Heywood, Yaoping Hu, Keith Humphrey, Lorna Jakobson, Karin Harman James, Tom James, Bob Kentridge, Grzegorz Króliczak, Jonathan Marotta, Robert McIntosh, Ravi Menon, Mark Mon-Williams, Kelly Murphy, Sukhvinder Obhi, Marie-Thérèse Perenin, David Perrett, Nichola Rice, Yves Rossetti, Thomas Schenk, Igor Schindler, Philip Servos, Jennifer Steeves, Chris Thomas, Kenneth Valyear, Lynne Mitchell, Tutis Vilis, David Westwood, David Whitney, and Haitao Yang. We would particularly like to thank Robert McIntosh, Kenneth Valyear, and David Westwood, for their insightful comments on an earlier draft of the Epilogue, and Kenneth Valyear and Grzegorz Króliczak for their assistance in preparing the figures and illustrations.

University of Durham   A.D.M.
University of Western Ontario   M.A.G.

Foreword to the First Edition

Lawrence Weiskrantz

Emeritus Professor of Psychology,
University of Oxford

We are in the midst of a fascinating rethink about brain mechanisms of vision, to which David Milner and Mel Goodale have made seminal contributions. Not only has it become clear that there are multiple visual *systems* in the primate brain, but increasingly there is switch away from a simplistic modular view to one in which the focus is on the dynamics of the various 'streams', and their interactions with each other. This book is welcome not only as a review of physiological and anatomical evidence for multiple channels, but as a treatment in which the biological demands of the behaving organism are given their rightful priority in functional interpretations. They have dared to venture into enquiries that go to the heart of such issues, for example, 'what is visual perception for?' and 'why is blindsight blind?', together with discussions of space perception, agnosia, unilateral neglect, and other topics which it is refreshing, not to say useful, to find in a single volume. Above all, they review the evidence about the relationship between perception and action on which their own contributions have been both ingenious and penetrating.

Much of that work has been based on research with single subjects, especially Patient D.F. in whom the importance of perceptual mechanisms geared to action, in contrast to judgmental 'seeing', were revealed. This represents another trend in modern visual research—the intensive and repeated testing of single subjects who show especially interesting functional dissociations. Such observations reveal what must be explained by the physiology, but they also point the way to such possible explanations. Thus, the work on D.F. casts an entirely different light on the role of the so-called dorsal visuo-cortical stream in which demands for action are incorporated in what has tended to be considered heretofore as a relatively passive processor of perceptual space. It is interesting that an earlier multiple visual system hypothesis of some 30 or 40 years ago, namely between cortical and midbrain pathways postulated to be processing 'what' and 'where' respectively, has been overtaken by a focus on separate intra-cortical streams. Both authors have also contributed to this earlier body of research, and perhaps the time is approaching when both the intra-cortical and extra-cortical hypotheses can be joined.

In their Preface, the authors express their confidence that they will be 'comprehensively shot at if not down'. That is what a good book should achieve especially when, as in this case, there is a good empirical base. As Voltaire put it, 'God is on the side not of the heavy battalions, but of the best shots.' These authors aim well, and this book should make a stimulating and durable contribution.

Preface to the First Edition

This book has emerged from somewhat serendipitous beginnings. In 1989, one of us (A.D.M.) began to study an unusual patient with severe brain damage (D.F.) who suffered from a failure to recognize visual shapes ('visual form agnosia'). He discovered that this profound impairment was unaccompanied by any apparent difficulty in executing certain visually guided actions that required visual shape processing. The other author (M.A.G.) had already written a series of papers arguing that there exist multiple visuomotor systems within the mammalian brain, and that these systems may be quite distinct from what is generally regarded as visual 'perception'. We subsequently collaborated in further studies of the same patient.

We published two papers on this work in early 1991; but while they were in press, we became aware of a quite independent investigation of single neurones in the posterior parietal cortex of the monkey by a group of Japanese physiologists. This showed that not only was the machinery present in this part of the brain for organizing such simple visuomotor acts as watching and reaching toward objects shown to the animal, but also for visually controlling the monkey's grasp to match the particular sizes and shapes of objects. We were well aware of the pioneering and highly influential work of Mishkin, Ungerleider, and their colleagues at N.I.H., in which they first identified and then systematically explored the two major streams of visual processing in the cerebral cortex. We hypothesized that one of these streams, that passing dorsally from primary visual cortex to the posterior parietal lobule, might underly the visual guidance of actions such as those seen to be intact in D.F. The other stream, passing ventrally from primary visual cortex to the inferior temporal region, is generally accepted to be essential for visual shape recognition, and we attributed D.F.'s agnosia to a disruption of this stream.

We set out these ideas in a short article that appeared the following year (1992), and in a longer one the year after that. The present book represents a still further development of these themes, in which we raise ourselves yet further above the parapets. We confidently expect that by doing so we will be comprehensively shot at if not shot down, but we hope that in preparing their arms and ammunition, our critics will put our ideas to empirical test. If they do so, then this would be a sufficient vindication, in our view, of our efforts in writing this book. Science advances more by disproving hypotheses than by confirming them.

We wish to acknowledge the help given to us by colleagues in several countries through discussion and feedback. We are particularly indebted to David Carey, Michael Goldberg, Keith Humphrey, and Giacomo Rizzolatti, for their helpful comments on the draft manuscript of the book. Needless to say, they can take the credit for correcting our factual errors, but should take no blame for any errors in our interpretation. We thank Monika Harvey for her assistance with the bibliography, and Leslie Hamilton for preparing many of the figures and diagrams. We are also grateful to the Wellcome Trust for the provision of travel money to aid our collaboration in the final stages in the preparation of the book. Lastly, as will already be obvious, we owe an enormous debt of gratitude to D.F. for her tireless cooperation and for her friendship. Without her, this book would look very different.

University of St Andrews A. D. M.
University of Western Ontario M. A. G.

Figure Acknowledgements

We wish to thank the following publishers, and the authors of the works concerned:

Ablex Publishing Corporation, Inc., for permission to reproduce: Fig. 1 (p. 272), 2 (p. 274), and 3 (p. 275) in: Goodale, M.A. (1988). Modularity in visuomotor control: from input to output. In *Computational processes in human vision*, (ed. Z.W. Pylyshyn), pp.262–85. Academic Press, Inc., for permission to reproduce: Fig. 2 (p. 271) in: Ungerleider, L.G. and Brody, B.A. (1977). Extrapersonal spatial orientation: the role of posterior parietal, anterior frontal, and inferotemporal cortex. *Exp. Neurol.*, 56, 265–80. American Association for the Advancement of Science, for permission to reproduce: Fig. 1 (p. 1053) and 2 (p. 1055) in: Ingle, D. (1973). Two visual systems in the frog. *Science*, 181, 1053–5; Fig. 2 and 3 (p. 91) in: Duhamel, J.R., Colby, C.L. and Goldberg, M.E. (1992). The updating of the representation of visual space in parietal cortex by intended eye movements. *Science*, 255, 90–2; Fig. 1 and 3 (p. 686) in: Tanaka, K. (1993). Neuronal mechanisms of object recognition. *Science*, 262, 685–8; and, Fig. 4 (p. 742) in: Livingstone, M. and Hubel, D. (1988). Segregation of form, color, movement, and depth: anatomy, physiology, and perception. *Science*, 240, 740–9. American Psychological Association, Inc., for permission to reproduce: Fig. 6 (p. 233) in: Pohl, W. (1973). Dissociation of spatial discrimination deficits following frontal and parietal lesions in monkeys. *J. Comp. Physiol. Psychol.*, 82, 227–39. The American Physiological Society, for permission to reproduce: Fig. 2 (p. 1267) in: Dürsteler *et al.* (1987). Directional pursuit deficits following lesions of the foveal representation within the superior temporal sulcus of the macaque monkey. *J. Neurophysiol.*, 57, 1262–87. Elsevier Science Publishers, for permission to reproduce Fig. 1 (p. 414) and 2 (p. 415) in: Mishkin, M. *et al.* (1983). Object vision and spatial vision: two cortical pathways, *TINS* 6, 414–17; Fig. 4 (p. 397) in: Schiller, P.H. and Logothetis, N.K. (1990). The color-opponent and broad-band channels of the primate visual system, *TINS* 13, 392–8; and Fig. 5 (p. 307) in: Goldberg, M.E. and Colby, C.L. (1989). The neurophysiology of spatial vision. In *Handbook of Neuropsychology, Vol. 2*, (ed. F. Boller and J. Grafman), pp. 301–15. Wiley-Liss, Inc., for permission to reproduce Fig. 16 (p. 147) in: Distler *et al.* (1993). Cortical connections of inferior temporal area TEO in macaque monkeys. *J. Comp. Neurol.*, 334, 125–50. Masson, S.p.A., for permission to reproduce: Fig. 2 (p. 80) in: Habib, M. and Sirigu, A. (1987). Pure topographical disorientation: a definition and anatomical basis. *Cortex*, 23, 73–85. Oxford University Press, for permission to reproduce: Fig. 3 and 4 (p. 54) in: Ratcliff, G. and Davies-Jones, G.A.B. (1972). Defective visual localization in focal brain wounds. *Brain*, 95, 49–60; Fig. 2 (p. 712) and 3 (p. 713) in: Weiskrantz, L. *et al.* (1974). Visual capacity in the hemianopic field following a restricted occipital ablation. *Brain*, 97, 709–28; and Fig. 4 (p. 643) and 6 (p. 658) in: Perenin, M.T. and Vighetto, A. (1988). Optic ataxia: a specific disruption in visuomotor mechanisms. *Brain*, 111, 643–74. Macmillan Journals Ltd, for permission to reproduce: Fig. 2 (p. 155) in: Goodale, M.A. *et al.* (1991). A neurological dissociation between perceiving objects and grasping them. *Nature*, 349, 154–6. MIT Press, Inc., for permission to reproduce: Fig. 2 (p. 48), 3 (p. 49), 4 (p. 50), 6 (p. 52), and 7 (p. 53) in: Goodale, M.A. *et al.* (1994). The nature and limits of orientation and pattern processing supporting visuomotor control in a visual form agnosic. *J. Cognitive Neurosci.*, 6, 46–56. Pergamon Press plc, for permission to reproduce: Fig. 2 (p. 808) in: Jakobson, L.S. *et al.* (1991). A kinematic analysis of reaching and grasping movements in a patient recovering from optic ataxia. *Neuropsychologia*, 29, 803–9. The Society for Neuroscience, for permission to reproduce: Fig. 13(p. 3393) in: Hubel, D.H. and Livingstone, M.S. (1987). Segregation of form, color, and stereopsis in primate area 18. *J. Neurosci.*, 7, 3378–415; and Figs 5 (p. 149) 7 (p. 150) in: Saito, H., Yukie, M., Tanaka, K., Hikosaka, K., Fukada, Y., and Iwai, E. (1986). Integration of direction signals of image motion in the superior temporal sulcus of the macaque monkey. *J. Neurosci.*, 6, 145–57. Springer Verlag, for permission to reproduce: Fig. 5 (p. 313) in: Ellard, C. and Goodale, M.A. (1988). A functional analysis of the collicular output pathways: a dissociation of deficits following lesions of the dorsal tegmental decussation and the ipsilateral collicular efferent bundle in the Mongolian gerbil. *Exp. Brain Res.*, 71, 307–19; Fig. 3 (p. 191) in: Sakata, H. *et al.* (1992). Hand-movement-related neurons of the posterior parietal cortex of the monkey: their role in the visual guidance of hand movements. In *Control of Arm Movement in Space*, (ed. R. Caminiti, P. B. Johnson, and Y. Burnod), pp. 185–198; Fig. 1, 2, and 3 (p. 163) in: Perrett, D.I. *et al.* (1991). Viewer-centred and object-centred coding of heads in the macaque temporal cortex. *Exp. Brain Res.*, 86, 159–73; Fig. 2 (p. 479) in: Gordon, A.M. *et al.* (1991). Visual size cues in the programming of the manipulative forces during precision grip. *Exp. Brain Res.*, 83, 477–82; Fig. 6 (p. 513) in: Sheliga, B.M. *et al.* (1994). Orienting of attention and eye movements. *Exp. Brain Res.*, 98, 507–22: and Fig. 1 (p. 38) in: Marshall, J.C. and Halligan, P.W. (1993). Visuo-spatial neglect: a new copying test to assess perceptual parsing. *J. Neurol*, 240, 37–40.

American Physiological Society, for permission to reproduce: Figs. 1 (p. 3497) and 2 (p. 3498) in: Gonzalez, C.L., Ganel, T. and Goodale, M.A. (2006).

Hemispheric specialization for the visual control of action is independent of handedness. *J. Neurophysiol.*, **95**, 3496–3501. Cell Press, for permission to reproduce: Figs. 1 (p. 754) and 4 (p. 756) in: Tong, F., Nakayama, K., Vaughan, J. T. and Kanwisher, N. (1998). Binocular rivalry and visual awareness in human extrastriate cortex. *Neuron* **21**, 753–759; *and* Fig. 2 (p. 851) in: Prado, J., Clavagnier, S., Otzenberger, H., Scheiber, C., Kennedy, H. and Perenin, M. T. (2005). Two cortical systems for reaching in central and peripheral vision. *Neuron* **48**, 849–58. Elsevier B.V., for permission to reproduce: Fig. 5 (p. 96) in: Andrews, T. J. and Schluppeck, D. (2004). Neural responses to Mooney images reveal a modular representation of faces in human visual cortex. *Neuroimage* **21**, 91–98; *and* Figs. 1 (p. 11), 2 (p. 12) and 3 (p. 13) in: Króliczak, G., Heard, P., Goodale, M. A. and Gregory, R. L. (2006). Dissociation of perception and action unmasked by the hollow-face illusion. *Brain Research*, **1080**, 9–16. Nature Publishing Group, for permission to reproduce: Figs. 1 and 2 (p. 738) in: Flanagan, J. R. and Beltzner, M. A. (2000). Independence of perceptual and sensorimotor predictions in the size-weight illusion. *Nature Neuroscience* **3**, 737–741; Fig. 1 (p. 554) in: Cohen, Y. E. and Andersen, R. A. (2002). A common reference frame for movement plans in the posterior parietal cortex. *Nature Reviews Neuroscience* **3**, 553–562; Fig. 1 (p. 662) in: Rizzolatti, G., Fogassi, L. and Gallese, V. (2001). Neurophysiological mechanisms underlying the understanding and imitation of action. *Nature Reviews Neuroscience* **2**, 661–670; *and* Fig. 2 (p. 781) in: Schindler, I., Rice, N. J., McIntosh, R. D., Rossetti, Y., Vighetto, A. and Milner, A. D. (2004) Automatic avoidance of obstacles is a dorsal stream function: evidence from optic ataxia. *Nature Neuroscience* **7**, 779–784. Oxford University Press, for permission to reproduce: Fig. 7 (p. 2473) in: James, T. W., Culham, J., Humphrey, G. K., Milner, A. D. and Goodale, M. A. (2003) Ventral occipital lesions impair object recognition but not object-directed grasping: a fMRI study. *Brain* **126**, 2463–2475; *and* Fig. 2 (p. 1629) in: Rees, G., Wojciulik, E., Clarke, K., Husain, M., Frith, C. and Driver, J. (2000) Unconscious activation of visual cortex in the damaged right hemisphere of a parietal patient with extinction. *Brain* **123**, 1624–1633. The Royal Society of London, for permission to reproduce: Fig. 6 (p. 1810) in: Logothetis, N. K. (1998) Single units and conscious vision. *Philosophical Transactions of the Royal Society of London B: Biological Sciences* **353**, 1801–1818. The Society for Neuroscience, for permission to reproduce: Figure 1 (p. 3982) in: Tootell, R. B. H., Tsao, D. and Vanduffel, W. (2003) Neuroimaging weighs in: humans meet macaques in "primate" visual cortex. *J. Neuroscience* **23**, 3981–3989; *and* Figure 1 (p. 11057) in: Schwarzlose, R. F., Baker, C. I. and Kanwisher, N. (2005) Separate face and body selectivity on the fusiform gyrus. *J. Neuroscience* **25**, 11055–11059.

Contents

Chapter 1

Introduction: vision from a biological viewpoint

Vision, more than any other sensory system, provides us with detailed information about the world beyond our body surface. While much is understood about how the changing patterns of light striking the retina are transformed into neural impulses, far less is known about how the complex machinery of the brain interprets these signals. Although modern neuroscience is helping us to understand the operational characteristics and interconnectivity of the various components, the organizing principles of the visual system as a whole remain open to debate. In our view a useful first step in trying to establish these principles is to take an evolutionary perspective and to ask what the system is designed to do. In short, what is the function of vision? One obvious answer to this question is that vision allows us to perform skilled actions, such as moving through a crowded room or catching a ball. Such actions would be quite impossible without visual guidance. But, of course, vision allows us to do many other things that are equally important in our lives. It is through vision that we learn about the structure of our environment and it is mainly through vision that we recognize individuals, objects, and events within that environment. Indeed, this 'perceptual' function is the one most commonly associated with vision in people's minds.

The visual system then has to be able to accommodate two somewhat distinct functions—one concerned with acting on the world and the other with representing it. How does the brain achieve these different ends? In theory, a single multipurpose visual system could serve both the guidance of actions and the perceptual representation of the world. In practice, however, we believe that evolution has solved the problem of reconciling the differing demands of these two functions by segregating them in two separate and quasi-independent 'visual brains'. In brief, it is our contention that, despite the protestations of phenomenology, visual perception and the visual control of action depend on functionally and neurally independent systems.

At first sight, making a distinction between the visual control of action and visual perception might appear rather strange. After all, it seems a truism that to act upon an object one must perceive it. But this is only so if one uses the term 'perception' to refer generally to any processing of sensory input. Such usage of course is quite common in both visual science and in everyday language. But the word 'perception' can also be used in another more restricted sense to refer to a process which allows one to assign meaning and significance to external objects and events. This usage, which is most common in philosophical and psychological writings, often (though not always) carries experiential connotations and tends to be identified with one's phenomenological experience of the world. In the present book our use of the word approximates to this more restricted sense, in that we see perception as subserving the recognition and identification of objects and events and their spatial and temporal relations. In this sense, perception provides the foundation for the cognitive life of the organism, allowing it to construct long-term memories and models of the environment. It will therefore be clear that our use of the term 'perception' excludes such 'reflexive' phenomena as the processing of visual input in the control of pupillary diameter. But, more importantly, it also excludes more complex processing such as that required for the moment to moment control of many skilled actions such as walking or grasping. This distinction between the visual mechanisms underlying 'perception' on the one hand, and action on the other, is central to the arguments that run through the book.

In attempting to identify the brain mechanisms mediating these different uses of vision, we will focus particularly on the organization and interconnectivity of the 'visual areas' in the primate cerebral cortex. In the present chapter, however, it is first necessary to present an introductory overview of the input pathways of the mammalian visual system. Our brief account of the major retinal projections will provide a framework for more detailed discussions later in the book. We also review in the present chapter the role of vision in the control of motor output, suggesting that the earliest functions of vision, in evolutionary terms, were action- rather than perception-oriented.

1.1 **Input pathways of the mammalian visual system**

The retina, which on embryological grounds can be considered as part of the central nervous system, not only transduces the electromagnetic radiation striking the photoreceptors into physiological signals that can be understood by the brain, but it also performs several computations on those signals which involve combining information from a number of different photoreceptors.

Thus, by the time the sensory signals leave the eye on their way to the brain, a good deal of processing has already occurred. This processing, furthermore, is not uniform within the system. The ganglion cells, whose axons leave the eye and constitute the optic nerve, are heterogeneous in the kinds of information they convey. Some, for example, carry information that is particularly useful for an analysis of the spatial distribution of light energy striking the retina; others carry information that is more related to the temporal dynamics of the retinal array, arising, for example, from stimulus motion. Still others appear to be primarily concerned with the distribution of the different wavelengths of light entering the eye. Moreover, across different species, the signal transformations that occur in the retina vary enormously, no doubt reflecting the range of ecological niches in which mammals live.

A striking feature of the retinal neurones that project from the eye, and one that is often not appreciated, is that they travel to a number of distinct target areas in the brain (see Fig. 1.1). In other words, they do not form a set of parallel lines of information projecting together from one complex processing station to another, but instead diverge to very different processing targets right from the outset. (For a more comprehensive account of the structure of the primate visual system, readers are referred to the review by Kaas and Huerta (1988).) We shall argue later that this multiplicity of retinal projection sites is a reflection of the many different outputs that are elicited and controlled by visual stimuli, each of which is dependent on rather different kinds of visual information.

The two largest pathways from the eye to the brain in mammals are the retinotectal and the retinogeniculate. The phylogenetically older retinotectal projection, which is the most prominent visual projection in other vertebrate classes such as amphibia, reptiles, and birds, terminates in the optic tectum of the midbrain. Called the superior colliculus in mammals, this prominent and laminated structure is interconnected with a large number of other brain structures, including premotor and motor nuclei in the brainstem and spinal cord. It also sends projections, via thalamic nuclei, to a number of different sites in the cerebral cortex. Most functional accounts of the superior colliculus, particularly in primates, focus on its role in the control of saccadic eye movements; however, as we shall see, its evolutionary history indicates a broader repertoire than this.

The retinogeniculate projection, which terminates in the dorsal part of the lateral geniculate nucleus of the thalamus (LGNd), is the most prominent visual pathway in primates. In other vertebrate classes, such as amphibia, this pathway is barely evident. Only in mammals has this projection system become prominent. Neurones in the lateral geniculate nucleus project in turn

Fig. 1.1 Schematic drawing of the main projections from the retina to the central nervous system. The more prominent projections are marked with heavier arrows. LGNd, lateral geniculate nucleus, pars dorsalis; Parvo, parvocellular layers of LGNd; Magno, magnocellular layers of LGNd; Interlaminar, interlaminar region of LGNd; SC, superior colliculus; Pulvinar, pulvinar nucleus of the thalamus; LGNv, lateral geniculate nucleus, pars ventralis; NOT, nucleus of the optic tract; AOTd, dorsal terminal nucleus of the accessory optic tract; AOTl, lateral terminal nucleus of the accessory optic tract; AOTm, medial terminal nucleus of the accessory optic tract; SCN, suprachiasmatic nucleus.

to the cerebral cortex, with almost all of the fibres, in primates at least, terminating in the primary visual area, or striate cortex (often nowadays termed 'area VI') in the occipital lobe. This geniculostriate projection and its cortical elaborations probably constitute the best studied neural 'system' in the whole of neuroscience (see Chapter 2). This fact is perhaps not unrelated to the general belief that subjective visual experience in humans depends on the integrity of this projection system.

Despite the prominence of the retinotectal and retinogeniculate pathways, it is important to remember that there are a number of other retinal projections that are not nearly so well studied as the first two. One of the earliest projections to leave the optic tract consists of a small bundle of fibres that terminate in the suprachiasmatic nucleus, which, as its name implies, lies just above the optic chiasm in the hypothalamic area. This pathway appears to play an essential role in synchronizing an animal's circadian rhythm with the day–night cycle. There are also projections to the ventral portion of the lateral geniculate nucleus, the pulvinar nucleus, the nucleus of the optic tract, various pretectal nuclei, and a set of three nuclei in the brainstem known collectively as the nuclei of the accessory optic tract. The different functions of these various projections are not yet well understood.

Perhaps the best studied of these 'minor' retinal targets are the nucleus of the optic tract and the accessory optic nuclei which appear to play a critical role in the mediation of a number of 'automatic' reactions to visual stimuli. An example of this is provided by 'optokinetic nystagmus', the alternating pattern of slow pursuit and rapid resetting eye movements that occur when a patterned field sweeps the retina. The accessory optic nuclei have also been implicated in the visual control of posture and certain aspects of locomotion, by virtue of their probable role in processing the 'optic-flow' stimulation created as the animal moves through a visual environment. Retinal projections to one area in the pretectum are thought to be part of the circuitry controlling the pupillary light reflex. Almost nothing is known about the functions of projections to other parts of the pretectal nuclei or the functions of the projections to the ventral part of the lateral geniculate nucleus and the pulvinar. Indeed, it would not be an exaggeration to say that most visual scientists would be hard pressed to offer a functional account of any of these projection systems in the mammal. Of course, one reason for this dearth of information is quite obvious: most of the attention of the neuroscience community has focused on the cortical elaboration of the geniculostriate projections (and to a lesser extent, the superior colliculus). The fascination with the geniculostriate system stems directly from certain tacit assumptions underlying most contemporary visual science, assumptions which have not only shaped the nature of the research questions that have been asked but have also determined to a large extent the methodology that has been used to answer those questions.

1.2 The evolution of vision in vertebrates

1.2.1 The functions of vision

It is commonly assumed that vision in humans has a single function: to provide a unified internal representation of the external world which can then serve as the perceptual foundation for visually based thought and action. From this perspective, the task of visual science boils down to the problem of understanding how the spatiotemporal mosaic of light striking the retina is parsed into the array of discrete objects and events that comprise one's perceptual experience of the world. This idea that the ultimate function of vision is to deliver one's perception of the world has been an underlying assumption, generally implicit and unquestioned, for most theorizing about vision and the organization of the visual system. Thus, even though many workers in the field have found it useful to invoke notions of 'modularity' when discussing the organization of the visual system, and influential theorists such as Marr (1982) have postulated the existence of 'visual primitives' which are domain specific and relatively independent, the many different processes involved in transforming the 'raw' visual image are typically regarded as part of a single monolithic system dedicated to delivering a unified percept of the visual world. While this approach to vision has not prevented considerable advances at both the empirical and theoretical levels, it has concentrated almost entirely on the input side of visual processing and has virtually ignored the ultimate function of vision and the visual system, namely to ensure an effective and adaptive behavioural output.

One notable exception to this tradition is the work of J. J. Gibson (1977), who many years ago recognized the importance of vision in the control of action. Gibson challenged the classic distinction between 'exteroceptors' (sensory systems which provide information about extrinsic events) and 'proprioceptors' (sensory systems which provide information about one's own actions). According to Gibson, most sensory systems have both exteroceptive and proprioceptive functions. Thus, vision, for example, not only provides information about objects and events in the external world, but also plays an essential role in monitoring changes in the visual array brought about by one's actions in the world.

It is almost axiomatic that the control of motor output is precisely why vision evolved in the first place. Consider the phototactic behaviour of a light-sensitive creature, such as the water beetle larva (*Dytiscidae*), which uses light to find the surface of the water where it can obtain air (see Fig. 1.2). If larvae are placed in an aquarium that is illuminated from below, they will swim to the bottom and invert themselves, and will suffocate there unless the illumination is reversed (Schone 1962).

To account for this behaviour, it is not necessary to invoke perception or some sort of internal representation of the outside world within the larva's nervous system. All that is required is a simple visuomotor mechanism linking input to the required output. But this linkage need not be obligatory and reflexive. When the larva needs air, it will swim toward the light, and after replenishing its air supply, it will swim away from the light. Of course, a servomechanism of this sort, although driven by visual inputs, is far less complicated than even the simplest of vertebrate visual systems. Nevertheless, it can

Fig. 1.2 Drawing of the visually guided behaviour of a water beetle (*Dytiscidae*) in an aquarium that is illuminated from below. Rather than going up to the surface for air, the beetle swims to the bottom. Adapted from Schone (1962.)

be argued that vision in vertebrates ultimately serves the same function as it does in the water beetle larva, namely the distal control of motor output. Moreover, as we shall see, the control systems for different motor outputs in vertebrates are not associated with a single representation of the outside world but are instead mediated by relatively independent visuomotor modules.

1.2.2 Visuomotor modules in non-mammalian vertebrates

In a now classic series of studies of vision in the frog (*Rana pipiens*), Ingle (1973) showed that different patterns of visually guided behaviour in this species depend on entirely separate pathways right through from the retina to the motor nuclei. The first clear indication of the extent to which different visually guided behaviours are mediated by independent visuomotor pathways came from a 'rewiring' experiment carried out over 20 years ago (Ingle 1973).

The central nervous systems of frogs and many other non-mammalian vertebrates possess a characteristic that makes them particularly useful for studying the neural substrates of visually guided behaviour: the projections from the retina to the brain can be transected and induced to regrow to new locations. By studying the visually guided behaviour of such rewired animals, one can gain some insight into the neural substrates of the behaviour in the normal animal. Ingle (1973) used this technique to demonstrate that visually elicited feeding and visually guided locomotion around barriers are mediated by entirely separate visuomotor pathways. After unilateral removal of the frog's optic tectum, Ingle (1973) found, just as Bechterev (1884) had a century before, that the animal totally ignored small prey objects or large looming discs presented within the monocular visual field contralateral to the ablated tectum. Of course, when these stimuli were presented in the visual field opposite the intact optic tectum, the frog continued to respond vigorously, turning and snapping at the small prey objects and jumping away from the large looming discs. Over the next few months, however, there was a slow recovery and the frogs began to turn and snap in response to prey objects presented in their formerly 'blind' visual field. But, as Fig. 1.3 (left) illustrates, their responses were far from normal.

Instead of turning and snapping in the direction of the prey object, the frogs directed their responses toward a location nearly mirror symmetrical to the position of the stimulus. Similarly, when a large 'threatening' disc was suddenly introduced into the field opposite the lesion, instead of jumping away from the disc, the frogs jumped towards it. This mirror symmetrical behaviour was particularly evident in frogs in which the eye contralateral to the intact tectum had been removed, leaving only the eye contralateral to the ablated tectum.

Fig. 1.3 Illustration of prey-catching behaviour in a 'rewired' frog. The drawing on the left shows the relation between the location of a prey object (circles) and the frog's corresponding snap (crosses). The diagram on the right shows the rewired projections (dotted lines) from the retina of the remaining eye to the ipsilateral optic tectum. Inputs from loci A, B, and C on the retina now project to sites in the ipsilateral tectum that would normally receive input from corresponding loci in the retina of the contralateral eye. Thus, when these tectal sites are activated by stimulation on the ipsilateral side, they direct responses to contralateral locations as if those sites had been activated by the contralateral eye. The retinal input to the pretectum on the injured side of the brain remains normal. Adapted from Ingle (1973).

Histological analysis of the frogs' brains revealed that the optic tract, which had been transected when the optic tectum had been ablated, had regenerated and the sprouting axons, finding no tectum on that side of the brain, had crossed the midline and innervated the intact tectum on the other side. This meant that the retinal projections from the eye contralateral to the ablated tectum were actually projecting to the tectum on the ipsilateral side (Fig. 1.3, right). Electrophysiological experiments carried out in other rewired frogs showed that the aberrant projection was distributed across the ipsilateral tectum in a retinotopic fashion, with the fibres from the nasal portion of the retina, for example, projecting to that part of the tectum that normally received nasal retinal fibres from the contralateral eye. The mirror-symmetrical behaviour of the rewired frogs could now be easily explained. When prey objects or looming discs were presented to the eye ipsilateral to the remaining tectum, they elicited behaviour from the tectal circuitry that was appropriate for the location of stimuli within the visual field of the eye contralateral to the tectum.

It was not the case, however, that the entire perceptual world of the rewired frog was simply a mirror image of what it had been before. Not all visually guided behaviour was reversed in these animals. As Fig. 1.4 illustrates, when the same frogs that showed mirror-symmetrical feeding attempted to escape a tactile stimulus (a touch on the rear) by jumping away from it, they always oriented their jump correctly to avoid hitting a large barrier placed in front of them. The trajectories of their jumps, like those of normal animals, were optimally planned; the frogs jumped just enough to one side to avoid hitting the barrier but still got as far away from the tactile stimulus as they could under the circumstances. This was true even when the edge of the barrier was located within their rewired visual field. (It should be noted that such behaviour was also observed immediately after the unilateral tectal lesion, a period during which prey catching could not be elicited in the contralesional visual field.)

In other words, a rewired frog that showed mirror-symmetrical responses to prey stimuli or looming targets presented in the field contralateral to the ablated optic tectum could still circumvent barriers located in that same visual field quite normally. This result strongly suggests that one or more of the remaining normal retinal projections was responsible for such visual guidance of barrier avoidance, since only the retinal projections to the optic tectum had been rewired. Subsequent experiments by Ingle (1980, 1982) have shown that retinal fibres terminating in one of the pretectal nuclei, lying just rostral to the optic tectum, are critical for this visual skill. Thus, it would appear that there there are at least two independent visuomotor systems in the frog: a tectal system, which mediates visually elicited prey catching and predator avoidance and a pretectal system which mediates visually guided locomotion around barriers.

Fig. 1.4 Illustration of the barrier avoidance behaviour of the 'rewired' frogs shown in Fig. 1.3. The visible edge of the 15 cm high barrier was positioned randomly at 0, 45, or 90° from the midline of the frog. The black rectangles in the radial histogram mark the different directions in which all the rewired frogs in the group jumped at each of the three barrier locations, each rectangle corresponding to one jump. The lines show the jumps of one individual. It is clear that the frogs were jumping correctly and that there is no overlap between the direction of the jumps for the three barrier locations. Adapted from Ingle (1973).

More recent research suggests that the tectal system itself can be further subdivided (Ingle 1991). Turning towards a prey-like stimulus is controlled by a modular system that consists on the input side of projections from 'class II' retinal ganglion cells to superficial laminae in the optic tectum. These class II cells respond best to small moving spots in the visual field, a property that led to the apt name of 'bug detectors' (Lettvin *et al.* 1959; see Chapter 2, Section 2.1.2). Tectal cells in these laminae then give rise in turn to projections, largely crossed, to nuclei in the pons, medulla, and spinal cord that control turning. In addition there is a 'visual escape' module that mediates rapid jumping away from large looming stimuli, which receives input projections from a quite different set of retinal ganglion cells, including class IV (and perhaps some class III) cells. These axons end in tectal laminae much deeper than those receiving input from the class II cells. Moreover, the tectal output fibres that trigger visually elicited escape appear to be largely uncrossed and to project to nuclei in the rostral medulla. This duplex account of tectal function is further complicated by the fact that certain other components of prey catching, such as snapping, are not dependent on the same crossed tectofugal projections that mediate turning towards prey. Moreover, there is a good deal of evidence to suggest that the sensitivity of these different systems can be modulated to some degree by other sensory inputs as well as by the animal's experience with particular food items and predators (Ewert 1987). Nevertheless, it would not be a misrepresentation to say that the different classes of visuomotor behaviour that depend on tectal circuitry are highly modular in their organization.

It should be emphasized that the modular organization of these different visuomotor systems (the two or more tectal systems and the pretectal system that mediates visually guided barrier avoidance) is not limited to separate input pathways but instead extends right through to the motor nuclei that encode the movements produced by the animal. Indeed, one might characterize the organization of the visual midbrain not as a visual system, nor even as a set of visual subsystems, but rather as a set of visuomotor subsystems.

The fact that the frog possesses this parallel set of independent visuomotor pathways does not fit well with the common view of a visual system dedicated to the construction of a unified representation of the external world. Although the outputs from the different visuomotor systems need to be coordinated, it would clearly be absurd to suppose that the different actions controlled by these networks are guided by a single visual representation of the world residing somewhere in the animal's brain. There is clearly no single representation or comparator to which all the animal's actions are referred.

Vision in the frog, like vision in other organisms, did not evolve to provide perception of the world in any obvious sense, but rather to provide distal sensory control of the movements that the animal makes in order to survive and reproduce in that world. Natural selection operates at the level of overt behaviour; it cares little about how well an animal 'sees' the world, but a great deal about how well the animal forages for food, avoids predators, finds mates, and moves efficiently from one part of the environment to another. To understand how the visuomotor systems controlling these behaviours are organized, it is necessary to study both the selectivity of their sensory inputs and the characteristics of the different motor outputs they control.

1.3 **Mammalian vision**

1.3.1 **Traditional approaches**

Such modularity is not limited to amphibia. Other vertebrate classes, including mammals, also show evidence of independent and parallel visuomotor pathways (Goodale and Graves 1982; Goodale and Milner 1982; Ingle 1982, 1991; Goodale 1983*a*, 1988). The evidence is limited, however, not because investigators have looked for it and failed to find it, but because almost all studies of vision in mammals (including humans) have approached the problem in perceptual and cognitive terms and have largely ignored the visual control of motor output. Indeed, a theoretical commitment to vision *qua* perception has shaped the methodology used to study vision and the visual system of animals in most laboratories throughout this century. Instead of examining the relationship between motor outputs and visual inputs (in a manner similar to that employed by investigators studying vision in the frog and other amphibia), investigators working with mammals have typically looked at the performance of their subjects on some form of visual discrimination task (Fig. 1.5).

The use of the visual discrimination paradigm is quite consistent, of course, with the assumption that the ultimate function of the vision is perceptual in nature. Given this assumption, then, by varying the stimulus parameters and training conditions on a visual discrimination task, one should be able to gain

Fig. 1.5 Examples of the different kinds of apparatus used to study visual discrimination learning in animals. (A) An operant chamber for testing pigeons. (B) A jumping stand for testing rats. (C) A Wisconsin General Testing Apparatus for testing monkeys. Very different responses are used in each case—pecking in the pigeon, jumping in the rat, and reaching and grasping in the monkey. It is assumed that the form of the motor response is not important, only the choice that the animal makes.

useful insights into how normal and brain-damaged animals extract information from the stimulus array and how they code and store that information. According to this argument, it does not matter what actual motor behaviour is required of the animal in such tasks. The animal could be pressing a lever, jumping from one platform to another, running down an alley-way, pulling a string, pushing aside the cover of a food well, or picking up an object. All that matters is that the animal discriminates among the relevant visual stimuli. It is this discriminative decision, not the motor act, that is of primary importance. From this point of view, it is clearly pointless to look at different motor outputs, since, except for a few visual reflexes, the visually guided behaviour of the animal is always generated on the basis of the internal representation or model that the visual system provides. Accordingly, any modularity in the visual system is limited to the input side and the different inputs are combined (eventually) into some sort of integrated representation.

The idea that one motor response can be commandeered by the visual system as easily as any other, provided the right kind of training paradigm is used, pervaded behaviorism and consequently physiological psychology, for most of this century. For example, Skinner (1938) and his disciples believed that it was possible to establish any stimulus–response association by appropriate reinforcement and were deeply suspicious of any suggestion that certain motor outputs enjoyed privileged access to a given sensory input. But the idea that vision can be studied quite independently of motor output came to extend far beyond behaviorism and still permeates most contemporary psychological and physiological accounts of visual function, including those information-processing theories that have rejected the basic tenets of behaviorism. For most investigators, the study of vision is seen as an enterprise that can be conducted without any reference whatsoever to the relationship between visual inputs and motor outputs. This research tradition stems directly from phenomenological intuitions that regard vision purely as a perceptual phenomenon.

The same approach characterizes *a fortiori* the majority of studies in human vision. Psychophysical studies, for example, typically require subjects to indicate whether or not they can detect a particular stimulus or whether two stimuli are the same or different. Most studies of vision in patients with brain damage have taken the same kind of 'perceptual' approach and have concentrated on how well such individuals 'see' the world. Because the investigator is interested in the subject's percepts of the stimuli in question, the choice of response mode is generally assumed to be a simple matter of convenience. It could be a verbal utterance, a keystroke on a computer, a button press, an eye movement, the rotation of a knob, or, perhaps, a pantomimed matching response. Again it is supposed that it is the subject's decision that is critical and that the nature of the response is irrelevant. The notion that different motor outputs might have preferential access to different visual inputs is not seen as an issue in most contemporary accounts of visual processing. Modularity on the output side, when it is considered at all, is assumed to be largely independent of input modularity and the province of quite separate subdisciplines such as motor physiology and motor-skills psychology.

There are, however, some striking exceptions to this research tradition. The most notable example is in the study of eye movements. Here, perhaps because the spatial and temporal characteristics of the movements are so obviously related to the nature of the visual array, investigators have routinely recorded the movements directly while at the same time systematically manipulating the characteristics of the controlling stimuli. In this way the activity of single cells in the superior colliculus and other visuomotor structures have been shown to be related not only to the characteristics of the visual stimulus (and other sensory inputs, such as those provided by the vestibular system), but also to the characteristics of the motor output. On the basis of this kind of electrophysiological work, together with information derived from anatomical studies and behavioural lesion studies, investigators have made substantial progress in working out the control systems that link visual input with oculomotor output. Indeed, oculomotor systems, particularly the control of saccadic eye movements, probably constitute the best understood set of visuomotor systems in mammals (for reviews of work on the superior colliculus, see Sparks and Hartwich-Young (1989) and Sparks and May (1990)). To achieve this understanding, of course, it has been necessary to study the motor outputs of these systems as thoroughly as their visual inputs. Such progress would not have been possible within the psychological tradition discussed above, in which visual processing is regarded as something quite independent of the motor outputs it might ultimately guide.

1.3.2 Visuomotor modules in mammals

But apart from eye movements, there has been little work on the neural substrates of visuomotor control in mammals. Part of the reason for this, of course, is that measuring behavioural actions, until recently, has been technically difficult. Recording the movements of the limb and hand during an act of prehension, for example, is a much more challenging task than recording an eye movement. The mathematical models for hand and limb movements are also more complex, involving many more degrees of freedom. But the main barriers to the study of visuomotor control, as we have already suggested, have been philosophical rather than practical. For most researchers, the study of vision is an endeavour quite independent of the study of motor control.

The few studies that have looked in detail at visuomotor control systems in mammals have found that they are organized, at the subcortical level at least, in much the same way as they are in amphibia. In many mammals, for example, retinal projections to the superior colliculus (the homologue of the optic tectum) appear to play an important role in mediating brisk eye, head, and body movements to novel and baited targets that are initially presented in the visual periphery. Thus, lesions of the superior colliculus in a variety of mammals, including rats, hamsters, gerbils, cats, and monkeys, disrupt or dramatically reduce the animal's ability to orient to visual targets, particularly targets presented in the visual periphery (see the review by Goodale and Milner (1982)). Conversely, stimulation of this structure, either electrically or pharmacologically, will often elicit contraversive movements of the eyes, head, limbs, and body that resemble normal orienting movements (see the review by Dean *et al.* (1989)). The orienting behaviour that appears to be mediated by the superior colliculus has been characterized by some writers, most notably Hess *et al.* (1946), as a 'visual grasp reflex' (*visueller Greifreflex*), a rapid shift in gaze that brings a stimulus originally located in the visual periphery into the central vision where it can be scrutinized in more detail.

The idea of a 'visual grasp reflex' may usefully describe one function of this orienting behaviour in some species, such as the cat and monkey, which possess a well-developed area centralis or fovea. Yet it cannot explain why such movements are also evident in many rodent species in which retinal ganglion cell density (and, thus, visual sensitivity) varies only slightly across the retina (Sengelaub *et al.* 1983; Dreher *et al.* 1984). Instead of placing the stimulus on the fovea, the rapid orientation movements that are subserved by the superior colliculus in rodents may rather serve to position a stimulus so that it can be approached and grasped with the mouth and forelimbs. Furthermore, by positioning the stimulus directly in front of the animal's nose and mouth, such behaviour would put the stimulus in a convenient position for olfactory, gustatory, and tactile exploration. Indeed, pharmacological stimulation of some sites in the rodent colliculus, in addition to producing contraversive movements of the head and body, will elicit biting and gnawing movements (Kilpatrick *et al.* 1982). In other words, orienting towards the stimulus is not so much a metaphorical 'visual' grasp, but rather the precursor to an actual one. (For a more detailed discussion of this issue, see Goodale and Carey (1990).) Thus, the projections to the superior colliculus, in rodents at least, appear to be remarkably similar in their function to the visuomotor modules controlling feeding in the frog.

This evident homology in functional architecture is further supported by the recent demonstration that visually elicited orienting and pursuit movements in the rodent, like the turning components of visually elicited feeding in the frog, depend on descending projections from the superior colliculus to the contralateral brainstem and spinal cord (Ellard and Goodale 1986, 1988; Dean *et al.* 1989; see Fig. 1.6). Unlike the amphibian system, however, the orientation system in rodents and other mammals is influenced by descending projections from visual areas in the cerebral cortex to both the superior colliculus itself and its target nuclei in the brainstem and spinal cord (for a review, see Goodale and Carey (1990)). Nevertheless, the apparent similarities in the neural substrates of visually elicited orientation in the rodent and visually elicited feeding in the frog are striking and argue for a common evolutionary heritage. Indeed, the participation of collicular networks in the control of saccadic eye movements in the primate can be seen to reflect in part a further development in this same evolutionary history. A discussion of the role of the tectospinal tract in predation throughout vertebrate evolution can be found in a recent review by Barton and Dean (1993).

There are further parallels between mammals and amphibians in their visuomotor modularity. In particular, a second projection system in the

Fig. 1.6 Illustrative drawings of different classes of responses elicited from microstimulation of the superior colliculus in the Mongolian gerbil (Meriones unguiculatus). (A) Orienting responses, characterized by smooth head and body turns made in a direction contralateral to the site of electrical stimulation (indicated by the black dot in one of the two colliculi drawn on the gerbil's head). (B) Escape responses, characterized by rapid running movements (with minimal head turning) made in a direction ipsilateral to the stimulation site. The contraversive orienting responses, but not the ipsiversive escape responses, are eliminated by sectioning the dorsal tegmental decussation which contains the descending projections from the superior colliculus to the contralateral brainstem and spinal cord. For more information, see Ellard and Goodale (1986).

rodent, from the retina to the superior colliculus and from there to targets in the ipsilateral brainstem, appears to mediate visually elicited escape reactions in a manner remarkably similar to that which we have described in the frog. Thus, lesions of the superior colliculus in rats and gerbils dramatically reduce escape responses to threatening visual stimuli, such as an unexpected overhead movement (for example, Goodale and Murison 1975; Ellard and Goodale 1988). Conversely, electrical or pharmacological stimulation of the superior colliculus in the rat and gerbil will sometimes elicit freezing, ipsiversive 'cringing' and turning movements, or explosive startle reactions that resemble responses to sudden or threatening visual stimuli (Ellard and Goodale 1986; Dean *et al.* 1989). Moreover, as Fig. 1.7 illustrates, lesions that interrupt the uncrossed tectal projections to the brainstem in the gerbil eliminate escape reactions to large looming visual targets while transections of the descending crossed pathways do not (Ellard and Goodale 1988). Like the frog then, the rodent appears to have a 'duplex' optic tectum, with a largely crossed tectofugal pathway mediating orienting movements of the head and body and a largely uncrossed tectofugal pathway mediating a constellation of escape behaviours. The evident homology is further extended by the observation that these two efferent projections originate from cells in the superior colliculus that are located in different laminae and that have different visual response characteristics (Westby *et al.* 1990). For instance, cells that respond to stimuli in the upper visual field tend to be associated with the 'escape' pathway, while those in the lower field are typically linked with the 'approach' system.

Finally, there is evidence that a visual projection from the retina to the pretectum mediates barrier avoidance, much as in the frog. Thus, as can be seen in Fig. 1.8, gerbils with lesions of the pretectal nuclei, like frogs with similar lesions, have difficulty negotiating large barriers placed in front of them (Goodale and Milner 1982; Goodale 1983*b*). Unfortunately, little as yet is known in detail about the neural architecture of this visuomotor module in mammals.

In summary, the modular organization of visuomotor behaviour in representative species of at least one mammalian order, the rodents, appears to resemble that of much simpler vertebrates such as the frog and toad. In both groups of animals, visually elicited orienting movements, visually elicited escape, and visually guided locomotion around barriers are mediated by quite separate pathways from the retina right through to motor nuclei in the brainstem and spinal cord. This striking homology in neural architecture suggests that modularity in visuomotor control is an ancient (and presumably efficient) characteristic of vertebrate brains.

Fig. 1.7 The proportion of trials in which visually elicited escape responses were observed in gerbils with different surgical lesions of the midbrain visual pathways. The stimulus used to elicit escape was a black rectangular target that was suddenly introduced into the visual field above the animal. SH, sham operations; D, interruption of contralateral descending output from the superior colliculus (dorsal tegmental decussation); LT, interruption of the descending ipsilateral projections from the colliculus (lateral tegmental region); SC, lesions of the superior colliculus itself. The LT and SC groups showed the fewest escape responses. From Ellard and Goodale (1988).

Two important questions remain however. Does this kind of modular organization, in which both input and output lines are specified, extend to visual projection systems within the cerebral cortex, including the cortical elaborations of the geniculostriate system? And does the visual system of 'higher' mammalian orders, such as the primates, in which the geniculostriate system is so well developed, show evidence of functional modularity similar to that seen in less complex vertebrate groups?

In mammals, of course, particularly in primates, not all visual processing is linked directly to specific kinds of motor output. The world of a monkey is much more complex and unpredictable than that of a frog and more flexible information processing is required. Identifying objects and events in that world and establishing their causal relations could not be mediated by simple input–output systems like the ones controlling feeding in the frog. Nevertheless, it is a truism that all visual processing systems ultimately serve to guide behaviour, otherwise they would not have evolved at all. This point was appreciated by the late Otto Creutzfeldt (1981, 1985), who recognized the crucial

Fig. 1.8 (A) Schematic diagram of barrier task showing the path followed by a normal gerbil running through a semicircular arena towards a target door for a food reward. A barrier, made of transparent plastic and covered with vertical black stripes, was positioned between the entrance and the target door. Over trials, the position of the barrier and the target door were randomly varied. The position of the gerbil's head was recorded at approximately 60 Hz and a line was drawn through the longitudinal axis of the head and through the two eyes on each frame. (B) Graph showing the percentage of trials on which different groups of gerbils successfully avoided the barrier. SH, sham operations; SC_1 and SC_2, lesions of superior colliculus; PT, lesions of pretectum; VC, lesions of visual cortex.

importance of output connections in any full description of the functions of cortical visual areas. We endorse this view and will explore it in the next chapter. As we shall see, despite the complexity of their interconnections, primate cortical visual areas can be divided into two functional groupings: one with rather direct links to motor control systems and the other with connections to systems associated with memory, planning, and other more 'cognitive' processes.

It is our view that this second group of visual areas subserves an intermediate goal in the guidance of behaviour, specifically the formation of perceptual representations of objects and of their relationships. Such representations are necessary if behaviour is to be guided intelligently by events that have occurred at an earlier time, allowing, for example, a mate or a prey object to be categorized correctly and, thus, acted upon appropriately. This use of vision in the categorization and recognition of objects must rely on stored information that can be abstracted from particular viewpoints or contexts in which the object might be seen. Furthermore, to permit maximum flexibility this system must be free from rigid linkage to particular possible responses, though the system would be essential for the selection of goals and the selection of actions relating to those goals. This perceptual system would by its nature have to be independent of particular motor outputs.

In contrast, the *execution* of such an action may be controlled by dedicated visuomotor channels not dissimilar in principle to those found in amphibia. For example, as we have already indicated, much of the control of saccadic eye movements in primates, including humans, depends on the sensorimotor transformations that are carried out in the superior colliculus. In higher mammals, however, this basic tectal circuitry is modulated by projections from visual areas in the cerebral cortex both to the superior colliculus itself and to motor nuclei in the brainstem (cf. Bruce 1990). Thus, even though the superior colliculus still plays a pivotal role in the control of saccadic eye movements, it has become part of a cortically modulated system. As will become clear in subsequent chapters, it is our contention that this dedicated oculomotor system operates as one of a set of interacting visuomotor systems or modules in the cerebral cortex. These modules support a range of skilled behaviours such as visually guided reaching and grasping, in which a high degree of coordination is required between movements of the fingers, hands, upper limbs, head, and eyes. We will also argue that the visual inputs and transformations required by these visuomotor systems differ in important respects from those leading to the visual perception of objects and events in the world. Indeed, it is possible that mechanisms for perceptual representation, supplementing those controlling action, have emerged only in higher mammals such as primates; they may not be evident at all in the simpler visual systems of amphibia and other less complex vertebrates.

In summary, we are suggesting that two separate networks of areas have evolved in the primate visual cortex: a perceptual system which is indirectly linked to action via cognitive processes, and a visuomotor system which is intimately linked with motor control. Of course, other divisions of labour have been proposed in previous discussions of the visual system, but the functional emphasis has always been on the features of the visual array that are analysed rather than the nature of the outputs that are controlled. One of the most pervasive of these schemes has been the distinction between 'what' versus 'where'. It is appropriate here to give a brief review of the development of that particular dichotomy—perhaps the best known functional distinction in visual neuroscience—before developing our own hypothesis in the ensuing chapters.

1.3.3 'Two visual systems' hypotheses

In the late 1960s, a number of different functional dichotomies of the visual system were proposed, most of them contrasting the functions of the phylogenetically older pathway from the retina to the superior colliculus with those of the more recently evolved geniculostriate system. For example, Trevarthen (1968) suggested, primarily from evidence derived from 'split-brain' monkeys and humans, that the midbrain system mediates what he called 'ambient' vision, while the geniculostriate system mediates 'focal' vision. He thought of this distinction primarily in terms of the different action systems that might be served by the two visual pathways: ambient vision guiding whole-body movements such as locomotion and posture, and focal vision guiding fine motor acts such as manipulation. This distinction was an important one to make, since it implied that the visual pathways do not constitute a unitary system but instead consist of at least two independent channels from the retina to the brain.

The most influential of the 'two visual systems' hypotheses proposed at this time, however, was that of Schneider (1969), who argued that the retinal projection to the superior colliculus enables organisms to localize a stimulus in visual space, while the geniculostriate system allows them to identify that stimulus. Like Trevarthen's (1968) model, Schneider's (1969) two visual systems model represented a significant departure from earlier 'monolithic' descriptions of visual function and introduced a more modular approach. But the notion of 'localization' that Schneider (1969) proposed was poorly defined and failed to distinguish adequately between the many different patterns of spatially organized behaviour, only some of which (as is now known) depend on the participation of collicular mechanisms. Indeed, although the putative function of the superior colliculus that Schneider (1969) put forward included elements reminiscent of the 'visual grasp reflex', the emphasis was on the nature of the visual coding—seen as enabling stimulus localization—rather than on the nature of the response. Within the framework of this two visual systems model, a considerable range of behaviours was thought to depend on spatially coded visual information within the superior colliculus. For example, localizing a food object during visually elicited prey catching and localizing the edge of a barrier during visually guided locomotion, would both, in Schneider's view, depend on the same localization mechanism in the superior colliculus. As we have seen, later research showed that both in the frog and in the gerbil, these two behaviours in fact depend on separate visuomotor systems, only one of which involves the superior colliculus. Nevertheless, even though Schneider's (1969) two visual systems model is no longer as influential as it once was, the distinction between object identification and spatial localization—between 'what' and 'where'—has persisted in visual neuroscience and represents one of the major watersheds of present-day thinking about the functional organization of the visual system.

In a much-cited paper, in particular, Ungerleider and Mishkin (1982) concluded that 'appreciation of an object's qualities and of its spatial location depends on the processing of different kinds of visual information in the inferior temporal and posterior parietal cortex, respectively' (p. 578). Here one sees the same distinction between identification and localization suggested earlier by Schneider (1969). Now, however, the functional dichotomy is kept entirely cortical and the putative division between 'what' and 'where' is mapped on to two diverging streams of output from the striate cortex which had been identified in the primate brain, one progressing ventrally to the inferotemporal cortex and the other dorsally to the posterior parietal cortex (see Fig. 1.9). It is notable that this conceptualization places the 'where' pathway firmly within a perceptual framework, rather than identifying it with a system for the spatial control of motor orientation as Schneider's (1969) model had.

Ungerleider and Mishkin's (1982) functional distinction (see also Mishkin *et al.* 1983; Ungerleider 1985) has been widely considered to provide a unifying framework for theorizing about higher visual processing in the primate brain and to encompass neatly a large body of knowledge ranging from human neuropsychology to monkey neurophysiology. Their distinction between two visual systems, one specialized for object vision, the other for spatial vision, now permeates most cognitive, computational, and philosophical accounts of vision designed to relate to the neural hardware. Vaina (1990), for example, sets out to show how the computational constraints imposed on visual representations can be accommodated within Ungerleider and Mishkin's (1982) distinction between the ventral and dorsal systems. It would perhaps not be an exaggeration to say that this 'two cortical visual systems' model has been the most influential account of higher visual organization in neuroscience throughout the 1980s. It should be noted, however, that notwithstanding the great influence that their synthesis has had within

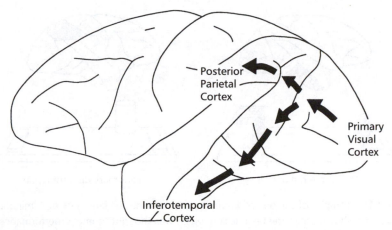

Fig. 1.9 A schematic diagram of Ungerleider and Mishkin's original (1982) model of the two streams of visual processing in the primate cerebral cortex. The brain illustrated is that of a macaque monkey.

cognitive neuroscience, Ungerleider, Mishkin, and their colleagues have now modified the 1982 model by acknowledging the important role played by the dorsal stream in visuomotor control (for example, Boussaoud *et al.* 1990; Haxby *et al.* 1993).

The main evidence for Ungerleider and Mishkin's (1982) position was derived from behavioural experiments in which the visual discrimination abilities of monkeys with lesions of inferotemporal cortex or posterior parietal cortex were compared (Fig. 1.10). Monkeys with inferotemporal lesions show profound impairments in visual pattern recognition (see the review by Gross (1973)), while this is not true for monkeys with posterior parietal lesions. In contrast, these parietal-lesioned animals may show greater impairment in their ability to use a spatial 'landmark' as the discriminative cue in a choice task. According to Ungerleider and Mishkin's (1982) model, the two lesions disrupt different neural circuits: one specialized for the perception of objects, the other for the perception of the spatial relations between those objects. The emphasis in their account therefore is a distinction based primarily on stimulus attributes or features. Indeed, the central behavioural evidence for the theory was derived from the traditional visual discrimination paradigm which, as we indicated earlier, focuses on the animal's decision about the stimulus array rather than on the animal's visuomotor behaviour. We will critically review this behavioural evidence in Chapter 4, since it constitutes the linchpin of the Ungerleider and Mishkin (1982) model.

Object discrimination   Landmark discrimination

Fig. 1.10 Examples of the object discrimination task and the landmark discrimination task, each shown under the brain lesion which was thought to impair performance most. In the object discrimination task, the monkey learns to choose a particular object, the position of which is varied randomly from trial to trial. In the landmark discrimination task, the monkey learns to choose the food well closer to the landmark, the position of which is varied randomly from trial to trial. Adapted from Mishkin *et al.* (1983).

Our own account of the distinction between the dorsal and ventral projections takes a rather different approach. We accept that the two visual projection systems in the cortex are anatomically separate (and perhaps of independent evolutionary lineage; Pandya *et al.* 1988). We consider it unlikely, however, that they evolved simply to handle different aspects of the stimulus array, as the distinction between 'what' versus 'where' would suggest. Instead, we propose that the anatomical distinction between the ventral and dorsal streams corresponds to the distinction we made earlier between perceptual representation and visuomotor control. In other words, the reason there are two cortical pathways is that each must transform incoming visual information for different purposes (Goodale and Milner 1992; Milner and Goodale 1993). In the following chapters, we present the evidence for this new 'two visual systems' hypothesis and try to apply it to an understanding of the effects of brain damage in both humans and monkeys.

Chapter 2

Visual processing in the primate visual cortex

Parallel processing of sensory information in the vertebrate visual system is apparent even as the retinal fibres leave the eye on their way to the brain. Not only do the fibres project to a number of independent nuclei in the forebrain and midbrain, as we saw in Chapter 1, but they are already differentiated and partially segregated with respect to the kinds of information they convey to those targets. In this chapter, we first review the evidence for differential coding of information in the retinal projections. We then trace the visual projections through the primary visual cortex to higher visual processing areas in the cerebral cortex, paying particular attention to the electrophysiology of the different pathways and their interconnectivity. In the final sections of the chapter, we show how the organization of the different visual processing systems in the cortex can be related to the functional demands of visual perception, on the one hand, and the visual control of action, on the other.

While our review of the relevant neuroanatomy and electrophysiology is by no means exhaustive, a certain amount of detail is necessary so that we can develop a coherent and well-founded framework for interpreting the neuropsychological observations discussed in later chapters.

2.1 Evidence for parallel processing in retinal ganglion cells

2.1.1 'On' and 'off' responses

The coding properties of a neurone in the visual system can be explored physiologically by plotting its 'receptive field', that is, the area of the visual field within which a light stimulus can influence the firing of the cell. In pioneering work over 50 years ago, Hartline (1938) noted that some axons of retinal ganglion cells in the frog produce action potentials only when a light stimulus appears, while others respond only when a light stimulus is withdrawn and still others respond to both events. He also observed that these responses could be attenuated if regions adjacent to the excitatory area were stimulated, suggesting some form of lateral inhibition within the retina itself. Kuffler's (1953) successful application of single-unit recording techniques to the mammalian retina revealed a similar pattern of firing in the ganglion cells of the cat. Some cells, the so-called on-centre cells, fire when a light stimulus comes on in the centre of the cell's receptive field while others, the off-centre cells, fire when the light is extinguished. Surrounding this central region, Kuffler (1953) observed, is a concentric annulus from which responses of the opposite sign can be elicited. In the 40 years since Kuffler's (1953) first description of the antagonistic centre–surround receptive field of the cat ganglion cell, single-unit recording studies have been applied with great effect to the ascending visual projections in both the cat and monkey and have followed the processing of sensory information from the retina to the striate cortex (V1) and well beyond. Most notable were the studies of Hubel and Wiesel (1959, 1962, 1968, 1970), which provided clear evidence for increasingly complex analysis of the visual array as one moved higher and higher through the geniculostriate pathway.

2.1.2 X, Y, and W cells

At the same time, detailed analyses of the responses of retinal ganglion cells in a number of vertebrate species were revealing more complex receptive field properties than were first suspected. The elegant work of Lettvin *et al.* (1959) showed that some ganglion cells in the frog were sensitive to movement while others were sensitive to boundaries, and that at least four different functional classes of ganglion cells could be identified on the basis of their selectivity for particular visual stimuli. Some cells, for example, appeared to be highly sensitive to visual stimuli that could be said to resemble moving bugs or flies. These 'bug detectors' were later shown to project to those laminae in the optic tectum of the frog that have been implicated in the visual guidance of prey catching (see Chapter 1). Thus, the bug-detecting ganglion cells could be regarded as the first component of a visuomotor module dedicated to the elicitation and control of the movements comprising visually guided feeding. But while the discovery of different functional classes of ganglion cells in the frog fits well with the idea developed in Chapter 1 that different visual pathways evolved to control different kinds of motor output, similar observations in the mammalian retina, as we shall see, have not been interpreted in this way.

Perhaps the most influential distinction that has been made in ganglion cell types in the mammalian retina is the one first reported by Enroth-Cugell and Robson (1966). On the basis of a detailed analysis of the response characteristics of ganglion cells in the cat retina, these investigators distinguished between two classes of cells, which they named X and Y. The significance of this discovery became apparent during the next few years as the properties of the two populations of ganglion cells were further explored (for reviews, see Rodieck (1979) and Lennie (1980)). It was found that X cells sustain their responses for as long as the stimulus is present in the receptive field. In addition, X cells have relatively small receptive fields (providing sensitivity to high spatial frequencies) and their axons show medium conduction velocities. In contrast, Y cells respond transiently to visual stimuli and have relatively large receptive fields (providing sensitivity to only low spatial frequencies) and rapidly conducting axons. A third class of ganglion cells, the so-called W cells, was also discovered (Stone and Hoffman 1972); these cells have the most slowly conducting axons of all and a broad range of different response characteristics.

As one might expect, a number of competing hypotheses were soon put forward to account for these differences in responsivity (for a review, see Schiller (1986)). According to some of these hypotheses, the X cells are responsible for the analysis of spatial pattern and the Y cells for temporal pattern. In other accounts, the function of the X cells is still seen as being involved in the analysis of spatial pattern, but the Y cells are believed to transmit high-speed information about the spatial location and movement of visual stimuli. Still other hypotheses have suggested that while the Y system provides information about basic forms in the visual array, the X system provides greater spatial resolution and position sensitivity. All of these early hypotheses, it is worth noting, emphasize the contribution of the different systems to visual perception. Except for the observation that the Y cells project heavily to the superior colliculus (the mammalian optic tectum) and are therefore presumably involved in the stimulus control of saccadic eye movements, little attention was paid to the possibility that these different systems might have evolved to control rather different classes of motor behaviour. The two classes (the W system, which also projects to the superior colliculus, as well as to the interlaminar layers of the LGNd, was rarely discussed) were instead conceived as parallel channels delivering information about different visual attributes for the purpose of constructing a coherent perceptual representation of the external world.

2.2 Parallel channels within the primate geniculostriate pathway

2.2.1 Magno and parvo channels

In the mid-1980s, a similar but more ambitious account of parallel processing began to emerge in the context of the primate visual system. As we shall see, according to this account, two parallel pathways can be followed from the retina through the lateral geniculate nucleus and striate cortex and then deep into the inferior temporal and poserior parietal regions of the primate brain (Maunsell 1987; Livingstone and Hubel 1988). The starting point for this model was the observation that a distinction between X-like and Y-like ganglion cells is present in the primate retina (for example Dreher *et al.* 1976; Sherman *et al.* 1976). Although there is not complete agreement on the nature of the differences between these two classes, a number of distinctive anatomical and physiological features have been described (Schiller and Logothetis 1990; Merigan and Maunsell 1993). One class of primate ganglion cells (the so-called Pα, A, or parasol cells) have relatively large cell bodies with radiating dendrites. Like the cat Y-cells, the Pα cells have large receptive fields, respond transiently to visual stimulation, and have rapidly conducting axons. All three of the cone-type photoreceptors that have been described in the Old World monkeys appear to converge upon these cells, giving them spectrally 'broadband' properties. The second class of primate ganglion cells (the Pβ, B, or midget cells) have medium-sized to small cell bodies and rather small dendritic arbours. Like the cat X-cells, the Pβ ganglion cells have small receptive fields, respond in a sustained fashion to visual stimulation, and have somewhat slower conduction velocities. In contrast to the Pα cells, the receptive field centre of most Pβ cells reflects input from only one or two cone types. Since complementary spectral information is received from the surround regions within the receptive field of these Pβ neurones, they are frequently characterized as forming a 'colour-opponent' channel.

The anatomical distinction between the two channels is preserved at the level of the primate lateral geniculate nucleus (LGNd) with the Pβ ganglion cells projecting to the four parvocellular layers and the Pα ganglion cells projecting to the two magnocellular layers (Dreher *et al.* 1976; Leventhal *et al.* 1981). The physiological differences between the two channels also appear to be preserved (and even enhanced) at the level of the LGNd neurones upon which the ganglion cells synapse. The most influential account of these differences was put forward by Livingstone and Hubel (1988) who argued that the so-called parvo and magno divisions differ physiologically in four major ways—colour, temporal resolution, contrast sensitivity, and acuity. The parvo system, according to Livingstone and Hubel (1988), is colour selective and relatively slow with low contrast sensitivity and high spatial resolution, while the magno system is colour-blind and relatively fast, with high contrast sensitivity and low spatial resolution. Thus, the differences between the magno and parvo systems in the LGNd are similar in many ways to the differences we have already seen in the response characteristics of the Pα and Pβ ganglion cells that project differentially to them.

As Fig. 2.1 illustrates, the two channels stay separate even as they progress to the primary visual cortex (V1). Here the magnocellular LGNd axons terminate in sublayer $4C\alpha$, and the parvocellular axons beneath them in $4C\beta$ (though both also send some projections to layer 6). The outputs from these two sublayers of layer 4C project in turn to other layers in V1, with sublayer $4C\alpha$ projecting to layer 4B and sublayer $4C\beta$ to layers 2 and 3.

In layers 2 and 3, a further (until recently anatomically covert) subdivision in the visual system was discovered. Histochemical techniques developed by Wong-Riley (see Schiller 1986) in which tissue is stained for the enzyme cytochrome oxidase have revealed a regular pattern of spots or 'blobs' of high oxidative metabolism across the striate cortex (Horton and Hubel 1981; Hendrickson 1985). The photomicrograph in Fig. 2.2 shows the distribution of cytochrome oxidase blobs in a tangential section of monkey striate cortex. According to Hubel and Livingstone (1987), although the blobs and the interblob regions both receive inputs primarily from the parvo system (via sublayer $4C\beta$), the neurones within the two subdivisions appear to be somewhat

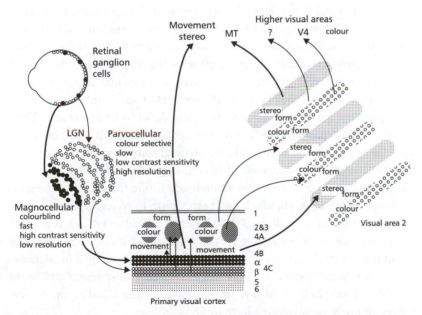

Fig. 2.1 Schematic diagram of the functional and anatomical segregation of the magno- and parvocellular pathways in the primate visual system according to Livingstone and Hubel (1988). The differential projections to the lower layers and the subdivisions of the upper layers of the primary visual cortex and to the subdivisions (stripes) in visual area V2 are shown. MT, middle temporal area; V4, visual area 4; LGN, lateral geniculate nucleus (dorsal part).

different in terms of their electrophysiological characteristics. Moreover, there was also evidence that the blobs receive an input from the magno system.

Thus, by the late 1980s, it appeared that there were three distinguishable streams of processing passing through V1: one projecting from the magnocellular layers of LGNd to sublayer 4Cα and from there to layer 4B, a second from the parvocellular layers of LGNd to sublayer 4Cβ and from there to the interblob regions of layers 2 and 3, and, finally, a third projecting from the parvocellular layers of LGNd to sublayer 4Cβ and from there to the blobs of layers 2 and 3 (along with a smaller input from the magno system). Livingstone and Hubel (1984; Hubel and Livingstone 1987) have been prominent in exploring the respective cell properties of these three streams. They showed that cells in the blobs are predominantly colour selective in a 'double-opponent' fashion. Most have simple (usually circular or elliptical) receptive fields, in the centre of which light of a fairly narrow wavelength band activates the cell but light of a complementary colour inhibits it, while in the surround of the receptive field, the opposite relationship holds. Most of these 'blob cells' have little or no orientation selectivity, binocularity, or selectivity for movement direction and they prefer relatively low spatial frequencies. In contrast, the cells in the interblob regions have relatively little colour sensitivity (though more than cells in the magno system). They do, however, show tuning for high spatial frequencies (enabling them to provide fine visual acuity) along with selectivity for stimulus orientation and often for binocular disparity. Unlike the blob cells, some of the interblob cells have selectivity both for a particular orientation and for colour (recently studied in detail by Lennie *et al.* (1990)). As De Yoe and Van Essen (1988) have commented, these cells might be able to signal the orientation of an edge which is defined entirely on the basis of chromatic contrast, that is, one invisible to a colour-blind visual system.

In contrast to either of these two subdivisions within the superficial layers of the striate cortex, layer 4B, which had been shown to receive projections primarily from the magnocellular LGNd layers (via sublayer 4Cα), contains a high proportion of cells selective for the direction of stimulus motion. Like cells in the interblob regions, however, cells here also have a high incidence of orientation selectivity and are sensitive to binocular disparity. But like the 'broad-band' cells in LGNd which provide most of their visual input, the cells in layer 4B rarely show colour selectivity.

(It should be noted here that the idea of only two geniculostriate channels, the magno and the parvo, may be an oversimplification. Hendry and Yoshioka (1994) have recently shown that there are prominent and direct projections to V1 from neurones located in the interlaminar regions lying in between the well-known magno and parvo layers of LGNd. These neurones, which Hendry and Yoshioka (1994) have likened to the W system in the cat (see Casagrande 1994), project directly to the blobs of V1 and, thus, may play a significant role in determining the visual properties of cells in these regions.)

2.2.2 Magno and parvo projections to the Extrastriate Cortex

Livingstone and Hubel (1988) presented additional evidence which suggested that the parvo and magno systems remain segregated well beyond the striate cortex. Thus, for example, layer 4B, which receives input primarily from the magno system, projects directly to an area usually known as MT (Lund *et al.* 1975; Maunsell and Van Essen 1983*b*). This area, the middle temporal area (sometimes called V5) is, as we shall see later, particularly concerned with the processing of visual motion.

But the main target for projections from the striate cortex or area V1 is the adjacent area V2 (part of Brodmann's area 18), which like V1 also shows a regular pattern when stained for cytochrome oxidase. Instead of small round or elliptical blobs, however, tangential sections through area V2 show a pattern of alternating dark and light stripes which run approximately perpendicular to the border between areas V1 and V2 (see Fig. 2.2). There are typically two kinds of dark stripes, thick and thin, which alternate with the pale stripes in which the cytochrome oxidase staining is less dense. These three histologically distinct subdivisions in V2 are reciprocally connected

Fig. 2.2 Photomicrographs of slices parallel to the cortical surface through the upper layers of V1 and V2 in macaque (left) and squirrel monkey (right). The small dark spots are the 'blobs' in V1 stained for cytochrome oxidase. The stripes in V2, bordering V1, can also be seen. In the squirrel monkey cortex in particular, the thin and thick stripes and the paler interstripe regions can be clearly seen. A, anterior; P, posterior; M, medial; and L, lateral. Adapted from Hubel and Livingstone (1987).

with the three subsystems in V1 described earlier. Thus, layer 4B is connected to the thick stripes, the blobs to the thin stripes, and the interblob regions to the pale stripes (or interstripe regions). Although the visible difference between 'thick' and 'thin' stripes is less clear in Old World than in New World monkeys and even less clear in humans (Wong-Riley *et al.* 1993), it may reasonably be assumed that blobs connect preferentially with alternate dark stripes in all primate species.

Electrophysiological investigations have shown that many of the properties of cells in the three subdivisions of V2 reflect those of the cells in the antecedent subsystems of V1 (Livingstone and Hubel 1984). Like many of the cells in layer 4B of V1, which receive inputs primarily from the magno pathway, the majority of the cells in the thick stripes are tuned for retinal disparity, motion direction, and orientation. Cells in the thick stripes, then, would appear to be particularly adapted for extracting stereoscopic information about depth and motion. Cells in the thin stripes, like the cells in the V1 blobs with which they are connected, show no evidence of orientation or direction selectivity but over half of them are colour coded. Like the colour-sensitive cells in the blobs, these cells are of the double-opponent process type. Thus, the thin stripes, like the blobs, contain cells that are particularly well-suited for the processing of colour information. The remainder of the cells in the thin stripes are rather broadly tuned for wavelength. Cells in the pale stripes, like their counterparts in the interblob regions of V1, are orientation selective but unlike the majority of interblob cells, many of them are also 'end-stopped', responding best to short but not long edges or lines. Hubel and Livingstone (1987) found none of these cells to be explicitly tuned for colour (though more recent studies have tempered this conclusion; Merigan and Maunsell 1993). The interblob–pale stripe channel appears instead to encode information about the shape or configuration of visual stimuli.

Beyond V2, the parallel structure of the projections is much more difficult to establish. Nevertheless, Livingstone and Hubel (1988) made a strong argument that the separation of the parvo and magno systems continues deep into extrastriate visual areas. Area MT, for example, which as we noted earlier receives input directly from layer 4B in area V1, also receives input from the thick stripes of V2 (De Yoe and Van Essen 1985; Shipp and Zeki 1985). Electrophysiological recordings from MT and the neighbouring area MST (medial superior temporal area) have shown that cells respond best to moving patterns, including objects moving in depth, and that they code for both the direction and speed of stimulus motion (see Maunsell and Newsome (1987) for a review). Furthermore, the response characteristics of cells in these areas are often holistic in nature, reflecting the motion of configurations rather than of figural elements (Movshon *et al*. 1985). In contrast, cells in V1 and V2, which are presumed to provide the input to MT, respond only to the motion of individual pattern elements within the stimulus.

Other prestriate visual areas appear to receive a very different set of inputs. Area V4, for example, first identified by Zeki (1971, 1973) and found by him to contain a preponderance of cells that code for colour, receives input from the thin stripes of V2, which similarly contain colour selective cells (De Yoe and Van Essen 1985; Shipp and Zeki 1985). There is also evidence that the pale stripes of V2 project to V4, though perhaps with a distribution different from the thin stripes (Zeki and Shipp 1989). Many cells in V4, irrespective of their colour sensitivity, are also selective for stimulus orientation (Tanaka *et al*. 1986; Desimone and Schein 1987). There are also projections from the thin and pale stripes in V2 direct to the visual area TEO in the temporal lobe (Nakamura *et al*. 1993).

2.3 Does magno/parvo map onto dorsal/ventral?

2.3.1 The Livingstone and Hubel proposal

It was evidence such as that discussed above that led Livingstone and Hubel (1988) to propose that the parvo and magno channels remain segregated well beyond the primary visual cortex. Indeed, they went on to suggest that the ventral and dorsal projection streams emanating from the striate cortex, which had been identified earlier by Ungerleider and Mishkin (1982), might represent the continuation of the parvo and magno systems, respectively. According to this view, the parvo channel, remaining independent from the eye to the inferotemporal cortex, plays an essential role in object identification, while the magno channel, running in a quite separate course from the retina through to the posterior parietal cortex, is critical to the localization of objects in the visual field. In short, the 'what' and 'where' pathways originally described by Ungerleider and Mishkin (1982) could now be traced back to the cytological subdivisions of LGNd.

Livingstone and Hubel's (1988) conception of the distinction between the magno and parvo channels, however, was much more detailed than the hypothesis put forward by Ungerleider and Mishkin (1982). In establishing the differences in processing between the two channels, Livingstone and Hubel (1988) appealed to the apparent correlation between a broad range of human psychophysical data and the electrophysiological characteristics of the parvo and magno pathways. They suggested that a larger 'magno system' might be primarily concerned with global spatial organization: 'deciding which visual elements, such as edges and discontinuities, belong to and define individual objects in the scene, as well as determining the overall three-dimensional organization of the scene and the positions of objects in space and movements of objects' (p. 748). The 'parvo system', they argued, is more 'important for analyzing the scene in much greater and more leisurely detail' (p. 748). Thus, the parvo system is conceived of as being sensitive to details about the shape, colour, and surface properties of objects. Moreover, by correlating the multiple visual attributes of an object, the parvo system, which projects through to the temporal lobe, could identify that object and help to establish its associations with other objects and events in the animal's world.

2.3.2 Contrary evidence

Bold and exciting as Livingstone and Hubel's (1988) proposal was, it soon became apparent that there were some difficulties. First, psychophysical studies of monkeys with discrete lesions of the parvo- and magnocellular layers of LGNd revealed a pattern of deficits that do not conform to the distinctions made in the proposal (for reviews, see Schiller and Logothetis (1990) and Merigan and Maunsell (1993)). While it is true that lesions of the parvocellular but not the magnocellular layers severely compromise colour discriminations, other results do not fit so well with the division of labour that Livingstone and Hubel (1988) envisaged. Thus, monkeys with parvocellular lesions show deficits in fine (but not coarse) stereopsis, while no deficits in stereopsis are seen in monkeys with lesions of the magnocellular layers. This finding challenges the idea that the magno channel has exclusive responsibility for stereoscopic vision. Moreover, deficits in luminance contrast sensitivity following lesions of the parvo and magno pathways appear to depend on the spatial and temporal frequency of the stimuli presented (Schiller et al. 1990; Merigan et al. 1991a, b). Lesions of the magno pathway cause a dramatic decrease in contrast sensitivity for stimuli of high temporal but low spatial frequency, whereas lesions of the parvo pathway result in a complementary pattern of deficits, reducing sensitivity to stimuli of low temporal but high spatial frequency.

This behavioural evidence is supported by a number of electrophysiological studies of the response characteristics of retinal ganglion and geniculate cells in the two pathways, which show a large overlap in the range of effective stimuli in the spatial and temporal domains, even though the mean responses are rather different (see Merigan and Maunsell 1993). These results suggest that the specializations of the parvo and magno pathways, at least at the level of the retina and LGNd, are best understood in terms of a trade-off between the different requirements of spatial, wavelength, and temporal processing (Schiller and Logothetis 1990).

Of course, as we have seen, additional processing at the level of V1 and V2 modifies the response characteristics of the magno and parvo inputs enormously. Thus, it is entirely possible that by the time these inputs segregate in the dorsal and ventral pathways to the 'higher-order' visual areas, their response characteristics now correspond to the division of labour originally described by Ungerleider and Mishkin (1982) and refined by Livingstone and Hubel (1988). But even this position is difficult to maintain, since the anatomical segregation of the magno and parvo inputs to these areas has been found to be much less clear-cut than was originally thought. Much of the early evidence for a separation of inputs rested on the demonstration that the cytochrome oxidase compartments in V1 and V2 appeared to act as conduits for the magno and parvo inputs as they proceeded from LGNd to various extrastriate areas. But even Livingstone and Hubel realized that the segregation was not complete and noted that there was physiological evidence for a magno input to the blobs in V1 (for example, Livingstone and Hubel 1984).

More recent anatomical observations have confirmed this result (Fitzpatrick *et al.* 1985; Lachica *et al.* 1992). In fact, the blobs and the 'interblobs', which both receive parvo inputs from sublayer $4C\beta$ in V1, also appear to receive substantial magno inputs from layer 4B and sublayer $4C\alpha$, although the magno projections to the blobs are more numerous than those to the interblob regions. The pattern of interconnections between the stripes in V2 and the organization of the back-projections to these regions from higher visual areas are also not consistent with the notion of strictly segregated magno and parvo compartments. Thus, there are direct connections between the thick and thin stripes of V2 (Livingstone and Hubel 1984) and all three kinds of stripe receive back-projections from area V4 (Zeki and Shipp 1989).

These anatomical findings are supported by a number of physiological studies which suggest that the segregation between the magno and parvo projections to the striate cortex and beyond is far from complete. Early work by Malpeli *et al.* (1981), in which recordings were made from neurones in V1 after selective blocking of input from the two subdivisions of the LGNd, showed that up to 40 per cent of the neurones in V1 were affected by blocking either the magnocellular or the parvocellular layers. Later observations by Nealey and Maunsell (1994) confirmed this result and provided evidence for a large magno input to both the blob and interblob regions of V1. This mixing of inputs from the magno and parvo pathways from the LGNd is also reflected in the properties of units well beyond V1, in the dorsal and ventral projections to the posterior parietal and inferotemporal cortices. Thus, while inactivation of the magnocellular layers of the LGNd reduces the responsivity of almost all cells tested in MT, some cells in this dorsal-stream area are also affected by inactivation of the parvocellular layers, though the effects are much less substantial (Maunsell *et al.* 1990). In V4, however, which is part of the ventral stream, most neurones are affected equally by inactivation of either the parvocellular or magnocellular layers of the LGNd (Ferrera *et al.* 1992, 1994), a result which is quite consistent with the observation that inputs from both of these cytological subdivisions are present in the blob and interblob regions of V1.

In conclusion, the ventral and dorsal streams both appear to receive inputs from the magno and parvo pathways, although most of the input to the dorsal stream is magno in origin. The earlier suggestion that there is a one to one correspondence between these input channels and the cortical visual streams therefore appears to be incorrect.

2.3.3 Extrageniculate inputs

A full characterization of the inputs to cortical visual areas must take into account not only those derived from the LGNd, but also those derived from other retinofugal projection sites. One of the most important sources of extra-geniculate input to the cortex is the pulvinar, a complex nucleus in the poste-rior thalamus, which receives input from the superior colliculus (Chow 1950; Benevento and Fallon 1975; Kaas and Huerta 1988; Robinson and McClurkin 1989) and, indeed, directly from the retina (Campos-Ortega *et al.* 1970; Itaya and Van Hoesen 1983; Nakagawa and Tanaka 1984). Furthermore, the LGNd itself receives input from the superior colliculus in addition to its main retinal input (Benevento and Yoshida 1981) and has some projections which, while quite sparse, bypass the striate cortex and terminate directly in extrastriate cortical regions (Fries 1981; Yukie and Iwai 1981; Cowey and Stoerig 1989; Girard and Bullier 1989).

The regions of the pulvinar nucleus that send information directly to the dorsal and ventral streams are largely separate from one another, with only a slight overlap within the medial subdivision of the nucleus (Baleydier and Morel 1992; Baizer *et al.* 1993). Most areas of the posterior parietal cortex (including areas FST and MST, which both lie in the depths of the superior temporal sulcus) are linked mainly with the medial pulvinar (Asanuma *et al.* 1985; Schmahmann and Pandya 1990; Boussaoud *et al.* 1992; Cavada and Goldman-Rakic 1993), which in turn receives inputs from only the interme-diate and deep laminae of the superior colliculus (Benevento and Fallon 1975; Benevento and Standage 1983). Most neurones in these collicular lami-nae have oculomotor properties. In contrast, the inferotemporal cortex receives its projections mainly from the lateral subdivision of the pulvinar (though partly also from caudal parts of the medial subdivision). The lateral pulvinar receives information both from the superficial layers of the superior colliculus and from certain pretectal nuclei, all of which receive input directly from the retina (Benevento and Standage 1983). In other words, dorsal-stream areas are linked to a pathway from the superior colliculus to the thalamus that is apparently concerned with visuomotor control, while the ventral stream is linked with a parallel projection system from the colliculus to the thalamus which is directly fed from the retina but not explicitly concerned with eye movements.

Recent electrophysiological studies of several extrastriate visual areas have demonstrated an important functional contribution of the first, but not yet of the second, of these input pathways from the superior colliculus. Gross and his colleagues, for example, have examined the effects of lesions of the striate cortex, lesions of the superior colliculus, and lesions of both structures on the receptive field characteristics of cells in areas MT (Rodman *et al.* 1989, 1990; Gross 1991). They found some reduction in overall visual responsiveness in MT cells following lesions of the striate cortex but only very slight changes in responsivity following lesions of the superior colliculus alone. In neither case was there any change in the pronounced directional selectivity of the motion-sensitive cells in this dorsal-stream region. Combined lesions of both structures, however, completely eliminated the visual responsiveness of all MT neurones whose receptive fields were in the retinotopic region that corresponded to the two lesion sites. These results suggest that in the absence of the striate cortex, many of the cells in MT still receive input about stimulus motion that originates in the superior colliculus. This input is probably conveyed to area MT via the pulvinar, although it is just possible that it passes from the superior colliculus via a circuitous route involving the LGNd and areas V2 and V4, which in turn project to MT.

In a recent study in which area V1 was temporarily inactivated by cooling, Girard *et al.* (1992) have confirmed that motion-direction information remains available to MT neurones through other routes, although their observations suggest a role for V1 in refining the directional tuning of MT cells. These authors have also observed that a substantial proportion of neurones in the dorsal visual area V3A (adjacent to area V3, which itself lies immediately anterior to V2) similarly retain visual responsiveness during inactivation of V1. Yet in the same cooling experiments they found almost no such surviving neuronal responses in area V3 itself (Girard *et al.* 1991a). Whatever the precise route(s) through which visual inputs can reach areas MT and V3A under these circumstances, it is abundantly clear that visual processing in the dorsal stream is influenced by inputs from the superior colliculus as well as from the geniculostriate pathway.

In marked contrast, the visual responsivity of cells in the inferotemporal cortex is completely eliminated following lesions of the striate cortex, while lesions of the superior colliculus have no detectable effect on the response characteristics of the cells (Rocha-Miranda et al. 1975). Other cortical visual areas too are silenced during inactivation of V1, including V2 (Girard and Bullier 1989), V3 (Girard et al. 1991a), and V4 (Girard et al. 1991b). Thus, the evidence indicates that visual processing in the ventral stream is predominantly dependent on visual input from the geniculostriate pathway, whereas processing in the dorsal stream also depends substantially on inputs from the superior colliculus (probably via the pulvinar). It remains a puzzle, therefore, what functional contribution the well-established collicular–pulvinar projections to the ventral stream are making. It is possible that some subtle effects on neuronal responses in ventral areas—perhaps attentional in nature—would be detectable after collicular lesions in unanaesthetized monkeys.

2.3.4 **Summary**

Evidence from a large number of anatomical, electrophysiological, and psychophysical studies suggests that two independent channels from the retina, a colour-opponent channel and a broad-band channel, project to separate cytologically defined layers in the LGNd. The spatiotemporal characteristics of these two channels are different and complementary (see Fig. 2.3). The four parvocellular layers of the LGNd, which receive input from the colour-opponent channel, and the two magnocellular layers, which receive input from the broad-band channel, project in turn to area V1 in the cerebral cortex. But despite early suggestions of a continued anatomical segregation between the magno and parvo inputs both within the primary visual cortex and beyond, there is now considerable evidence that the two classes of input are heavily intermingled. The dorsal stream of projections from the striate cortex through to the posterior parietal region, although largely magno in origin, also contains a significant if small parvo input. The ventral stream of projections is even more mixed, with probably as many inputs from the magno as the parvo system. In addition to the input to visual cortical areas that arises from retinal projections to the LGNd, there is a significant contribution from the superior colliculus (via tectopulvinar and perhaps tectogeniculate routes). This input is, however, much more evident in the dorsal than in the ventral stream of processing.

Fig. 2.3 Schematic diagram showing differences in the processing capacity for the parvocellular (colour-opponent or C-O) and magnocellular (broad-band or B-B) channels for spatially and temporally modulated stimuli. In the spatial domain, the processing capacity of the broad-band channel drops off more rapidly than the colour-opponent channel with increasing spatial frequency (that is, fine-grain structure). In the temporal domain, the opposite is the case and the processing capacity of the colour-opponent channel drops off more rapidly than the broadband channel. Adapted from Schiller and Logothetis (1990).

2.4 The organization of the dorsal and ventral streams: a proposed model

Despite the fact that the dorsal and ventral steams cannot be regarded as simple extensions of the parvo and magno channels, recent advances in tract tracing studies have not seriously questioned the existence of two separate streams as formulated by Ungerleider and Mishkin (1982) over 10 years ago. That is, the anatomical separation of these two streams of processing is not disputed. Instead, recent studies have served to flesh out in much more detail the intermediate steps intervening between V1 and the higher cortical regions (see Fig. 2.4). It is true that there is evidence for much more cross-talk between the systems than was originally thought, but the distinction between a dorsal stream projecting to the posterior parietal lobule and a ventral stream projecting to the inferotemporal cortex has been repeatedly confirmed (Morel and Bullier 1990; Baizer *et al.* 1991; Felleman and Van Essen 1991; Young 1992).

Given their existence and taking into account the evident difference in emphasis between the dorsal and ventral streams in their relative use of magno and parvo inputs, respectively, it still remains to be established how the functional 'roles' of the two streams should best be characterized. Indeed, it might even be the case that the evidence would lead one to the conclusion that their roles did not differ at all: that one was merely a 'backup' for the other.

As we have seen, Ungerleider and Mishkin (1982) originally conceived of the division of labour between the two systems as a simple partitioning of the analysis performed on the visual array. They assumed that the dorsal stream computes one visual attribute of a stimulus, its location, while the ventral stream computes and collates other visual attributes, such as size, shape, orientation, and colour. Their distinction was thus primarily in terms of input processing: one system for spatial vision, the other for object vision. Even the more detailed account put forward by Livingstone and Hubel (1988), in which the dorsal and ventral distinction was translated into a distinction between the magno and parvo channels, respectively, is essentially an elaboration of the account put forward earlier by Ungerleider and Mishkin (1982). Both accounts focus entirely on the role of these two pathways in their differential processing of incoming visual information and the products of this processing are each seen as contributing ultimately to a single combined representation of our visual world that provides the foundation for thought and action.

Our perspective on the division of labour between the dorsal and ventral streams is to place less emphasis on input distinctions (for example, object location versus intrinsic object qualities) and to take more account of the output characteristics of the two cortical systems. As we have already seen in Chapter 1, separate processing 'modules' have evolved in non-human vertebrates to mediate the different visually guided behaviours that such organisms exhibit. Thus, in the frog, for example, there are independent modules controlling visually elicited prey catching and visually guided avoidance of barriers during locomotion. In mammals, including primates, the principle of independent visuomotor modules is generally accepted in relation to the control of certain classes of visually guided behaviour such as saccadic eye movements, where projections from the eye to the superior colliculus (and, thence, to various premotor nuclei in the midbrain and pons) have been shown to be particularly important (though, in primates, possibly not essential). In primates, this principle can be extended to other more recently evolved behavioural skills such as visually guided prehension, a skill which is particularly well developed and appears to involve cortical circuitry.

The programming and on-line control of a particular action typically requires a unique set of transformations of the visual array, so that each component of the action can be correctly executed with respect to the goal object. Reaching out and grasping an object, for example, is a complex act requiring coordination between movements of the fingers, hands, upper limbs, torso, head, and eyes. The visual inputs and transformations required for the orchestration of these movements will be equally complex and differ in important respects from those leading to the identification and recognition of objects and events in the world. Thus, to fixate and then reach towards a goal object, it is necessary that the location and motion of that object be specified in egocentric coordinates (that is, coded with respect to the observer). But the particular coordinate system used (centred with respect to the retina, head, or body) will depend on the particular effector system to be employed (that is, eyes, hand, or both). Similarly, to form the hand and fingers appropriately for the grasp, the coding of the goal object's shape and size would also need to be largely viewer based, that is, the object's structure must be coded in terms of its particular disposition with respect to the observer. In addition, since the relative positions of the observer and the goal object will change from moment to moment, it is obvious that the egocentric coordinates of the object's location and its surface and/or contours must be computed on each occasion that the action occurs. A consequence of this last requirement will be that the visuomotor system is likely to have a very short 'memory'.

But as we indicated in Chapter 1, the expansion of visual areas in the primate cerebral cortex reflects not only the refinement of visuomotor control, but also the emergence of representational systems that are linked to processes of perception and cognition. In sharp contrast to the viewer-based coding required for visuomotor control, visual coding for the purposes of perception must deliver the identity of the object independent of any particular viewpoint. This could be accomplished by constructing a network of multiple views so that object identity can be accessed by transforming or interpolating any particular view of an object with respect to that network (for example, Tarr and Pinker 1989; Bülthoff and Edelman 1992). Alternatively, a particular view of an object could be transformed to some sort of canonical or prototypical view (for example, Palmer *et al.* 1981). Whatever the particular coding mechanisms might be (and they could vary across different classes of objects), the essential problem for the perceptual system is to code (and later recover) object identity—thus approximating what Marr (1982) called an 'object-centred' description. It is objects, not object views, that the perceptual system is ultimately designed to deliver. As a consequence, human perception is characterized by 'constancies' of shape, size, colour, lightness, and location, so that the enduring characteristics of objects can be maintained across different viewing conditions. The outputs provided by this type of processing are well suited for the long-term storage of the identities of objects and their spatial arrangements.

Clearly then, the output requirements for a visual coding system serving the visual control of action are bound to be quite different from the requirements for a system subserving visual perception. We suggest that it is these fundamental differences in the required transformations of incoming visual information that has driven the evolution of separate streams of processing in the primate visual cortex. In the remaining sections of this chapter, we introduce some of the neuroanatomical and physiological evidence in the monkey that suggests that networks of cells in the dorsal stream perform the computations and transformations required for visually guided actions, while networks in the ventral stream permit the formation of perceptual and cognitive representations of the enduring characteristics of objects and their relations. In later chapters, we will come back to this and other evidence from both monkeys and humans to flesh out the basic premise that the division of labour in cortical visual systems is based on a distinction between the requirements for action and perception and that this division cuts right across any distinction between spatial and object vision.

2.5 Visual processing within the dorsal stream

2.5.1 Neuronal activity and visuomotor guidance

Neuroanatomical studies of the dorsal stream have revealed a complex pattern of connectivity. Indeed, the connectional anatomy summarized in Fig. 2.4 includes only the inputs arising from V1 and does not include the important projections from the pulvinar which, as we saw earlier, convey critical inputs (mainly from the superior colliculus) to this region. Moreover, as is evident in Fig. 2.4, there are a number of different routes from V1 to higher-level visual areas in the posterior parietal cortex, which we will often refer to collectively as the posterior parietal (PP) lobule or region. (This region corresponds loosely to what some writers refer to as area 7 or area PG.) One set of inputs arrives via area MT, which, as we saw earlier, receives largely magno input from layer 4B in V1 as well as from the thick stripes of V2. Fed by MT, areas MST and FST then project to area 7a (Boussaoud *et al.* 1990). Additional visual inputs from areas V2 and V3 reach the posterior parietal cortex via area V3A and also via the parieto-occipital area (PO); both V3A and PO also send projections via the dorsal prelunate area DP (see Fig. 2.4). Although all three

Fig. 2.4 Schematic diagram of the major projections to the dorsal and ventral streams. V1–V4, visual areas 1–4; V3A, visual area 3A; PO, parieto-occipital area; MT, middle temporal area (sometimes called V5); DP, dorsal prelunate area; VIP, ventral intraparietal sulcus area; LIP, lateral intraparietal sulcus area; 7a, parietal area 7a; MST, medial superior temporal area; FST, fundus of the superior temporal sulcus; PP, the posterior parietal complex; STS, anterior complex within the superior temporal sulcus; IT, inferotemporal complex. Not all known connections are shown and those within the PP complex are omitted. The new area AIP is also omitted from within the PP complex. Adapted from Distler et al. (1993).

of these major routes originate mainly in layer 4B of the striate cortex, they may convey different visual information to the parietal cortex, as we shall discuss later. This multiplicity, along with differential collicular–pulvinar inputs, no doubt contributes to the considerable heterogeneity in response characteristics found in cells in the dorsal stream (for reviews, see Motter (1991) and Stein (1991)). The visual areas within the posterior parietal cortex are also intimately associated with adjacent regions that receive somesthetic input, particularly from receptor systems in the upper limbs, hands, and face.

One of the most striking characteristics of many cells in the dorsal stream, especially those within the posterior parietal area such as LIP and 7a (see Fig. 2.4), is that they are virtually silent to visual stimulation while the animal is under anaesthesia. This lack of responsivity under anaesthesia is not a characteristic of cells in V1 itself, nor indeed of cells in areas within the ventral stream of projections from V1 to the inferotemporal cortex; only cells in the posterior parietal region appear to be silenced. Thus, it was only when investigators became able to monitor the activity of single units in alert monkeys during the performance of simple visuomotor acts, that the visual response characteristics of cells in the posterior parietal cortex were uncovered (Hyvärinen and Poranen 1974; Mountcastle *et al.* 1975). It soon became apparent that the properties of many of these cells could not be accounted for in terms of visual stimulation alone. In fact, the responses of most neurones in the posterior parietal cortex appear to be conjointly tuned for specific concurrent behaviours of the animal with respect to the visual stimulus that is presented (for reviews, see Lynch (1980), Andersen (1987), and Stein (1991)).

As we shall see in the following pages, different subsets of cells have been described which respond specifically when the monkey fixates a stationary visual stimulus, when it pursues a stimulus moving in a particular direction, when it makes a saccade towards a stimulus, when it reaches for a stimulus, and when it grasps a stimulus object. There is a continuing controversy between those who stress the central importance of this correlation of cell activity with ongoing behaviour (for example, Mountcastle *et al.* 1975) and those who argue that the cells are primarily visual, though modulated by the attentional significance of the stimulus (Robinson *et al.* 1978). Most recent attempts to separate sensory from motor-related cell properties, however, have confirmed that the response characteristics of most cells in this region cannot be fully specified unless both sensory and movement-related modulation is taken into account (Andersen 1987; Taira *et al.* 1990; Colby and Duhamel 1991). Whether one should label these cells as sensory, motor, or sensorimotor, is controversial. Nevertheless, it is generally accepted that the cells play a crucial role in the transformation of information from visually based to motor-based coordinates. (Of course, there are also cells which appear only to be visually driven or 'light-sensitive', though they may always be antecedent to visuomotor cells.)

The routes by which sensory information can reach these visuomotor cells are now reasonably well documented, though the precise nature of the information conveyed through each of them remains unclear. The source of the motor properties of these cells remains obscure, though several possibilities exist. As we argue later, projections from more unequivocally motor-related areas in the frontal lobe (specifically the 'frontal eye fields' and premotor cortex) could convey precise information about eye, hand, and limb movements to the posterior parietal region. Other projections, from the deep layers of the superior colliculus (via the pulvinar), which presumably could code information about saccadic eye movements, might also play an important role. The motor properties of posterior parietal cells could even originate within the parietal lobe itself, as first suggested by Mountcastle *et al.* (1975), who referred to the cells as 'command neurons', a view still held, although in modified form, by several authors (for example, Andersen *et al.* 1992).

2.5.2 Coding of space for action

While all visually guided actions take place in space, the spatial coding required will vary according to the action performed. In other words there is no single representation of space in the brain, but instead multiple effector-specific coordinate systems (for a recent discussion of these issues, see Rizzolatti *et al.* (1994)). Evidence for these multiple systems can be seen in the spatial coding shown by cells in the dorsal stream, as summarized below.

As already mentioned, the activity of many cells in the parietal cortex is associated with saccadic eye movements. Many of the cells in the lateral intra-parietal area (LIP), for example, fire prior to and during the execution of a visually elicited saccade. How is the necessary spatial coding achieved in this area for the amplitude and direction of the eye movement to be specified?

Although this is a matter of current controversy, one possibility has been proposed by Andersen and his colleagues. They discovered that many cells in areas 7a and LIP have gaze-dependent responses; in other words, where the animal is looking (that is, the position of the eye in the orbit) deter-mines the amplitude of the cell's response to a visual stimulus in its recep-tive field (Andersen *et al.* 1985, 1990*b*. Such modulation or 'gating' by gaze direction could permit the computation of the 'true' (head- or body-related) coordinates of the stimulus independent of retinal location. In other words, it could be used to transform the retinal coordinates of the stimulus into head-based coordinates. It is possible that as a result, individ-ual parietal cells may be able to code this transformed information explicitly (see Galletti *et al.* 1993), but, in any case, certainly assemblies of cells of the kind described by Andersen and colleagues in these areas could do so col-lectively (Andersen *et al.* 1990*b*; Mazzoni *et al.* 1991). Independent evidence for head-based coding comes from the reports of Shibutani *et al.* (1984) and Kurylo and Skavenski (1991) that microstimulation of certain parts of areas 7a and LIP elicits saccadic eye movements coded for a particular final location that is fixed relative to the head. In these cases, the amplitude and direction of the elicited saccade (with respect to the head) clearly must vary as a function of the eye's initial position in the orbit. These 'goal-directed' saccades contrast with the 'fixed vector' saccades typically observed at stimulation sites elsewhere in the primate cortex and superior colliculus, where the same amplitude and direction of saccade (with respect to the head) is evoked irrespective of the eye's position in the orbit.

A second possible mechanism for spatial coding in posterior parietal areas such as LIP has emerged from recent work by Duhamel *et al.* (1992). This group has shown that some LIP cells appear to shift their receptive field transiently just before the animal makes a saccadic eye movement, so that stimuli that will fall on that receptive field after the eye movement is completed actually influence the cell's activity before the eye movement occurs (see Fig. 2.5). In addition, many cells will respond when an eye movement brings the site of a previously flashed stimulus into the cell's receptive field. Taken together, these results suggest that a network of cells in the posterior parietal cortex anticipates the retinal consequences of saccadic eye movements and updates the cortical representation of visual space to provide a continuously accurate coding of the location of objects in the world.

Both of these forms of spatial coding, of course, would only be of value over rather short time spans, since every time the animal moved its body, the usefulness of the coding would be lost. In other words, such egocentric spatial coding would be useful for guiding action in the present but not for storing spatial information for use very far in the future. It would provide useful information about object location for calibrating the amplitude and direction of an immediate movement of the eye and perhaps the limb, but not for the long-term storage of information about the relative location of that object *vis-á-vis* other objects in the world.

As we discuss in more detail later in this chapter, area LIP has substantial reciprocal connections with the part of the frontal lobe known as area 8 (frontal eye fields), stimulation of which has long been known to give rise to a range of eye movements. In an analogous fashion, parietal area 7b (lying anterior to 7a), which contains many of the so-called 'reach' cells described by Mountcastle and his colleagues (Mountcastle *et al.* 1975), is intimately connected with another part of the frontal cortex, sector F4 of premotor area 6. While there has been little investigation of the visual coding of stimulus location in area 7b, the coding used by cells related to arm movements in sector F4 has been extensively investigated (for example, Fogassi *et al.* 1992). It has been found there that coding in head-based coordinates is the norm. It is possible that in area 7b, the coding of space to guide reaching takes into account not only the position of the goal object but also the starting position of the limb. Certainly there is behavioural evidence that goal-directed aiming movements of the limb are organized eventually in shoulder-centred coordinates and not solely in retinocentric coordinates (Flanders *et al.* 1992).

2.5.3 Coding of visual motion for action

In many everyday visuomotor actions performed by primates, the target object is moving and it will be necessary not only to track that motion, but

Fig. 2.5 A neurone in cortical area LIP which anticipates a stimulus to be brought into its receptive field by an eye movement. (A) Response to a visual stimulus in the cell's receptive field during a steady fixation task. (B) Response in a saccade task in which the monkey makes a gaze shift that brings the stimulus into the receptive field. The neurone begins to respond to the stimulus well before the saccade has occurred, as shown by the third display, which is aligned on the beginning of the saccade. The point fixated by the monkey is shown as a dot, the visual stimulus as a star, the receptive field of the cell as a dashed circle, and the saccadic eye movement as an arrow. The monkey's line of gaze is shown by the plots of eye position in the horizontal (H) and vertical (V) directions. The raster displays show neuronal responses for 16 consecutive trials. Adapted from Duhamel *et al.* (1992).

also to try to anticipate it. Furthermore, not only are actions guided by independently moving objects, such as a potential prey or conspecific, but actions themselves generate movement within the retinal array, which in turn, can be used to control the amplitude and direction of those actions. It is not surprising therefore to find that many neurones in the dorsal stream of the monkey, most notably within area MT, are selective for the velocity and direction of a visual stimulus (Maunsell and Van Essen 1983*a*). In the neighbouring area MST also, which receives its visual input mainly from area MT, many of the cells are movement-selective, but, in addition, many of them vary in response amplitude as a function of the animal's behaviour with respect to the stimulus. In particular, tracking a moving target with the eyes, rather than maintaining stationary fixation, is associated with an optimal response of many of these motion-sensitive cells in area MST (Komatsu and Wurtz 1988). Furthermore, experiments showed that many of these neurones continued to respond during pursuit eye movements of the appropriate speed and direction even when the visual stimulus itself was interrupted (Newsome *et al.* 1988). In addition, the firing of some of these cells is associated not only with the eye movements made by the animal as it pursues a visual target, but also with the accompanying head movements. Thus, for many of the cells in the lateral portion of MST ('MSTl'), the preferred directions for the moving visual stimulus are closely correlated with the preferred directions of movement of the eyes and head (Thier and Erickson 1992). It is notable that areas MT and MSTl (unlike ventral-stream areas such as V4) send substantial functional projections to the nuclei of the optic tract and accessory optic tract (Hoffmann *et al.* 1991, 1992). These nuclei are sensitive to moving patterns and have been implicated in the visual control of pursuit (Hoffmann and Distler 1989).

In addition, as Fig. 2.6 illustrates, there is specificity in parts of area MST (and in MT also) for relative motion, size change, and for the rotation of an object in the frontoparallel plane or in depth (Saito *et al.* 1986). Such changes would need to be incorporated in sensorimotor algorithms for the on-line adjustments of the moving limb as it is directed towards a moving target. Recent kinematic studies of catching in humans (Savelsbergh *et al.* 1991) have shown that the acceleration of the moving limb is controlled by the rate of expansion of the target image on the retina, which is a typical example of the kind of stimulus change that excites cells in area MST. One of the critical computations for this control is thought to be the 'tau margin', which is essentially the inverse of the rate of expansion of the target image on the retina and which predicts the 'time to contact' with the target stimulus (Lee 1976). Whether cells in areas MT or MST or elsewhere in the dorsal stream carry out this computation is not known; the appropriate tests have not been carried out. It is interesting to note, however, that cells in the nucleus rotundus of the pigeon (a structure that is widely believed to be homologous with the primate pulvinar) are sensitive to time to contact with an approaching visual stimulus in a manner consistent with the computation of the tau margin (Wang and Frost 1992). Another function apparently served by cells in the dorsal stream that code for 'looming' objects (perhaps when too close or too rapid to catch) is that of eliciting blinking in anticipation of the imminent collision. As first discovered by Ferrier (1875), electrical stimulation of sites within the posterior parietal cortex frequently elicits blinking, and, within area 7a, more than half of the cells recorded code for expanding retinal images (Shibutani *et al.* 1984), the kind of stimulus change that is likely to elicit blinking.

Fig. 2.6 Response properties of cells in the dorsal stream that are sensitive to motion. (A) Cells in area MST sensitive to radial movement. Cell 1 is sensitive to changes in the size of a circle, but not to the radial flow of a wide field of dots. Cell 2 is sensitive to the radial flow field but not the size change in the circle. Cell 3 is sensitive to both. (B) Example of a cell in area MT sensitive to rotation in the frontoparallel plane. This cell was sensitive to counterclockwise rotation. It was not sensitive, as the bottom two panels indicate, to straight movements in the frontoparallel plane. Adapted from Saito et al. (1986).

But as well as providing information about the movement of individual objects in relation to the observer, it is likely that many directionally selective cells in the dorsal stream participate in the direct visual monitoring of the moving limb during prehension. Most visually responsive neurones in area 7a, for example, respond best to stimulus movement toward the centre of the visual field and many of them are also selective for movement in depth (Motter and Mountcastle 1981). These cells would thus be activated by the arm as it passes through the lower portion of the visual field *en route* towards a target (Motter 1991). They could therefore provide visual information to the numerous reach cells that respond better when the monkey reaches in the light than in the dark (MacKay 1992).

A less direct form of self-monitoring is available through the activation of dorsal-stream cells by wide-field visual information reflecting the rate and direction of locomotion of the observer through the environment. Many of the visual cells in the dorsomedial part of MST (MSTd) are strongly driven by such large-scale 'optic-flow' fields (Tanaka and Saito 1989; Duffy and Wurtz 1991). The concept of optic flow was first described in detail by Gibson (1950, 1966) and refers to the changes in the retinal array that occur as an organism moves through the world and the images of objects, surfaces, and other contours stream across its retina. Various dynamic aspects of the array such as shear, expansion, and rotation can be used to control the speed and heading of locomotion through the world (Lee and Thomson 1982; Koenderink 1986). Indeed, as we have already seen, the expansion of the visual array or a portion of that array, can be used to predict time to contact; this would be a useful parameter in the control of locomotion with respect to a goal or barrier.

Although the critical experiments have yet to be done, it is likely that many of the neurones sensitive to optic flow that have been found in area MST (and area 7a, which also contains neurones with large-field properties; Motter and Mountcastle 1981) play an important role in the visual control of locomotion in primates. Furthermore, some motion-sensitive cells in area MSTd have an opposite preference for motion direction according to whether the disparity between the retinal images of the stimulus on the two eyes is 'crossed' or 'uncrossed'. Thus, motion and depth information are combined within these cells in such a way that they could simultaneously monitor visual information at different distances as the monkey locomotes through the environment (Roy *et al.* 1992). It is interesting that, as mentioned earlier, there are neural projections from areas MT and MST to the nuclei of the optic tract and the accessory optic tract (Hoffmann *et al.* 1991). As well as participating in ocular pursuit, these nuclei are believed to be intimately involved in processing optic flow in both lower (Simpson 1984; Simpson *et al.* 1988) and higher

(Grasse and Cynader 1991) mammals. It is possible that the descending pathways from area MST allow the cortex to exert a refining influence on more primitive subcortical structures, through the provision of more elaborate visual coding.

Yet it is by no means the only role of area MT to provide motion analysis for the visual control of action in areas such as MST. Although it is primarily a processing station within the dorsal stream, area MT also projects to areas such as V4 which lie primarily within the ventral stream (Maunsell and Van Essen 1983b; Ungerleider and Desimone 1986). As we shall discuss in a later section, it is likely that such dorsal to ventral projections provide essential information for the perception and recognition both of the nature of an object or animal that is moving and of the nature of the motion itself.

2.5.4 Coding of object properties for action

We have argued in the preceding sections that much of the space and motion coding in the dorsal stream is related to the control of action. But of course, actions are most often directed at objects, not simply at points in space. To pick up a coffee cup, it is not enough to know its location: it is also necessary to know its size, shape, and orientation.

Not surprisingly, therefore, visual information about such object properties has been found to play a critical role in the control of skilled actions such as manual prehension. In particular, the classic work of Jeannerod (Jeannerod and Biguer 1982; Jeannerod 1988) showed clearly that the anticipatory posture of the hand and fingers while reaching for a goal object reflects the orientation and size of the object and that this posture is largely determined by visual input. Therefore if, as we argue here, the posterior parietal cortex performs the sensorimotor transformations required for such actions, then we would expect there to be cells or circuits in this region sensitive to the visual appearance of the objects that are to be grasped.

Early electrophysiological investigations of the posterior parietal area reported that there are visually responsive 'manipulation' cells, which fire optimally when the monkey reaches out and picks up an object (Hyvärinen and Poranen 1974; Mountcastle et al. 1975). Moreover, such cells, in contrast to the 'reach' cells we discussed in Section 2.5.2, are not sensitive to the spatial location to which the movement of the arm is directed. More recently, it has been demonstrated that over half of these manipulation cells are selective for the actual visual appearance of the object to be grasped (Taira et al. 1990; Sakata et al. 1992; see Fig. 2.7). Since these cells, which are found in the anterior intraparietal area (area AIP) on the ventral bank of the intraparietal sulcus, are not tied to a particular spatial or retinal location, many do not have a definable

Fig. 2.7 A neurone in the posterior bank of the monkey's intraparietal sulcus (area AIP) which responded preferentially to a small manipulandum requiring a finger–thumb precision grip. This cell responded best during a visually guided pulling of the object (A), though it responded also to a pull made in the dark (C). Importantly, it responded well to the object even when no response was permitted (B). The raster displays show neuronal responses for 12 consecutive trials. They are aligned on the moment of pressing a lap-level key in (B) and (D) and on release of the key in (A) and (C). The triangles on the rasters and the lines below the histograms indicate the durations of the key press and of the object grasp. Adapted from Sakata et al. (1992).

receptive field. Nevertheless, they are visually driven, responding selectively to the size and/or orientation of the object. Many of these manipulation neurones are tied, to varying degrees, both to object properties and to the movements of the hands and fingers that are appropriate for those properties.

The route by which the visual information required for object coding reaches these cells is at present unknown, although area V3A and the dorsal part of area V3, both rich in orientation-selective cells, are likely way stations. Another possibility would be a route via area V4, since this too has connections with parts of the posterior parietal cortex. Inputs through any of these routes could explain the existence of cells in the parietal cortex sensitive to the orientation of luminous bars (Sakata *et al.* 1992); these may in turn provide orientation information to the manipulation cells. It is most unlikely, however, that the shape coding in manipulation cells is dependent on input from the higher-level modules within the ventral stream that support the perception of object qualities. Evidence against this possibility is that monkeys with profound deficits in object recognition following inferotemporal lesions are nevertheless still adept at visuomotor skills. They are as capable as normal animals at picking up small food objects (Klüver and Bucy 1939), at catching flying insects (Pribram 1967), and at orienting their fingers in a precision grip to grasp morsels of food embedded in small oriented slots (Buchbinder *et al.* 1980; see Glickstein *et al.* 1998). Therefore, although the experiments have not yet been done, we would predict that the visuomotor properties of cells in the dorsal stream would survive large ventral stream lesions.

Many of the cells studied by Taira *et al.* (1990) were sensitive not only for the shape of an object but also for the appropriate motor act performed in grasping it. This motor information may reasonably be assumed to come from the rostral sector of inferior area 6 (area F5), a part of the frontal lobe known to be intimately connected with this part of the parietal lobe (Godschalk *et al.* 1984; Matelli *et al.* 1986) and whence neurones project directly to motor cortex (area 4). Cells in this premotor area include ones with motor and visuomotor properties associated with grasping behaviour (Rizzolatti *et al.* 1988) and Sakata *et al.* (1992) proposed that they provide a feedback message to enable a 'matching' process between sensory input and motor output to take place in the parietal cortex.

It is important to note that the existence of manipulation cells within the posterior parietal cortex that are sensitive to the intrinsic visual properties of objects but not their location would make no sense in the context of a dorsal system specialized for spatial perception. As we have already pointed out, however, such cells would be expected to exist within a system dedicated to the sensorimotor transformations underlying the visual control of action.

That is, both 'what' and 'where' would have to be coded in a dorsal stream specialized for visuomotor control and the evidence indicates that both of these aspects are indeed coded.

2.5.5 Modularity within the dorsal stream

2.5.5.1 Visual inputs

The different cell types discussed in the above sections, which are associated both with particular visual inputs and with the co-occurrence of particular motor adjustments, are partially segregated into different regions within the dorsal pathway. This modular arrangement is no doubt a reflection of the role that each region plays in the distinctive sensorimotor transformations required for different components of actions. As Stein (1992) has suggested, different networks within the posterior parietal region appear to constitute a distributed set of transformational algorithms for converting sensory vectors into other reference frames or motor coordinate systems. Different actions require the participation of different subsets of these algorithms. An action as simple as picking up a ball, for example, requires the coordination of a number of different effector systems including movements of the eyes, head, arm, hand, fingers, and body, each of which is controlled to some degree by visual inputs. The set of transformational algorithms required for that action will be very different from those required for throwing the ball or catching it. As a consequence, a full understanding of the distribution of functions within the dorsal stream will require a mapping of both the inputs and the outputs relating to the different systems, a task made even more complex by the considerable anatomical overlap between different functional modules.

As was discussed earlier (see Fig. 2.4), there appear to be at least three routes from V1 to the posterior parietal cortex, though all three pathways are cross-connected. The most prominent of these passes through area MT, located dorsally within the posterior bank of the superior temporal sulcus, while the second one involves area V3A, located largely in the anterior bank of the lunate sulcus, and the third implicates area PO, which lies medially, mainly in the parieto-occipital sulcus. We have seen that area MT has a preponderance of cells that are selective for motion direction (for a review, see Zeki (1990c)); V3A on the other hand has a preponderance of neurones that are orientation-selective (Gaska et al. 1988), while PO seems to be specialized for dealing with stimuli located in the peripheral visual fields (Gattass et al. 1985).

It would of course be premature to speculate in detail as to the visual transformations for which these three routes might be specialized. Nevertheless, our discussion above suggests that while the first must contribute widely to the delivery of visual information necessary for many tasks including ocular pursuit and the guidance of locomotion and posture, the second may be primarily concerned with providing the visual information to guide control of manual grasping. Area PO, the least well studied, may be involved in providing the visual information for directing saccadic eye movements and/or manual reaching to peripheral stimuli (Colby *et al.* 1988; Galletti *et al.* 1991). As mentioned earlier, there is preliminary evidence that some neurones in area PO appear to code for location in craniocentric rather than retinocentric coordinates (Galletti *et al.* 1993). But it should be cautioned that the segregation of cell properties in these dorsal visual pathways is not strict. For example, most neurones in area V3A code for stimulus orientation, but their visual responses also depend on the animal's direction of gaze (Galletti and Battaglini 1989). Yet the computations leading to such 'gaze modulation' are generally regarded as constituting an initial stage in the transformation of stimulus location from retinal to head-centred coordinates (Andersen *et al.* 1985; see Section 2.5.2). In other words, as Zeki (1990*a*) has pointed out, both 'what' and 'where' appear to be coded conjointly in single neurones in this part of the dorsal stream.

2.5.5.2 Parietofrontal modules

Modularity is clearly seen within the posterior parietal cortex itself and is further reflected in the selective links each region has with separate areas within the premotor and prefrontal regions of the frontal cortex (Petrides and Pandya 1984; Cavada and Goldman-Rakic 1989*b*). Indeed, there appear to be a number of anatomically and functionally distinct parietofrontal circuits or modules. Some of the clearest examples of this modularity involve three small neighbouring areas in and around the monkey's intraparietal sulcus, each of which is connected with separate regions of the premotor cortex. For example, as we mentioned in an earlier section, area LIP has strong reciprocal links with the frontal eye fields. Like the superior colliculus, to which they both project, these areas are both strongly implicated, probably in complementary ways, in the control of saccadic eye movements (Bruce and Goldberg 1984). Interestingly, the frontal eye fields also receive direct projections from other dorsal-stream areas such as MST and FST (Boussaoud *et al.* 1990), areas which are concerned, among other things, with the control of pursuit eye movements. These connections may therefore constitute a second quasi-independent parietofrontal circuit, concerned with a kind of eye-movement control quite distinct from the saccadic system.

In contrast to the frontal eye fields, which lie within and anterior to the arcuate sulcus in the monkey, the frontal areas concerned with limb movements lie in the premotor cortex just behind this sulcus. For example, as our earlier discussion indicated, the visual control of reaching movements of the arm is underpinned by a parietofrontal circuit involving the ventral intraparietal area (VIP)—which borders on area LIP—and sector F4 of inferior premotor cortex. This part of premotor cortex was implicated in the control of arm movements by Rizzolatti and Gentilucci (1988). Since sight of the arm plays an important role in the control of such movements, it is interesting to note that area VIP, with which sector F4 is connected, itself receives input from area MT (Maunsell and Van Essen 1983b; Ungerleider and Desimone 1986) and has a high degree of selectivity for the direction of moving stimuli. A third component of this 'reaching circuit' is area 7b, with which sector F4 is also interconnected in addition to its connections with VIP. Area 7b, as we mentioned earlier, contains many 'reach' neurones.

Finally, very recent research has revealed yet another link between the intraparietal region and the premotor cortex of the frontal lobe. Area AIP, which as we saw earlier contains visual neurones related to grasping movements of the hand (Taira et al. 1990) and the F5 sector of the inferior premotor cortex where neurones have been also shown to fire in association with visually guided grasping (Rizzolatti et al. 1988) are themselves interconnected (G. Rizzolatti, personal communication).

Thus, the dorsal stream blends, in a modular fashion, into the premotor areas of the frontal lobe, forming a complex parietofrontal visuomotor system. But the posterior parietal cortex also has extensive connections with even more anterior areas, in the prefrontal cortex. These include area 46, which lies in and around the sulcus principalis, an area in the monkey that has long been implicated in spatial short-term memory through classical lesion studies (for a review see Fuster (1989)). Some cells here have been found to code spatial location over a short delay, while others code a delayed directional response, which might be manual (Niki and Watanabe 1976) or oculomotor (Funahashi et al. 1989). The fact that this memory coding can be tied to particular effector systems may relate to the observation of Cavada and Goldman-Rakic (1989b) that there are separate projections from discrete parts of the posterior parietal cortex to different portions of area 46.

2.5.5.3 Descending projections

As we mentioned earlier in this chapter, there are ascending links between the visual midbrain and the dorsal stream, via the pulvinar nucleus. But to complete the picture of extended modularity, it should be added that the dorsal stream also sends extensive descending projections to brainstem structures. Thus, it is notable that most if not all of the dorsal-stream areas send projections to the superior colliculus. The visual control of eye movements presents a clear case in point. Area LIP projects strongly to the intermediate and deep layers of the superior colliculus (Asanuma *et al.* 1985; Lynch *et al.* 1985), which, as we saw earlier, are intimately involved in oculomotor control (Sparks and Hartwich-Young 1989). Indeed, inactivation of the magnocellular LGNd inputs to the cortex silences visual responses in these deeper layers of the superior colliculus, which do not receive a direct retinal input (Schiller *et al.* 1979): presumably this must reflect a magno-based route through the dorsal stream, including area LIP. Thus, the downstream connections of LIP (and of other parts of the dorsal stream) are consistent with the notion that they play an important role in modulating phylogenetically older brainstem networks concerned with the visual guidance of saccadic eye movements.

But the superior colliculus is not the only target for corticofugal projections from the dorsal stream. Other anatomical studies have revealed that posterior parietal areas, including areas PO (Glickstein *et al.* 1980) and LIP (May and Andersen 1986), also send extensive projections to nuclei lower in the brainstem, especially those in the dorsolateral region of the pons (Glickstein *et al.* 1985). Areas earlier in the dorsal stream, including MT (Maunsell and Van Essen 1983*b*, Ungerleider *et al.* 1984), FST, and MST (Boussaoud *et al.* 1992) also project to the same pontine nuclei. These pontine nuclei are closely linked with the cerebellum and pontocerebellar circuits such as these have been implicated in the subcortical organization of visuomotor skills (Glickstein and May 1982), a view which would reinforce the suggestion that the dorsal stream may provide a modulatory influence (perhaps by virtue of more refined visual coding) on the activity of subcortical visuomotor networks. The extent of these corticopontine projections from dorsal-stream areas contrasts strikingly with the apparently complete absence of such projections from the inferotemporal cortex (Glickstein *et al.* 1980, 1985; Baizer *et al.* 1993; Schmahmann and Pandya 1993).

A final group of descending connections from the dorsal stream goes to the corpus striatum, a complex of structures lying deep within the cerebral hemispheres. While both the inferotemporal and posterior parietal cortices send projections here (to the caudate and putamen), they do so in a segregated fashion (Baizer *et al.* 1993). Indeed different parts of the posterior parietal cortex individually project to segregated regions in the caudate and putamen (Cavada and Goldman-Rakic 1991), supporting the idea that they may be outposts of different visuomotor subsystems within the dorsal stream. Recent work by Graziano and Gross (1993) has revealed that in the parts of the striatum where dorsal-stream areas project, neurones can be found with many interesting visuomotor properties in common with cells in the parietal and premotor cortices. One of the new properties that has been discovered in some of these neurones is an arm position-dependent visual sensitivity, that is, the cell fires to visual stimuli in its receptive field, only when the monkey's arm is positioned in that same part of space. The same cell also shows sensitivity to tactile stimulation of the relevant arm (independent of its position in space). The putamen is intimately connected with those parietal and premotor cortical areas (7b, VIP, and F4) that appear to be implicated in the control of reaching and which may also code space in body-related coordinates. For example, Caminiti *et al.* (1991) have provided evidence that neurones in area F4 associated with reaching have different directional preferences according to the location of the monkey in the work space; these cells could form the basis of an arm-centred coding system.

2.5.5.4 Distributed control

In summary then, the parietal cortex would appear to provide crucial visual information to a number of motor-related structures both in the frontal cortex and in the basal ganglia and brainstem. The functional modularity of these interconnections can be seen most clearly in the specificity of the links between corresponding parts of the parietal and frontal lobes, but it probably extends subcortically as well. Presumably, as we suggested at the beginning of this section, different combinations of these functional modules will be recruited in the programming and control of various complex movements such as reaching and grasping.

It is appropriate here to return to a matter that we raised when discussing the properties of cells in the posterior parietal cortex. There has been much debate as to whether cells in the dorsal stream are 'sensory' or 'motor' in nature. It is our view that this debate is fundamentally misguided. If these areas are involved, as we have proposed, in transforming retinal information into motor coordinates, then the cells and networks mediating such transformations are, by their nature, neither sensory nor motor. It is arguable that the terms 'sensory' and 'motor' are too closely tied to the periphery of the central nervous system to be useful when characterizing the computations and functional architecture of the highest levels of the brain. In other words, there is no hard and fast line to be drawn at any point within the parieto-frontal–subcortical circuits we have described, where cells on one side are 'visual' and on the other side 'motor'. They constitute a set of semi-independent distributed control systems and the properties of individual cells will ultimately have to be understood in that context.

2.6 Visual processing within the ventral stream

2.6.1 Neuronal coding for visual perception and recognition

The ventral or occipitotemporal stream of processing, as classically defined (Ungerleider and Mishkin 1982), consists of projections from V1 to the inferotemporal cortex via a number of routes involving areas V2, the ventral portion of V3, V4, and TEO (which lies at the posterior border of the inferotemporal area). As Fig. 2.4 indicates, however, there is considerable cross-talk between the ventral and dorsal streams; the anterior portions of the superior temporal sulcus, in particular, are intimately connected with both projection systems.

As we noted earlier, progressively more detailed coding of visual features can be observed as one moves from V1 through V2 and V3 to V4. This progression in the specificity of coding becomes even more pronounced in the inferotemporal cortex, where cells show quite remarkable specificity in their responses to visual stimuli. The selectivity of neurones in the inferotemporal cortex for the intrinsic figural and surface properties of visual stimuli has been known for well over 20 years (Gross *et al.* 1972; Gross 1992) and pre-dates the earliest work on visual processing in the posterior parietal cortex. In fact, the longer history of electrophysiological work on the inferotemporal cortex is a testament to the fact that anaesthesia has little effect on the responsivity of inferotemporal cells; in sharp contrast, advances in exploring the properties of neurones in the posterior parietal region had to await the development of techniques for recording from awake animals.

Many of the inferotemporal cells recorded in this early work appeared to respond best to rather complex visual stimuli, such as hands, faces, and the type of spiky outline exemplified in a bottle brush (Gross *et al.* 1972, 1985). More recent work has confirmed such findings, showing that these cells, particularly in the more anterior parts of the inferotemporal cortex, are remarkably selective in their responses to object attributes (Tanaka *et al.* 1991; Kobatake and Tanaka 1994). Other recent work has shown that cells sensitive to similar stimulus features are clustered together in columns through the depth of the inferotemporal cortex, as sketched in Fig. 2.8 (Fujita *et al.* 1992). There is also evidence that colour-sensitive cells in the inferotemporal cortex include the whole range of different perceptible hues and saturations (Komatsu *et al.* 1992). As noted in an earlier section, much of this coding in the inferotemporal cortex is primarily dependent on visual inputs arriving through the geniculostriate system. The visual information thus provided seems likely to be very comprehensive in nature, since the work of Ferrera *et al.* (1992, 1994) shows that both the magno and parvo channels contribute substantially to neuronal activity in area V4.

It was discovered early on that many of the cells in this region have large receptive fields, almost always including the fovea and usually extending across the vertical meridian well into both half-fields. This is a feature that allows the cells to generalize across the visual field and code the intrinsic

Fig. 2.8 The organization of cells sensitive to object features in the inferotemporal cortex. (A) Method used to determine which particular feature an inferotemporal cell was responding to. A cell that responded to a tiger head was tested successively with various features of that stimulus until it was determined that it 'liked' an open rectangle with two black rectangles. (B) A highly schematic representation of the kind of 'columnar' arrangement of cells responsive to similar features observed in the inferotemporal cortex. Adapted from Tanaka (1993).

features of an object independent of its location. More recent work has extended these observations and has shown that not only do many cells in the inferotemporal cortex and in neighbouring regions in the superior temporal sulcus (area STP) have remarkable categorical specificity (for example, for faces), but some of them maintain this selectivity irrespective of viewpoint (Perrett *et al.* 1984, 1991; Hasselmo *et al.* 1989). Also many cells generalize their selective response to faces over a wide range of size, colour, lighting, and optical transformations (see Perrett *et al.* 1987; Hietanen *et al.* 1992). In short, there is evidence that some 'face' neurones in the temporal cortex code for object-centred visual descriptions (see Fig. 2.9). It should be pointed out, however, that most cells in these regions do respond better to one view of a face than another and that these 'viewer-centred' cells are presumably func- tionally important in their own right. It has been suggested that many of the properties of the object-centred cells might be derived through convergence of inputs from a number of viewer-centred cells, each contributing informa- tion about a different view of the object in question (Perrett *et al.* 1987). However, it has also been argued that such simple convergence might be only

Fig. 2.9 The responsivity of three cells in the rostral STS sensitive to faces. The top panel shows a 'viewer-centred' cell sensitive to a particular view of a face. The middle panel shows a bimodal 'viewer-centred' cell. The bottom panel shows an 'object-centred' cell showing little selectivity between views of faces. The dashed lines show the mean responsivity to control stimuli and the rate of spontaneous activity. Adapted from Perrett et al. (1991).

part of the story and that much of the information about objects that is processed within the inferotemporal cortex and neighbouring areas might depend on population or ensemble coding (Desimone and Ungerleider 1989). For certain biologically-important categories, such as faces, it might be important to have single-neurone coding of object-centred descriptions, in order, for example, to facilitate rapid response. In general, however, the use of more economical coding strategies, such as ensemble coding and the coding of prototypical views, may be the rule.

We noted earlier in this chapter that pathways exist for visual motion information to pass to the ventral stream from area MT and that this information may be important in the recognition of the identity of moving objects (for example, the type of animal), as well as of the significance of the actions being performed by another animal. In recent years, evidence has emerged for the involvement of temporal-lobe systems in dealing with both of these forms of perceptual analysis. A good demonstration of the way in which motion can contribute to the process of object identification is provided by the recent experiments of Sáry et al. (1993). These authors have provided examples of cells in the inferotemporal cortex which respond to a particular shape, even when the contours of that shape are defined by the relative direction of motion of pattern elements making up the shape and its background, rather than by differences in other features such as luminance or texture.

As mentioned earlier, it is likely that the necessary input for computing such contours from motion reaches the ventral stream via projections from area MT to V4. Area MT, of course, is traditionally placed in the dorsal stream and indeed makes crucial contributions to the motion analysis needed for the dynamic control of action, such as ocular pursuit. But there is also now good evidence that damage to area MT impairs not only such skills as visual pursuit, but also the perception of motion and motion-defined form. For example, both MT lesions (Marcar and Cowey 1992; Schiller 1993) and V4 lesions (Schiller 1993) impair a monkey's ability to use motion boundary information to discriminate between shapes. But as indicated by the work of Sáry et al.(1993), the actual recognition of shapes defined through motion is probably mediated by generalized 'shape' cells in the inferotemporal cortex, dependent for their visual information on inputs from MT via V4. One would predict therefore that following lesions of area MT, inferotemporal cells would no longer respond to motion-defined form.

The significance of patterns of moving elements in the visual array for signalling what another animal is doing is exemplified in the research of Perrett and his colleagues (Perrett et al. 1990; Oram and Perrett 1994). They have reported that patterns of 'biological motion'—spatiotemporal sequences of moving dots that yield coherent percepts of, for example, a person walking (for example, Johansson 1973)—selectively activate cells in area STP in the same way as the sight of a wholly visible person in locomotion. At a still higher level than this, the 'meaning' of a viewed action, like the identity of an object, should generalize across a number of different viewpoints. For example, one recognizes the significance of another person's action in picking up a piece of food no matter which direction one sees it from. Similarly a person walking forwards will be seen as such, no matter whether that person is moving left-wards or rightwards with respect to the observer's line of sight. Individual neurones with precisely this kind of 'object-centred' coding of motion have been described in area STP of monkeys (Perrett *et al.* 1989).

It has already been noted that anaesthesia has little effect on the visual selec-tivity of cells in the ventral stream, a finding that suggests that cells in the ven-tral stream are not involved in the on-line control of the behaviour of the animal. This conclusion is supported by more recent studies that have used unanaesthetized monkeys; in none of these studies has there been any report that concurrent motor behaviour affects the responsiveness or response char-acteristics of cells in occipitotemporal areas. It is also interesting that it has recently been discovered that cells in area STP which are sensitive to visual movement produced by the experimenter are insensitive to the sight of limb movements produced by the monkey itself (Hietanen and Perrett 1993). In contrast, as we mentioned earlier, many motion-sensitive cells in the parietal cortex may be specifically implicated in the visual monitoring of the monkey's own arm movements during reaching (Motter and Mountcastle 1981). In other words, one stream is concerned only with the world 'out there' inde-pendent of the observer, while the other is concerned only with the observer's actions within that visual world.

2.6.2 **What is visual perception for?**

The properties of cells in the inferotemporal cortex are entirely consistent with what would be expected in a system that is concerned with the recogni-tion of objects, scenes, and individuals, where enduring characteristics rather than the moment to moment changes in the visual array are of primary con-cern. In sharp contrast, therefore, to the action systems in the posterior pari-etal cortex, the object-based coding computed by the ventral system would provide the basic raw material for recognition memory and other long-term representations of the visual world. There is extensive evidence for the neu-ronal encoding of such visual memories in the medial and anterior regions of the inferior temporal lobe, in the perirhinal cortex, and in related limbic areas (Fahy *et al.* 1993; Li *et al.* 1993; Nishijo *et al.* 1993). Moreover, within the ventral system itself, there is evidence that the responsivity of cells can be modulated by the reinforcement history and prior occurrence of the stimuli employed to study them (Richmond and Sato 1987; Haenny and Schiller 1988; Maunsell et al. 1991). Other recent work suggests that cells in the inferotemporal cortex may play a role in comparing current visual inputs with recalled visual patterns presumably stored in other regions such as the medial temporal cortex or other limbic structures (Eskandar et al. 1992a, b). Of course these forms of modulation of inferotemporal cell activity were revealed only when investigators began to record from unanaesthetized alert monkeys, but the changes in cell activity observed related not directly to the concurrent behaviour of the animal but rather to its past experience with the stimuli. In contrast, in the dorsal stream the opposite pattern—an 'on-line' rather than 'off-line' relationship to behaviour—is seen. That is, many of the cells in this stream are closely related to the concurrent behaviour of the animal, yet there is comparatively little evidence that they are modulated by the effects of previous exposure to the stimuli or to reinforcement contingencies (Maunsell and Ferrera 1993). Indeed Rolls et al. (1979) showed that reaching and fixation cells in the posterior parietal cortex responded equally well to both attractive and aversive objects, for example when a single object was successively made 'positive' or 'negative' through conditioning.

The ventral stream's role in the longer-term modulation of behaviour rather than in on-line control is clearly reflected in its pattern of subcortical connections. Recent studies (Baizer et al. 1993; Schmahmann and Pandya 1993) have confirmed earlier studies (Whitlock and Nauta 1956; Glickstein et al. 1985) in showing that unlike posterior parietal areas (see above), the inferotemporal cortex sends few if any projections to either the superior colliculus or to pontine nuclei, areas we have seen to be implicated in the visual control of eye and head movements. (Although Webster et al. (1993) have recently reported that area TEO does project to the superior colliculus, the target for these fibres is the superficial visual layers, rather than the deeper parts which receive from the dorsal-stream cortex.)

Instead, Baizer et al. (1993) describe strong reciprocal connections between the inferotemporal cortex and the amygdala (see also Iwai and Yukie 1987; Webster et al. 1991), a structure lying deep within the temporal lobe. This structure has very few if any interconnections with the posterior parietal cortex. A series of studies in the laboratories of Mishkin and Gaffan (for example, Spiegler and Mishkin 1981; Gaffan et al. 1988) have provided strong support for the view that the amygdala is intimately concerned in the process of learning to associate visual stimuli with reward. In addition, the amygdala has been implicated in social and emotional responses to visual signals, both through lesion studies (Kling and Brothers 1992) and most recently through single-unit recording studies (Brothers and Ring 1993). It would seem therefore that the visual routes both to associative learning and to social behaviour pass through the ventral rather than the dorsal stream.

It cannot be denied, of course, that all visual processing ultimately serves action and it is therefore not surprising that the parahippocampal gyrus, a structure closely associated with medial temporal structures such as the hippocampus and amygdala, does have outputs to pontine nuclei in the brainstem (Schmahmann and Pandya 1993). But the fact that these non-visual structures concerned with learning and memory (see Mishkin and Murray 1994) intervene between the ventral stream and its ultimate motor outputs merely serves to confirm the 'off-line' nature of the visuomotor control ultimately exerted by the ventral stream.

2.7 Conclusions: perception versus action

The electrophysiological evidence and the patterns of connectivity of the dorsal and ventral streams of processing reviewed in this chapter suggest strongly that the division of labour proposed by Ungerleider and Mishkin (1982) fails to capture the functional essence of the two streams. Their distinction between spatial vision and object vision ('where' versus 'what'), like Livingstone and Hubel's (1988) later account of processing in the extrastriate cortex, is essentially an extension of the parallel input processing that is already segregating at the retinal level. In other words, Ungerleider and Mishkin's (1982) model was one based more on putative requirements for the analysis of the visual array than on requirements for the control of behaviour. This emphasis on input rather than output considerations is, of course, quite consistent with the theoretical commitment to vision *qua* perception that has dominated most accounts of the visual system in this century. But as we pointed out in Chapter 1, vision in vertebrates evolved in response to the demands of motor output, not for perceptual experience. Even with the evolution of the cerebral cortex this remained true, and in mammals such as rodents the major emphasis of cortical visual processing still appears to be on the control of navigation, prey catching, obstacle avoidance, and predator detection (Dean 1990). It is probably not until the evolution of the primates, at a late stage of phylogenetic history, that we see the arrival on the scene of fully developed mechanisms for perceptual representation. The transformations of visual input required for perception would often be quite different from those required for the control of action. They evolved, we assume, as mediators between identifiable visual patterns and flexible responses to those patterns based on higher cognitive processing.

Thus, while it is true that different channels in the mammalian visual system are specialized for different kinds of visual analysis (broad band versus colour opponent; magno versus parvo), at some point these separate inputs are combined and transformed in different ways for different purposes. In other words, both cortical streams process information about the intrinsic properties of objects and their spatial locations, but the transformations they carry out reflect the different purposes for which the two streams have evolved. The transformations carried out in the ventral stream permit the formation of perceptual and cognitive representations which embody the enduring charac-teristics of objects and their significance; those carried out in the dorsal stream, which need to capture instead the instantaneous and egocentric features of objects, mediate the control of goal-directed actions.

Chapter 3

'Cortical blindness'

3.1 **Introduction**

In Chapters 1 and 2, we have advanced the idea that the division of labour between the ventral and dorsal streams of processing can be best characterized in terms of a distinction between the roles of vision in perception and action, respectively. In doing so, we have restricted our discussion to studies of the anatomy and physiology of visual pathways in non-human primates. What needs to be addressed now is whether or not these ideas have any relevance for understanding the human visual system. Can they be used, for example, to explain some of the visual deficits and spared visual abilities in human beings who have cortical brain damage?

One way of approaching this question is to consider what would be expected to happen if either the dorsal or ventral stream were to be effectively deprived of its visual input. As Ungerleider and Mishkin (1982) established, both the dorsal and ventral streams diverge anatomically from the primary visual cortex, but, as we noted in Chapter 2, the dorsal stream also has substantial inputs from several subcortical visual structures in addition to the input from V1 (sketched in Fig. 3.1). In contrast, the ventral stream appears to depend on V1 almost entirely for its visual inputs. Consequently, damage to V1 while not directly invading either of the two processing streams, would effectively denervate the ventral stream, but would leave the dorsal stream with many of its associated structures, such as the superior colliculus, intact. Therefore, it would be expected that a patient who suffered damage to V1 would suffer a near-total loss of visual perception of the world, but might still be able to perform certain actions under visual control. That is, the patient should be able to show at least a limited repertoire of visually guided actions, despite having no visual experience of the stimuli guiding those actions. The past 20 years have in fact seen several descriptions of just such patients and indeed their spared visual abilities in many cases do seem to be explicable in these general terms.

Fig. 3.1 Schematic diagram showing major routes whereby retinal input reaches the dorsal and ventral streams. The inset shows the cortical projections on the right hemisphere of a macaque brain. LGNd, lateral geniculate nucleus, pars dorsalis; Pulv, pulvinar nucleus; SC, superior colliculus.

3.2 **'Blindsight': action without perception?**

3.2.1 **'Cortical blindness'**

Traditionally, patients with extensive damage to area V1 have been regarded as 'cortically blind', since they fail to acknowledge seeing stimuli in the affected parts of their visual field. (In clinical contexts the term 'cortical blindness' is generally reserved for patients who have bilateral damage to the primary visual cortex or the underlying white matter that forms the 'optic radiations'. But in the present context we use the term more broadly to include cases where the field defect follows from similar but unilateral damage. In such cases the blind area or 'scotoma' is restricted to one visual hemifield.) Despite this terminology, given that their visual brain structures have not been totally deafferented, such patients should not be completely insensitive to visual input. It should be possible, indeed, to demonstrate that their behaviour can be controlled by visual information—information that is presumably provided by intact subcortical visual structures in conjunction with cortical structures in the dorsal stream that receive input from those subcortical structures. What these patients should not in general be able to do is process visual information within the ventral stream, which depends primarily on V1 for its visual inputs. It should be impossible for these patients to give any kind of perceptual report about their visual experiences (except for certain special exceptions; see Section 3.4 for a more precise statement).

The definition of 'cortical blindness' is in fact based on only one particular index of visual capacity—namely that of perceptual report (for example, 'Can you see this light?'). Yet even though a patient might be unable to report changes in the overall light level in the visual field contralateral to the V1 lesion, the patient's pupillary diameter might change by reflex action in response to that variation. This visual reflex would clearly not be possible in a truly blind person, for example one with a severed optic nerve—but it often does occur in 'cortically blind' patients (Koerner and Teuber 1973).

The paradoxical term 'blindsight' (initially coined by Sanders *et al.* 1974), refers to all such 'unconscious' visual capacities that are spared in cortically blind parts of the visual field. Yet blindsight is only paradoxical if one's concept of 'sight' is equated with visual awareness. Within the framework that we have introduced in Chapter 1, the paradox disappears. Visual awareness, we suggest, can characterize activity in only one part of the visual system, namely the ventral stream of processing through to the temporal lobe (see also Chapter 7). Visual processing, however, takes place in the dorsal stream too and may continue to do so even after severe damage to area V1.

3.2.2 The pupillary response and GSR

As already mentioned, pupillary control provides clear evidence for one visuomotor system that operates quite independently of visual awareness in man. This system, however, may not be able to influence voluntary action and has therefore in the past been dismissed as 'purely reflexive'. Yet recent work (Weiskrantz 1990) shows that the pupillary response is sensitive to far more than just light intensity, and, thus, calls for a re-evaluation of this prejudice. Although the nature of the response may be simple, its determinants are certainly not. The pupil has been found to be sensitive to variations of stimulus motion, spatial frequency, and possibly colour, all within a patient's 'blind' visual field (Weiskrantz 1990).

It is true of course that control of the pupil is mediated by a primitive pathway in evolutionary terms and its direct (retinal) inputs may still only code for light intensity even in higher mammals. An important component in this pathway seems to be the olivary pretectum, which is known both to receive axons directly from retinal ganglion cells as well as being involved in the control of the pupil (see Simpson 1984). In man, however, extrastriate cortex (presumably within the dorsal stream) must also play a part in mediating the visual processing for pupillary control, since hemidecortication (a surgical procedure which leaves no cortex at all in one hemisphere) abolishes all of the effects except that of light intensity (Weiskrantz 1990).

In some ways, the pupillary response resembles another 'involuntary' response, the change in skin conductance known as the GSR. Both responses may be regarded as 'vegetative' (involuntary) components of the orienting reflex (Sokolov 1960). Furthermore, in the absence of V1, the GSR resembles the pupil in showing clear phasic responses to 'unseen' light flashes within the scotoma (Zihl *et al.* 1980). Although the neural pathway underlying this phenomenon is unknown, it does seem that the superior colliculus is a plausible participant, since electrical stimulation there results in a variety of autonomically mediated changes (Keay *et al.* 1988).

It is a matter of terminology whether or not these two examples of visual control, whose existence has been demonstrated despite the presence of cortical blindness, are regarded as 'behavioural' in nature, although both pupil size and hand sweating may well have indirect behavioural effects by generating social signals. Certainly they both provide clear examples of visual processing that can proceed through to an efferent response, in the absence of a functioning geniculostriate system.

3.2.3 Guidance of reaching and grasping

Of rather more neuropsychological interest have been the many reports that patients with cortical blindness in one visual hemifield ('hemianopia') can use spatial information to guide their actions within the blind field (for a review, see Weiskrantz (1986)). The first report showed this by asking three incredulous patients to move their eyes toward a light that they insisted they could not see (Pöppel *et al.* 1973). Their eye movements were inaccurate, but none the less bore a statistically significant relationship to the location of the light, at least over an eccentricity range of 20–30°. Weiskrantz *et al.* (1974) found a similar result (up to approximately 20°) with their much-studied patient D.B. (see Fig. 3.2), but went on to show much higher spatial accuracy when D.B. was asked to make pointing movements with his arm, as shown in Fig. 3.3. Confirmatory support was soon provided by Perenin and Jeannerod (1975), who reported evidence for accurate pointing within the blind fields of six hemianopic patients.

Further, Zihl (1980; Zihl and Von Cramon 1980) found that the accuracy of saccadic responses themselves can be improved markedly as a consequence of training, just as had been earlier found in monkeys (Mohler and Wurtz 1977). The training can consist of many trials of attempted saccadic eye movements toward the 'unseen' stimuli (Zihl 1980) or simply of many trials of attempted stimulus detection, in which the subjects were asked to signal stimulus occurrence by blinking (Zihl and Von Cramon 1980). Whether or not there were any accompanying saccadic eye movements in addition to the blinking in the

Fig. 3.2 Graph showing accuracy of saccades made by blindsight patient D.B. into his 'blind' hemifield to a 2° target presented at different eccentricities. The dotted line indicates trials in which a target was present; the solid line indicates blank control trials. The bars above and below the points on the line indicate the range of obtained eye positions on target and blank control trials respectively. Adapted from Weiskrantz *et al.* (1974.).

latter study is unknown. In any case, it is clear that considerable visual control of the direction and amplitude of both eye and arm movements can be developed in cortically blind patients.

A potential problem with this research is that none of the patients tested had complete cortical blindness, so that the intact (or relatively intact) parts of their visual fields could have been aiding performance. This could have come about either through inaccurate ocular fixation, such that the stimulus was occasionally directly received in a 'good' part of the field, or indirectly, through the scattering of light from the stimulus onto a 'good' retinal region (Campion *et al.* 1983). In the latter case, the patient might (perhaps unwittingly) infer the approximate location of the light from the amount of scattered light seen: the more the light, the nearer its source to the edge of the scotoma.

There are, however, two good reasons for rejecting these arguments as a general explanation of apparent blindsight (which is not to say that they might not account for some of the published reports). First, Weiskrantz (1987) has shown that D.B. is unable to point to a stimulus if it falls on the natural blind spot (the part of the retina where the optic nerve leaves the eye), within his scotoma, even though he can point accurately to the same stimulus when placed elsewhere in his scotoma. This dissociation cannot be encompassed by either the faulty-fixation or the scattered-light hypotheses. Both hypotheses would predict D.B. to perform equally well whether the stimulus fell within or outside the blind spot in the scotoma, since both hypotheses assume that those regions outside the blind spot are as blind as the blind spot itself.

Fig. 3.3 Averaged aiming responses made by D.B. with his finger towards targets of different diameter and eccentricity presented in his 'blind' hemifield. The series was conducted in order from (a) through to (e). Vertical bars indicate the range of observed end points at each eccentricity. In condition (e), blank trials were randomly interspersed between stimulus trials and the mean response position and range for blanks are shown to the right of the experimental results. Adapted from Weiskrantz et al. (1974.).

Second, Perenin and Jeannerod (1975, 1978) tested patients with a severed optic chiasm (the crossing point of optic nerve fibres from each eye to the opposite side of the brain) as controls for their cortically blind patients. These control patients could have no residual vision in the temporal hemianopia present in either eye, since this hemianopia was caused by an interruption of the actual optic nerve fibres from the corresponding (nasal) hemiretinae. However, they should have been able to use scattered light in the intact hemi-field as easily as the cortically blind patients. (They could equally have exploited faulty fixation, but in fact the authors excluded trials where any sub-ject made a clear, 5° or more, ocular deviation.) Despite this, the control patients were unable to point to visual targets accurately when tested under conditions where the cortically blind patients were able to perform well.

If one accepts the fact that patients with cortical blindness can indeed move their eyes and hands accurately towards visual stimuli that they cannot 'see', the question remains as to what pathways underlie this residual ability. First of all, the fact that they cannot report the stimuli, we would argue, is a conse-quence of the loss of visual input to the ventral stream. It is this pathway, we assume, which is essential for our perception of the world and (perhaps by virtue of its associated experiential content) facilitates recognition and mem-ory. Being therefore subjectively blind, the patient is unable to report the pres-ence of a target stimulus, even though some non-geniculostriate visual structures will still be processing that stimulus.

Weiskrantz et al. (1974) and others have attributed the residual visuomotor ability in their cortically blind patients to the 10 per cent or so of the optic fibres that terminate in the superior colliculus (Perry and Cowey 1984). As we saw in the first two chapters, this midbrain structure has long been implicated in the control of saccadic eye movements (for example, Sparks and May 1990) and could therefore, in theory at least, organize and initiate such movements in cortically blind patients. But the superior colliculus not only has important 'downstream' connections to eye-movement control centres, it also sends extensive projections to dorsal-stream areas in the cortex via the pulvinar nucleus of the thalamus and indeed, receives direct projections back from them (see Chapter 2). To the extent that such dorsal stream structures have remained intact, therefore, the cortices of cortically blind patients would presumably continue to receive visual input through this tectopulvinar route. As we saw in Chapter 2, there are networks of neurones in the parietal cortex of the primate brain which are intimately involved in the control of saccadic eye movements and others which are concerned with manual reaching towards visual targets. Thus, in some cortically blind patients, these dorsal-stream networks could probably continue to participate in the control of spatially organized eye and hand movements. It is known that in at least some dorsal-stream structures, many cells continue to show relatively normal responses to visual stimuli after lesions of V1 and could therefore play a role in blindsight (see Chapter 2 and Gross (1991)). In addition, cortical control structures in the frontal lobe, such as the frontal eye field, are interconnected with structures in the dorsal stream and exert a modulatory influence on ipsilateral tectal eye-movement mechanisms (Bruce 1990), as well as on other brainstem structures involved in visuomotor guidance (Stein and Glickstein 1992).

But not all forms of blindsight require the participation of the dorsal stream. In some studies (for example, Perenin and Jeannerod 1978), the cortical blindness of the patients resulted from hemidecortication during childhood, performed as a surgical treatment for severe infantile hemiplegia. This means that not only did the patients have no intact striate cortex on the damaged side of the brain, they did not have any intact visual cortical areas on that side and indeed would have had rather little undegenerated tissue in thalamic nuclei, including the LGNd and pulvinar, on the damaged side. Of course, one can still explain the preserved control of saccadic eye movements in the blind field of these patients by appealing to the intact retinal pathway to the superior colliculus, from which there are well-known downstream projections to structures concerned with eye (and in some species head) movements. But their remarkably accurate reaching behaviour is more difficult to account for, since there is no direct physiological evidence that the colliculus plays any role in the control of limb movements. Indeed, movements of the arm such as those involved in reaching are generally believed to depend on networks in the cerebral cortex.

Nevertheless, there is fragmentary evidence to support the idea that the superior colliculus can play a crucial role in the control of reaching. For example, in an early study referred to in Chapter 1, Hess *et al.* (1946) found that electrical stimulation of the midbrain in cats not only produced turning movements of the eye and head (the so-called 'visual grasp reflex') but would also sometimes elicit reaching movements of the forelimb in the same direction. A later study by Solomon *et al.* (1981) showed directly that the superior colliculus was involved in mediating reaching towards a visual target following V1 lesions in monkeys: although the animals retained this ability after V1 lesions alone, they then lost it after an additional lesion of the colliculus. And yet more recent evidence for a role of the colliculus in visually guided reaching comes from a study which describes cells in the deep collicular layers in monkeys that fire in close association with such movements (Werner 1993).

Of course, in all these studies the motor cortex was intact and this may have been a necessary part of the circuitry for executing the reaching responses apparently initiated in the superior colliculus. It remains to be seen, for example, whether the neurones discovered by Werner (1993) depend upon the integrity of the ipsilateral motor cortex for their reach-related properties: if so, they would not be able to mediate reaching in hemidecorticate patients. In other words, it would still remain a puzzle how patients with hemispherectomy can reach accurately to a visual target in their blind field. One possibility is that even though the retinotectal pathway would no longer have access to cortical motor structures on the damaged side of the brain in such patients, it might be able to gain access, via the intercollicular commissure and the thalamus, to cortical mechanisms in the intact hemisphere. This could allow the intact cortex to generate pointing responses with either hand.

It is clear from our discussion in this chapter so far that we do not consider blindsight to be well characterized as 'unconscious perception', as many writers would have it. We believe that it is more correctly seen as a collection of residual visuomotor responses that may depend on a variety of relatively independent circuits in the superior colliculus and dorsal stream. This idea is strengthened by the observation that the accuracy of localization in blindsight depends on the nature of the response used. If there were a single visual representation that could be used to generate whatever response was required, this would not be expected. Yet, as we have seen, visually guided saccadic eye movements in cortically blind patients are generally much less accurate than visually guided limb movements (Weiskrantz *et al.* 1974; Perenin and Jeannerod 1978). Such a finding is consistent with the observation that different semi-independent subsystems within the dorsal stream, superior colliculus, and perhaps other subcortical centres, have responsibility for the visual control of different effector systems. To put it another way, the coding of egocentric visual space differs according to the response system used. (It should be noted that there has been little attempt to prevent eye movements when blindsight patients are asked to point. But the argument for the participation of two quasi-independent visuomotor modules would remain equally strong even if the superiority of pointing over saccadic localization were simply an additive effect of using two effector systems cooperatively.)

If one accepts that visual input about spatial location can gain access to dorsal stream structures in blindsight, then one can go on to ask whether or not other kinds of information about the visual world can also be delivered to these visuomotor networks. Might a cortically blind patient, for example, show some ability to use visual information about the local features of objects to organize and execute well-formed grasping responses? On the face of it, this would be possible only if the tectopulvinar and other extrageniculate inputs to the dorsal stream could code the size, shape, and/or orientation of objects without the participation of V1. As yet there is no physiological evidence for this possibility. Although many neurones in the inferior pulvinar of monkeys are selective for stimulus orientation (Bender 1982), this property is permanently lost when area V1 is removed (Bender 1983). While there is some recovery of visual responsiveness in these pulvinar cells after a few weeks, this does not extend to a recovery of orientation selectivity. That kind of selectivity in pulvinar neurones may in fact depend crucially on prominent cells deep in layer 5 of area V1 which are known to project to the inferior pulvinar.

But of course there is orientation coding in area V1, despite its absence in the LGNd: in other words, the absence of such coding in the pulvinar would not preclude orientation being constructed in the extrastriate cortex from pulvinar inputs. It turns out that in fact some patients with blindsight do seem to have a residual ability to use shape and size information. The first evidence for this was reported by Marcel (1983): two cortically blind patients were described as showing 'better than chance preparatory adjustments of the wrist, fingers, and arm in reaching for objects of differing shape, location, and distance in the blind field' (p. 276). While it is unclear how good these visuo-motor abilities were, nor how well the testing was restricted to scotomatous retinal regions, Marcel's (1983) evidence suggests that extrageniculate pathways may be able to provide the necessary visual information about orientation and size for organizing grasping, without the mediation of V1. This would of course be consistent with the idea that the visual 'manipulation' neurones in the parietal lobe described by Taira *et al.* (1990) in the previous chapter could function to guide grasping using solely tectopulvinar visual inputs (see also Chapter 4).

This interpretation has now been strengthened by new quantitative evidence from Perenin and Rossetti (1993) in tests carried out with a completely hemianopic patient. When asked to 'post' a card into an open slot placed within his scotoma at different angles, this patient demonstrated moderately accurate (and statistically well above-chance) orientation of the card, using either hand. Yet when asked to make perceptual judgements of the slot's orientation, either verbally or by manual matching, the patient was unable to perform better than chance in this half of his visual field. Perenin and Rossetti (1993) also demonstrated that the patient could reach out and grasp rectangular objects with some proficiency in his hemianopic field; as in normal subjects, the wider the object, the greater the anticipatory hand-grip size during reaching. Yet again the patient failed when asked to make perceptual judgements, whether asked to so verbally or manually: his attempts were uncorrelated with object size. The authors conclude that orientation and size can be processed in cortically blind visual fields, but only when used to guide a motor action and not for 'more elaborate' perceptual tasks. We will consider this matter further in the next section.

As we noted earlier, Weiskrantz and his colleagues (Sanders *et al.* 1974) coined the term 'blindsight' to highlight the apparent paradox that, despite the absence of primary visual cortex and of conscious sight, a patient may be accurate at pointing to a source of light. Equally paradoxical, however, is the converse problem of patients with 'optic ataxia' (see Chapter 4): they are unable to use visual information accurately to guide motor acts such as reaching and grasping, though they still retain conscious sight of the objects they are unable to reach towards. (The reaching disability of these patients, who generally have occipitoparietal lesions, cannot be attributed to a motor deficit, since reaching can be well performed under non-visual guidance.) But within the framework we have proposed, in which visual perception and visual guidance are vested in separate systems, these complementary puzzles are easily resolved. We can simply argue that the dorsal visual stream mediates accurate reaching in blindsight but is disabled in optic ataxia, while inputs to the ventral stream permitting visual awareness of the stimulus are intact in optic ataxia but disrupted in blindsight.

3.2.4 Detection and discrimination in blindsight

Detection of a light stimulus in a normal subject is normally assumed by researchers in visual psychophysics to be synonymous with conscious perception of that stimulus. Consequently, they assume that the mode of reporting detection is of little importance. In blindsight, however, where such 'conscious' visual processing is not available, the mode of response has been found to play a role just as important in stimulus detection as we described above in stimulus localization.

Zihl and von Cramon (1980) asked hemianopic patients to report when a light had come on in their blind field, either by blinking, by pressing a button, or by saying 'yes'. After several training sessions, detection using either the manual or eyelid response showed great improvement, but accuracy remained very poor when the subjects gave their judgements verbally. Evidently the training had had differential visuomotor effects, rather than a general effect upon visual sensitivity which affected all response modalities equally. Equally striking results have recently been reported by Marcel (1993), even in the absence of training. His hemianopic patient, G.Y., was asked to report in the same three ways as Zihl and von Cramon's (1980) patients, whenever he felt that a light had come on in his blind field (which it did in 50 per cent of the trials). Blinking was found to be significantly more accurate than finger responses, which in turn proved a significantly more sensitive index than verbal responses. This trend of decreasing accuracy was paralleled by a trend of increasing response latency. In one of Marcel's (1993) experiments, this same result was found even when the three responses had to be made on the very same set of trials. Thus, for example, G.Y. might detect a stimulus manually on a given trial while failing to acknowledge the same stimulus verbally (or occasionally the converse).

The first puzzling aspect of these data is that blindsight patients can make any kind of verbal response, however inaccurate, to a visual stimulus, given our proposals that residual vision in blindsight depends upon intact visuomotor systems in the dorsal stream and elsewhere. Unlike the visuomotor control of saccades and pointing movements the relationship between any of the responses used and the visual stimulus detected in the above experiments was an arbitrary one. Nevertheless, although no overt visually directed movement (for example, a saccade) might be made, it can be assumed that there would still be activity generated in visuomotor control circuits in the dorsal stream. Such weak activity might be able to guide more arbitrary forms of response under circumstances where stronger signals, for example in the ventral stream, are absent. Indeed even when eye movements or other directed responses are actively suppressed, computations may be performed upon the inputs resulting from stimuli presented in the blind field, providing a variety of subtle cues ranging from efference copy of the motor commands to feedback from isometric contractions of the eye or limb musculature. These weak signals might vary as a function not only of the presence of a target but also, as we shall argue below, of its location or orientation. In this way a blindsight patient might be able to use information derived from visuomotor control systems to generate above-chance performance even on a forced-choice test of detection or discrimination.

The second interesting aspect of these data is that they show that the nature of the response (blink, finger movement, or verbal response) used to signal stimulus detection seems to determine how well the visual information is able to influence behaviour. We would argue that a blink or a finger movement, although still rather arbitrary, might be influenced more directly by the partial activation of one or more of the dorsal-stream networks than a verbal response. In all cases, the responses would be associated with very low confidence levels because of the absence of a concomitant visual experience.

In stimulus detection, as in other instances of blindsight, the superior colliculus probably provides the major input route whereby visual information reaches the dorsal stream and other relevant brain areas. There is in fact strong evidence for the role of the colliculus in stimulus detection in monkeys after V1 lesions: Mohler and Wurtz (1977) showed that manual detection performance following recovery from such a cortical lesion was abolished by a subsequent collicular removal on the same side. In the case of detection using the blinking response, the superior colliculus may be more directly involved in bringing about the response, as well as in analysing the stimulus. Keay *et al.* (1988) have shown that the colliculus mediates a range of light-elicited autonomic responses. Since blinking itself is a defensive response, it is not surprising that it can be efficiently enlisted by blindsight patients to indicate the presence of a light. Moreover there is evidence dating back to Ferrier (1875) that electrical stimulation of sites in the posterior parietal cortex will elicit blinking in a monkey and recent work using neural imaging has shown that an equivalent area in humans is activated during eyeblinks (Hari *et al.* 1994).

Blindsight, of course, is defined by the absence of visual consciousness. It may still be that non-visual sensations will occur during a detection task. Patients who exhibit blindsight in fact often report 'feelings' that, at least in some cases, correlate with their visual successes. For example Weiskrantz *et al.*'s (1974) patient D.B. who sometimes described having 'feelings' that a stimulus had occurred, 'repeatedly stressed that he saw nothing at all in the sense of "seeing" and that he was merely guessing' (p. 721). We assume that these non-visual experiences (which vary from patient to patient) are associated with the activation of different visuomotor subsystems. Marcel (1993) goes so far as to argue that in each of the three response modalities used in his experiments, G.Y. was reporting a different kind of non-visual experience. If he is right, then in our terms, this would imply a distinct non-visual experiential state associated with each different visuomotor system activated. In any event, if parallel systems are being recruited as we have suggested, it may be that when monitored as a whole they can exceed the sum of their parts in determining detection responses. This would explain Marcel's (1993) observation that when asked simply to guess, G.Y. performed consistently better in the detection tasks than when asked to report on a 'feeling'.

Might the kinds of indirect cueing mechanisms we have postulated enable some cortically blind patients not only to 'detect' objects but also to 'discriminate' between them? While the evidence for such discrimination abilities is not widespread, there are some reports of residual vision for pattern or pattern elements in cortically blind fields. Weiskrantz *et al.* (1974), for example, found that D.B. was able to guess with better than chance success (70–80 per cent correct) as to whether he was being shown a circle or a cross, or a horizontal or a vertical line. But this does not mean that he has any ability to see the 'shape' of real objects, even in some unconscious sense. Indeed, D.B. cannot guess as to the sameness or difference between two oriented lines presented simultaneously in his scotoma, even though he can guess at an above-chance level at their identity when presented singly (Weiskrantz 1987). Furthermore D.B.'s ability to discriminate between shapes is best when orientation cues are plentiful (for example, X versus O) and falls almost to chance where they are less helpful. This suggests a lack of any combinatorial or 'Gestalt' processing of features one with another.

What kinds of visuomotor mechanisms might mediate such abilities? One possibility could be the partial activation or active suppression of voluntary or involuntary ocular scanning responses made to the stimuli. Such covert oculomotor responses would presumably differ as a function of the orientation of each of two different stimuli when they are presented separately. Alternatively or in addition, similar activation of other visuomotor structures might cause the patient to make overt or covert preparatory hand-turning movements, which would normally be a precursor for the picking up of an object at that orientation. In this case the patient might even use explicit self-cueing, when asked to guess the orientation of a stimulus. But when two stimuli are presented together, there would be little or no differential activation of these various visuomotor systems that could assist the patient in making informed guesses as to stimulus similarity or difference.

It is likely that self-cueing from preparatory motor acts of these kinds would depend upon visuomotor networks in the dorsal stream rather than on the superior colliculus alone, where there is no evidence for the coding of stimulus orientation. As discussed in the previous section, it is possible that projections from the colliculus, via the pulvinar, might provide the necessary visual inputs to the dorsal stream so that orientation can be computed. Such tectopulvinar visual inputs arrive at the cortex as early as cortical area V2. But since experiments have shown that neurones in neither V2 nor V3 retain their visual responsiveness when area V1 has been inactivated by cooling (Girard and Bullier 1989; Girard et al. 1991a), these areas can presumably play no role in blindsight. (It should be borne in mind, however, that these experiments were carried out acutely and that the tectopulvinar route to visual areas such as V2 might recover responsiveness over a longer time scale.) In area V3A, however, many neurones do continue to respond to visual stimuli when V1 is cooled (Girard et al. 1991a), suggesting this area as a possible arrival point for visual information to reach the dorsal stream. Indeed, cells in area V3A are coded for orientation just as precisely as cells in V1 (Gaska et al. 1988), and project to the dorsal prelunate area DP and area LIP (see Fig. 2.4, p. 40), which in turn have direct connections to area 7a (Andersen et al. 1990a).

If this way of thinking is correct, we would expect little if any pattern or orientation discrimination ability in blindsight patients with substantial occipitoparietal cortical damage. And indeed Perenin (1978) and Ptito et al. (1987)

found little evidence for such discrimination in their hemidecorticate patients. (The evidence was convincing in only one of Perenin's patients, who was operated on at the early age of 7 years; it may be that early rewiring is possible in such cases, permitting the use of the undamaged hemisphere. Although one other patient performed slightly above chance, a third performed significantly below chance. Thus, the evidence as a whole suggests that orientation discrimination in blindsight normally depends upon there being intact extrastriate cortical visual processing within the damaged hemisphere.)

Furthermore, the form that an intact ability of this kind might take will no doubt depend on which parts of the dorsal stream cortex are spared. As we saw in the previous section, the hemianopic patient of Perenin and Rossetti (1993) could demonstrate some intact discrimination of the orientation of a slot when asked to 'post' a card into it, but none when asked to indicate the orientation verbally or by manual pantomime. We would predict that this patient may have more extensive extrastriate damage in the superior parietal areas concerned with the visual control of eye movements than D.B., who presumably would have been able to judge the orientation better than chance. Yet Perenin and Rossetti's (1993) patient evidently has relatively little damage in the areas concerned with visually guided grasping. We would predict, in general terms, that the more intact the dorsal stream areas in the damaged hemisphere of a cortically blind patient, the better the blindsight, but also that the specific form of the blindsight will depend on the individual systems that are damaged. As yet it is difficult to test this idea in detail, but the increasing sophistication of imaging techniques may permit it in the future.

3.2.5 Colour processing in blindsight

It was first reported by Weiskrantz *et al.* (1974) that D.B. could guess with above-chance success as to whether a light flashed in his scotoma was green or red, despite variations in the luminance of the stimuli. More recently, a careful examination of ten patients by Stoerig (1987) has demonstrated that different cortically blind patients may have an 'unconscious' ability to detect either white light targets or coloured ones or both or neither. Furthermore, a patient unable to guess successfully as to the occurrence of a coloured light, may nevertheless be able to guess at an above-chance level whether a light is green or red.

Stoerig and Cowey (1989) went on to test the spectral sensitivity of three patients both in their field defect and at a symmetrical point in the intact hemifield. Although the patients were 'guessing' in their scotomas, their psychophysical thresholds were raised by only approximately 1 log unit, right across the visible spectrum. There was evidence that they were able to access cone as well as rod activity, since the photopic sensitivity curve showed the characteristic peaks and troughs whose positions indicate colour-opponent interactions. Moreover, the peak sensitivity shifted from short to medium wavelengths with the change from dark to light adaptation, as in a normal observer (the Purkinje shift).

These data allowed the same investigators to test for wavelength discrimination, between stimuli matched for their effective strength in the scotoma; each was set at 0.5 log units above threshold (Stoerig and Cowey 1992). Two patients were found to discriminate significantly better than chance with all three pairs of stimuli used. These results provide convincing evidence for wavelength discrimination after striate cortical damage and, thus, agree with some studies in the monkey literature (Schilder *et al.* 1972; Keating 1979).

At first sight, Stoerig and Cowey's (1992) findings do not fit in any simple way into our view of blindsight as a reflection of activity in the superior colliculus and the dorsal stream of visual processing in the cortex. There is little or no evidence that true colour or wavelength selectivity is present in the neurones of midbrain structures like the superior colliculus. What evidence there is for rudimentary wavelength selectivity in the colliculus (Kadoya *et al.* 1971) may derive from cortical rather than retinal inputs. Certainly none of the small Pβ cells, believed to be the sole carriers of chromatic information from the retina, project from the retina to the midbrain (Perry and Cowey 1984).

In contrast, wavelength selectivity is common throughout the geniculostriate parvocellular channel, especially in its branch via the 'blobs' in area V1 and, thence, to the thin stripes of V2 and on to area V4 (De Yoe and Van Essen 1988; Zeki and Shipp 1988). However, a small number of cells (a few thousand) project directly from the parvocellular LGN layers to areas V2 and V4 (Benevento and Yoshida 1981; Fries 1981) and are known to survive V1 destruction in the monkey (Yukie and Iwai 1981; Cowey and Stoerig 1989). These therefore constitute the most plausible candidate for providing the necessary information to subserve colour discrimination in blindsight. There is indeed now evidence that an intrinsic group of specialized 'interneurones' survive in the LGNd, despite the otherwise total degeneration there that follows V1 lesions in monkeys, and that these interneurones receive a direct visual input from the retina and in turn synapse onto cells which project to areas V2 and V4 (Kisvárday *et al.* 1991; Cowey and Stoerig 1992).

It is unclear what function this projection pathway from LGNd to the secondary visual cortex might serve in the normal brain. It is possible, as argued above for the retinotectal pathway, that it has privileged functional connections to some specific output system. For example, it is conceivable that it might play a role in the observation that certain colours are more effective in eliciting saccadic eye movements than others (Doma and Hallett 1988).

Wavelength inputs could reach the dorsal stream either through area V2 or V4 (Maunsell and Van Essen 1983b). If they took only the former route, we could explain the absence of a perceptual experience of colour in patients whose guessing revealed 'colour blindsight'. (In contrast, an activation of 'colour cells' in area V4, part of the ventral stream, would be expected to give rise to experiences of colour.)

3.2.6 Motion processing in blindsight

The evidence for sensitivity to object movement in blindsight is well documented (for example, Bridgeman and Staggs 1982; Blythe et al. 1986, 1987). Indeed, most patients show better evidence for blindsight when stimuli are moving and some patients only show it then. It has been well known since the classic descriptions of Riddoch (1917) that patients tend to be better able to see an object when in motion in a defective part of the field than when stationary. Although Riddoch's (1917) descriptions are not clear on this point, some of his patients probably showed blindsight for motion, that is, were able to process motion information while not visually aware of the movement. There is now good evidence that some blindsight patients of this kind can discriminate even the direction of motion of a stimulus, at least crudely (Blythe et al. 1986, 1987). This indicates a capacity beyond the mere appreciation of greater 'salience' in a moving stimulus.

What has also now become clear, however, is that motion perception in the full sense of a reported awareness of movement in particular directions may co-occur with dense cortical blindness with respect to all other visual modalities. This has been recently documented by Barbur et al. (1993) in the hemianopic patient G. Y. It appears that under some circumstances G. Y. does not have blindsight for motion; he is actually able to perceive motion. Thus, 'cortically blind' patients may show sensitivity to stimulus motion in two quite different ways, that is with or without awareness. We will return to patient G. Y. in the next section.

As in the case of stimulus localization and detection, it seems likely that the superior colliculus must be implicated in mediating blindsight for stimulus movement. Many neurones in the primate colliculus are sensitive to motion and, moreover, moving stimuli are the most effective in eliciting orienting head and eye movements, in which the superior colliculus is known to play an important role (Sparks 1986). It is unlikely, however, that this circuitry on its own could mediate the residual ability of many blindsight patients to discriminate the direction of motion, since tectal neurones are not well tuned for direction in primates (Goldberg and Wurtz 1972). It is more likely that for such abilities, intact projections (via the pulvinar) to the dorsal stream are required. As mentioned in Chapter 2, not only does area MT in monkeys have a large concentration of direction-selective neurones, but these neurones continue to show such selectivity after ablation of area V1 (Rodman *et al.* 1989). Subsequent ablation of the superior colliculus abolishes this selectivity (Rodman *et al.* 1990). Consequently, the tectopulvinar route to MT must be a strong candidate for subserving directional motion processing in blindsight.

If this is so, it is interesting to recall that area MT provides the major input to area MST, where (in its lateral subdivision) neuronal activity is intimately associated with the occurrence of pursuit movements of head and eye. Furthermore, pursuit eye movements to foveated moving stimuli remain accurate in monkeys following the removal of V1 (Segraves *et al.* 1987). In contrast, saccadic eye movements to such moving stimuli in the same animals are faulty, despite being accurate to stationary objects (Segraves *et al.* 1987). This suggests that visual inputs signalling stimulus motion cannot be provided to *saccadic* control systems through the tectopulvinar–MT pathway.

It is tempting in the light of this evidence to speculate that the direction-of-motion discrimination often observed in blindsight may be attributable to self-cueing from real or incipient pursuit eye movements mediated by the lateral MST. A first prediction from this idea would be that the greater the restriction placed upon a patient's eye movements, the poorer performance would be. Secondly, since such a cortical pursuit pathway would be lost following hemispherectomy, there should be no blindsight for movement direction in these patients. This is borne out by recent evidence: although hemispherectomized patients can detect movement (Ptito *et al.* 1991), they nevertheless fail to discriminate its direction (Perenin 1991) or velocity (Ptito *et al.* 1991). Finally, one would predict that patients who do have discriminative blindsight for motion should be able to show good oculomotor pursuit. Some years ago, pursuit eye movements were tested in one patient with bilateral cortical blindness by surrounding him with a large moving striped display. The normal observer will make slow pursuit eye movements alternating with rapid catch-up flicks, that is, show optokinetic nystagmus (OKN). This patient's eyes were observed to follow the pattern and to display relatively normal OKN, despite his having no perceptual experience of the motion (ter Braak *et al.* 1971). Similarly, OKN has been found to be preserved in monkeys following removals restricted to V1 (Pasik and Pasik 1964).

Despite these data, however, the use of brain systems which are specialized for OKN and pursuit cannot explain all residual motion sensitivity in human cortical blindness, since some blindsight patients able to guess motion direction correctly fail to show OKN (Perenin 1991). But despite the absence of OKN, moving pattern elements might have been capable of driving other action systems in these patients. For example, whole-field motion will often occur on the retina as a direct correlate of the observer's own bodily motion. As we saw in Chapter 2, there is good evidence that such self-produced visual motion (optic flow) is important in the guidance and control of motor action, especially whole-body locomotion and the maintenance of postural stability (Lee and Thomson 1982). Perhaps, then, the partial activation of mechanisms dedicated to the processing of optic flow can provide cortically blind patients with some useful cues for discriminating the direction of motion. There is preliminary evidence to suggest that such processing may still be possible in cortically blind patients: Mestre *et al.* (1992) found that simulated optic flow in the form of expanding 'cloudburst' patterns could be accurately detected and discriminated in a patient with almost-complete bilateral V1 damage. They also observed that their patient could walk quite successfully through a cluttered environment and they argue that his sensitivity to optic-flow cues may have enabled him to do this.

As indicated in Chapter 2, cortical networks in areas MT and MST probably play an important role in the guidance of locomotion (and posture) by means of optic flow fields. Of course subcortical structures such as the accessory optic nuclei, where many neurones have been found to be sensitive to whole-field stimulation (Grasse and Cynader 1991), are almost certainly also involved. These brainstem structures have interconnections with cortical area MT and adjacent areas in the superior temporal sulcus of the monkey (Hoffman *et al.* 1991). It therefore seems likely that in higher mammals at least, they have become integral parts of larger vertically organized circuits for the visual guidance of locomotion and posture.

3.3 Why is blindsight blind?

The argument of this chapter has been that blindsight is a set of visual capacities mediated by the dorsal stream and associated subcortical structures. It has been implicitly assumed that the processing underlying blindsight occurs without the intervention of the ventral stream, which has been in effect visually deafferented by the striate lesion. But it is known that in the monkey at least, the two cortical streams are not hermetically sealed from one another: in particular, area MT sends substantial projections to area V4 (Maunsell and Van Essen 1983*b*; Ungerleider and Desimone 1986). Indeed, we argued in Chapter 2 that this pathway probably underlies the normal subject's visual perception of motion. Why then, cannot motion information processed in area MT reach visual awareness in the ventral stream in patients with V1 lesions?

The answer seems to be that this can indeed happen: patient G.Y. described earlier can have a perceptual awareness of visual motion, despite having apparently suffered complete destruction of area V1 in the left hemisphere. And evidence from positron-emission tomography (PET) imaging suggests that the human equivalent of area MT is activated by moving stimuli in G.Y. (Barbur *et al.* 1993) much as it is in normal human subjects (Zeki *et al.* 1991). The question, therefore, is why this does not happen more often, that is, why most other cortically blind patients sensitive to stimulus motion appear to lack awareness of that motion. We suggest that the answer must lie in the variable extrastriate damage that accompanies V1 damage in human subjects. Where this damage invades the dorsal stream (for example, area MT), we must predict little residual visual ability at all (aware or unaware). Where the extrastriate damage invades occipitotemporal areas (for example, area V4) instead, we would predict blindsight, but no visual awareness. Only where the damage spares both ventral and dorsal stream areas would one expect to see preserved islands of conscious vision, as in patient G.Y. The magnetic resonance imaging (MRI) scan of this patient would be consistent with such a rather 'clean' lesion of V1, but to test our predictions fully, further research combining imaging procedures with detailed visual testing needs to be done in patients whose lesions extend dorsally and/or ventrally beyond V1.

3.4 Conclusions

Blindsight is paradoxical only if one regards vision as a unitary process. Once it is accepted that the mechanisms capable of providing perceptual experience are separate from those underlying the visual control of action, the paradox disappears. In most cortically blind patients, retinal stimulation can no longer lead to the perceptual experience of 'sight', but in some at least such stimulation can still gain access to visuomotor control mechanisms. Not only can patients with blindsight move their eyes, hands, or body under visual control, they can also use subtle internal or external cues generated by these control mechanisms to make informed guesses about the nature of the visual world they cannot 'see'.

The very term 'blindsight' is in our view a misleading one, in so far as it seems to imply (and has often been taken to imply) that the residual abilities are a form of 'unconscious perception' rather than a collection of visuomotor skills and strategies. It is our contention (see Chapter 7) that while 'unconscious perception' need not be a meaningless phrase, it can probably only be mediated by the ventral stream and only be seen under special conditions such as inattentiveness or a pathological disorder of attention.

Chapter 4

Disorders of spatial perception and the visual control of action

Humans and monkeys with lesions of the posterior parietal cortex often have difficulty in reaching out to grasp objects in the visual field. Such deficits, of course, are entirely consistent with our proposal that the dorsal stream of visual projections, which terminates in this area, plays a critical role in the visuomotor transformations underlying the distal control of manual prehension and other skilled visuomotor acts. Most previous interpretations of these deficits, however, have dealt with them as part of a more general disturbance in spatial perception rather than as a disorder that is limited to the visual control of particular movements. But as we noted in Chapter 1, the use of a general phrase like 'disturbance in spatial perception' carries with it the implicit assumption that the computations underlying the visuospatial control of motor output and those underlying the perception of spatial relations rely on a single unitary process and share the same neural substrate. Indeed, this was the point of view implied by Ungerleider and Mishkin (1982) in their original 'two cortical visual systems' theory, which distinguished between object vision and spatial vision and located the latter in the dorsal stream of projections to the posterior parietal cortex.

In sharp contrast to this now widely accepted characterization of the visual processing of spatial location, we wish to argue that the relevant computations for the control of spatially directed movements are carried out by neural systems that are quite independent of those underlying much of what is called 'spatial perception'. Furthermore, we wish to argue that different kinds of actions will often require rather different transformations of the spatial information available. As already indicated in previous chapters, we propose that many of these visuomotor transformations rely on algorithms embodied in circuitry within the dorsal stream, whereas circuitry in the ventral stream may support the visual processing of spatial information to be used for purposes of perception and cognitive manipulation. Moreover, since actions such as grasping are clearly directed at objects rather than at disembodied locations, additional information about the objects, such as their size, shape, and local orientation must also form part of the required set of visuomotor transformations underlying the control of the constituent movements. We maintain that the neural systems carrying out these object-related computations also reside in the dorsal stream.

In this chapter, we review the behavioural and neuropsychological evidence for these proposals in some detail and also attempt to draw functional limits on the two visual processing streams. We point out that while one can ask which stream supplies the visual data for 'spatial cognition' when it is required, there is no need to assume that either stream performs those high-level computations itself, nor even that such cognition always needs visual inputs at all. We speculate that a non-visual (supramodal) system may handle such cognitive manipulations.

4.1 Space: egocentric and allocentric coding

Establishing the spatial location of an object is clearly important for the moment-to-moment interactions that we might need to have with that object. If one wishes to offer a friend a drink, for example, one needs to know both the location of the glass of whisky and the location of the friend. Knowing the locations of the relevant objects will enable one to direct both a smile and the drink in the correct direction. Indeed, the computation of the exact position of one's friend's hand is critical if one is to pass the glass successfully from one's own hand to theirs. But often these same locational properties are not at all important to the nature of the interactions themselves (why they are performed, and their content or semantics), nor are they intrinsically important to remember later. They are important only for the performance of the required actions at the time.

Yet in other contexts, the spatial location of objects and object parts (or more properly, visual stimuli) *is* important for our perception and memory of the external world. The recognition of objects and their interrelations depends upon the visual system's ability to compute the relative location of stimuli impinging on the retina. Without such information, the content of the visual array would be indecipherable. In fact, spatial information is primary since the very configuration of an object can be known only by computing the spatial distribution of elements within the visual array. And even after objects have been individuated and identified, additional semantic content can be gleaned from knowing something about the relative location of the objects in the visual world.

Thus, spatial information about the location of objects in the world is needed both to direct actions at those objects and also to assign meaning and significance to them. In this respect, spatial information is no different from other properties of objects that are processed by the visual system, such as shape, size, and orientation, which are also critical to both action and perception. This does not mean, however, that spatial location is coded in the same way for these different purposes, nor does it mean that the same systems or processes provide spatial information to be used in these different ways. As we have already suggested, two broadly different sets of computations, each involving various properties of objects, including location, are computed by two separate cortical systems: a parietofrontal system for visuomotor control and an occipitotemporal one for visual recognition (see also Goodale and Milner 1992; Milner and Goodale 1993). This position obviously contrasts with the currently widespread assumption that the visual information required for mediating the perception of spatial relationships is received through the dorsal stream.

Once one has changed perspective from thinking in terms of a unitary 'spatial perception' to thinking of the ways in which spatial information is used in a variety of human activities, further observations can be made. The first is that there is unlikely to be a unitary spatial coding system even for visuomotor control: there are many visually guided activities, involving different effector combinations and modulated by different kinds of visual information. Thus, it is not surprising to see a set of quasi-independent but interactive networks in the parietal and frontal cortices, visuomotor modules leading to different outputs and influenced by different inputs. It is to be expected, in fact, that 'space' will be coded in different ways for different purposes in different subsystems (cf. Feldman 1985; Rizzolatti *et al.* 1994).

Perhaps the most basic distinction that needs to made in thinking about spatial vision is between the locational coordinates of some object within the visual field and the relationship between the loci of more than one object (cf. Kosslyn 1987). In many discussions of spatial processing, these two modes of description have been grouped together as if they achieved the same end and as if they might plausibly depend on the same brain mechanisms. However, this is because most discussions neglect the different ways in which we need to use spatial information. Of course, at the most general level, all forms of spatial coding do serve a single function: to allow the organism to select a particular object so as to be able to act upon that object. But this formulation hides a lot of variation. Depending on the needs and circumstances of the observer, there will be a trade-off between the accuracy and flexibility of the underlying coding mechanisms that index and locate the intended goal object.

Thus, the most primitive form of localization is simply to specify where on the retinal surface the image of an object is located. But although the specification of the retinal coordinates of an object may be accurate and may require no information about other objects (provided the target object is indexed in some way), this form of localization has limited usefulness. It might be used, for example, in guiding saccadic eye movements, and there is evidence to suggest that such coding systems are indeed used by control systems in the superior colliculus and in certain loci in the posterior parietal and frontal cortices. But unless the organism remains perfectly stationary, a coding mechanism based solely on retinal coordinates would be useless by itself for any coding of location over time. For less immediate but still relatively short-term purposes, it is necessary to have a mechanism for recoding position that does not depend on the observer remaining stationary.

One important form of spatial recoding would be to modulate the retinal information as a function of eye position with respect to the head, thus allowing the computation of location in head-based rather than retina-based coordinates. The evidence thus far indicates that transformations of this kind are characteristic only of dorsal stream circuits. As we saw in Chapter 2, such modulation is already apparent as early as visual area V3A (Galletti and Battaglini 1989) and is a frequent feature of the visuomotor cells in area 7a (Andersen et al. 1985) and LIP (Andersen et al. 1990b). Modulation occurs for moving visual stimuli as well: some motion-sensitive cells in the lateral region of area MST, for example, are modulated by the head and eye movements that are produced when the monkey visually pursues the moving stimulus. Thus, by the time visual information about spatial location reaches premotor areas in the frontal lobe, it has been considerably recalibrated by information derived from eye position and other non-retinal sources (Gentilucci et al. 1983).

The evidence indicates that multiple egocentric coordinate frames are found within parietofrontal systems, each presumably being suitable for the control of different kinds of spatially directed acts. Thus, for example, egocentric frames of reference that are head and/or body centred would provide the observer with information that would allow accurate reaching for objects despite movements of one's eyes and head. There is the additional problem, of course, of specifying the required motor coordinates for limb and hand movements with respect to their initial position in space (for a discussion of this issue, see Flanders et al. (1992)).

A very different kind of spatial coding is required for the guidance of behaviours that depend on more permanent features of the environment through which we move. Finding our way from one's house to one's place of work requires spatial knowledge in a form that transcends particular movements of the eye, head, and body. For this degree of generality, no kind of egocentric coding is of any utility: one has to sacrifice precision for flexibility. With the exception of 'dead reckoning,' which is extremely computationally demanding, the only way to code the location of an object once the observer has begun to move around is to locate the object relative to the location of other relatively stationary objects in the environment. This kind of 'allocentric' coding allows an observer to generalize over longer time scales while moving around in the environment and would be essential for constructing any useful long-term memory of spatial location. Although such allocentric coding will suffer from the drawback that it is less accurate than egocentric, coordinate-based coding, it will serve as a 'ball park' mechanism, getting the observer sufficiently near the goal object to enable an egocentric coordinate system to operate. It is important to note that in order to store the spatial relations of objects, it also necessary to store the identities of the objects themselves. This simple logical point makes it impossible for any allocentric coding system to operate without information about object identity. In contrast, provided an object has been indexed or 'flagged' in some way, egocentric coding of its location does not require information about the object's identity.

Thus, allocentric coding, but not egocentric coding, would appear to require the participation of the object recognition systems in the ventral stream. In fact, as we hinted earlier, the systems for object and allocentric coding are necessarily symbiotic, in the sense that each depends crucially upon the other. The parsing of the visual scene into a spatial array of discrete objects requires a kind of 'boot-strapping' operation whereby the two processes can work in a mutually cooperative manner. Indeed a number of computational approaches to object recognition have recognized the necessity for such an interplay between feature analysis and spatial coding (McCarthy 1993). Once this parsing has been achieved, the spatial relations between objects can be incorporated into a 'cognitive map' that is independent of the observer's movements and viewpoint. The storage of such maps may involve structures such as the medial temporal cortex and the hippocampus (see, for example Rolls (1991)), where individual cells coding allocentric visual location can be found (Tamura *et al.* 1990; Feigenbaum and Rolls 1991). Only egocentric coding of space has ever been discovered in dorsal-stream neurones and, indeed, our theoretical position would predict the absence of allocentric coding. In fact if allocentric spatial coding were ever discovered in dorsal stream neurones, it would constitute clear evidence against our view of dorsal stream function, and instead would favour the conceptualization put forward by Ungerleider and Mishkin (1982).

In Chapter 3 we discussed the effects of selectively depriving the extrastriate cortex of visual input as the result of damage to the striate cortex, V1. In this and the next chapter, we look at the direct effects of damage to the dorsal and ventral streams themselves. First, we present evidence that damage to the human dorsal stream results in severe disturbances in the visual control of actions of the eye, hand, and body, but need not interfere with the ability to identify objects or their spatial interrelations. We then describe the closely analogous behavioural disorders that are caused by posterior parietal lesions in monkeys. The visuomotor disorders observed after parietal damage in both human and monkey are clearly consistent with the electrophysiological evidence for networks of cells in the posterior parietal lobe associated with the visual control of eye movements and reaching and grasping movements (Chapter 2). We then examine critically the evidence that disorders of 'spatial perception' present any kind of a unitary syndrome and argue instead that different extrastriate areas are implicated in different aspects of human spatial performance. We conclude this chapter by critically examining the data that have been used to argue for a disorder of 'spatial perception' following posterior parietal lesions in monkeys, and suggest that they can be better accounted for in visuomotor terms.

4.2 Disorders in the visual control of action: the Bálint–Holmes syndrome

4.2.1 Disorders of reaching: 'optic ataxia' or 'disorientation'?

Bálint (1909) described a patient who had bilateral brain infarcts in the parietal region and who suffered from an inability to reach out accurately for visible objects when using his right hand. Bálint (1909) called this reaching disorder 'optic ataxia', although he believed it to be an integral part of a larger cluster of symptoms, including an inability to move ocular fixation ('gaze paralysis' or 'sticky fixation'; Benson 1989), that have collectively become known as Bálint's syndrome. As Bálint (1909) himself noted, a purely sensory or perceptual account of the reaching deficit would not suffice, since the patient could use visual information to guide the movements of his left hand quite accurately. Yet nor would a purely motor deficit explain the misreaching, since Bálint's (1909) patient could perform movements directed toward his own body quite accurately, presumably on the basis of tactile and proprioceptive information. Since Bálint's (1909) initial observations, optic ataxia has been repeatedly described, though often under different names (for example, 'visual disorientation', Brain (1941), 'defective visual localization', Ratcliff and Davies-Jones (1972), and 'visuomotor ataxia', Rondot *et al.* 1977).

As indicated in Fig. 4.1, optic ataxia does not require a bilateral lesion, but can also occur after a unilateral lesion. In many of these cases, unlike Bálint's

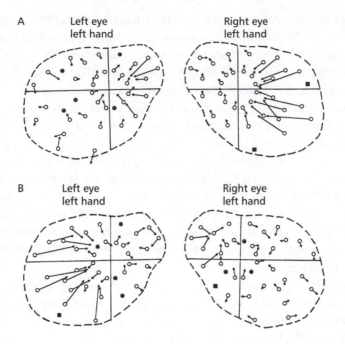

Fig. 4.1 Schematic diagram illustrating defective aiming movements in patients with lesions of the posterior cerebral cortex using different combinations of hand and eye. In both cases, damage included regions of the posterior parietal cortex. (A) Patient with left-hemisphere damage and hemiplegia. Aiming movements are grossly inaccurate in the right half field in both eyes. (B) Patient with right-hemisphere lesion. The deficits in aiming are largely confined to the left visual field in both eyes. Open circles indicate each target position, arrows indicate the location of the response, filled circles indicate accurate localization, and filled squares indicate targets not detected. Adapted from Ratcliff and Davies-Jones (1972).

(1909) patient, the misreaching affects only the contralesional visual field (Riddoch 1935; Cole *et al.* 1962; Ratcliff and Davies-Jones 1972). With a small lesion, optic ataxia may even be limited to only a single quadrant (Ross-Russell and Bharucha 1984). Since the standard tests are carried out with the head and eyes fixed, it is uncertain whether the disorder conforms to strict retinal coordinates or to head- or body-based coordinates. In any event, it is clear in these patients that no generalized motor disorder can explain the results, since a given arm is often able to point accurately towards targets in one visual field (or side) but not the other (Ratcliff and Davies-Jones 1972). On the face of it, such behaviour could be explained as a global deficit in spatial localization (albeit limited to one half of space) and, indeed, many of the reports of this disorder are described in these terms. Holmes (1919) regarded the disorder as 'the inability of the patients to determine the position in space, in relation to themselves, of objects which they saw distinctly' (p. 231). In other words, he attributed the disorder (which he called a 'disturbance of visual orientation') to a general loss of egocentric visuospatial coding.

The basic problem with this and other interpretations that postulate a generalized deficit in spatial coding, of course, is that in many patients the 'disorientation' shows effector specificity. Even when reaching is impaired whichever hand is used, several patients with optic ataxia can direct their eyes accurately towards targets that they cannot accurately reach for (Riddoch 1935; Ratcliff and Davies-Jones 1972). This shows clearly that in no sense can the misreaching in optic ataxia be attributed to a loss of 'the' sensory representation of space in such patients. Instead, such a result compels us towards the alternative view, that there are multiple spatial codings, each controlling a different effector system.

There are substantial variations in the pattern of reaching deficits in optic ataxia, even though a lesion to the same general region in the superior part of the parietal lobe appears to be responsible in virtually every case (Ratcliff and Davies-Jones 1972; Perenin and Vighetto 1988; Rondot 1989). For example, as Bálint (1909) originally found, a patient may be affected in both halves of the visual field, but only when using one arm (cf. Rondot 1989) and we have mentioned the quite different pattern where only one visual hemifield but both limbs are affected. In yet other patients, the disorder is only apparent when they reach with the contralesional arm and within the contralesional visual hemifield (Tzavaras and Masure 1976; Rondot et al. 1977). These variations can all be understood within the scope of a simple disconnection model (De Renzi 1982; Rondot 1989). It has to be assumed that the visuomotor network underlying reaching can be interrupted at different hypothetical points, the damage affecting either the earlier or later stages in the transformation from visual to motor coordinates for reaching (cf. Stein 1992).

It has been a long-running controversy as to whether the reaching disorder seen in Bálint's (1909) syndrome is of the same nature as that seen in Holmes's (1918) patients. McCarthy and Warrington (1990), for example, consider that the two are different and that, as argued by the original authors, one reflects a visuomotor disorder (that is, 'optic ataxia') while the other reflects a purely perceptual disorder (that is, 'visual disorientation'). Other writers, in contrast (for example, De Renzi 1982, 1985; Newcombe and Ratcliff 1989), consider the disorder to be essentially the same in both cases and as one symptom within a larger 'Bálint–Holmes' syndrome. We agree with the latter account and would argue that different but overlapping combinations of deficits are bound to arise after damage to the parietal lobe, because different visuomotor modules will be damaged to different extents in different patients.

It is likely that in both Bálint's (1909) and Holmes' (1918) patients the damage was rather extensive, disrupting more than one visuomotor module. Many of Holmes' (1918) patients, for example, had major deficits in gaze control as well as in reaching. Thus, a failure to make both accurate eye and hand movements to a specified object need not have been due to a global visuospatial deficit but simply due to damage to two quasi-separate visuomotor modules. Indeed, the fact that some of Holmes' (1918) patients could not even move their eyes accurately to command suggests that they not only had visuomotor deficits but also more basic motor or 'praxic' deficits. It is also likely that in some of Holmes' patients, the lesion invaded more inferior regions within the parietal lobe, well beyond the homologues of the visuomotor systems identified in the monkey. As we shall argue later, the parietal lobe has expanded greatly during the evolution of the human brain and has probably incorporated several new functions supplementary to those embodied within the dorsal stream.

The damage in Holmes' (1918) patients may even have included parts of the human homologue of the ventral stream, in which we have argued that allocentric coding is probably elaborated in the monkey. As we will describe later, difficulties in topological orientation are strongly associated with lesions of the occipitotemporal region in humans. Similarly, the deficits in distance estimation that were described in some of Holmes' (1918) patients are reminiscent of similar deficits in distance coding seen in monkeys with lesions of the inferotemporal cortex (Humphrey and Weiskrantz 1969).

In more recent work, patients with optic ataxia, many of whom had smaller lesions than those studied by Holmes (1918), have been examined in detail using quantitative measures. In the most comprehensive study to date, Perenin and Vighetto (1988) described the visual and visuomotor capacities of ten such patients. To compare perceptual reports of stimuli in the two visual hemifields, Perenin and Vighetto (1988) presented stimuli for only 0.2 s to prevent the patients from foveating them. Despite these short presentation times, the patients performed well above chance on judgements of spatial location and on the perception of orientation of a single line, within either half of the visual field. Furthermore, under more natural conditions, all the patients could give good verbal estimates of the distance and relative position of items throughout the visual field. Thus, it seems clear that their profound difficulties in reaching towards objects could not be accounted for simply in terms of a disturbance in some kind of global spatial representation. Unlike the gunshot-wound patients of Holmes (1918), these patients all had unilateral lesions, in many cases known to be restricted to the parietal lobe and in no case invading the temporal lobe.

4.2.2 Visually guided eye movements

As was indicated above, many patients with Bálint–Holmes syndrome have difficulty in using eye movements to transfer and maintain their gaze fixation with respect to relevant visual stimuli. Indeed, a number of studies have reported disturbances in various kinds of eye-movement control following damage to the posterior parietal cortex. For example, Pierrot-Deseilligny *et al.* (1987, 1991) have reported that unilateral lesions including the posterior parts of the intraparietal sulcus (the region specifically associated with optic ataxia by Perenin and Vighetto 1988) cause a slowed onset of saccades in response to visual cues. This slowing affects saccades made towards stimuli contralateral to the lesion more severely than ones made ipsilaterally (Sundqvist 1979; Nagel-Leiby *et al.* 1990) and it may be more severe after right parietal lesions than after left (Pierrot-Deseilligny *et al.* 1991). The slowing (and in some cases inaccuracy) of saccades may reflect a disorder of stimulus selection, rather than one of programming the saccadic act itself (Braun *et al.* 1992; see Chapter 7). Bilateral parietofrontal lesions may cause a severe paucity of visually elicited eye movements of all kinds (Pierrot-Deseilligny *et al.* 1988) in isolation, though in most cases such 'sticky fixation' is accompanied by optic ataxia (Hécaen and Ajuriaguerra 1954; Cogan, 1965; Tyler 1968; Pierrot-Deseilligny *et al.* 1986).

Other selective deficits in visually elicited eye movements were documented by Baloh *et al.* (1980): they described two patients with left occipitoparietal damage who both showed normal saccadic responses, but who failed to show normal pursuit eye movements when tested for optokinetic nystagmus (see Chapter 3). The slow phase of OKN was particularly affected in their patients. A more specific failure of pursuit eye movements to keep up with single targets moving towards the side of the lesion has been observed in other patients with parietal damage (see Troost and Abel 1982). A recent study by Morrow and Sharpe (1993) confirms that inferior occipitoparietal lesions are associated with this disorder in following targets moving in the ipsilesional direction. They also report evidence that a wider range of lesions may be able to cause a 'retinotopic' deficit, that is, one restricted to the pursuit of targets (moving in either direction) in the contralesional visual hemifield.

4.2.3 Disorders of grasping

When one attempts to pick up an object, one not only reaches towards its location in space, one also shapes the hand and fingers in anticipation of the object's size, shape, and orientation. In a series of classic studies, Jeannerod (1988) showed that these two components of prehension, which he termed the transport and grasp components, respectively, were temporally coupled, although he argued that they were largely independent. Later work by Jakobson and Goodale (1991) confirmed this observation, showing further that many of the same variables in the visual array affected both components. In Chapter 2, we described so-called 'manipulation' cells in the posterior parietal cortex that were modulated by the visual features of goal objects as well as by the grasping movements made by the monkey towards them (Taira *et al.* 1990). We believe that these cells form part of the control system for the grasp component of manual prehension. If this is the case, then one might expect that patients with optic ataxia following damage to the posterior parietal cortex might not only fail to reach in the right direction but also fail to orient their hand and form their grasp appropriately.

This possibility was first explored by Tzavaras and Masure (1976). Their two subjects, who both exhibited optic ataxia, were required to extricate a small object lodged in a groove that was presented at different angles from trial to trial. Video recordings showed clearly that one of the two patients not only failed to reach towards the object's location accurately, but also failed to orient his finger–thumb grip correctly, in both cases whenever he used his right (contralesional) hand to reach for targets within the right hemifield. A later study by Perenin *et al.* (1979) recorded a failure to rotate the hand appropriately in patients with optic ataxia as they attempted to reach towards and into an open slot. In yet another report, Damasio and Benton (1979) noted that when their optic ataxic patient tried to reach to pick up an object 'the hand was held with palm facing down, slightly cupped, with fingers close together and mildly flexed' (p. 171), though there was no paresis of grasp. Perenin and Vighetto (1983, 1988) subsequently reported quantitative data on errors in both the transport and grasp components of prehensive movements, initially in six and later in ten patients with optic ataxia. They found that the subjects all made errors in hand rotation as they reached towards a large oriented slot (see Fig. 4.2) and that the incidence of these errors, in relation to the hand and visual hemifield tested, closely followed the deficits seen in reaching accuracy.

All of Perenin and Vighetto's patients showed inaccurate reaching into the contralesional visual hemifield, whichever hand they used, and all showed few serious errors in reaching toward ipsilesional targets with the ipsilesional hand. Interestingly, however, Perenin and Vighetto reported that different overall patterns of optic ataxic deficit tended to be associated differentially with left and right hemisphere lesions. All except one of the left-hemisphere patients made

Fig. 4.2 Illustrations of errors made by a patient with optic ataxia when reaching out to pass the hand through an oriented slot. The figure shows normal responses (A), hand-orientation errors (B), and localization errors (C). The patient (case 2) had a tumour centred in the right parietal lobe, and examples are given of her reaching respectively into the right (A) and the left (B, C) hemifield, in each case with her left hand. Single frames are shown, each taken from films made on different test trials. (The authors wish to thank Dr M-T Perenin for providing this figure.)

reaching and hand-rotation errors whenever the contralesional (right) hand was used: even in the left visual hemifield. In contrast, the right-hemisphere damaged subjects made few errors in the right hemifield, even when using the left hand (see Fig. 4.3). Across these differential patterns of hand/field impairment, there was a strong association between impairments of the transport and the grasp components. Yet despite the failure of Perenin and Vighetto's (1988) patients to orient their hands appropriately or to reach towards the right location, they had little difficulty in giving perceptual reports of the orientation and location of stimuli in the contralesional visual fields.

While correct orientation of the hand is an important component of a well-formed grasp, it is not in itself sufficient. The opening of the hand must also be matched to the size of the goal object. In a normal grasping movement, the hand begins to open almost as soon as it begins to move towards the object, and reaches maximum aperture approximately two-thirds of the way through the action. As Fig. 4.4 (left) shows, this maximum aperture, while considerably larger than the object itself, is strongly correlated with the size of the object. Such 'grip scaling' might be expected to be absent or deficient in patients with lesions in the dorsal stream. The first investigation of this possibility was carried out by Jeannerod (1986). He filmed two optic ataxia patients while they reached out to pick up a small wooden sphere and measured the aperture between the thumb and forefinger during the course of each reach. Unlike normal subjects, there was no clear anticipatory adjustment of the grip size

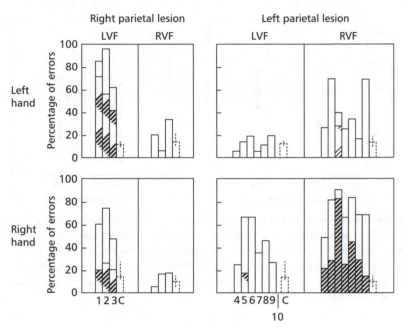

Fig. 4.3 Distribution of the localization errors across the different hand-hemifield combinations for individual patients with right and left posterior parietal damage, while reaching to an object under visual control. The number of errors is given as a percentage of the total number of trials for each hand-field combination for each patient. White bars, corrected errors; hatched bars, uncorrected errors; LVF, left visual field; RVF, right visual field. The performance of a group of control subjects for each hand-field combination is presented as a mean with a standard error bar (dashed: C). Although both sets of patients show a 'visual field effect' (making errors predominantly in the field contralateral to the lesion), the patients with left-hemisphere damage (with the exception of case 10) also show a 'hand effect' (making errors with the right hand in both fields). Adapted from Perenin and Vighetto (1988).

and, indeed, it was usually the palmar surface of the hand that first contacted the object. (This 'fanning' of the fingers has often been mentioned in qualitative descriptions of grasping in other optic ataxics; see, for example Perenin and Vighetto 1983, 1988.) The abnormality was particularly marked when the patients were unable to see their hand as it moved. Similarly, in more recent studies two patients with bilateral parietal lesions who had recovered from Bálint's syndrome (V.K., Jakobson *et al.* (1991) and R.V., Goodale *et al.* (1993)) showed only weak evidence for grip scaling (see Fig. 4.4). The patient V.K., furthermore, typically showed a succession of abnormal adjustments in her hand aperture during the course of the reach (see Fig. 4.5). Similar results have recently been reported by Jeannerod *et al.* (1994).

Fig. 4.4 Maximum grip aperture during grasping of objects of two different widths by a patient with bilateral occipitoparietal damage (V.K.) and an age-matched control subject (B.S.). While there is no overlap between the maximum grip apertures achieved by the control subject for the two objects, patient V.K. shows considerable overlap, often opening her hand wider for the 2 cm wide object than for the 5 cm wide object.

Fig. 4.5 Grip-aperture profiles for a patient with bilateral occipitoparietal damage (V.K.) and two age-matched control subjects (L.K. and B.S.) as they reached out to pick up a small wooden block using a precision finger grip. The grip aperture was measured as the distance between two infrared light-emitting diodes, one attached to the end of the index finger and another to the end of the thumb. V.K. not only took longer to initiate the grasping movement, but she also showed a much wider grip with repeated reposturing of the finger and thumb throughout the movement. Such reposturing was never observed in the control subjects.

To pick up an object successfully, however, it is still not enough to orient the hand and scale the grip appropriately; the fingers and thumb must be placed at geometrically appropriate opposition points on the object's surface. To do this, the visuomotor system has to compute the outline shape or boundaries of the object. In a recent experiment (Goodale *et al.* 1994*c*), the patient R. V. mentioned above was required to pick up a series of small, flat, non-symmetrical smoothly contoured objects which required her to place her index finger and thumb in appropriate positions on either side of each object. If the fingers were incorrectly positioned, these objects would slip out of the subject's grasp. Presumably, the computation of the correct opposition points ('grasp points') can be achieved only if the overall shape or form of the object is taken into account. Despite the fact that R.V. could readily distinguish these objects from one another, she often failed to place her fingers on the appropriate grasp points when she attempted to pick up the objects (Fig. 4.6).

In spite of these unequivocal demonstrations of the effects of parietal-lobe damage on the visual control of hand and finger movements, it should be emphasized that such deficits are not indissolubly coupled with misreaching. Thus, one of Tzavaras and Masure's (1976) patients misreached in contralesional hemispace (with either hand) but showed no clear deficit in grasping, and the patient V.K. described by Jakobson *et al.* (1991) showed the reverse dissociation in that the distance scaling of the transport component was

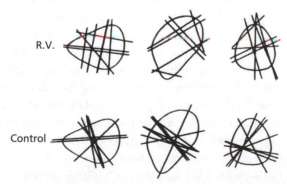

Fig. 4.6 The 'grasp lines' (joining the points where the index finger and the thumb first made contact with the shape) selected by a patient with bilateral occipitoparietal damage (R.V.) and a control subject picking up three different shapes. The four different orientations in which each shape was presented have been rotated so that they are aligned. The grasp lines selected by the control subject tend to pass through the centre of mass of the shape and the points of contact on the object boundary are quite stable. In contrast, R.V. often chose very unstable grasp points and the grasp lines often do not pass through the centre of mass of the object.

relatively well preserved. It must be inferred that if a lesion is small enough or suitably located, then in exceptional cases it may separately interrupt the control system for the grasp component or for the transport component. Nevertheless, in the normal brain we would suppose that the two subsystems would work intimately together in the production of each smoothly executed action.

The evidence showing that parietal damage in humans (and comparable damage in monkeys; see below) can cause deficits in the sensitivity of the grasp to various object parameters such as orientation, size, and shape, is consistent with our proposal that visual networks in the dorsal stream compute more than just spatial location. Although the data do not exclude the possibility that the requisite computations are carried out elsewhere (that is, in the ventral stream), we shall see in the next chapter that the lesion data provide no evidence for this. Such studies have provided no evidence for visuomotor disabilities following ventral-stream damage, even when visual recognition is profoundly impaired. In addition, although there are visually responsive cells within the dorsal stream and the frontal premotor cortex which appear to code the relevant object parameters for guiding grasping (Rizzolatti *et al.* 1988; Taira *et al.* 1990; see Chapter 2), no such visuomotor cells have ever been discovered in the ventral stream.

4.2.4 Evidence from monkeys

It was first observed over 100 years ago that monkeys with posterior parietal lesions suffer from reaching difficulties akin to those that Bálint (1909) described in his patient 20 years later. Thus, Ferrier and Yeo (1884) reported that a monkey with bilateral lesions of the 'angular gyrus' (a combination of the prelunate and inferior parietal gyri and, therefore, including most of the dorsal stream areas) 'was evidently able to see its food, but constantly missed laying hold of it at first, putting its hand beyond it or short of it' (p. 494). Ferrier (1886) went on to observe that a similarly lesioned monkey 'always exhibited some uncertainty or want of precision in its endeavours to seize things offered it, or to pick up minute articles of food from the floor, such as currants or grains of corn' (p. 282). In his Croonian Lectures, Ferrier (1890) observed that in yet a third similar monkey, 'vision gradually improved, but continued to be very imperfect, especially for minute objects, which it rarely, if ever, seized quite precisely; groping at them with the whole hand, and reaching short, or over, or to the side' (p. 57). These quotations give a very good flavour of the visuomotor problems of a parietal-lesioned monkey.

Misreaching in space is the most immediately obvious visual effect of posterior parietal cortex lesions in monkeys, just as it is ubiquitous in the Bálint-Holmes syndrome in humans (Ettlinger 1977). Furthermore, it has long been very clear that this parietal misreaching in monkeys is a visuomotor deficit rather than a deficit in spatial perception. For example, after unilateral lesions the reaching disorder is invariably restricted to the contralesional arm, that is, the identical visual information can be used to guide accurate reaching with the ipsilesional arm (Ettlinger and Kalsbeck 1962; Hartje and Ettlinger 1974; Faugier-Grimaud et al. 1978; Lamotte and Acuña 1978). Yet at the same time, a simple motor disorder is ruled out by the fact the same animals are able, once they have grasped a food object, to bring it efficiently and accurately to the mouth. (Curiously, when the cortex of the inferior parietal gyrus is temporarily deactivated by cooling, monkeys have been reported to misreach in contralesional space only (Stein 1978), which is more like the typical picture in human optic ataxia after a right parietal lesion. But Stein (1978) was still able to argue that this transient disorder, like that produced by tissue removal, was visuomotor rather than visual, since detection responses to the stimuli were found to be as rapid and accurate as normal.)

In addition, as Ferrier's (1890) descriptions indicate, monkeys with posterior parietal lesions fail to shape and orient their hands and fingers appropriately to pick up a food object. This again is strikingly similar to the picture in human optic ataxia described in Section 4.2.3 above. Almost a century after its discovery by Ferrier, the deficit in the visual control of precision grasp was confirmed quantitatively by Haaxma and Kuypers (1975), who made smaller lesions in the inferior parietal cortex designed to disconnect occipital from frontal areas. They used a board in which food morsels had to be dislodged from small grooves set at different angles, requiring the hand to be oriented correctly in order for the finger and thumb to grasp the food (cf. Tzavaras and Masure 1976). Despite the pronounced difficulties encountered by their monkeys on this task, Haaxma and Kuypers (1975) were able to show by means of discrimination training procedures that the animals were well able to tell apart the different orientations of the grooves and, indeed, there was no visuomotor impairment when the monkey used the hand ipsilateral to a unilateral lesion. Buchbinder et al. (1980) reported a similar deficit (described as 'irreversible') on this task, following dorsal-stream lesions which variably included the dorsal prestriate cortex, area PO, and posterior parts of area 7a. Yet they found no deficit in a control monkey given large inferotemporal lesions, despite a severe impairment in visual discrimination (see also Glickstein et al. 1998).

Lamotte and Acuña (1978) and Faugier-Grimaud et al. (1978) confirmed Haaxma and Kuypers' (1975) finding that this disorder in the shaping of the fingers in preparation for grasping was strictly linked to the contralesional hand following a unilateral posterior parietal lesion. This clearly rules out a perceptual deficit, since evidently the orientation and shape of the object are well-enough 'perceived' when the ipsilesional hand is responding. Faugier-Grimaud *et al.* (1978) also showed that the distal difficulty was not purely motor, since objects were grasped normally in response to tactile stimulation. As in humans, it is striking how closely impairments in the grasp and transport components of prehension are associated in these monkeys, though clearly the motor elements are themselves relatively independent. It is likely, however, that as in humans, these two visuomotor components will ultimately be dissociable with suitably discrete lesions.

Posterior parietal lesions in monkeys also impair visually elicited eye movements much as they do in humans. Lynch and McLaren (1989), for example, showed that monkeys trained to fixate a light and then to saccade to a visual target at right or left, responded with reliably increased latencies after partial lesions of the area. These lesions included the region now known as LIP, which plays an important role in visually guided saccade generation (see Andersen *et al.* 1992; Chapter 2). As first discovered by Ferrier (1875), electrical stimulation in various parts of the monkey's posterior parietal cortex provokes saccadic eye movements, but stimulation is effective in LIP with the shortest latencies and lowest currents (Shibutani *et al.* 1984; Kurylo and Skavenski 1991).

Saccades are not the only type of eye movement to be affected by lesions of the posterior parietal cortex. Lynch and McLaren (1983) had shown earlier, for example, that optokinetic nystagmus (OKN) is also disrupted. Thus, when a monkey with a posterior parietal lesion was placed in a full-field drum moving in the direction towards the side of its lesion, the speed of the animal's slow-phase OKN was abnormally reduced (although, curiously, the speed of its fast eye movements remained unaffected). Furthermore, the monkeys' ability to follow a single moving stimulus deteriorated when bilateral lesions were made (Lynch and McLaren 1982). In more recent work, even small unilateral lesions in the dorsal stream restricted to areas MT or MST have revealed clear deficits in ocular pusuit. Dürsteler and Wurtz (1988) and Dürsteler *et al.* (1987) have shown that damage to MST or to the part of MT corresponding to foveal vision caused impairments in both an initial saccade to catch up a moving stimulus and in maintaining smooth pursuit at the same speed as the target (see Fig. 4.7). Saccades to a stationary stimulus were normal. It is interesting that in their microstimulation studies of lateral parts of the posterior parietal cortex (probably in area MST) Kurylo and Skavenski (1991) were able to elicit slow eye movements resembling pursuit, though only when the experiment was run in darkness.

Newsome *et al.* (1985) found that discrete lesions in other parts of area MT caused a similar but more mild and transient difficulty in ocular pursuit,

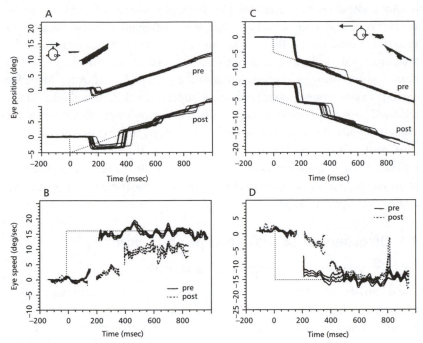

Fig. 4.7 Saccadic and pursuit errors before and after small neurotoxic lesions of area MST. Pursuit was initiated to a rightwardly- (A and B) or leftwardly-moving (C and D) target in the visual hemifield contralateral to the lesion (left in this case). (A) Position and (B) speed traces show deficits for pursuit of a target that was stepped 5° from the centre and moved to the right at 16°/s. Following the lesion, there was a saccadic overshoot of the target and pursuit was too slow: the monkey failed to match its eye speed to the target throughout the trial. (C) and (D) show position and speed records for a target step of 5° followed by target motion to the left, away from the side of the lesion. Again the saccade failed to take the motion into account following the lesion and pursuit was initially too slow. Reproduced from Dürsteler *et al.* (1987).

which they regarded as 'sensory' rather than visuomotor in nature. Later work confirms that lesions to MT cause disorders on non-motor tasks requiring motion processing (Newsome and Paré 1988; Marcar and Cowey 1992). These data suggest that MT must play some role in motion perception. But as we pointed out in Chapter 2, MT sends projections to the ventral stream as well as the dorsal. We believe it is through this cross-stream projection that the necessary inputs are provided for the perception of motion and motion-defined form.

In summary, the visuomotor effects of posterior parietal lesions in monkeys closely resemble the various visuomotor features of the Bálint–Holmes syndrome, such as optic ataxia. The deficits seen in the monkey can of course be readily understood by reference to the electrophysiology of these same dorsal stream areas, as described earlier in this book. Although of course we have no such direct evidence for the human brain, we consider it reasonable to infer that human disorders such as optic ataxia result from the disruption of homologous visuomotor systems within the parietal lobe. But the focus for damage to cause optic ataxia tends to be superior in the parietal lobe, in the region of the intraparietal sulcus (Ratcliff and Davies-Jones 1972; Perenin and Vighetto 1988). It would seem to follow, therefore, that the dorsal stream in man must pass superiorly within the parietal lobe. If so, then of course there remains a large expanse of human parietal cortex that remains as yet unaccounted for, parts of which will be damaged in most naturally occurring lesions of the parietal lobe.

4.3 Disorders of spatial perception in humans

4.3.1 Is 'visual–spatial agnosia' a myth?

The disorders considered in this chapter so far have been restricted to those where spatial information needs to be coded for the direct visual guidance of action. But impairments may be observed after brain damage in the performance of a wide variety of more cognitively complex spatial tasks, in which a more elaborate representation of space needs to intervene between vision and action. For example, a major right-hemisphere stroke can cause one to have difficulty in finding one's way around a once-familiar city or even within one's own home. Often such topographical disorders are associated with other 'spatial' problems such as dressing difficulty (Brain 1941; Paterson and Zangwill 1944, 1945). When tested in the clinic, such patients may be severely impaired at drawing a map of their native country or of the layout of their home. Generally these kinds of difficulty have been described in patients who have suffered either right-hemisphere or bilateral lesions (reviewed by De Renzi (1982, pp. 210–18)). On a smaller scale, a patient might be unable to copy a line drawing of a pattern composed of abstract shapes or to construct a pattern with blocks or matchsticks. Typical in this so-called 'constructional apraxia' is a failure to represent three-dimensionality, such as when drawing the Necker cube. These constructional disorders also tend to be more severe following right-hemisphere lesions, though they can also occur after left-sided damage (McFie and Zangwill 1960).

As we discussed in Section 4.1, these more complex abilities differ fundamentally from those of spatially guided movements of the hand or eye, which we considered in Section 4.2. Firstly, performance always depends on spatial properties that are intrinsically relational, not on where something is in relation to the observer but on where it is in relation to other things. No system which coded merely the locational coordinates of an item, without coding the nature of the item, could provide this. Secondly, in most cases reference has to be made to a medium- to long-term stored spatial representation for successful performance; this too of course would always require relational encoding. Accordingly, these more complex spatial abilities, because of their dependence on object identification and relatively long-term memory, might be expected to depend heavily on ventral-stream processing. This is not to say, of course, that they can be identified with damage to the ventral stream.

Early studies described several patients with extensive right-hemisphere damage in whom various combinations of these visuospatial disorders occurred, often along with 'hemispatial neglect' (a complex disorder affecting a patient's ability to explore and respond to stimuli in contralesional space) and/or various visuomotor elements of the Bálint–Holmes syndrome (for example, McFie *et al.* 1950; Ettlinger *et al.* 1957). All of these disparate symptoms were grouped together as components of a supposed syndrome of 'visual–spatial agnosia'. In fact, however, although many studies since the 1950s have supported a loose association of disordered spatial cognition (including hemispatial neglect) with right hemisphere damage, more 'visuomotor' symptoms such as constructional apraxia and optic ataxia regularly follow lesions of either hemisphere (De Renzi 1982, Chapter 9; Morrow and Ratcliff 1988*a*). This fact immediately suggests that different (though perhaps overlapping) neural systems have been damaged when combinations of visuomotor and visuospatial disorders are seen together.

Indeed, even the earliest papers describing 'visuospatial agnosia' contained dissociations among the visuomotor and visuospatial symptoms recorded, casting doubt on the existence of a single unitary syndrome right from the outset (see Ratcliff 1982). As early as 1941, Brain noted that misreaching and hemispatial neglect could be dissociated, although both were subsumed within 'visual disorientation' in his terminology. Ettlinger *et al.* (1957) gave several examples of patients whose deficits in 'spatial' tasks dissociated one from another and, indeed, co-existed with good visuomotor control. For example, patients numbers 1 and 3 in their report were both poor at constructional tasks, yet case 1 remained accurate at throwing darts at a target and case 3 was still able to thread a needle. Case 10 had hemispatial neglect and constructional apraxia, yet had no loss of topographical memory. Case 9 too had constructional difficulties without topographical disorder, but had no neglect. Case 5 was unimpaired on any of the small-scale spatial tasks given to him, nor did he have topographical difficulties yet he had a visuomotor problem of distance estimation. As the patient put it: 'It isn't the *judgement* of distance that is at fault, but instinctively *the space to allow* in judging distances, as in parking a car' (our italics). Finally, Godwin-Austen (1965) described a patient who showed gross visual misreaching and who also suffered from a deficit in visually guided saccadic eye movements and severe constructional apraxia. But despite these visuomotor difficulties and despite a large bilateral parieto-occipital lesion, the patient had no topographical disorder.

These multiple dissociations are not surprising in the light of more recent studies using computer-assisted techniques of X-ray tomography ('CT scans'), as illustrated in Fig. 4.8. These show that, as mentioned earlier, the brain damage in optic ataxia tends to be superior in the parietal lobe, in the region of the intraparietal sulcus (Perenin and Vighetto 1988). In contrast, other CT studies show that the focus for hemispatial neglect lies more ventrally in the region of the supramarginal and angular gyri (Heilman *et al.* 1983; Vallar and Perani 1986: see Chapter 7), while that for topographical disorientation lies still further ventrally, in a medial occipitotemporal location (see Chapter 5). More recent evidence still comes from PET scanning, carried out while normal volunteers performed visuomotor tasks (Grafton *et al.* 1992). During performance of a pursuit task in which subjects were required to track a moving target with their hand, there were clear signs of elevated cerebral metabolic activity in the superior parietal areas (as well as in primary motor and supplementary motor regions of the brain). This evidence is neatly consistent with the localization of optic ataxia in the more superior regions of the parietal lobe.

There is also evidence on the localization of the processes underlying cognitive manipulations such as 'mental rotation' based on the allocentric coding of spatial relationships. Haxby *et al.* (1991, 1993) have argued, on the basis of a series of PET studies, that superior parietal regions mediate these functions, as would be expected from Ungerleider and Mishkin's (1982) identification of the dorsal stream with spatial processing. In these experiments, the subjects performed matching tasks in which they were required to match either faces photographed from different viewpoints or relative spatial locations within a frame set at different orientations. It was found that the cerebral blood flow was greater in superior parietal areas during the performance of the spatial location task, while it was greater in occipitotemporal regions during the face-matching task. It would be expected from a range of studies (see Chapter 5) that face-processing tasks would invoke occipitotemporal rather than parietal mechanisms, but the results from the spatial task would seem to conflict with our proposal that visuomotor functions are associated with the superior parietal lobe. There is, however, an alternative account which would be more compatible with our position and, indeed, with the PET results of

Fig. 4.8 Reconstructions of the regions of overlap of lesions that result in optic ataxia (black) or visual neglect (cross-hatched). The optic ataxia lesions were taken from CT reconstructions reported by Perenin and Vighetto (1988); the site is based on six lesions in the left hemisphere and two in the right hemisphere. The neglect lesions, which were all in the right hemisphere, were taken from a study by Vallar and Perani (1986). The site represents the overlap of lesions in seven patients showing severe neglect. This area shows close correspondence to the site identified by Heilman *et al.* (1983). Since different numbers of patients contributed to these drawings, there is probably no significance in the apparently different sizes of the areas of overlap.

Grafton *et al.* (1992) discussed above. It seems likely that to solve the spatial problem, larger and more numerous eye movements would be required, since the subject has to make more back and forth scanning movements to solve the task. If so, then in this task one would predict a greater activation of superior parietal regions, since these are known to be involved in visually guided saccadic eye movements (Pierrot-Deseilligny *et al.* 1991; see Section 4.2.2). This possibility highlights the enormous difficulty in constructing fully watertight experimental designs in brain-imaging studies. But until the patterns of visually evoked eye movements in different tasks are measured and/or equated, the localization of mental rotation processing must remain open to question.

In our view, the evidence for separating the anatomical loci underlying optic ataxia and other visuomotor deficits from those underlying neglect and topographical disorders is fairly clear. But there is also evidence that deficits on different visuospatial cognitive tasks can be mutually dissociated. For example, patients described by Ratcliff and Newcombe (1973) and Newcombe *et al.* (1987) performed poorly on a stylus maze task but at the same time were unimpaired on the Semmes locomotor navigation task and in some cases on a spatial memory task involving pointing at objects in a remembered sequence. De Renzi and Nichelli (1975) described two individual patients who were severely impaired on spatial short-term memory but performed normally on stylus maze learning, while a third patient showed the reverse pattern. These dissociations may reflect the use of two different representational systems, each necessarily based on the allocentric coding of spatial location, but perhaps one more closely associated with the ventral stream than the other. As we discuss in the next chapter, topographical agnosia can now be unequivocally associated with occipitotemporal damage, but perhaps tasks requiring such visuospatial skills as manipulating imaginal representations of objects or layouts may depend on a more 'general-purpose' system lying outside either of the two visual streams.

4.3.2 Higher level representations of space: a confluence of the dorsal and ventral streams?

It is important to emphasize that the existence of a deficit on a 'spatial' task following a parietal lesion does not imply that the deficit results from a disruption of dorsal stream function. We would propose instead that a good deal of visuospatial cognitive processing in the human brain depends on the integrity of convergent networks in the inferior parietal and parietotemporal cortex and that the major visual input to these structures comes from the ventral stream. In the monkey, such polysensory systems exist in area STP within the superior temporal sulcus (Seltzer and Pandya 1978), in the caudalmost portion of area 7a (Jones and Powell 1970), and in ventral parts of area POa also in the parietal lobe (Seltzer and Pandya 1980). These areas probably receive converging inputs from both the dorsal and ventral visual streams (as well as from other sense modalities) and should thus properly be regarded as part of neither. Indeed, the suggestion has been made that visual projections through the superior temporal sulcus to area STP might constitute a 'third stream' of visual processing (Boussaoud et al. 1990; see also Morel and Bullier 1990; Baizer et al. 1991).

It is not implausible to speculate that these polysensory networks in parietal cortex and the superior temporal sulcus will have expanded considerably in size and in computational capacity during hominid evolution. In the monkey, there is evidence that neurones in these areas have congruent visual and somatosensory egocentric receptive field properties (Mistlin and Perrett 1990; Duhamel et al. 1991). It is possible that their human homologues might have become able to support forms of spatial cognition that are unavailable to the monkey (for example, the manipulation of spatial images, thus allowing the use of pictorial maps). We would argue that although everyday human route-finding activities generally involve the use of the visual modality, they do not always: therefore those visual inputs must be able to access a supramodal representation.

Evidence for the participation of supramodal systems in the control of spatially organized behaviour comes from studies that have employed a laboratory-based map-reading task (Semmes *et al.* 1955). In this task, the subject has to navigate a locomotor route through a matrix of points arranged on the floor by referring to a map. What is important for our arguments is that parietal lobe-injured patients who are impaired at locomotor navigation with a visual map are also impaired with a tactual map (Semmes *et al.* 1955). Normal subjects, of course, can use either map to find their way. This result suggests that structures in the parietal lobe are critical for the manipulation of stored spatial representations, whether visually or tactually derived (see Ettlinger 1990).

It may not be too fanciful to speculate that these hypothesized supramodal representational systems in the human parietal lobe form the neural substrate that allows us to construct and manipulate visual and tactual images. Subjectively at least, imagery offers a powerful means by which one can manipulate representations of the world so as to permit flexible action based on those representations. As mentioned in the previous section, laboratory tasks of 'mental rotation' attempt to tap this kind of ability, typically by asking subjects to judge whether or not two different pictures represent the same object, though depicted at different orientations (see Corballis 1982). There is evidence that this ability is especially vulnerable to right posterior brain damage (Butters *et al.* 1970; Ratcliff 1979), though some studies have also shown effects of left hemisphere damage (see Corballis 1982; De Renzi 1982, pp. 178–9). It will be interesting to see how future imaging research teases out the relative localization of different types of mental rotation task performance: we would expect inferior parietal areas to be more implicated than more superior regions, especially where three-dimensional representations of objects need to be accessed (Milner and Goodale 1993).

This admittedly speculative account may appear to depart a good deal from the emphasis that we have been putting on the role of the posterior parietal cortex in visuomotor control. That visuomotor role, however, for which we have adduced evidence primarily from non-human primates, still remains in dorsal parts of the human parietal lobe; it has been added to rather than changed. What we are suggesting is that new functional areas may have emerged ventrally within the human parietal lobe which can co-opt some of the transformational algorithms that originally evolved for the control of movement. Thus, some forms of mental rotation and map reading (where one moves from one set of coordinates to another) may make use of the viewer-based representations that those dorsal-stream algorithms deliver. What is very different about these putative new parietal systems is that unlike the ancient visuomotor networks, they can be experienced in the form of mental imagery and manipulated consciously.

4.3.3 Is the right parietal lobe 'dominant' for space?

Although one of the most pervasive features of the human cerebral hemispheres is the fact they are functionally asymmetric, this does not seem to impinge greatly upon the organization of the dorsal visual stream. Both hemispheres seem to be roughly equally implicated in the on-line visual control of motor activity. Nevertheless, the detailed pattern of impairment in optic ataxia does seem to be dependent on the side of the brain that is damaged (Perenin and Vighetto 1983, 1988). As we saw earlier, left-parietal lesions typically cause visuomotor difficulties throughout the visual field, which are most severe when the contralesional hand is used; this pattern approximates to that seen in parietal-lesioned monkeys (for example, Lamotte and Acuña 1978). In contrast, right-hemisphere cases of optic ataxia typically show the visuomotor disorder in both hands, but only in the left visual field. Presumably the evolution of a special role of the human left hemisphere in the motor programming of complex action sequences (Kimura 1982; De Renzi 1989; Goodale 1990) has interacted asymmetrically with the more ancient visuomotor structures in the dorsal system inherited from our primate ancestors. (It should be noted that although visuomotor mechanisms may be rather symmetrically disposed between the two hemispheres, mechanisms for motor execution and initiation are more lateralized, for example, in the control of eye movements (Girotti *et al.* 1983). Such motor asymmetries are discussed further in Chapter 7).

As we have seen earlier, however, the functional asymmetry of the human brain becomes rather more clearly apparent when cognitive manipulations of allocentric spatial information are considered. Right-hemisphere lesions tend to affect these capacities more severely than those on the left (for a review, see Morrow and Ratcliff (1988a)). (In contrast the left inferior parietal cortex has come to participate in the programming of sequential action patterns (Kimura 1993) and in processes underlying the visual recognition of symbols such as words.) What then is the nature of this apparent dominance of the human right inferior parietal cortex for visuospatial skills?

The answer may lie in the fact that although the human dorsal stream may not be greatly lateralized in function, the ventral stream is. For example, the clinical evidence on topographical disorders summarized in the next chapter strongly implicates occipitotemporal structures specifically in the right hemisphere (Landis *et al.* 1986; Habib and Sirigu 1987). Laboratory tests have shown that, although right occipitoparietal lesions can impair stylus maze learning (Newcombe and Russell 1969), so can lesions of the right temporal lobe (Milner, 1965). It is our view that the role of the right temporal lobe in route finding may arise from the fact that allocentric coding necessarily requires the participation of recognition systems fed from the ventral stream. But anatomical studies in the monkey show that the major neural projections from the temporal cortex to other cortical areas go principally to areas in the same hemisphere (for example, Felleman and Van Essen 1991). Therefore, if the right inferior parietal lobe does have a special role in performing cognitive operations based upon allocentrically coded information, this may follow rather directly from the fact that the right occipitotemporal region plays an important role in providing that information. In other words, the oft-claimed right hemisphere dominance for 'space' may derive merely from a right hemisphere dominance for visual perception in general.

4.4 'Visuospatial' deficits in the monkey

4.4.1 The landmark task

As mentioned in Section 4.2.4 above, failures of reaching and grasping have been observed in parietally damaged monkeys for over a century. These deficits are more correctly regarded as part of a 'visuomotor syndrome' rather than as 'disorders of spatial perception'. Another kind of visuomotor deficit that can often be seen in these monkeys is inaccurate jumping (Ettlinger and Wegener 1958; Bates and Ettlinger 1960). Of course different kinds of visual information would be used to guide reaching and jumping, so that this associated deficit does not argue for a single global disorder of 'spatial perception'. Nevertheless, some authors have argued that a generalized visuospatial disorder does follow posterior parietal lesions in monkeys (Pohl 1973; Ungerleider and Mishkin 1982). The major plank in their argument has been an impaired performance on the 'landmark task' (first devised by Davis *et al.* (1964)) following posterior parietal lesions. Indeed, this deficit has often been regarded as diagnostic of a visuospatial perceptual deficit in monkeys, with only rare sceptical voices, notably that of the late George Ettlinger (1990), questioning this interpretation.

The landmark task involves the choice between two food wells on the basis of the proximity of a landmark object placed somewhere between the two (see Fig. 1.10). The task has two versions and both require the monkey first to learn to choose whichever food well has the landmark cue adjacent to it. In one version the monkey is then required to learn the reversal—that is, to choose consistently the food well not adjacent to the landmark—and having learned this, to revert to the original task and so on, through several such reversals. In the other version of the landmark task, the monkey is always rewarded for choosing the food well nearer to the landmark, but training passes through more and more difficult stages in which the landmark is shifted inwards from the rewarded food well (increasing the so-called S–R separation), progressively closer to the midpoint between the two food wells (cf. Davis *et al.* 1964). In this second version, most of the training is performed pre-operatively, and post-operatively the monkeys are typically only retested on the final stage of the task.

Pohl (1973) used both versions of the task, starting with the reversal version. It was found that monkeys with bilateral ablations of the posterior parietal cortex performed poorly compared with controls, particularly on later reversals. Animals with lesions of the inferior temporal cortex, however, were also significantly impaired, tending to do worst on the earlier reversals (see Fig. 4.9, left). In a later study, Ungerleider and Brody (1977) also used the landmark reversal task and they too found that both parietal and temporal lesions caused significant impairment on the task. In this case the pattern was reversed, with the later reversals tending to be more impaired after inferior temporal lesions and the earlier ones more impaired after parietal lesions (see Fig. 4.9, right).

In Pohl's (1973) second experiment, he used the S–R separation version of the task; in this case parietal damage was clearly more severe in its effects than inferior temporal damage. Nevertheless, the inferotemporal lesion again appears to have caused some impairment, though it is unclear how much, since no unoperated animals were tested. Later investigators have usually adopted this S–R separation version of the task and a parietal deficit has usually (Milner *et al.* 1977; Mishkin *et al.* 1982; Latto 1986) but not always (Ridley and Ettlinger 1975) been reported. It has also been reported that a deficit follows combined unilateral lesions of the posterior parietal cortex and the contralateral area V1 (Mishkin and Ungerleider 1982), indicating that striate inputs to the posterior parietal area are important for the task. Unfortunately, none of these confirmatory studies included monkeys with inferior temporal lesions.

It has been a common but incorrect assumption (for example, Wurtz *et al.* 1984) that animals with inferotemporal lesions are unimpaired on the landmark task. In fact the evidence indicates a clear impairment after either posterior parietal or inferotemporal lesions, although it may sometimes be more severe in the former case. The interesting question is whether the two lesions affect the task for different reasons and, if so, what those reasons might be. To determine the answers to these questions, it is necessary to consider just what it is that the monkey has to do to solve the landmark task. Because the landmark and the food well sites may be separated by several centimetres, the

Fig. 4.9 The performance of monkeys with various circumscribed cortical lesions on the landmark reversal task, in the experiments of Pohl (1973) and Ungerleider and Brody (1977). The asterisks mark where the performance of monkeys with lesions was significantly different from that of the normal (NC) monkeys (p < 0.05). Although the monkeys with parietal (PP) lesions were impaired in both experiments, so were the monkeys with inferotemporal (IT) lesions. Animals with dorsolateral frontal (LF) lesions were impaired in neither experiment. The numbers of animals in each experimental group is indicated in brackets. Adapted from Pohl (1973) and Ungerleider and Brody (1977).

monkey is required to shift its gaze away from one of the food wells to the landmark, to determine the landmark's relative location, and to make a choice on that basis. Therefore, any disruption of the monkey's ability or inclination to redirect its gaze may be expected to result in learning deficits on the task. Even normal monkeys are notoriously inclined not to 'look before they leap' in laboratory test situations, looking only at the place where food is likely to be found. Whenever a monkey fails to look at the landmark, its choice of food wells on that trial will inevitably fall close to chance levels. Not surprisingly, therefore, normal monkeys find the landmark task very difficult to learn and many fail the task altogether (Pohl 1973). If posterior parietal lesions reduce the likelihood of the monkey's orienting toward the landmark still further, then very poor performance on the task is to be expected.

There are ways of counteracting this putative orienting failure. For example, using some means of attracting the lesioned monkey's gaze to the landmark should help it to perform the task. Such an effect has been found in unpublished research by A. Cowey (personal communication): while a landmark consisting of a steady light on a TV screen revealed the usual parietal deficit, the use of a flashing light permitted the same monkeys to perform without impairment. Another way to encourage monkeys to direct their gaze at the landmark is to 'bait' it with a raisin: this has been found to improve choice accuracy in both normal (Sayner and Davis 1972) and parietal-lesioned (Milner *et al*. 1977) monkeys. Presumably, in taking the bait, the monkey tends to look where its hand goes (Cowey 1968) and this helps it to code the position of the cue. Indeed even in the absence of baiting, many monkeys spontaneously acquire the habit of touching the landmark prior to making their food well choice; they presumably acquire this habit because it makes them better at performing the task. Given the well-known effect of posterior parietal lesions on reaching, it is perhaps not surprising that such lesions reduce this tendency to touch the landmark (Milner *et al*. 1977). This provides a second reason to expect fewer glances at the landmark during individual trials on the task following parietal lesions, thereby further impairing choice performance.

If these arguments are correct, then posterior parietal lesions should also cause a deficit in a task where a separated cue provides only symbolic information (for example, by its colour) for choosing between the two food wells. Yet since the spatial location *per se* of the separated cue would not now have any significance, a deficit in spatial discrimination (as proposed by Pohl (1973) and by Ungerleider and Mishkin (1982)) should cause no impairment. In practice, posterior parietal lesions do impair performance where the correct choice depends on the nature rather than the location of the separated cue in this way (Bates and Ettlinger 1960; Mendoza and Thomas 1975; Lawler and Cowey 1987).

If success on these tasks really does depend on the production of orienting eye movements to the relevant cue, then one would have to predict that any lesion impairing visually elicited eye movements should disrupt performance. Evidence for this is provided by an experiment by Kurtz and Butter (1980) in which monkeys with lesions of the superior colliculus were shown to be impaired on a colour discrimination task in which the stimulus and response sites were separated. Indeed the more the separation, the worse the deficit observed. Eye movement recordings revealed that these deficits were closely associated with failures to shift gaze to the stimuli. While we do not have such direct evidence of gaze-orienting failures during the landmark task following posterior parietal lesions, we do know that even unilateral posterior parietal lesions increase the latency of visually elicited saccadic eye movements (Lynch and McLaren 1989) in monkeys, just as in humans (see Section 4.2.2).

We conclude that it is reasonable to argue that the landmark deficit after bilateral parietal lesions is due to a failure to orient the head and eyes toward a visual cue, rather than being due to a failure of spatial discrimination. The nature of the inferotemporal deficit on landmark tasks, however, remains obscure. One possibility is that monkeys with ventral-stream damage might suffer from a deficit in engaging visual selective attention, as has been suggested from studies of lesions damaging areas TEO and V4 (Cowey and Gross 1970; Schiller 1993). Alternatively, the poor performance of monkeys with inferotemporal lesions on the landmark task may simply be one example of the global perceptual disorder that has been so often described in these animals. In particular, their difficulty might be due to a failure of allocentric coding of the relative locations of landmark and food wells, a form of coding that we have argued is carried out in the ventral stream.

If so, one could make the following paradoxical prediction: bringing the two food wells close together (for example, only 5–10 cm apart) in the landmark task should still reveal a deficit in inferotemporal monkeys, but not in parietal monkeys. This is because the reduced distances should make it less necessary for the monkey to make shifts of ocular fixation in order to see the landmark while looking at one or other food well, yet the task would still require the processing of the relative (allocentric) locations of the landmark and the food wells. A similar prediction could be made using yet another variation of the landmark task. If the monkey were required to respond to the landmark on each trial (for example, using a touch-screen) prior to making its choice, the present hypothesis would leave the inferotemporal deficit unchanged while abolishing the parietal deficit. Both predictions are opposite to what would be predicted on the hypothesis that posterior parietal lesions disrupt the allocentric coding of spatial location.

4.4.2 Route finding

Finally, a source of evidence that has been widely regarded as supporting a 'spatial perception' formulation of posterior parietal function in monkeys is that of route finding. For example, monkeys with parietal lesions have been observed to have great difficulty in finding their particular home cage when released into a common housing area (Ettlinger and Wegener 1958; Bates and Ettlinger 1960; Sugishita et al. 1978). While it is possible to interpret this deficit as resulting from spatial disorientation, Ettlinger and Wegener (1958) attributed it instead to the disruption caused by inaccurate jumps executed by the monkey in the course of making its way to the cage. Such jumping errors were observed to be as great as 30 cm. In other words, an equally plausible explanation of the findings can be framed in terms of disordered visuomotor guidance.

In another, more direct, test of route finding, Traverse and Latto (1986) observed impaired performance in a pre-operatively learned locomotor maze in two out of their four monkeys with posterior parietal lesions. In this case, it is unlikely that inaccurate jumping could explain the apparent deficit. Nevertheless, the two monkeys who did poorly on the pre-operatively learned task went on to learn a new route faster than controls, suggesting that whatever their problem, it was not one of route finding *per se*. It would be interesting to test the maze-learning abilities of inferotemporal-lesioned monkeys; we would expect them to be unable to recognize environmental landmarks and, hence, to have more consistent trouble in finding their way.

On a smaller spatial scale of route finding, stylus maze learning has been found to be impaired after posterior parietal lesions in monkeys (Milner *et al.* 1977). However, the authors also tested their monkeys' ability to guide a stylus along a route that lacked blind alleys and found a comparable and correlated impairment. Petrides and Iversen (1979) reported a similar deficit in visuomotor guidance after parietal lesions restricted to the inferior parietal lobule, using a related task requiring monkeys to move an object along a bent wire. These findings support the conclusion by Milner *et al.* (1977) that the difficulty their monkeys had with negotiating the maze could be attributed to impaired visuomotor coordination.

4.4.3 Behavioural deficits caused by posterior parietal lesions

In summary then, the deficits observed on formal behavioural testing after posterior parietal lesions in monkeys seem to be explicable more satisfactorily in terms of failures of visual guidance of gaze, hand, arm, or whole body movement, than as failures in the visual perception of location. The behavioural evidence thus complements the physiological studies summarized in Chapter 2. In our view, the totality of evidence from non-human primate research is quite inconsistent with a characterization of the dorsal stream as the 'pathway for spatial vision' (Desimone and Ungerleider 1989).

Broadly speaking, the behavioural picture after posterior parietal lesions bears a strikingly close resemblance to the constellation of symptoms seen after human parietal damage in the Bálint–Holmes syndrome and its variants. There is, in contrast, no compelling evidence in the monkey for homologues of the failures of 'spatial cognition' seen after posterior lesions in humans. The absence of such deficits may be due to the fact that such cognitive capacities are poorly developed in the monkey, so that impairments are difficult to detect. In any event, the lesion evidence from monkeys provides no support for the suggestion that the disorders of spatial cognition found in humans can be directly traced to damage to the dorsal stream of visual processing.

4.5 **What is the visual function of the parietal lobe?**

We have tried to demonstrate in this chapter that the widespread view of the parietal end-point of the primate dorsal visual stream as the seat of visuospatial perception is probably incorrect. We have argued that spatial processing is a characteristic of both the dorsal and the ventral visual streams: visual space is coded, differently, in both streams. We have presented evidence that the spatial coding found in the dorsal stream has more to do with the guidance of particular forms of action than with the representation of allocentric space. In fact we can see no convincing lesion evidence that the dorsal stream underlies visuospatial perception in either monkeys or humans. We believe instead that spatial perception, in the full sense, is associated more with the ventral stream than it is with the dorsal stream. This view will be supported in the next chapter, where we will present evidence that damage to the ventral stream can produce not only profound deficits in object identification, but also great difficulties in encoding the spatial layout of the environment. Yet the egocentric coding of space for the control of actions is generally spared in these patients.

For cognitive manipulations of space, the egocentric information processed in the dorsal stream would be of no possible utility alone. Therefore we have speculated that an expanded area in the human brain, homologous with polysensory areas already identifiable in the monkey's superior temporal sulcus and parietal cortex, may be able to transform visual information derived from both cortical streams (as well as from other sense modalities) into an abstract spatial representation. As we will suggest in Chapter 7, damage to representational networks of this kind may give rise to errors of size and distance perception, that is, the damaged part may cause perceptual underestimations of less well-represented parts of the visual array. Such perceptual distortions occur in 'perceptual' forms of unilateral visual neglect (Milner *et al.* 1993; Milner and Harvey, 1995) and there are hints that they may occur in different forms after damage to different parts of the parietal lobe (von Cramon and Kerkhoff 1993).

If these hypothesized networks depend crucially on visual inputs from the ventral stream and in humans there is a right-hemisphere dominance for ventral-stream processing (see Chapter 5), then it would be expected that a similar dominance would automatically extend to the right inferior parietal region's role in abstract visuospatial processing. Historically, the occurrence—and with large lesions the co-occurrence—of impairments on quite different 'spatial' tasks following right posterior damage in humans led naturally to a tendency to attribute all these difficulties to a disruption of some quasi-unitary faculty of spatial perception. Of course, impairments of spatial cognition will sometimes be associated with optic ataxia and other visuomotor disorders, especially after right hemisphere damage, since large lesions are sure to damage several different brain systems. But it is a mistake to suppose that all these impairments are a reflection of damage to a single system for visuospatial perception. *A fortiori*, it is dangerous to identify such visuospatial deficits with damage to the dorsal visual stream.

Chapter 5

Disorders of visual recognition

We saw in Chapter 3 that damage to the primary visual cortex can cause a profound loss of awareness of the visible world. Yet surviving pathways appear to provide sufficient visual information to allow the brain to mediate a range of visual tasks in the absence of such awareness. We further argued that input to the dorsal stream (via intact tectothalamic pathways) could be responsible for many of the spared functions in such patients. We assumed that because the ventral stream is effectively deprived of any visual input after V1 damage, these patients have no conscious perception of the objects and events in the world to which they can react. But of course more direct evidence should be available from studying patients with damage to the ventral stream itself: lesions which might spare the primary visual cortex completely. Such damage, in severe cases, can result in a variety of visual recognition deficits, which collectively are known as 'visual agnosia'. By definition, agnosic patients do not fail to recognize something because they fail to 'see' it; in other words, the recognition deficit can not be attributed to cortical blindness or other 'sensory' disorders. Instead, agnosic patients have a problem in recognizing objects which they have no difficulty in consciously detecting. And as we shall see, lesions of the ventral stream can also result in disorders in the recognition of spatial relations *between* objects in the world.

5.1 Types of agnosia

It is not the purpose of this book to attempt any detailed account of the range of different forms of visual agnosia that have been documented. Comprehensive treatments of the literature can be found in the recent books by Farah (1990) and Grüsser and Landis (1991). Instead, our aim is to illustrate how agnosia fits into the scheme of cortical visual processing that we proposed in Chapter 2.

As early as 1890, the neurologist Lissauer distinguished two broad forms of visual object agnosia. Patients suffering from what he termed 'apperceptive agnosia' were thought to be unable to achieve a coherent percept of the structure of an object. In contrast, patients with what he termed 'associative agnosia' were thought to be able to achieve such percepts but still be unable to recognize the object. Thus, in Lissauer's (1890) scheme, an associative agnosic would be able to copy a drawing even though unable to identify it, while an apperceptive agnosic would be unable to copy or identify the drawing. Lissauer (1890) argued that the apperceptive agnosic had a disruption at a relatively early stage of perceptual processing while the disruption in the associative agnosic was at a higher 'cognitive' level of processing where percepts would normally be associated with stored semantic information. As argued by Humphreys and Riddoch (1987), the pattern of disorders of object recognition that have been described in the more recent literature does not fit perfectly into such a simple serial scheme of classification. Yet despite this, Lissauer's (1890) distinction has remained useful over the century intervening since its publication and still serves as a convenient if crude initial means of classifying individual patients. Furthermore, it seems reasonable to endorse the traditional view that agnosias with clearly 'apperceptive' features reflect damage at a relatively early stage of the visual recognition networks.

We have suggested in Chapter 2 that an important role of the ventral stream of corticocortical projections in the monkey is the extraction of a viewpoint-independent description or coding of an object or scene. It is our contention that apperceptive visual agnosias reflect, in their different ways, damage to the human equivalent of this ventral stream and that the unifying characteristic of all of them is that they reflect a failure to achieve such abstract coding (cf. Cowey 1982; Ratcliff and Newcombe 1982; Warrington 1985a). We would further argue that for any 'semantic' or 'associational' system to operate as the final stage of recognition, it must necessarily receive its inputs processed up to this abstract level via the ventral stream. Therefore, we would suggest that any (rare) unequivocally 'associational' agnosias must result from the disconnection of structures that depend on outputs from the ventral stream, while at the same time the integrity of that ventral stream is in large part maintained. In this broad sense, we suggest, Lissauer's (1890) original conception of agnosia can be mapped onto the successive stages of processing in the ventral stream.

Most recent writers on the topic of apperceptive agnosias have distinguished between the relatively mild conditions where view-generalized coding seems to be the primary disorder and those more profound cases where a basic disorder of shape perception is present (Warrington 1985a; Humphreys and Riddoch 1987; Farah 1990; Grüsser and Landis 1991). According to Warrington (1985a), the latter more radical type of loss should be regarded as 'pseudo-agnosic', but most other writers consider it to be the paradigm case of apperceptive agnosia (for example, Alexander and Albert 1983; Benson 1989; Grüsser and Landis 1991). In this more basic disorder (named 'visual form agnosia' by Benson and Greenberg (1969)), not only is there a failure to recognize objects, there is also a failure even to perceive their shape. In our conceptualization, visual form agnosia probably reflects a major visual deafferentation of the ventral areas. The patient may not have lost the machinery to construct an abstract representation from visual information about shape and contour, but must at least have suffered an interruption of the crucial inputs that could furnish that information.

A corollary of this view is that many cases of apperceptive agnosia should retain intact visual and visually guided abilities of a kind that do not require explicit recognition of either the goal objects or their spatial location. After all, in many of these patients the dorsal stream is presumably still intact. As we have repeatedly argued in previous chapters, information about motion, orientation, size, shape, and location is used by this stream in the visual control of a range of skilled actions. Thus, such patients might be expected to show some evidence that they can use visual information to interact efficiently with objects that they are unable to recognize. Clues that this might be so can be gleaned from several clinical descriptions of agnosic patients in the literature. For example, Benson and Greenberg's (1969) visual-form agnosic patient Mr S 'could navigate corridors successfully in his wheelchair' (p. 83) and, more recently, Campion (1987) reported that the similar patient R.C. 'could negotiate obstacles in the room, reach out to shake hands and manipulate objects or to reach a cup of coffee' (pp. 208–9).

Of course, this expectation would not extend to all patients with apperceptive agnosia. In some cases the lesion may be so extensive that it includes dorsal as well as ventral structures and in other cases motor structures in the cortex, basal ganglia, and cerebellum may be affected. In all such cases visuomotor skills would be expected to suffer impairment along with visual recognition (for example, Wechsler 1933; Alexander and Albert 1983, case E.S.).

5.2 Visual form agnosia

5.2.1 Pathology

This most severe form of apperceptive agnosia follows gross bilateral damage to lateral parts of the occipital lobes. Curiously, the clearest cases that have been described in the literature have nearly all resulted from an anoxic episode, in which carbon monoxide poisoning probably also made a major pathological contribution. For example, in 1944, Adler described a comparatively mild visual form agnosia in a young woman who was overcome by smoke fumes in the Cocoanut Grove nightclub fire of 1942, a disaster in which 491 people died. This patient (H.C.) was tested again in a follow-up study by Adler in 1950 and, uniquely, again studied 40 years later by Sparr *et al.* (1991).

One of the most famous examples and the patient whose condition gave rise to the descriptive term we have adopted here, 'was found stuporous on the bathroom floor after having been exposed to leaking gas fumes while showering' (Benson and Greenberg 1969 pp. 82–3). The visual abilities of this patient (Mr S) were studied in great detail by Efron (1969). Two other clear examples of visual form agnosia have received detailed experimental study since then: R.C., who suffered CO poisoning while trapped inside a foundry chimney (Campion and Latto 1985) and D.F., who like Mr S, was asphyxiated as a result of a faulty gas water heater while taking a shower (Milner *et al*. 1991).

Pathology of this kind does not result in discrete lesions in a single brain area; however the damage is not uniformly diffuse throughout the brain either. The most vulnerable brain tissues appear to be in so-called 'watershed' areas, lying in the border regions between the territories of different arterial systems. One such region is the lateral occipital lobe: others are the premotor areas, the hippocampus, the cerebellum, and the basal ganglia (Hoyt and Walsh 1958; Richardson *et al*. 1959; Plum *et al*. 1962; Adams *et al*. 1966; Brierley and Excell 1966; Ross-Russell and Bharucha 1978; Howard *et al*. 1987). Within these regions, which suffer damage to different relative extents in different patients, particular subareas and even specific laminae may be differentially vulnerable (see also Section 5.3.3 below). Although no post-mortem data are yet available on any of the well-studied patients with visual form agnosia, MRI scans on two of them indicate the existence of dense necrosis in the lateral occipital cortex bilaterally (Milner *et al*. 1991; Sparr *et al*. 1991).

The above cases, though of differing severity, form qualitatively a rather uniform group in terms of both pathology and symptomatology. But the most celebrated case of apperceptive agnosia (Schn) suffered a traumatic injury to the brain during the trench warfare in the First World War (Goldstein and Gelb 1918; summarized in English by Landis *et al*. (1982)). A symptomatically very similar case (Mr X) but whose brain pathology derived from mercury poisoning, was described more recently by Landis *et al*. (1982). In many ways the visual symptoms of these two patients resemble visual form agnosia and for present purposes they will be regarded as falling into that category. However, they both differed from the other cases of visual form agnosia in that they spontaneously adopted a strategy of 'tracing' either with the hand or the head, which allowed them to recognize forms, and furthermore, they were both able to recognize their own handwriting. Inevitably, the detailed pattern of their brain damage will have differed from that present in the cases of carbon monoxide poisoning, and it may have left certain systems intact that were damaged or inaccessible in those other cases.

5.2.2 The symptoms of visual form agnosia

An excellent description of the agnosic difficulties present in a typical patient is provided by Efron (1969). His patient, Mr S, had profound deficits in object and pattern recognition; he failed to recognize familiar faces and was unable to identify or copy line drawings of common objects or even simple geometric shapes. When he was shown real objects, however, he was sometimes able to make reasonable guesses at the object's identity by virtue of surface properties such as colour, reflectance, and texture. He was able to do this through having relatively well-preserved colour discrimination, brightness discrimination, and visual acuity. However, these efforts were always 'educated guesses' and frequent errors were made. Mr S also had difficulty in segregating stationary objects from their background and would often make errors in trying to trace around an object where colour was an insufficient cue to the object's outline. Simple geometric shapes could not be correctly named. Mr S, however, was essentially normal when he was asked to identify objects and shapes on the basis of haptic information. Hence, his problem was a visual one and did not reflect a general failure in accessing stored information about shapes and objects.

Efron (1969) hypothesized that Mr S's basic disorder was one of visual contour—and, hence, shape—discrimination. He accordingly devised a quantitative test for shape discrimination, in which the subject had to judge whether pairs of rectangles (one square, the other oblong) were alike or different. All of the shapes were matched for surface area, so that overall brightness could not be used as a cue (see Fig. 5.4). Mr S was found to be unable to perform these comparisons with oblongs of even a 2:1 side ratio and performance never exceeded 90 per cent correct even with 9:1 ratio oblongs (at which point the possibility of local brightness differences could have come into play).

The 'Efron rectangles' have now become a standard diagnostic test for this form of agnosia (see Warrington 1985a, b). It should be noted, however, that it is not entirely clear what aspect(s) of shape discrimination the Efron test is tapping. The task could be performed without the ability to discriminate true shape (that is, 'square' versus 'oblong'), if the patient were either able to use linear size (that is, width) differences or perhaps use orientation (that is, is the predominant axis of the shape horizontal or vertical or neither?). The fact that patients like Mr S cannot perform the Efron task suggests that they fail to use any of these possible cues, except possibly with the easiest exemplars. This is borne out by specific tests, as described below, showing that patients with visual form agnosia have severe difficulties even with orientation and width discrimination.

5.3 **Patient D.F.: a case history of visual form agnosia**

5.3.1 **Deficits in visual perception**

By far the most extensively tested patient with visual form agnosia is D.F. Psychophysical assessment and visual perimetry showed that her severe recognition disorder cannot be explained by low-level visual deficits (Milner *et al.* 1991). For example, she is generally able to detect flashes of light throughout her central visual fields out to 30°. Her detection of fine (high spatial frequency) grating patterns is normal, although she is quite unable to indicate their orientation. It is notable, however, that she shows an impairment in her detection of low spatial frequency gratings, which has remained over the period we have been seeing her and is present whether the stimuli are stationary or drifting. A recent example of her performance in detecting static gratings is shown in Fig. 5.1. In other tests, D.F. has been found to show a normal frequency threshold for the detection of visual flicker, at least within the parameters tested, and like Mr S, she shows remarkably well-preserved colour

Fig. 5.1 The detection of grating patterns of different spatial frequency by patient D.F. and by a control subject (H.B.S.). Each trial consisted of a warning tone followed by a grating of a given fineness bounded by a circular aperture (the higher the spatial frequency, measured in cycles per degree of visual angle, the finer the spacing of the 'stripes' forming the grating). The contrast of the grating varied from trial to trial depending on the subject's performance: it was reduced by one step after two successive correct detections or increased after one failure to detect. By means of this 'staircase' procedure, the contrast zeroed in on the 'threshold' values shown in these graphs. The data points are the means of five determinations at each frequency tested (D.W. Heeley and A.D. Milner, unpublished observations).

discrimination and, indeed, reports a vivid experience of colour. In fact she is much better at discriminating between fine shades of colour than among comparably fine shades of grey (Milner and Heywood 1989).

In contrast to her relatively normal low-level visual functions, D.F.'s ability to recognize or discriminate between even simple geometric forms is grossly impaired. For example, like other patients with visual form agnosia, D.F. is severely impaired on the Efron test, only achieving above-chance levels of discrimination with rectangles exceeding a 2:1 ratio. It is not surprising, therefore, that she has great difficulty in recognizing line drawings; in one test, for example, she could name correctly only 11 per cent of 120 standard drawings of common objects. Furthermore, her ability to copy such drawings is remarkably poor (see Fig. 5.2; and Humphrey *et al.* 1994).

In another test of visual recognition, D.F. correctly identified only one of a series of 16 letters and digits. Her erroneous responses were often not visually similar to the target item (for example, S for P, K for 5, O for R, and so on) and different items were sometimes misidentified as being the same. In marked

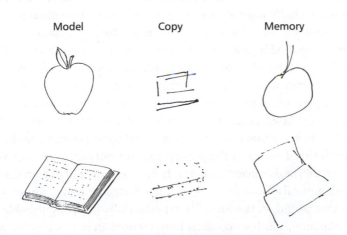

Fig. 5.2 Examples of the ability of D.F. to recognize and copy line drawings. She was able to recognize neither of the two drawings on the left. Nor, as the middle column shows, was she able to make recognizable copies of those drawings. (Although in her copy of the book D.F. did incorporate some of the elements from the original drawing—the small dots representing text, for example—the drawing as a whole is poorly organized.) D.F.'s inability to copy the drawings was not due to a failure to control her finger and hand movements during drawing since on another occasion, when asked to draw an apple or an open book, she produced reasonable renditions, presumably on the basis of long-term memory (right-hand column). When she was later shown the drawings she had produced from memory, she had no idea what they were.

contrast to her inability to recognize objects, letters, or digits visually, however, D.F. is adept at the tactual recognition of common objects and of three-dimensional, alpha-numeric shapes (matched in size to the two-dimensional characters used in visual testing). For example, she recognized 12 out of 16 three-dimensional alpha-numeric shapes, when allowed to explore them tactually. Moreover, her ability to print single letters or numbers to dictation was near perfect (14 items out of 16). In addition, as Fig. 5.2 illustrates, she could also draw simple objects from memory.

When real objects, rather than line drawings, are shown to D.F., she is often able to identify them, particularly when they are 'natural' objects such as fruit and vegetables. Systematic examination of this ability, however, has revealed that, like Mr S, she is using surface properties, particularly colour and fine texture, rather than outline shape, to identify the object (Humphrey *et al.* 1994). This ability to identify real objects as opposed to line drawings of objects (or black and white slides) has been reported by a number of investigators of visual agnosia (for a review, see Farah (1990).

Thus, D.F.'s pattern of visual deficits, like those of most other visual form agnosics, is largely restricted to deficits in form perception. Her colour perception is essentially normal, she can perceive fine texture differences, and she also appears to have some appreciation of allocentric space. This latter ability is exemplified by her normal performance on a simple left–right discrimination in which she was asked to indicate whether the red block of a red and white pair was on the left or right. The apparently specific sensitivity of form perception to anoxia and other brain insults is a puzzle (which we will discuss later). Our interpretation of apperceptive agnosia (see Section 5.1 above) would predict, however, that some patients should suffer from generalized losses in the perception not only of form, but also of colour, texture, and allocentric space. Indeed, lesions causing an extensive occipitotemporal disconnection should result in a global apperceptive agnosia that would, in the limit, be experientially indistinguishable from cortical blindness, which we consider to result from an isolation of the ventral stream from visual inputs (see Chapter 3).

5.3.2 Preserved visuomotor abilities

D.F., like most previously described visual form agnosics, recovered, within weeks, the ability to reach out and grasp everyday objects with remarkable accuracy. We have discovered recently that she is very good at catching a ball or even a short wooden stick thrown towards her (Carey *et al.* 1996). This latter skill demands accurate coding and extrapolation of a complex dynamic stimulus. She negotiates obstacles in her path with ease and can follow a moving light with her eyes. These various skills suggest that although D.F. is poor at the perceptual report of object qualities such as size and orientation, she is much better at using those same qualities to guide her actions.

We have examined D.F.'s spared abilities to use visual information in a series of experimental studies. In the initial experiments, Milner *et al.* (1991) used a vertically mounted disc in which a slot of 12.5 × 3.8 cm was cut: on different test trials, the slot was randomly set at 0, 45, 90, or 135°. We found that D.F.'s attempts to make a perceptual report of the orientation of the slot showed litle relationship to its actual orientation and this was true whether her reports were made verbally or by manually setting a comparison slot. Remarkably, however, when she was asked to insert her hand or a hand-held card into the slot from a starting position an arm's length away, she showed no particular difficulty, moving her hand (or the card) towards the slot in the correct orientation and inserting it quite accurately. Video recordings showed that her hand began to rotate in the appropriate direction as soon as it left the start position. In short, although she could not report the orientation of the slot, she could 'post' her hand or a card into it without difficulty.

These findings were confirmed and extended in a second series of studies (Goodale *et al.* 1991): D.F. performed with normal accuracy in her 'posting' of a solid plaque into a slot (see Fig. 5.3, bottom). In contrast, it was found that her attempts to match the target orientation by rotating the same plaque without moving it towards the slot were near-random (Fig. 5.3, top). A similar dissociation was found with solid rectangular blocks when presented on a table-top at different orientations; perceptual judgements were poor, yet grasping movements to pick them up were performed accurately and were preceded by normal anticipatory orientation of the hand during the course of the reaching movement.

The perceptual matching task and the posting task used in this study might appear superficially similar to one another; in both cases, the subject had to rotate the plaque to 'match' the orientation of the target slot. However, there is a crucial difference. In the perceptual matching task, what subjects were doing by rotating the hand-held card was to report their perception of the slot. The particular form in which this reporting was done was essentially arbitrary. For example, we could have asked them to draw the slope of the slot on a piece of paper. In the posting task, in contrast, subjects were executing a natural goal-directed movement which requires an obligatory rotation of the hand in order to perform the action successfully. Acts such as this are non-arbitrary and require no explicit perception of the orientation of the hand or the slot. Primates and other animals capable of prehension have had to deal with

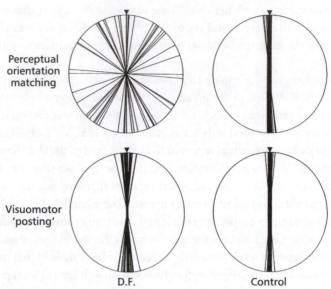

Perceptual orientation matching

Visuomotor 'posting'

D.F.   Control

Fig. 5.3 Polar plots illustrating the orientation of a hand-held card in two tasks of orientation discrimination, for D.F. and an age-matched control subject. On the perceptual matching task, subjects were required to match the orientation of the card with that of a slot placed in different orientations in front of them. On the posting task, they were required to reach out and insert the card into the slot. The correct orientation has been normalized to the vertical. Adapted from Goodale *et al.* (1991).

problems of this kind throughout their evolutionary history and have presumably evolved dedicated visuomotor systems for their solution.

Similar dissociations between perceptual report and visuomotor control were observed in D.F. when she was asked to deal with the intrinsic properties of objects such as their size and shape. Thus, D.F. showed excellent visual control of anticipatory hand posture when she was asked to reach out to pick up blocks of different sizes that she could not discriminate between perceptually. In one such test, solid blocks of matched top surface area, comparable to the two-dimensional rectangles devised by Efron (1969), were used, as illustrated in Fig. 5.4. Normal subjects adjust their finger–thumb separation in advance of arrival at the object during such reaching behaviour (Jeannerod 1986; Jakobson and Goodale 1991; see Chapter 4), reaching a maximum grip aperture at approximately 60 per cent of the way towards the object. This maximum aperture is strongly related to the width of the object (see Fig. 5.5).

As can be seen from the lower half of Fig. 5.6, D.F. behaved quite normally in the visual control of her grip size while reaching. Yet when she was asked to use her finger and thumb to make a perceptual judgement of the object's

Fig. 5.4 Diagram illustrating the range of a typical set of 'Efron rectangles', in this case in the form of solid plaques. These shapes all have the same surface area but differ in the ratio of their length and width. Different studies (for example, Efron 1969; Warrington, 1985 *a, b*; Goodale *et al.* 1991; Milner *et al.* 1991) have used different ranges of length-width ratios, but the principle is the same.

Fig. 5.5 The relationship between the forefinger–thumb grip aperture and object size, for a normal subject reaching out and grasping a small block of three different sizes placed 30 cm away.

width on a separate series of trials (in a manner analogous to the matching task she had carried out earlier with the card and slot), her responses were unrelated to the actual stimulus dimensions and showed high variation from trial to trial (upper half of Fig. 5.6). The normal controls, of course, had little difficulty indicating the width of the blocks using their index finger and thumb and their responses were well correlated with the object dimensions. D.F.'s accurate calibration of grip size contrasts markedly with poor perform-ance of optic ataxic patients with occipitoparietal damage, such as patient V.K. described in Chapter 4.

Finally, D.F.'s sensitivity to the outline shape of objects was tested using the technique described in Chapter 4. In that experiment, our patient R.V., who showed optic ataxia after biparietal lesions, was unable to position her fingers appropriately on the edges of asymmetrical, smoothly contoured objects that she had no difficulty distinguishing. D.F.'s performance on these tests yielded

Fig. 5.6 The relationship between object width and thumb—index finger aperture on a matching task and a grasping task for the patient D.F. and two age-matched control subjects (C.G. and C.J.). When D.F. was required to indicate how wide the block was by opening her finger and thumb, her matches were unrelated to the object width and showed considerable trial to trial variability (upper right graph). When she reached to pick up the block, however, the size of her anticipatory grasp was well-correlated with the width of the block (lower right graph). Adapted from Goodale *et al.* (1991).

a completely complementary pattern of results, that is, she was able to position her fingers correctly but was quite unable to discriminate one object from the other (Goodale *et al.* 1994c). D. F.'s performance is contrasted with that of R. V. in Fig. 5.7.

Taken together, these findings strongly indicate the preserved operation in D.F. of a system for visuomotor control of manual actions on the basis of orientation, size, and shape. Indeed we have recently confirmed that both orientation and size in concert can successfully guide D. F.'s hand and fingers. She was able to reach out and grasp solid plaques of different dimensions, placed at different orientations on a table in front of her, with an accuracy equal to that of normal controls (Carey *et al.* 1996). If then we make the plausible assumption that the ventral stream is severely compromised in D. F., it is likely that the calibration of her residual visuomotor skills must depend on intact mechanisms within the dorsal stream. The visual inputs to this stream, which provide the necessary information for coding orientation, size, and shape,

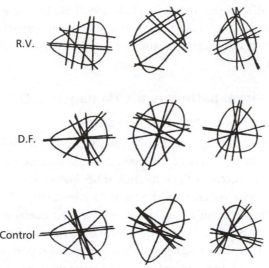

Fig. 5.7 The 'grasp lines' (joining points where the index finger and the thumb first made contact with the shape) selected by the patient D.F. (visual form agnosia), the patient R.V. (optic ataxia), and a control subject, when picking up three different shapes. The four different orientations in which each shape was presented have been rotated so that they are aligned. The grasp lines selected by D.F. and the control subject are virtually identical and pass approximately through the centre of mass of the shape. Moreover, both D.F. and the control subject tended to choose stable grasp points on the object boundary. Their performance contrasts with that of R.V., the patient with dorsal stream damage, who was discussed in Chapter 4.

could arise from V1 or from the tectopulvinar route or from both. Indeed, both routes would appear to be available to D.F. since MRI evidence indicates a substantial sparing of V1 in this patient and no suggestion of collicular or thalamic damage.

As summarized in Chapter 2, cells certainly exist in the dorsal stream of monkeys that appear to be intimately involved in the visual guidance of movements made by the hand, eye, arm, and fingers and, indeed, by the whole body in locomotion. In the case of grasping, the work of Sakata and his group (Taira *et al.* 1990; Sakata *et al.* 1992) indicates that some of these visuomotor cells are orientation and/or size selective. At the present time their sensitivity to shape has not yet been fully investigated. Moreover, it is not yet known whether lesions to the ventral stream in a monkey would leave these physiological properties intact. Nevertheless, extensive damage to the monkey's ventral stream does appear to leave a wide range of visuomotor skills intact (see Section 5.6). In the meantime, therefore, it would seem reasonable to assume that the cells discovered by Sakata *et al.* (1992) are indeed still functional following ventral stream disruption and, further, to hypothesize that the human analogues of these cells are able to mediate prehension and other visual skills in D.F.

5.3.3 What visual pathways are damaged in D.F.?

5.3.3.1 The cause of D.F.'s visual form agnosia

Although we now have an increasingly clear picture of D.F.'s visual abilities, the precise functional nature of her lesion still remains obscure. Any hypothesis has to take into account the full range of her known abilities and disabilities, along with what we currently know of the cortical organization of vision in primates. That is, it must explain not only how her dorsal stream seems to be able to operate well in the visual control of her actions, but it must also explain how she is able to make confident perceptual reports of surface features such as colour and fine texture, while being unable to perceive figural properties such as size, orientation, and shape.

It is our guess that the effective cortical damage, which is located mainly in the lateral prestriate cortex, must disrupt large parts of the human equivalents of V2, V3, and V4 (Clarke 1993; Zilles and Schleicher 1993). though there is probably selective necrosis within these areas rather than a complete destruction. Such a belief would be broadly consistent with the evidence from the MRI pictures undertaken a few weeks after D.F.'s accident (Milner *et al.* 1991). The MRI also suggests that area V1 is largely intact, but since D.F. has little or no awareness of shape or even orientation, we assume that neither the 'magno' nor the 'parvo interblob' channel is able to send information to the ventral stream (see Fig. 5.8). Recent evidence indicates that in fact the interblob regions of area V1 receive inputs from the magno as well as the parvo channels (Nealey and Maunsell 1994) and contain cells with well-defined orientation tuning (see Chapter 2). The simplest assumption, therefore, is that these interblob regions in D.F. are no longer able to convey information to the ventral stream, thus depriving it of both magno- and parvo-derived information about form. In other words, we suggest that D.F.'s ventral stream has been deprived of visual form information from all sources, which would explain both her visual form agnosia and her lack of awareness of visual orientation, size, and shape.

If this hypothesis is correct, D.F.'s residual vision must owe very little to the parvo interblob channel, since this channel seems to send few or no outputs to the dorsal stream in the normal brain, which is dominated by inputs from the magno channel (Maunsell *et al.* 1990). The magnocellular channel is

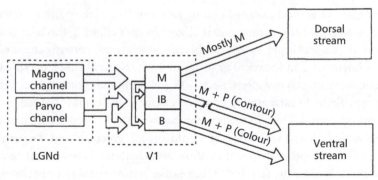

Fig. 5.8 Schematic diagram illustrating the magno and parvo inputs into the primary visual cortex (V1) and then to the dorsal stream. LGNd: lateral geniculate nucleus, pars dorsalis; M, magno channel within the visual cortex; P, parvo channel; IB, interblob region of V1; B, blob region of V1. The diagram illustrates our hypothesis that the magno and parvo inputs from the interblob regions of V1 to the ventral stream have been compromised in D.F., leaving the (mainly magno) projections to the dorsal stream and the (mainly parvo) 'blob' projections to the ventral stream, largely intact.

characterized by a tuning to low spatial frequencies; thus the fact that D.F. has impaired sensitivity to such frequencies in her psychophysical judgements (Milner *et al.* 1991) is consistent with a failure of this channel to pass information to her ventral visual areas (see Fig. 5.8).

5.3.3.2 The mediation of D.F.'s residual visual abilities

As the main input to the dorsal stream derives from the magnocellular system (Maunsell *et al.* 1990), we assume that it is this channel that provides most of the information about orientation, size, and position to the visuomotor structures in D.F.'s cortex. Even a complete necrosis of cells in cortical areas V2, V3, and V4 could still leave visuomotor abilities intact, since there exist direct neural projections from V1 to key areas in the dorsal stream such as MT, V3A, and PO (Zeki 1969, 1980; Colby *et al.* 1988). In addition, as we have already indicated, there is no evidence to suggest that D.F.'s tectothalamic pathways to MT and other dorsal-stream areas are damaged. This would provide an alternative route through which D.F.'s dorsal stream could receive orientation and size information rather than via the striate cortex.

There is indirect evidence, however, that the striate cortex does actively process orientation information in D.F. In a recent study, Humphrey *et al.* (1991) tested D.F. for the so-called McCollough effect (McCollough 1965). In this task, the subject is first exposed for some 15–20 min to alternating horizontal and vertical coloured grating patterns. One of the patterns, say the horizontal, is always red; the other is always green. Following this adaptation period, the subject is presented with black and white test patterns containing either horizontal and vertical gratings or both. Normal subjects typically experience strong colour after-effects when viewing these patterns such that they see colours in each grating complementary to the colours viewed in the adaptation period. Thus, in the present example, they would report that the horizontal black and white grating would appear 'greenish' and the vertical one 'pinkish'. In other words, they show an orientation-contingent colour after-effect. Despite the fact that D.F. in earlier testing could not discriminate between the two black and white gratings used in the test phase, after adaptation with the coloured gratings she showed a normal and vivid orientation-contingent colour after-effect. This striking observation must mean that, at some stage in D.F.'s visual system, colour and orientation processing are interacting. Since there is no evidence of colour processing in the tectothalamic pathways, the presence of a McCollough effect in D.F. argues that orientation processing is preserved within her geniculostriate system, within the same subsystems that ultimately yield her colour phenomenology (see Humphrey 1996).

Electrophysiological data from the monkey lead us to assume that D.F.'s colour perception must be mediated by the ventral stream. Therefore, we suggest that her 'parvo blob' channel may retain relatively intact connections through V1 and V2 to V4 and the inferotemporal complex. While this channel might provide the wavelength information needed for colour perception, however, it would not furnish the information about edge orientation or size needed for her to perceive shape (Livingstone and Hubel 1984; Chapter 2). Nevertheless, it is possible that a range of information about the surface characteristics of objects may be conveyed to the ventral stream through this route. This could explain D.F.'s vivid visual experiences of textures, colour, and fine detail (Milner et al. 1991) and her dependence on such qualities when attempting to identify objects and pictures. The spatial resolution of the 'blob channel', while not as good at the neuronal level as the parvo-interblob channel, may still be sufficient to mediate D.F.'s normal ability to detect fine gratings, whose orientation she can yet only guess at.

It has been suggested to us by John Allman (personal communication) that one reason why the blob projections and the dorsal route via MT have apparently been spared in D.F. is that these brain systems are rich in cytochrome oxidase and other associated enzymes, such as lactase dehydrogenase (LDH). The high levels of LDH, an enzyme for anaerobic energy production, in these regions would allow them to sustain function during the anoxia caused by carbon monoxide poisoning, while areas in the surrounding regions, such as the interblob regions of area V1, would be much more vulnerable. This argument, however, is weakened by the observation that apparently similar anoxic pathology can produce quite different behavioural deficits, including symptoms from the Bálint–Holmes complex, as well as achromatopsia (for example, Ross-Russell and Bharucha 1978). The cellular aetiology responsible for the pattern of loss in D.F. and similar patients, therefore, remains obscure.

5.3.4 Limits on D.F.'s visual coding for action

5.3.4.1 Temporal limitations

D.F.'s ability to scale her grasp to the size of a goal object is remarkable, but nevertheless has certain revealing limitations. In one study, we examined the effects of interposing a temporal delay between showing an object to D.F. and then allowing her to reach out to grasp it unseen (see Goodale *et al.* 1994a). In normal subjects, grip size still correlates well with object width, even for delays as long as 30 s. In D.F., however, all evidence of grip scaling had disappeared after a delay of only 2 s (see Fig. 5.9). This failure cannot be attributed to a general impairment in short-term memory since D.F. has only a mild impairment when tested in more 'cognitive' (auditory-verbal) tasks. It is important to note that even the grasping movements made by normal subjects in the delay condition look very different from those directed at objects that are physically present. In short, the normal subjects were 'pantomiming' their grasps in the delay conditions and, in doing so, were relying upon a stored perceptual representation of the object they had just seen (see Chapter 6). We believe that D.F.'s problem in the delay condition arises from the fact that she cannot use a stored percept of the object to drive a pantomimed grasping movement because she never 'perceived' the goal object in the first place.

In summary, the behaviour of the normal subjects and of D.F. in delayed grasping is consistent with an assumption that visuomotor mechanisms within the dorsal stream operate very much in the 'here and now' and that movements generated after even short delays require stored representations of objects which have been derived through some quite separate 'perceptual' system. We assume that such representations would have to be supplied by structures associated with the ventral stream and thus would be unavailable in D.F. This issue will be returned to at greater length in Chapter 6.

5.3.4.2 Limits imposed by the nature of the response

We have already seen that D.F. can use the orientation of a target to control the orientation of her hand in a 'posting' task (see Fig. 5.3). The question arises, however, as to whether or not she can use the orientation of a more complex

Fig. 5.9 Graphs illustrating the changes in the finger–thumb grip aperture shown by (A) a normal subject and (B) D.F. when asked to reach towards an object which they had been shown 2 s earlier but which is no longer visible. (During the 2 s interval, subjects kept their eyes closed.) As in a normal reach (left), the normal subjects continue to show grip scaling in the absence of the object (right), but no such scaling is evident in the grasps shown by D.F. in the delay condition.

target stimulus to control hand rotation during posting. We explored this question by asking her to post a T-shaped object (see Fig. 5.10) into a T-shaped aperture. On different test trials, the target aperture was presented at different orientations, such that its principal axis was oriented at −30, −60, +30, or +60° off the vertical. As might be expected from D.F.'s known ability to post a card or plaque through a single slot, she succeeded in smoothly posting the T-shape on many of the trials. However, she did make errors in approximately half of the trials and these errors were almost always of approximately 90° magnitude (Fig. 5.10).

This result confirms that D.F. is able to use the orientation of one visible edge to determine her manual posting behaviour, but suggests that she cannot combine two components to form a visual 'shape' to guide such actions.

Fig. 5.10 Diagrams and polar plot of responses of D.F. in the 'T-posting' task. As both the diagrams and the polar plot indicate, in approximately half the trials D.F. was quite accurate, while in the other half she rotated the T-shaped insert approximately 90° from the correct orientation. Adapted from Goodale *et al.* (1994*b*).

It is important to note, however, that the main behavioural variable that was measured in this experiment, the orientation of the hand-held rectangular or T-shaped card, depended directly on the orientation of the wrist. This element of prehension may be particularly sensitive to the orientation of a target object, but relatively insensitive to other figural components of the object. In contrast, actual grasping movements of the hand and fingers have to be sensitive to just such figural components. And as we discussed in Section 5.3.2, D.F. is able to use information about the outline shape of objects to position her fingers on points which maximize the stability of her precision grip, even though, of course, she remains unable to discriminate perceptually between such objects. Unlike the posture of the fingers during grasping, then, rotation of the wrist in the T-posting experiments may have been driven not by the outline shape of the aperture, but rather by a single dominant axis present in the display. It can probably be assumed as a general rule that constraints will be imposed on the visual computations underlying skilled motor behaviours as a function of the particular motor outputs required.

5.3.4.3 Visual cues to orientation available to D.F.

The contours or boundaries of a target shape can theoretically be defined in many different ways. For example, they could be defined by differences in brightness, differences in visual texture, or even differences in depth.

Boundaries can even be extracted on the basis of more subtle organizing principles—principles that were set out in classic studies by the Gestalt psychologists. One of the most useful of these principles is that of similarity. According to this principle, elements in the visual image that are similar in appearance will be seen as belonging to the same object or subregion (that is, will be grouped together). Similarity may be defined by one or more of a set of elementary visual attributes (for example, intensity, colour, size, shape, and orientation). Grouping according to similarity (like the other Gestalt grouping principles) is a useful image-processing strategy because it reflects the high probability that real-world elements with the same visual appearance are likely to be parts of the same object or members of the same object class (for example, leaves of a tree). Another Gestalt principle is good continuity— a boundary is seen as continuous over space if the pattern elements (that is, edges) which make it up can be linked continuously along a curved or straight trajectory.

Our initial work indicated that D.F. was unable to make use of either similarity or good continuity to identify boundaries or edges (Milner *et al*. 1991). As in the classic Gestalt studies which established the importance of these organizing principles, however, the tests we used required a perceptual report. D.F. was asked to give a verbal label for the orientation or shape that was defined by the pattern elements. An important question remained, therefore: Could D.F. make use of these grouping principles to guide actions, such as reaching out to insert the hand or a hand-held card into a slot with a single axis of elongation? This might be possible, given that she can use luminance to guide such responses even though she cannot judge the orientation of a luminance-defined slot perceptually. To test for this, it was necessary to devise varieties of the card-posting task where there was no aperture physically present, but instead only a rectangular target represented graphically within a two-dimensional pattern. This gave us independent control over the different cues defining the target. In one version of the task, the subject is asked to place an ink mark on an elongated rectangular target printed on a piece of paper, by stamping it with a thin rectangular block inked at one end. As would be expected from her card-posting abilities, D.F. could accurately stamp such a target shape when it was defined by sharp luminance contours of various kinds (Fig. 5.11).

In contrast, when faced with a rectangular shape whose contours were defined by the collinear termination of a set of parallel lines, giving 'good continuity' (Fig. 5.12), D.F.'s responses were frequently found to be controlled by the orientation of the stripes rather than of the slot. Where the orientation of the stripes matched that of the target (Fig. 5.12A), performance was good, but where they

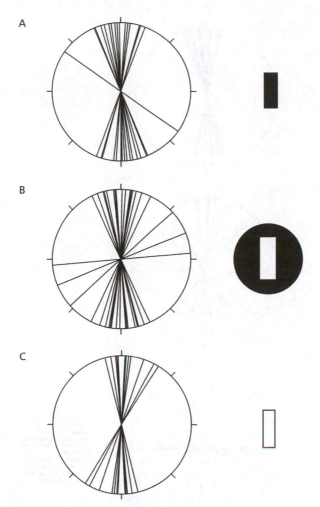

Fig. 5.11 Polar plots of the final position of a hand-held block as D.F. reached out and 'stamped' it endways onto the type of figure indicated. The actual oriention of the rectangular target has been normalized to vertical. (A) Dark rectangle on light background. (B) Light rectangle on dark background. (C) Outline rectangle on light background. Adapted from Goodale *et al.* (1994*b*).

were orthogonal to the target orientation, many responses were made at right angles to the target, especially with thick high-contrast stripes (Fig. 5.12B and C). Furthermore, as Fig. 5.13 shows, D.F. was equally deficient in her ability to use the principle of similarity to control her hand orientation while stamping the target slot. Thus, while the spared visuomotor system controlling 'posting' behaviour in D.F. can use luminance-defined contours, it appears to have little sensitivity to contours defined by good continuity or similarity.

Fig. 5.12 Responses to targets consisting of different arrangements of square wave gratings. (A) A 'missing' rectangular target on a parallel background of fine lines. (B) A missing rectangle on an orthogonal background of fine lines. (C) A missing rectangle on an orthogonal background of thick high-contrast stripes. See Fig. 5.10 for more details. Adapted from Goodale *et al.* (1994*b*).

The overriding tendency of D.F.'s visuomotor system to rely on luminance-defined edges may reflect the fact that the dorsal stream is not capable of utilizing more subtle cues to demarcate the boundaries of goal objects. These factors may only play a role within the perceptual domain. As we discuss in the next chapter, the visual information for efficient online control of action must be

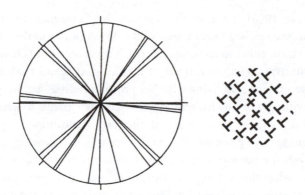

Fig. 5.13 Responses to a rectangular target defined by the similarity of the textural elements. See Fig. 5.10 for more details. Adapted from Goodale *et al.* (1994*b*).

reliably and rapidly processed. If the boundaries of a goal object can only be determined by reference to more computationally expensive algorithms, then the dorsal stream may have to rely on a circuitous route involving perceptual machinery in the ventral stream that is clearly quite capable of such analysis.

5.3.5 Tricks and strategies

In one recent experiment, we asked D.F. to 'stamp' not directly onto the stimulus rectangle that was provided, but to do so instead on a separate blank piece of paper, copying the orientation of the target rectangle in doing so. We predicted poor performance, since the task would not tap the kind of direct visuomotor skill for which we hypothesize that the dorsal visual stream is specialized. In fact the task approximates to the manual modes of perceptual report on which we have repeatedly found D.F. to perform at low levels (for example, Goodale *et al.* 1991; Milner *et al.* 1991). As it turned out, she performed surprisingly well—but video evidence reveals that she achieved this by subterfuge. Instead of moving the stamp directly towards the blank paper while looking at the target, as a normal subject would, she can be seen to initiate a movement first towards the target (approximately one-third of the distance) and then to transfer the hand posture achieved over to the blank sheet.

In another recent experiment, in which D.F. was asked to pick up (say) the square, when both a square and a rectangular plaque were presented together, she again did somewhat better than one might have predicted given her failure to discriminate between them verbally. Closer examination revealed, however, that rather than always reaching for the square (or the rectangle) directly, as normals subjects do, she often changed course mid-flight

(Murphy *et al.* 1996). It may be that she was able to monitor the aperture of her grasp as she reached towards one of the objects and was then able to use this information either to continue her reach trajectory or to change it.

From a number of observations of this kind, it seems that during the course of several years of living with her profound visual handicap, D.F. has acquired, wittingly or unwittingly, tricks or adaptive habits to overcome her perceptual difficulties. To some extent, the results of our own experimental studies seem to have given her the confidence to try to develop such strategies. In effect, she can monitor her intact visuomotor skills to some degree, so as to use what she is doing to inform her overt perceptual judgements (without affecting, we believe, her perceptual experience). Related observations can be found in the older literature, as we noted earlier. Goldstein and Gelb (1918) discovered that their apperceptive agnosic patient Schn was able to report on the shape of a geometric form or the identity of a letter only after laboriously tracing around it with hand or head movements. When these were prevented, he was unable to do the task. It seems that this patient had spontaneously acquired a strategy whereby he could monitor his own movements (perhaps proprioceptively) and it was only by these means that he could arrive at veridical perceptual reports. A very similar phenomenon has been reported by Landis *et al.* (1982). Their patient Mr X depended predominantly on monitoring his own left-hand movements in tracing letters and other shapes in order to identify them. Again this was the only way he could arrive at a 'perceptual' judgement.

It would seem that these two patients had shape recognition difficulties just as profound as those of D.F., but they had the advantage over her in being able to guide the hand around the contours of a visual shape. These observations are, of course, interesting confirmations of the ability of severely agnosic patients to guide their actions using form information they cannot use for perception. D.F., however, is unable to trace in this way, perhaps because of a more extensive lesion: as a result she cannot use the strategy of monitoring such tracing behaviour. The less severely affected but otherwise similar patients H.C. (Adler 1944) and Mr S (Efron 1969) on the other hand, did retain some ability to trace shapes with a finger. It is, of course, difficult to know how a patient who is able to monitor his or her own actions then proceeds to some kind of recognition. It may be that some patients, particularly those capable of tracing an outline, can construct a subjective visual image from proprioceptive inputs; indeed, such imagery might be a necessary part of the tracing strategy. It is unclear at present whether or not such mediation is involved in D.F.'s case.

5.4 'Apperceptive agnosia' and the right hemisphere

5.4.1 'Transformation agnosia'

In a systematic series of studies, Warrington and her colleagues have documented a reliable deficit in patients with posterior right hemisphere lesions in the recognition of objects when those objects are presented at an unusual viewing angle (Warrington and Taylor 1973; Warrington 1982). A similar problem was found in these patients when objects were depicted in other atypical viewing conditions, such as when photographed under unusual lighting (Warrington 1982). The deficit appears to be most profound following damage to the parietotemporal region of the right hemisphere. Such lesions may also impair the recognition of forms and drawings when this is made difficult by other means, such as overlapping one figure with another (De Renzi *et al.* 1969). Warrington (1982) conceptualizes the deficit in recognizing objects in unusual views or lighting conditions as arising from a failure of 'perceptual classification', that is, a failure to relate different pictorial exemplars to the same three-dimensional object. This notion resembles Marr's (1982) interpretation of the same data, which led him to the assumption that visual object recognition depends crucially on constructing and accessing a viewpoint-independent ('object-centred') representation in the brain.

Warrington takes this argument a step further by suggesting that severe cases of failure to recognize 'unusual views', when shape discrimination (as measured by performance on the Efron rectangles, for example) is intact, constitute the only true form of apperceptive agnosia (Warrington 1985*a*; Warrington and James 1988). This view is controversial, however, and it is even debatable whether 'agnosia' is an appropriate term for this disorder, since the patients have no recognition difficulty when objects are viewed from a conventional angle (Farah 1990; Grüsser and Landis 1991). Logically, furthermore, the spared ability to recognize prototypical views would seem to imply in Warrington's terms that the coded representation of the object, presumably object-centred, is intact. That is, Warrington's theory would imply only a failure of access to stored representations from an 'unusual view' input, with visual access from more typical inputs remaining unaffected.

Terminology apart, however, it is clear that a distinct disorder of recognition often exists after these posterior right-hemisphere lesions, which we may refer to (following Humphreys and Riddoch 1987) as 'transformation agnosia'. It is possible that more recent approaches to understanding object recognition may provide a more satisfactory framework for understanding the disorder than that of Marr (1982) (see Chapter 2). For example, if in general there is separate coding of different views of an object in the ventral stream and these representations subserve recognition by interpolative or ensemble processing, then it is conceivable that a lesion might impair the accessibility of less frequently encountered representations. Such difficulties would not constitute a true agnosia, however, unless extensive enough to prevent access to even frequently encountered views.

We have argued in Chapter 2 that the ventral stream is crucially involved in visual recognition processes and that these processes entail access to object-based coding of objects (for example, ensembles of multiple view-dependent representations, prototypical representations, or even in certain special categories, object-centred representations). We shall present behavioural evidence later in this chapter (Section 5.6) that the inferotemporal and neighbouring cortical areas in monkeys are intimately concerned with just the kind of cross-viewpoint generalization that would presumably depend upon such representations. But of course such processing occurs in both of the monkey's hemispheres. Two interrelated puzzles, therefore, present themselves: first, how is it possible for a unilateral (right-hemisphere) lesion to impair this process in humans (when it doesn't in monkeys) and, second, why does a unilateral left-hemisphere lesion not affect it in humans (Warrington 1985a)?

Clearly any answer to these questions must implicate a phylogenetic change, presumably one associated with the evolution of cerebral dominance for praxis, language, and/or gesture (Kimura 1993), through which certain processes concerned in visual recognition have become lateralized into the right hemisphere in humans. One possibility, for example, would be that both humans and monkeys have bilateral temporal-lobe areas which hold object-based representations of the world, but that in humans, the transformation of an unusual view of an object to its stored prototypical representation is less efficient in the left than in the right hemisphere. Alternatively, it is possible that there is simply a less complete ensemble of representations available in the left hemisphere. (These ideas could be tested using surgically 'split-brain' patients. Presumably callosal (or anterior-commissural) connections would be needed for an unusual view seen through the right hemifield to gain access to the more comprehensive right-hemisphere recognition system (Gross et al. 1977). In contrast, familiar views should be recognizable in either hemifield in such patients.)

Finally, Warrington (1982) has suggested that specific recognition disorders such as prosopagnosia are just different forms of transformation agnosia, that is, that in all cases the root problem is one of perceptual 'classification' through accessing object-centred descriptions. In prosopagnosia, a patient suffers from severe difficulties in recognizing familiar or famous people by their faces (Michel *et al*. 1989; Grüsser and Landis 1991, pp. 264–8). Warrington's theory would readily account for the fact that the right hemisphere appears to be always damaged in prosopagnosia. In support of her theory, she has presented preliminary evidence that there may exist rather selective forms of transformation agnosia in which patients have difficulty in matching different views of faces (Whiteley and Warrington 1977). Of course, it may be argued that these are not typical cases of prosopagnosia. Certainly a unitary characterization of prosopagnosia has difficulties with the undoubted heterogeneity of symptom patterns that have been recorded (Jeeves 1984; De Renzi 1986; McNeil and Warrington 1991).

5.4.2 Topographical agnosia

The ability to find one's way around familiar environments is sometimes referred to as 'topographical orientation' and deficits in this ability are called 'topographical agnosia' or 'topographical disorientation'. This disorder, then, is one that is commonly regarded as spatial in nature and which therefore might be expected from Ungerleider and Mishkin's (1982) hypothesis to result from lesions in the parietal area. From our point of view, however, topographical orientation must rely on the allocentric coding of spatial location and this in turn will crucially depend on the availability of stored information about the identity of fixed objects or landmarks. It follows therefore that topographical agnosia should be more likely to result from damage to ventral structures, which we have argued are concerned with the perception not only of objects, but also of their spatial relations.

Jackson (1876) was perhaps the first to put on record a patient with this kind of difficulty: a 59 year old woman found herself unable to find her way through once-familiar streets in her London East End neighbourhood and her difficulty was associated with prosopagnosia. She turned out to have a lesion caused by a large tumour centred in the posterior right temporal lobe. Another striking example, from more recent times, is provided by Pallis (1955). He described a patient who was quite unable to recognize places in his home town and, therefore, frequently got lost. Investigations revealed that he had an upper visual-field defect, indicative of ventral damage posteriorly within the hemispheres and as in Jackson's (1876) patient, his place-recognition disorder was associated with other visual disorders, including prosopagnosia and achromatopsia (loss of colour perception). From these two classic case reports, it would appear that topographical agnosia not only results from damage to the occipitotemporal pathway, but like transformation agnosia, arises from damage to the right rather than the left hemisphere.

Much of our urban route finding is normally dependent on the recognition of landmarks or 'nodes', to which we learn to attach information as to the direction of locomotion needed to locate some further node (Byrne 1979, 1982). We are much better at using such 'network' knowledge to guide our topographical orientation than at acquiring 'vector' knowledge (a spatial or cognitive map) of the environment (Byrne 1979). Patients such as Pallis's (1955) can be regarded as exemplifying the role of occipitotemporal structures in the recognition of objects in places, that is, the nodes as proposed by Byrne (1979). Other patients appear to have little difficulty recognizing the landmarks but, having done so, are unable to recall which way they must then turn (De Renzi et al. 1977; Habib and Sirigu 1987). In either case, it is network rather than vector knowledge that seems to be disturbed.

There have been two important reports each of which summarizes several cases of topographical disorder, including both of the subtypes just distinguished (Landis et al. 1986; Habib and Sirigu 1987). Both groups of investigators used CT evidence to localize the brain damage in their patients and both conclude that the critical area lies in the right medial occipitotemporal region (see Fig. 5.14). This appears to hold good irrespective of whether the patient's problem is in recognizing a place or in orienting with respect to a place, or both. This CT evidence is consistent with earlier reports, such as those of Jackson (1876) and Pallis (1955) mentioned above. Moreover, like the patients described in those earlier papers, many of the patients in the more recent studies had other perceptual problems as well as topographical agnosia. For example, seven of Landis et al.'s (1986) 16 patients with topographical agnosia also suffered from prosopagnosia. In contrast, although some showed indications of hemispatial neglect, none showed any sign of optic ataxia.

The evidence therefore strongly supports our suggestion that the visual recognition of places and routes is a function of the ventral stream rather than the dorsal. We assume that the codes for neighbouring places and the routes between them are associated with each other through medial temporal and limbic mechanisms which receive substantial inputs from the human equivalent of the inferotemporal cortex. Indeed McCarthy (1993) has recently described a patient with a topographical disorder whose lesion principally affected medial right temporal-lobe structures including the hippocampus and amygdala. Similarly, monkeys with hippocampal lesions have particular difficulty in remembering where an object has been seen before (Parkinson et al. 1988). As we noted in the previous chapter, physiological studies have revealed cells in the monkey hippocampus that respond to places in the environment coded allocentrically (for example, Feigenbaum and Rolls 1991). For example, Rolls and O'Mara (1993) describe cells that respond to a 'view' of

Fig. 5.14 Reconstructions from CT scans of four lesions resulting in topographical agnosia. The individual lesions are outlined in dashed lines. The black area indicates the site of overlap in the four lesions. As the diagram shows, the lesions are all on the medial surface of the right hemisphere in the occipitotemporal region, with the area common to the four lesions centred on the parahippocampal region. Adapted from Habib and Sirigu (1987).

part of the environment irrespective of the monkey's viewpoint. Interestingly, they also describe a subset of hippocampal cells that are responsive during whole-body motion between particular places (see also O'Mara *et al.* 1994). There is therefore good reason to believe that the hippocampus and its visual inputs could constitute the seat of normal topographical orientation in primates. That this spatial system is, furthermore, of some evolutionary antiquity is suggested by the large number of studies of non-primate mammals, principally rodents, showing deficits in spatial navigation following damage to the hippocampus (O'Keefe and Nadel 1978: Morris *et al.* 1986). It is possible that its existence paved the way for the evolution of the ventral visual stream.

Notably, it is the right occipitotemporal pathways rather than the left that seem to play the major role in human topographical orientation. This result is in agreement with earlier experiments using the stylus maze in which patients with right-temporal lobectomies were the most impaired, especially those with more medial lesions invading the entorhinal and hippocampal areas (Corkin 1965; Milner 1965). More recent small-scale tests of spatial memory have shown that right temporal-lobectomized patients have difficulty in remembering where they have seen particular objects before (Smith and Milner 1981) and in remembering the exact spatial locations of elements in a complex pictorial scene (Pigott and Milner 1993).

As we have already seen, the occipitotemporal region typically damaged in topographical agnosia (specifically the fusiform and lingual gyri) is also implicated in other disorders of visual recognition such as prosopagnosia, and seems to lie squarely within the territory of the ventral visual stream of the right hemisphere. As discussed in the next section, damage to this region in the left hemisphere is associated with pure alexia or 'word blindness' (Damasio and Damasio 1983; De Renzi *et al.* 1987) and perhaps also with associative object agnosia (for example, McCarthy and Warrington 1986). Furthermore, medial occipitotemporal damage in either hemisphere can cause achromatopsia in the opposite field of vision (Damasio and Damasio 1983: Zeki 1990*b*). These various disorders are often present in combination, but they can occur separately.

We suggest, therefore, that in this region of the ventral visual system, separate modalities of visual recognition must be to some extent segregated from each other. Indeed in humans they appear to be partially segregated even between left and right hemispheres. Just as we have argued for the dorsal visual system, therefore, we consider that there must be quasi-independent networks operating at this stage within the ventral stream. Experimental support for this idea comes from electrophysiological studies such as those alluded to in Chapter 2 which have shown that there are neurones in the monkey's temporal cortex that are preferentially activated by the sight of faces (Perrett *et al.* 1982, 1987; Desimone 1991).

5.5 'Associative agnosia' and the left hemisphere

As mentioned above, damage to the fusiform and lingual gyri in the left hemisphere is likely to cause pure alexia, rather than prosopagnosia or topographical agnosia (see Grüsser and Landis 1991). This suggests that the left hemisphere plays a special role in reading words. Either hemisphere may be able to process individual letters, but perhaps only the left hemisphere has the combinatorial system permitting access from these letter codes to lexical representations. In fact, pure alexia may result from a more general inability to construct perceptual wholes from parts, which when severe could cause a form of object agnosia (Farah 1990) as seen in the patient H.J.A. (Riddoch and Humphreys 1987). In support of this idea, Farah (1991) has pointed out that object agnosia (even of the so-called 'associative' variety) never occurs without either prosopagnosia or pure alexia, while the latter two conditions are never seen together in the absence of object agnosia. She argues that the syndrome of 'object agnosia with prosopagnosia' results primarily from a right occipitotemporal lesion, while 'object agnosia with pure alexia' would follow from a left occipitotemporal lesion.

Farah's (1990, 1991) suggestion is that 'associative agnosia' following left hemisphere damage may always have more to do with the integration of parts of an object or figure than with a failure to relate visual with semantic processing. This idea would fit with the almost ubiquitous reports of such integrative difficulties ('piecemeal processing') in case descriptions of patients with putative associative agnosia. It is, however, at variance with all other models of associative agnosia and new evidence needs to be found that might help to test the hypothesis.

It seems, in any event, that different visual recognition processes depend asymmetrically upon ventral-stream structures in the human cerebral hemispheres. In contrast, it is unlikely that visuomotor control systems are asymmetrical to anything like the same extent: optic ataxia occurs equally often after damage to either parietal lobe (Perenin and Vighetto 1988). There may be subtle differences in the form this disorder takes according to which hemisphere is damaged (see Chapter 4), but not in its degree of severity or its frequency of incidence. Presumably, the efficient on-line visual control of effector systems on both sides of the body demands a symmetrical distribution of visuomotor networks in the brain. It is therefore unlikely that a lateralized visuomotor network would have evolved. On the other hand, the perceptual system does not have these constraints, since its outputs are not tied closely to any particular effector system. The computational machinery underlying different kinds of visual recognition could therefore have become lateralized to either hemisphere as a result of quite independent forces of natural selection.

5.6 Agnosia in monkeys?

Our arguments for conceptualizing the ventral stream as a system for the generalized visual coding of objects and their relationships were built upon physiological and anatomical evidence provided by the Old World monkey. Logic therefore requires us to argue that making lesions of the ventral system in such animals should create a model of visual agnosia. Such a model should not only include the recognition deficits seen in human visual agnosia but also the spared visuomotor abilities.

5.6.1 Recognition deficits

In point of fact, such a model long antedates the physiology: it was described first by Brown and Schäfer (1888) and then more fully by Klüver and Bucy (1937). Klüver and Bucy (1937) made large bilateral resections of the temporal lobe in monkeys and the eponymous syndrome that resulted included what the authors themselves termed 'visual agnosia'. Amongst other difficulties, the monkeys were observed to be unable to distinguish food from non-food objects using vision alone and to be unable to learn new visual discriminations between patterns for food reward. In more recent times, it became apparent that these visual components of the Klüver–Bucy syndrome did not depend on a resection of the entire temporal lobe. Removal of the inferotemporal (IT) cortex—a complex of areas lying ventrally below the superior temporal sulcus, including various subdivisions of area TE along with area TEO—was sufficient (Mishkin 1954; Mishkin and Pribram 1954). This cortical region is, as was pointed out in Chapter 2, the culmination of the ventral stream of cortical visual projections. Such a stream of processing was itself predicted by crossed lesion and disconnection studies some years ago, which showed that cortical links between the geniculostriate system and the inferotemporal cortex were crucial for visual pattern discrimination in the monkey (Ettlinger 1959; Mishkin 1966).

Like human visual agnosia, the inferotemporal monkey's recognition deficits cannot be explained by 'low-level' sensory impairments. Large bilateral lesions of the inferotemporal cortex have been found to have no residual effect on flicker detection (Symmes 1965) or light thresholds (Bender 1973) and they leave a monkey with intact visual fields (Cowey and Weiskrantz 1963, 1967) and normal visual acuity (Weiskrantz and Cowey 1963). Attempts to pin-point the precise nature of the visual disorder after inferotemporal lesions have produced rather inconclusive results (Gross 1973; Dean 1976, 1982). For example, the animals are impaired not only on perceptual and attentional tests, but also on mnemonic tests. Nevertheless, a partial fractionation was achieved, in which lesions located rostrally in the temporal lobe (in middle/anterior TE) tended to have a predominantly mnemonic effect, while those located more caudally (in posterior TE/TEO) had a predominantly perceptual or attentional effect (Iwai and Mishkin 1969; Cowey and Gross 1970).

We argued in Chapter 2 that the ventral stream may be crucially involved in visual recognition processes and that these processes entail access to some form of viewpoint-independent representations of objects, faces, etc. Behavioural evidence for this comes from the experiments of Weiskrantz and Saunders (1984). They trained monkeys to distinguish between different solid shapes and showed by transfer tests that inferotemporal lesions selectively impaired the ability to maintain performance across different viewpoints. They also found an impairment in the monkey's ability to recognize objects under changed conditions of lighting and shadow. In related work, monkeys with inferotemporal lesions have been found to lack size constancy when performing choice discrimination tasks (Humphrey and Weiskrantz 1969; Ungerleider et al. 1977): apparently they fail to use information about object distance correctly when estimating size. In other words, these studies provide direct evidence that the inferotemporal cortex is a crucial part of the circuitry required for accessing the generalized structural coding of objects independent of particular viewing conditions.

Paradoxically, inferotemporal monkeys are able to learn to discriminate mirror-image patterns more easily than one might expect from the performance of normal animals on this kind of problem (Gross 1978; Holmes and Gross 1984; Gaffan *et al.* 1986). Perhaps, if the inferotemporal monkey lacks the object constancy mechanisms that make the normal monkey see the two mirror-image patterns as equivalent, it is able to treat the two stimuli as different in a way that the normal monkey cannot. Thus, despite its visual learning deficits, the inferotemporal monkey can perform relatively better on this problem than on others. Findings like these lend further support to our proposal that the ventral stream is more concerned with object-based coding than with egocentric coding.

The information that is useful for a long-term memory system is information about the relatively enduring characteristics of objects, their associations, and their spatial relationships. The evanescent images that objects cast upon the retina are of little lasting value in themselves. In other words, the perceptual constancies—our tendency to perceive objects as the same despite changes in their position, distance, inclination, lighting, etc.—are precisely what a memory system needs. The memory system needs to know about objects, not about unique images on the retina. It is thus no accident that the inferotemporal cortex lies at the interface between vision and memory. It enables learning about new objects and the recognition of old ones. It also injects an element of stability into the visual world: we do not perceive an object as changing or metamorphosing into a different object whenever its retinal size or orientation varies or when its precise colouring—in terms of the reflected wavelengths of light—varies. A system yielding such an instability of the visual world would be a poor one for dealing with the real world of objects that an animal has to deal with. Similarly, we need to be able to recognize whether we are looking at the same or a different object from one minute to the next and our ability to do that will depend upon our mnemonic representation of the object(s) in question.

It has been suggested (for example, Dean 1976, 1982) that inferotemporal lesions cause an impoverishment in the monkey's ability to represent fully the qualities of an object in memory, that is, that the object is 'categorized' in too broad a manner. Thus, for example, an inferotemporal monkey will tend to generalize from a training stimulus to a wider range of test stimuli than a normal monkey (Butter *et al.* 1965; Dean 1978). However, these results need not be seen as reflecting a structural failure to establish precise representations, but might instead reflect a strategy for coping with a failure to access object-based representations. In such circumstances, where all views of a given object look like different objects, all the monkey has to fall back on is its ability to treat retinally similar stimuli as equivalent. Thus, in essence, it might come to misclassify similar patterns—which actually derive from different objects—as if they derived from the same object. By the same token, the agnosic patient D.F. may appear to 'overgeneralize' when she misnames a spoon as a knife; in fact she is simply resorting to a strategy of guessing on the basis of what to her is visual similarity.

5.6.2 Spared visuomotor abilities

As we indicated earlier, it is necessary for a satisfactory animal model of visual agnosia to show a sparing of visuomotor skills: if not, then it is unlikely that studies of the monkey will help us to understand such sparing in the human agnosic. In fact there are several anecdotal indications of such sparing in the literature. Thus, in their classic paper, Klüver and Bucy (1938) described a monkey after bilateral resection of the temporal lobe as follows:

'From the very beginning the monkey had no difficulty in promptly picking up objects. There was never any fumbling around. In grasping or reaching for stationary or moving objects, the movements of the hands and fingers were definitely guided by the position and the form of the object until contact was established. The ability to localize position in space and to recognize the shape of objects did not seem to be impaired even if the objects were placed on surfaces exhibiting complex visual patterns' (p. 34).

And also

'The animal when turned loose in a room would jump from the floor to stands or tables 85 cm high without hesitation and apparently used visual cues in space without the slightest difficulty. In other words, she showed no visual defect when climbing, running or jumping around' (pp. 35–6).

There seems little doubt, then, that even radical ablations like those made by Klüver and Bucy (1938) left several visually guided skills largely intact. Yet their monkeys failed to recognize even simple everyday food items. Consequently, it is not surprising that visuomotor skills survive smaller lesions restricted to the inferotemporal cortex. Pribram (1967), for instance, made the memorable observation that monkeys with inferotemporal removals, which failed to learn a pattern discrimination despite many weeks of training, nevertheless remained far more adept than he was at catching gnats flying within the cage room. Butler (cited by Gross 1973) similarly observed that inferotemporal monkeys could track and seize a rapidly and erratically moving peanut. Other investigators have confirmed that inferotemporal-lesioned monkeys do not bump into obstacles or misjudge distances when jumping. The distinction then, in inferotemporal monkeys as in human agnosics, seems to be between tasks where the animal has to recognize an object or pattern (on which they fail) and tasks where the animal has to interact with the object or pattern (on which they pass).

Although the observations of spared visuomotor abilities in monkeys with ventral stream lesions provide some support for the arguments we have been developing, more formal assessment of such abilities needs to be done. It is our suspicion that such testing will reveal well-preserved visuomotor skills in monkeys with lesions either of V4 or of the inferotemporal cortex. A small beginning has been made by Buchbinder *et al.* (1980) who found that one monkey with large bilateral inferotemporal lesions had no difficulty in orienting its finger–thumb 'pincer grip' under visual guidance to dislodge morsels of food lodged in small grooves set at different orientations (see Chapter 4, Section 4.2.4 and Glickstein *et al.* 1998).

5.7 **Summary**

In this chapter and the previous one, we have reviewed a wide range of behavioural studies of both brain-damaged monkeys and humans in which the damage has been largely restricted to either the dorsal or the ventral stream of visual processing. We believe that the functional model that we have proposed provides a useful framework for understanding this body of data. In the next chapter, we examine how the model can help to explain some intriguing dissociations between perception and action in normal subjects.

Chapter 6

Dissociations between perception and action in normal subjects

6.1 Introduction

The control of skilled actions directed at everyday objects imposes requirements on visual processing that are different from those leading to the recognition of those objects. For example, the visuomotor systems mediating prehension, when confronted with a goal object—particularly a novel one—must compute the size, shape, orientation, and distance of the object *de novo*. Moreover, the temporal constraints on the control of prehension, particularly on the amendments made during its execution, demand that the underlying computations be both fast and robust. In addition, because the required actions must be matched to the location and disposition of the object with respect to the observer, the required computations must be organized within egocentric frames of reference.

In the previous three chapters we have reviewed the evidence from a wide range of neuropsychological studies to suggest that there is a clear dissociation between the visual pathways supporting perception and action in the cerebral cortex. One of the most compelling examples of this dissociation is provided by the patient D.F., who shows intact visuomotor behaviour despite her profound perceptual deficits. But it must follow from our arguments that even in neurologically intact individuals, the visual information underlying the calibration and control of a skilled motor action directed at an object will not always mirror the perceptual judgements made about that object. In this chapter, we review some of the evidence for such dissociations in normal subjects and discuss some of the reasons why these dissociations are important.

6.2 Different frames of reference for perception and action

There have been a number of studies of aiming and grasping showing that such movements can be adjusted 'on-line' as the movements unfold. In a typical experiment, on-line adjustments are provoked by introducing a sudden perturbation in the location (or size) of the goal object during the execution of the movement (for reviews of these experiments, see Jeannerod (1988), and Goodale and Servos (1996)). In some cases, the amendments to the motor act are made even though the subject does not perceive the change in the particular parameter of the object that is responsible for that amendment.

One of the clearest examples of such a dissociation comes from experiments in which the position of a target is moved unpredictably during a saccadic eye movement (Bridgeman *et al.* 1979, 1981; Hansen and Skavenski 1985; Goodale *et al.* 1986). In these experiments, subjects typically fail to report the displacement of the target even though a later correction saccade and even a manual aiming movement directed at the target will accurately accommodate the shift in position. To understand just how such dissociations can occur during a visually guided act such as pointing to a target, it is necessary to describe the organization of the constituent movements in some detail.

When one reaches toward a target that suddenly appears in the peripheral visual field, not only does the arm extend toward the object, but the eyes, head, and body also move in such a way that the image of the object falls on the fovea. Even though the motor signals reach the ocular and brachial musculature at much the same time (Biguer *et al.* 1982), the saccadic eye movements directed at the target (because the eye is much less influenced by inertial and gravitational forces than the limb) are typically completed while the hand is still moving. Indeed, the first and largest of the saccades made towards the target is often completed before (or shortly after) the hand has begun to move. A second saccade—the so-called 'correction saccade'—puts the image of the target on the fovea. This means that during the execution of the aiming movement, the target, which was originally located in the peripheral visual field, is now located either on or near the fovea. Theoretically then, detailed information about the position of the target provided by central vision (coupled with extraretinal information about the relative position of the eye, head, body, and hand) could be used to correct the trajectory of the hand as it moves toward the target.

Goodale *et al.* (1986) were able to demonstrate that this information is indeed used to amend the motor program during its execution by changing the position of the target as the movement unfolded. In their experiment, subjects were asked to move their finger from a central target to a new target (a small light) that appeared suddenly in their peripheral visual field (see Fig. 6.1A). In half the trials, the peripheral target stayed in position until the subject had completed the aiming movement. In the remainder of the trials, however, the target was displaced to a new position 10 per cent further out from where it had originally appeared. This sudden displacement of the target occurred just after the first saccadic eye movement had reached its peak velocity. The two kinds of trials, which are illustrated in Fig. 6.1(B), were presented

A

B

Fig. 6.1 (A) Schematic diagram of apparatus used by Goodale *et al.* (1986) to study the accuracy of pointing to targets moved during a saccadic eye movement. The upper surface consisted of a matrix of light-emitting diodes (LEDs) each of which could be independently illuminated. C represents the LED which was illuminated to present the central target and E represents a target that was presented in the peripheral visual field. When the subject looked through the semi-reflecting mirror placed between the LED matrix and the pointing surface, he saw a virtual image of one of the LEDs (C' or E') on the pointing surface. Vision of the hand could be prevented by turning off all the illumination below the semi-reflecting mirror. By recording eye movements on-line, it was possible to produce a second displacement of the target (E') just as the eye movement reached peak velocity. (B) Cartoon illustrating the spatiotemporal organization of the movements of the target, eye, and hand on single-step ('normal') and double-step ('displacement') trials. The duration of the hand movement is indicated by d. The second displacement on double-step trials was triggered when the first saccade reached peak velocity. Vision of the hand was prevented as soon as the hand began to move. Adapted from Goodale (1988).

in random order and the subjects were not told that the target would sometimes change position during the first eye movement.

The effects of this manipulation on the aiming movements and correction saccades were clear and unambiguous. As Fig. 6.2 illustrates, the final position of the finger in trials in which the target was displaced during the saccadic eye movement was shifted (relative to 'normal' trials) by an amount equivalent to the size of the target displacement. (Similarly, the correction saccade, which followed the first saccade, always brought the target, displaced or not, onto the fovea.) In other words, subjects corrected the trajectory of their aiming movement to accommodate the displacement of the target that occurred on some of the trials. Moreover, as Fig. 6.3 illustrates, the duration of limb movements made to a displaced target corresponded to the duration of the movement that would have been made had the target been presented at that location right from the start of the trial. Thus, no additional processing time was required on displaced-target trials.

These findings strongly suggest that when rapid eye and hand movements are directed at a visual target, an initial set of signals is sent to the muscles controlling both the eye and the hand based on information about the position of the target that is available from the peripheral retina and extraretinal sources. After the first saccade, however, more precise information about target position is provided from foveal or parafoveal regions of the retina and can be used to 'fine-tune' the trajectory of the hand (and set the amplitude of the final correction saccade). If this hypothesis is correct, then it becomes much clearer why the duration of a limb movement is the same for a given position of the target, independent of whether the target appeared there initially or was moved to that position from another during the first saccade. In either case, the same post-saccadic information would be used to update motor signals controlling the trajectory of the hand (provided the target displacement during the saccade was not too large). In other words, the apparent 'correction' in the trajectory that occurred on displaced-target trials was nothing more than the normal updating of the motor programming that occurs at the end of the first saccade on an ordinary trial.

In spite of the fact that the visuomotor systems mediating the aiming movement appeared to be exquisitely sensitive to changes in the position of the goal object in these experiments, the subjects' perception of these events was quite different. At no time during these experiments, in fact, did the subjects realize that the target had jumped to a new location while they were reaching towards it. Nor did the subjects detect anything different between normal and displaced-target trials. Indeed, even when subjects were told that the target would be displaced during the eye movement on some trials and were asked to

Fig. 6.2 Frequency distributions of the final position of the index finger on 'normal' and 'displacement trials'. The distributions on normal trials are indicated by the oblique hatching running up to the left. The distributions on the displacement trials are indicated by the oblique hatching running up to the right. Overlap in the two distributions is indicated by cross-hatching. The size and direction of the second jump of the target on displacement trials is indicated by the small arrows on the abscissa. Adapted from Goodale (1988).

Fig. 6.3 Mean duration of hand movements plotted as a function of their amplitude on normal and displacement trials. The amplitude–duration curve for normal trials is indicated by a solid line and filled circles. The amplitude–duration curve for displacement trials is indicated by a dotted line and open circles. As the graph shows, the two lines fall on top of one another. Adapted from Goodale (1988).

indicate after each trial whether or not such a displacement had occurred, their performance was no better than chance. The failure to perceive stimulus change, particularly in position, during saccadic eye movements is well-known and is sometimes termed 'saccadic suppression' (for example, Volkmann *et al.* 1968; Bridgeman 1983). These and other experiments using the same paradigm (for a review, see Goodale (1988)) have consistently shown that subjects fail to perceive changes in target position even though they modify their visuomotor output to accommodate the new position of the target.

In fact, had the subjects perceived the change in target position that occurred on displaced-target trials and, on the basis of this perception, quite 'deliberately' altered the trajectory of their reach, then the duration of the movements on these trials would have fallen well outside the amplitude–duration curve (see Fig. 6.3) obtained on normal, no-displacement, trials. The fact that this did not occur is additional evidence that the subjects were treating normal trials and displaced-target trials in an identical fashion and, as we have already argued, suggests that the 'correction' observed on displaced-target trials is nothing more than the fine-tuning of the trajectory that occurs at the end of the first saccade in the normal course of events. Later experiments by D. Pélisson (personal communication) have shown that if the displacement of the target during the first saccade is made large enough, subjects will perceive the change in target position. When this happens, the subjects show a large readjustment in the trajectory of their reach that falls well outside the normal amplitude–duration curve for movements to targets that are initially presented in those locations. In short, the 'leap' into conscious perception is associated with a failure to make efficient on-line adjustments in motor output.

But provided the displacement of the target during the first saccade is not too large (less than 10 per cent of the original distance of the target from the midline), subjects fail to perceive the shift in position. This failure may reflect a broad 'tuning' of perceptual constancy mechanisms that preserve the apparent stability of a target in space as its position is shifted on the retina during an eye movement. Such mechanisms are necessary if our perception of the world is to remain stable as our eyes move about, but if the perceptual system is largely object based, as we have argued in earlier chapters, the spatial coding of these mechanisms would not need to be finely-tuned. The action systems controlling goal-directed movements, however, need to be much more sensitive to the exact position of a target and, as a consequence, they will compensate almost perfectly for real changes in target position to which the perceptual system may be quite refractory. Thus, because of the different requirements of the perception and action systems, an illusory perceptual constancy of target position may be maintained in the face of large amendments in visuomotor control.

Similar dissociations between perceived position and pointing responses have also been observed in experiments in which subjects viewed both their hand and the target stimulus through prismatic lenses that shifted the visual array a few degrees (less than 3°) to the left or right (Jakobson and Goodale 1989). Despite the shift in the array, subjects (who were not told that they were looking through prisms) were just as accurate at pointing to the target as they were when no prisms were present (see Fig. 6.4). Thus, on the first trial with the prisms, they compensated for their initial heading error by correcting the trajectory of their hand as it moved towards the target. (Of course, had they not been able to see their hand, they would have shown the usual errors on the first few trials that are typically seen in prism experiments.) Yet, despite the adjustments made in their motor behaviour in response to the prismatic distortion of visual input, the subjects remained quite unaware of the relatively large shift in the stimulus field. Again, perception appears to be refractory to changes in the visual display to which the visuomotor systems are exquisitely sensitive.

Complementary dissociations between perception and action have also been observed, in which perception of a visual stimulus can be manipulated

Fig. 6.4 The mean pointing errors of subjects looking through five diopter right-deviating prisms. Their errors when they are looking through the prisms (Exp) are no different from the pre-exposure or post-exposure conditions (Pre and Post). The small triangles indicate the errors that would be expected if they did not correct for the displacement in their visual array. Subjects remained unaware of the fact that their visual array was displaced. Adapted from Jakobson and Goodale (1989).

while visuomotor output remains unaffected. Bridgeman *et al.* (1981), for example, have shown that even though a fixed visual target surrounded by a moving frame appears to drift in a direction opposite to that of the frame, subjects persist in pointing to the veridical location of the target. In the context of the arguments that we have been developing, however, such a result is not surprising. Perceptual systems are largely concerned with the relative position of stimuli in the visual array rather than with their absolute position within an egocentric frame of reference. For action systems of course, the absolute position of a visual stimulus is critical, since the relevant effector must be directed to that location. Thus, a perceived change in the position of a target can occur despite the fact that the motor output is unaffected. Similarly, as we saw in the experiments by Goodale *et al.* (1986), a 'real' change in the position of a target (within an egocentric frame of reference) can produce adjustments to motor output even though that change is not perceived by the subject.

But even when a real change in the position of a goal object is perceived, there is evidence that the visual processing that mediates that perception can take far longer to carry out than the processing underlying adjustments to the trajectory of the motor response directed at that object. In a recent experiment by Castiello *et al.* (1991), subjects were asked to indicate (using a vocal response) when they perceived a sudden displacement in the position of an object to which they were directing a grasp. On displacement trials, in which the object was displaced at the onset of the grasping movement, the vocal response was emitted 420 ms after the onset of the movement. In contrast, adjustments to the trajectory of the grasping movement could be seen in the kinematic records as little as 100 ms after movement onset, that is, more than 300 ms earlier than the vocal response. (A number of control experiments were run to make sure that the result was not due to interference effects.) The authors concluded that the delay between motor correction and the vocal response reflects the fact that perceptual awareness of a visual stimulus takes far longer to achieve than adjustments to the ongoing motor activity provoked by the visual stimulus. Processing time, of course, is likely to be a much more critical constraint for visuomotor networks than for the perceptual networks supporting conscious awareness.

In previous chapters, we have argued that the clear functional dissociation between visual perception and visuomotor control can be mapped onto the well-known distinction between the ventral and dorsal streams of visual processing. In developing the argument for separate visual pathways, we have suggested that perception demands transformations of the incoming visual data that are rather different from those required for visuomotor control and that it is these differences that lie at the root of the division of labour between the dorsal and ventral streams. The primary purpose of perception is to identify objects and places, to classify them, and to attach meaning and significance to them, thus enabling later responses to them to be selected appropriately. As a consequence, perception is concerned with the enduring characteristics of objects so that they can be recognized when they are encountered again in different visual contexts. Thus, the apparent constancy of target position observed in the experiments described above (for example, Goodale *et al.* 1986) can be seen as part of a constellation of perceptual constancies by means of which the size, shape, colour, lightness, and relative location of objects are preserved across a variety of viewing conditions.

In contrast, the computations required for the control of movement must be viewer based; in other words, both the location of the object and its disposition and motion must be encoded relative to the observer. Moreover, because the position of a goal object in the action space of an observer is rarely constant, such computations must be undertaken every time an action occurs and, if possible, be updated during the execution of that action. As we have already suggested, it is this concern with the location and disposition of objects in egocentric space that helps to explain why, in the Goodale *et al.* (1986) study, the aiming movements of subjects are sensitive to shifts in the location of the target even though those shifts in location are not perceived. We would suggest that all of the various discrepancies that have been observed between the visuomotor performance and perceptual reports of normal subjects may reflect the differential processing characteristics of the dorsal and ventral streams (and their associated networks). Such a hypothesis, however, can only be substantiated through direct neuropsychological and neurophysiological observations.

6.3 Movements to remembered places: a possible role for perception in the control of action?

Throughout the previous section, we have emphasized that motor outputs, such as saccadic eye movements and visual-guided limb movements, are directed to the location of the target within egocentric frames of reference, which may or may not be coincident with the perceived location of the target. There are special circumstances, however, where motor output can be driven by the perceived (allocentric) position of a target rather than by its absolute (egocentric) coordinates. Wong and Mack (1981), for example, showed that while saccades made to visible targets are driven by the retinal location of those targets rather than by their perceived location, saccades to a remembered target are made to the perceived rather than the retinal location it previously occupied. In their experiments, a small target was presented within a surrounding frame and after a 500 ms blank, the frame and target reappeared, but now with the frame displaced a few degrees to the left or right. The target itself was presented at exactly the same location as before. Yet instead of perceiving the frame as having changed position, subjects had the strong illusion that it was the target that had moved, in a direction opposite to that of the actual displacement of the frame. This illusion was maintained even when the target was displaced in the same direction as the frame, but by only one-third of the distance. In this latter condition, the perceived change in target position following the blank period and the actual change of target position on the retina were in opposite directions. Yet despite the presence of this strong illusory displacement of the target, subjects consistently directed their saccades to the true location of the target (that is its location in retinal, not perceptual, coordinates). So far then, these findings are similar to those outlined in the previous section in which motor output has been shown to be driven by egocentric spatial information that is quite independent of the subjects' perception. In a second very similar experiment, however, when subjects were asked to look back to the 'original' location of the target after making their saccade to its new location, these memory-driven saccades were made to a location in perceptual, not retinal, coordinates. In other words, the 'look-back' saccade was made to a location that corresponded with the subjects' perceptual judgement about the previous location of the target—a judgement that was determined by the relative location of the target in the frame rather than by its absolute location in egocentric space.

The suggestion that memory-driven saccades may be driven by visual information very different from normal target-directed saccades (and by inference may depend on separate neural pathways) is consistent with a number of other observations showing that the kinematic profiles and trajectories of saccades to remembered targets can be very different from those of target-directed saccades. Thus, saccades made 1–3 s following the offset of a target light were 10–15 ms slower and achieved lower peak velocities than saccades directed towards an identical target that remained illuminated (Becker and Fuchs 1969). In addition, the coupling between peak velocity and movement amplitude appears to be much more variable in saccades made to remembered rather than to visible targets (Smit *et al.* 1987). Memory-driven saccades also appear to be less accurate than those made to visible targets (Gnadt *et al.* 1991): these errors were seen even when the delay between target offset and the initiation of the saccade was as short as 100 ms. Moreover the amplitude of the errors increased as the delay was lengthened systematically up to 2 s.

This observation led Gnadt *et al.* (1991) to propose that in the oculomotor system a transition between visually linked and memory-linked representations occurs during the first 800–1000 ms following offset of a visual target and that 'the "memory" of intended eye movement targets does not retain accurate retinotopic registration' (p. 710).

In summary, these differences in saccadic dynamics and accuracy suggest that the neural subsystems for the generation of saccades to remembered locations are to some degree independent from those subserving normal target-driven saccades (see, for example, Guitton *et al.* 1985; Wurtz and Hikosaka 1986). Indeed, if, as the work by Wong and Mack (1981) described above suggests, memory-driven saccades are computed in perceptual rather than egocentric coordinates, then the visuomotor transformations mediating those saccades may use the same visual information that underlies perceptual reports of spatial location. At present, of course, all of this is purely speculative. One useful avenue of research might be to explore the visual coordinate systems used by those regions of the prefrontal cortex, such as area 46, which have been implicated in the control of memory-driven saccades (Funahashi *et al.* 1989; see Chapter 2). It is not clear at present whether the neurones in this area related to memory-driven saccades use the same visual coordinate systems as target-driven saccades. To answer this question, single-unit studies of area 46 could, for example, borrow some of the techniques used by Wong and Mack (1981) in their studies of human subjects making memory-driven saccades. Certainly area 46 is interconnected, not only with the dorsal stream (Cavada and Goldman-Rakic 1989b; Seltzer and Pandya 1989), but also with the inferotemporal cortex (Barbas 1988); the ventral stream inputs might provide allocentric perceptual information about target position that could be used to drive a delayed saccade.

As we saw in Chapter 3, even some patients who show a profound hemianopia following damage to the primary visual cortex can generate saccades to visual targets presented in their blind field. We argued that they probably do this on the basis of intact retinal projections to the superior colliculus, which has downstream projections to the premotor nuclei in the brainstem controlling eye movements and upstream links, via the pulvinar, with visuomotor networks in the dorsal stream. It would be our prediction that such patients should be unable to generate saccades guided by the location of remembered targets in their blind field. Since the location of the target would not have been perceived in the first place, the patient should be unable to retain it for longer than a fraction of a second for the purpose of saccadic guidance.

Like eye movements, pointing movements are most accurate when directed to still-visible targets and errors accumulate as the length of the delay period between target viewing and movement initiation increases (Holding 1968; Elliott and Madalena 1987). Indeed, Elliott and Madalena (1987) have suggested that a visual representation of the environment which would be useful for guiding manual aiming movements does not persist for longer than 2 s. It is reasonable to suppose that, like the visuomotor mechanisms mediating saccadic eye movements, the action systems underlying the control of pointing work optimally in 'real time' with visible targets. Once the target is gone and some time has elapsed (2 s or more), the production of a pointing movement, like the saccadic eye movements discussed earlier, may have to be referred to earlier perceptual representations of the target—representations that depend on neural circuitry different from that mediating pointing movements to visible targets. Again, just as was discussed for saccadic eye movements, one might expect that 'blindsight' patients with lesions of the primary visual cortex, who can often point accurately to targets they cannot perceive in their hemianopic visual field, would nevertheless have great difficulty pointing accurately to remembered targets in that field (since they did not 'see' those targets in the first place). Such experiments, however, have yet to be carried out.

6.4 Illusory size distortions

There are many examples of visual illusions in which perception of the relative size of objects does not correspond to their real size. One such illusion is provided by the so-called 'Titchener circles' in which two target circles of equal size are presented, each surrounded by a circular array of either smaller or larger circles. Subjects typically report that the target circle surrounded by smaller circles appears larger than the other target circle (see Fig. 6.5, upper part). By differentially adjusting the real size of the two targets, they can be made to appear equivalent in size, as shown in the lower part of the figure. Although the perception of size is clearly affected by such contextual manipulations, it is possible that the processing responsible for the illusion occurs wholly within the ventral stream. If so, then the calibration of size-dependent motor outputs, such as grip aperture during prehension, might not be affected.

To test this idea, Aglioti *et al.* (1995) used a variation of the Titchener illusion in which two thin 'poker-chip' discs were used as the target circles. Subjects were asked to pick up the target disc on the left if the two discs appeared equal in size and to pick up the one on the right if they appeared different in size. Subjects used their right hand and their finger–thumb grip aperture was monitored using optoelectronic recording equipment. The relative size of the two discs was randomly varied so that in some trials the discs appeared perceptually equivalent but were physically different in size and in

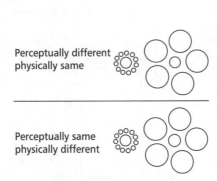

Perceptually different
physically same

Perceptually same
physically different

Fig. 6.5 Diagram showing the 'Titchener circles' illusion. In the top figure the two central discs are of the same actual size, but appear different; in the bottom figure, the disc surrounded by an annulus of large circles has been made somewhat larger in size in order to appear approximately equal in size to the other central disc.

other trials they were physically equivalent but perceptually different. Under the conditions used, most of the subjects needed a difference of at least 2 mm between the diameters of the two discs for them to perceive the discs as identical in size. All subjects treated discs that were actually physically different in size as perceptually equivalent and they treated discs that were physically identical as perceptually different.

In contrast, however, the scaling of the subjects' grip aperture (measured before contact with the disc) proved to be quite immune to the illusion. As Fig. 6.6 illustrates, the difference in grip aperture for the larger and smaller target discs was the same in trials in which the subject believed the two discs to be equivalent in size (even though they were different) as it was in trials in which the subject believed the two discs to be different in size (even though they were identical, either both larger or both smaller). In short, grip size was determined entirely by the true size of the target disc. Thus, the very act by means of which subjects indicated their susceptibility to the visual illusion (that is, picking up one of the two target circles) was itself uninfluenced by that illusion.

These results indicate that the visual mechanisms underlying perception and visuomotor control can operate independently, in normal subjects, not only in the domain of spatial coding, but also in the domain of object coding. Just as the perception of object location appears to operate within relative frames of reference, so does the perception of object size. Although we often make subtle relative judgements of object size, we rarely make absolute judgements. In contrast, when we reach out to pick up an object, particularly one we have not seen before, our visuomotor system has to compute its size accurately if we are to pick it up efficiently, that is, without fumbling or readjusting

Fig. 6.6 The maximum aperture between the index finger and thumb on trials in which subjects reached to one of the target discs under the two different conditions illustrated in Fig. 6.5. As the two bars on the right-hand side of the graph illustrate, even when subjects perceived the two different discs as identical, they continued to scale their grip appropriately, opening their hand significantly wider for the slightly larger of the two discs. As the bars on the left-hand side of the graph illustrate, the same veridical scaling was observed in trials in which the two target discs were the same size, either both the standard size or both slightly larger.

our grip. It is not enough to know that the target object is larger or smaller than neighbouring objects; the visuomotor systems controlling hand aperture must compute its absolute size. For this reason, one might expect grip scaling to be refractory to sizecontrast illusions and, indeed, to other size illusions.

A discussion of the possible causes of the Titchener illusion is not necessary here, though several ideas have been suggested. One hypothesis is that some sort of image-distance equation is contributing to the illusion, such that the array of smaller circles is 'assumed' by the perceptual system to be more distant than the array of larger circles; as a consequence, the target circle within the array of smaller circles will also be perceived as more distant (and therefore larger) than the target circle of equivalent retinal image size within the array of larger circles. In other words, the illusion may be simply a consequence of the perceptual system's attempt to make size constancy judgements on the basis of an analysis of the entire visual array. Mechanisms such as these, in which the relations between objects in the visual array play a crucial role in scene interpretation, are clearly central to perception and on our model likely to be associated with the ventral stream. In contrast, the execution of a goal-directed act such as prehension depends on size computations that can be restricted to the target itself. Moreover, the visual mechanisms underlying the control of the grasping movements must compute the true distance of the object (presumably on the basis of reliable cues such as stereopsis and retinal motion). As a consequence, computation of the retinal image size of the object coupled with an accurate estimate of distance will deliver the true size of the object for calibrating the grip.

6.5 **Grasping remembered objects**

There may well be many other examples where, despite visual illusions affecting size perception, actions based upon the size of the stimuli are unaffected. But not all actions dependent upon visual size information will be immune to the influences of the perceptual system. For example, there is evidence that grasping movements directed toward remembered objects are very different from those directed towards visible objects. Thus, work by Goodale *et al.* (1994*a*) has shown that the imposition of a delay of only 2 s between object viewing and movement execution produces a dramatic alteration in the kinematics of the grasp. As Fig. 6.7 illustrates, not only were movements to the remembered object slower than movements made to an object that was still present, but the path followed by the hand was more curvilinear, rising higher above the surface on which the object had been presented. Subjects also showed 'abnormal' pre-shaping of the hand in-flight during reaches directed at remembered objects. When subjects attempt to grasp an object that is presented to them without the interposition of a delay, the opening of the hand invariably exceeds the width of the object at some point during the movement, reaching maximum aperture approximately 70 per cent of the way through the movement (Jakobson and Goodale 1991). As the action reaches completion, however, the aperture is reduced prior to the hand closing on the object. This pattern of hand opening and closing produces a prominent peak in the grip-aperture profile. In contrast to this normal pattern, when a 2 s delay was introduced between object viewing and movement execution, subjects typically adopted a smaller, fixed grip aperture and maintained this hand posture until the movement was completed (Goodale *et al.* 1994*a*).

Taken together, these results suggest that normal visuomotor programs were not being implemented when grasping movements were made in the delay condition. Indeed, both the appearance of the movements in this condition (in which the object was no longer present) and the reports of the subjects

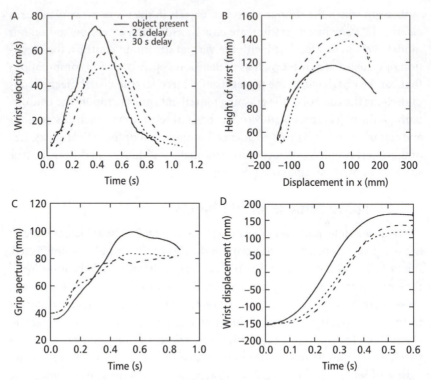

Fig. 6.7 Representative plots showing various kinematics of grasping movements made to 'present' versus 'remembered' objects. (A) Velocity profiles of wrist. (B) Path of wrist above table surface. (C) Grip aperture measured between index finger and thumb. (D) Displacement of wrist along table towards object or remembered object location. Reaches made to remembered objects (broken lines) look very different from reaches made to objects that are still present. Yet there is little difference between reaches to remembered objects after a 2 or a 30 s delay. Adapted from Goodale *et al.* (1994a).

themselves suggested that such actions might be best characterized as 'pantomimed' rather than as simply delayed. As Goodale *et al.* (1994a) have proposed, subjects may have been extracting the information needed to scale their grasp from a stored percept of the object rather than from the visual information provided by the usual on-line visuomotor networks (or stored parameters derived from this information). In other words, they may have been using stored representations of the object provided by the ventral stream in default of visual information being available directly to the visuomotor networks in the dorsal stream which normally control goal-directed actions.

Support for the idea that the programming of these delayed or pantomimed reaches depends on information derived from earlier perceptions of the goal object rather than stored visuomotor parameters comes from the performance of the patient D.F. on the delay task. As we indicated in Chapter 5, despite the fact that this patient has a profound visual form agnosia, she grasps objects of different sizes, orientation, and shape without difficulty—objects that she cannot identify, describe, or even tell apart. Although she is unable to indicate the size of an object, either verbally or manually, the aperture of her grasp is well scaled to the size of that object when she is asked to pick it up. As far as can be seen, her visuomotor behaviour appears quite normal. But as briefly mentioned in Chapter 5, when D.F. was tested in the delay condition, a deficit was suddenly revealed. Even after a delay of just 2 s, she appeared to have 'lost' all information about object size needed to pre-shape her hand in flight (see Fig. 5.9, p. 138). This result is readily explained in the context of the argument outlined above. If D.F. had no percept of the object in the first place, we assume that after a delay she could not fall back on the kind of stored information about object size that would be available to normal subjects. Thus, when no object was present to drive her visuomotor control systems in 'real time', there would be no visual guidance of her performance at all.

Additional evidence that D.F.'s difficulty is clue to an initial failure in her perception of the object comes from experiments in which she was asked to pretend to pick up familiar objects of known size, such as a hazelnut, a table tennis ball, and a grapefruit. Here, where she could presumably call upon her general knowledge and her long-term memory of objects, she showed appropriate scaling of her grip aperture as a function of the size of the imagined object. Thus, D.F.'s difficulty in the delay task, where blocks of varying size were presented randomly, was not a difficulty with pantomime *per se*, but instead reflects her profound inability to construct enduring percepts of object features directly from the sensory array in a 'bottom-up' manner.

We have argued that unlike D.F., normal subjects were able to bridge the 2 s delay by relying on stored perception-based representations of the object. Indeed, for the systems underlying visual learning and recognition, which presumably rely on these perceptual representations, a retention interval of 2 s is trivial. Clearly, we are capable of remembering the characteristics of objects we have seen only once for extremely long periods of time. Moreover, as we have outlined in Chapter 2, there are many visual units in the ventral stream and associated areas that show long-term changes in their response characteristics as a function of earlier exposure to the visual stimuli to which they are responsive. As we have argued in this chapter, however, the visuomotor networks controlling actions such as grasping appear to operate in real time with little or no memory.

This is not to suggest that memory about objects does not influence motor behaviour or that memory is not used to optimize motor performance. After all, we can and do use information about objects, such as their function, weight, fragility, temperature, and friction coefficients, in planning movements directed at those objects (for example, Johansson 1991). In addition, we all know that our performance of many motor skills improves with practice. Yet when we perform an action, however well rehearsed and informed we might be about the intrinsic characteristics of the goal object, we still must compute the instantaneous egocentric coordinates and local orientation of the target object to execute that action. Here we cannot rely on memory, because, of course, the precise position of the object with respect to our own body coordinates can vary enormously from one occasion to the next. For this reason, it would not be useful to store such coordinates (or the resulting motor programs) for more than a brief period (certainly less than 2 s) before executing the action. Instead, visuomotor systems would be expected to update motor programmes quickly on the basis of new visual information. The rapid decay of the egocentrically coded information underlying goal-directed actions such as saccadic eye movements, pointing, and grasping would be expected to be reflected in the response characteristics of visual units in the dorsal stream that are presumed to play a critical role in the production of these actions (see Chapter 2).

6.6 Differences between perceptual and visuomotor memory

As we indicated in the previous section, while the calibration of grip aperture and other parameters of grasping are computed in real time on each occasion an object is encountered, other aspects of motor programming are influenced by experience and, thus, must rely on some form of mnemonic representation of the goal object and its intrinsic characteristics. But even here, the nature of these representations may be very different from those contributing to the perception of the objects. One example of how experience can generate different long-term representations for perception and action comes from work on the programming of grip force when picking up objects. In an impressive series of experiments, Johansson, Gordon, and their colleagues (e.g. Gordon *et al.* 1991 *a, b*) have shown that previous experience with an object can affect the manipulative forces that are applied to that object during the execution of a precision grip. What is more surprising is that the forces used to grip and lift novel objects are scaled to the size of the objects (Gordon *et al.* 1991 *a, b*). Moreover, the fact that these forces are generated as soon as contact is made with the goal object must mean that their calibration is determined by the visual features of the object rather than on the basis of somatosensory feedback. This suggests that visual information about the target object may access stored internal knowledge of the 'normal' relationship between physical properties of objects such as size and weight, information that would be important in specifying the parameters of manipulative actions directed at unfamiliar objects (Johansson 1991).

When the expected relationship between size and weight is violated by using objects of the same weight but different sizes (see Fig. 6.8), subjects continue to scale their grip and load forces according to the visual appearance of the object and not its weight, even after many trials (Gordon *et al.* 1991 *a, b*). But despite the fact that subjects apply the least amount of force when lifting the smallest box in a series, they report that the smallest box feels heavier than the larger ones. In other words, the subjects show the familiar size–weight illusion in which the smallest of a series of objects of the same weight is typically perceived as heavier than the other members of the series (while, conversely, the largest object is perceived as the lightest). Thus, it could not be the subject's perception of the object's weight that determines the calibration of the grip and lift forces, since if that were the case, they should apply the largest forces to pick up the smallest box and the smallest forces to pick up the largest one.

Clearly, subjects must be continuing to rely on some sort of algorithm or internal model about the relationship between size and weight, rather than on their conscious perception of the weight of the different objects. In fact, their reliance on such a stored model might offer a convenient explanation for the generation of the size–weight illusion itself. If the visuomotor systems controlling prehension generate the forces for grasping and lifting an object on this basis, then the discrepancy between perceived size and the apparent difficulty in lifting small as opposed to large objects (of equal weight) might create the illusion of greater weight in the smaller object. In any case, it appears that the relatively long-term internal model of object size–weight relations that sets grip and lift forces on the basis of visual information is not influenced by normal perceptual judgements about object weight.

6.7 Perceptual stability and postural adjustment

Other visuomotor systems in human beings also seem to operate independently of perceptual phenomenology. A clear example of such a dissociation can be seen in the normal postural adjustments made by a standing subject to the small shifts in the visual array that occur as the body moves slightly with respect to the world. To study this phenomenon, Lee and Lishman (1975) had

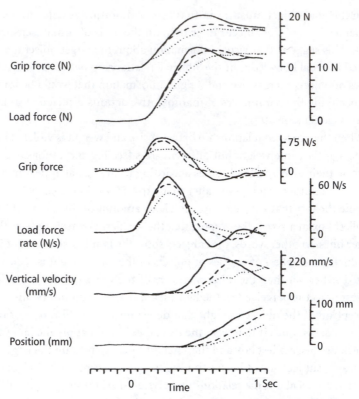

Fig. 6.8 Picking up boxes of different sizes but identical weights. The mean grip force, load force, grip force rate, load force rate, vertical velocity, and vertical position are shown as a function of time for each box size. The three boxes were all picked up by means of a force transducer attached to the top surface of the box. The results with the large box are indicated by a solid line, the medium box by a dashed line, and the small box by a dotted line. Adapted from Gordon *et al.* (1991*a*).

subjects stand in a room which was in fact suspended from the ceiling of a larger room and as a consequence could be gently oscillated back and forth while the subjects stood on the unmoving floor of the larger room (Fig. 6.9). Although subjects were not aware that the room was swaying back and forth, they invariably made postural adjustments commensurate with the oscillations of the room. Moreover, they did not realize that they were swaying. Of course, we make such postural adjustments with respect to the visual array all the time and for the most part remain quite unaware that we are making them. Only when we attempt to maintain a difficult posture (such as standing on one leg) with our eyes closed do we even appreciate the contribution that vision makes to the maintenance of an upright stance.

Fig. 6.9 Schematic drawing of apparatus used in 'moving room' experiments by Lee and Lishman (1975). The subject stands on a fixed floor within a small moveable room that is suspended from the ceiling of a larger fixed room. When the suspended room is moved back and forth a few centimetres, the subject adjusts his posture accordingly (presumably on the basis of the visual flow field generated by the moving room). Although subjects show postural sway, they typically remain unaware that the room is being moved back and forth.

6.8 Distance judgements and the calibration of locomotion

Our perception of real distance in the spatial array beyond our extrapersonal space is rarely as veridical as the calibration of motoric output directed at targets in that array. In a recent series of experiments, Loomis *et al.* (1992) showed that when subjects standing in an open field were required to match the distance between two markers placed in depth on the ground some distance in front of them, they made systematic and large errors in their estimates. Similar kinds of distortions in the perception of distance in extrapersonal space have been observed by other investigators (Wagner 1985; Toye 1986). Nevertheless, when the same subjects were required to walk with their eyes closed toward targets placed at the same distances, they were quite accurate. In other words, 'the distortion in the mapping from physical to visual space evident in the matching task does not manifest itself in the visually open-loop tasks' (Loomis *et al.* 1992, p. 906). Yet again, it seems that our visuomotor systems are much less easily fooled than our perceptual systems and these data provide still further evidence for separately coded representations of spatial location for perception and for action.

6.9 **Conclusions**

The evidence summarized in this chapter is far from an exhaustive review of relevant studies on normal subjects. Furthermore, it is likely that many new dissociations will be discovered in visual experiments in the future, for example, when the many patterns that give rise to visual illusions are examined in the context of manual or ocular actions carried out directly upon them. The flavour of such dissociations, has, however, been conveyed by the examples we have given. The intrinsic interest of these demonstrations, in most cases, has been that they highlight surprising instances where what we think we 'see' is not what guides our actions. In all cases, these apparent paradoxes provide direct evidence for the operation of visual processing systems of which we are unaware, but which can control our behaviour. They therefore provide powerful evidence for the parallel operation, within our everyday life, of two types of visual processing system, each apparently designed to serve quite different purposes and each characterized by quite different properties.

This inference has been acknowledged by various investigators in relation to the particular phenomena they have described, but it has not been generalized by them to arrive at the broader conclusion that underlies the thesis of this book. For example, we consider that the dissociations between the perception of position and the visual control of ocular saccades exemplified by the work of Goodale *et al.* (1986) are not just interesting oddities in the workings of the oculomotor system. Rather they point to the more general separation of the visual computations that lead to perception and those that guide action. We would like to argue that a perspective based upon neuropsychology and single-neurone electrophysiology can lead us to a more satisfying integration of these various dissociations in the visual science literature than is apparent from studying them in isolation. Such a perspective leads one not only to a hypothesis about a broad separation between two types of visual coding in the brain, but further offers a strong hypothesis as to the neural embodiment of that separation.

Of course one may consciously perceive many features of an object at the very same time as one examines it, reaches for it, or manipulates it. The studies in this chapter support our contention, however, that such perceptual processing is quite independent of the visual processing that actually governs those actions. Once this counterintuitive conclusion has been reached, one can begin to ask detailed questions as to what are the critical visual characteristics involved in the guidance of different actions. The anatomy and physiology of the two streams of cortical visual processing would lead to certain general expectations in this regard: in particular it would be predicted that only subsets of the information available to the ventral stream would be used by dorsal visuomotor systems. Thus, cues such as colour, texture gradients, specularities, shading, shadow, and transparency, which are all important elements in perception, may not affect the programming parameters and on-line control of actions directed at novel objects at all. While, for instance, one may see that a book is blue when reaching for it, the pathways concerned with organizing the reach and grasp movements need to 'know'—and are probably 'told'—nothing of that.

Studies of agnosic patients such as those on D.F. described in the previous chapter should provide strong pointers to what cues are in fact available to these dorsal systems. Physiological and behavioural considerations would lead to the expectation that cues such as optic-flow fields, object boundaries, retinal image size, and retinal disparity (and a variety of other distance cues) might be expected to be critical. Of course, in a less direct fashion, even 'ventral' cues such as colour can affect the ways in which we interact with the world. Such cues might invoke stored information about the nature of an object (via the ventral stream) which could help to determine the action programs initiated with respect to the object. But the on-line visual transactions guiding the action itself would probably not be open to such influences. In the final chapter, we will ask how the dorsal and ventral streams may interact with each other. We will also discuss the question of the relation of the two streams to phenomena of visual awareness and explore how they may relate to attentional phenomena.

Chapter 7

Attention, consciousness, and the coordination of behaviour

In the preceding chapters, we have reviewed a broad range of evidence which we believe converges on the idea that the division of labour between the ventral and dorsal streams of visual processing is best summarized as a distinction between coding for perception and coding for action. Although this account of cortical visual processing helps to integrate a number of disparate observations ranging from monkey electrophysiology to normal human behaviour, many questions remain unanswered. What, for example, is the internal functional organization of each of these streams? How do the two streams interact in the production of integrated patterns of behaviour? How do the phenomena of visual attention and consciousness map onto the two streams? And how does the puzzling syndrome of hemispatial neglect fit into this account of cortical visual processing?

At present there is little hard information that bears directly on these questions. Outlined below, however, are some tentative suggestions as to how they might be addressed in the future.

7.1 Streams within streams

In making the distinction between two broad categories of visual coding—one for perception and one for action—we recognize that within each of the streams of processing identified with these functions there are further subdivisions. Thus, as we indicated in Chapters 2 and 4, there appear to be quasi-separate systems or modules for the visual control of different actions, such as saccadic eye movements, reaching, grasping, ocular pursuit, and so on. Within the dorsal stream, it is likely that the various visuomotor transformations that contribute to the control of these different movements work to some extent within different egocentric coordinate systems. Thus, the control of saccadic eye movements could often be achieved through retinocentric coordinates, while the control of reaching is more likely to use head- or body-centred coordinates. There is considerable debate, however, about how these different coordinate systems are constructed and how they are used in the production of different actions (see Chapter 2, Section 2.4.2.2).

While there is also evidence for functional modularity in the ventral system, the distinctions appear to be based, not directly on the requirements of the ultimate motor outputs, but rather on the requirements of the different cognitive operations that need to precede such activities as social interaction, spatial navigation, and planning for action. Thus, for example, the subtle intraclass discriminations that are required for the recognition of faces and facial expressions may depend on coding strategies and mechanisms that are different and separate from those underlying broader interclass distinctions between different kinds of objects. While there is good electrophysiological and neuropsychological evidence to support the idea of modularity in the ventral stream (see Chapters 2 and 5), the taxonomy of these perceptual modules and their interrelations, particularly in the human brain, are not yet known. Thus, unlike the dorsal stream where it may be easier to see how different actions might demand different kinds of transformations of visual information, the underlying principles of modularity in the ventral stream remain to be elucidated.

But despite the fact that both streams appear to contain functional subdivisions, it is clear that each stream operates in an internally coordinated fashion. For example, when a monkey reaches out and grasps a moving insect, there must be a concerted action of several modules within the dorsal stream, permitting the monkey to saccade, to fixate and track the prey, and then reach out and finally grasp it. Similarly, the ventral stream appears to act in a concerted fashion in that different stimulus features (shape, colour, motion, etc.) are combined or bound together to yield a single integrated percept of an object, organism, or scene. It is possible that processes of selective attention play a major role in achieving this apparent internal orchestration within each of the two streams and even perhaps in interrelating the activity of the two streams to one another. It is to a consideration of such mechanisms that we now turn.

7.2 **Attention**

7.2.1 **Attention and consciousness**

The sensory systems of animals are bombarded every moment with a vast number of different stimuli, only some of which are of relevance to them. Therefore, to use the metaphor made famous by the late Donald Broadbent (1958), this massive amount of potential sensory information has to be somehow filtered if it is to be dealt with effectively and economically. That is, animals have to 'attend' to some stimuli and 'ignore' others. All organisms have this problem to face: even a lowly vertebrate such as the frog has to be able to exercise selective attention. This phenomenon has in fact been experimentally demonstrated: Ingle (1975) discovered that a frog is much more likely to snap at a potential prey object when the target location is 'primed' by a previous stimulus at that location. Evidently the effect of the prime was to attract the frog's attention to the primed location, since primes elsewhere were ineffective. The criterion for the successful operation of selective attention in this case is simply the more efficient detection of the target. In other words, in invoking the operation of selective attention we are not implying that the frog is conscious of the stimulus to which it attends (if indeed the frog is ever conscious of anything).

In discussions of human attention, however, the assumption tends to be made that attention and consciousness are inextricably linked. In the famous words of William James (1890),

> 'My experience is what I agree to attend to. . . . Every one knows what attention is. It is the taking possession by the mind, in clear and vivid form, of one out of what seem several simultaneously possible objects or trains of thought. Focalization, concentration, of consciousness are of its essence. It implies withdrawal from some things in order to deal effectively with others . . .' (pp. 402–3.)

We will discuss the linkage of attention with awareness later. However, James's (1890) conceptualization is important also because it introduces two aspects that have guided psychological research on attention over the past century. We have already mentioned the 'negative' function of attention in serving to cut down the vast array of sensory information that bombards the organism. But James (1890) also argues that this filtering has to be associated with a positive property of attention, whereby the 'important' information is somehow intensified or amplified so as to facilitate action or perception. In other words, selective attention has both 'costs' and 'benefits' (Posner 1980).

In Ingle's (1975) priming experiments with frogs, the index of selective attention was an overt movement by the frog. However, the actual 'switching' of attention to the primed location was not itself accompanied by overt movements. Indeed, the absence of such overt orienting movements on the part of a predator will presumably have a biological advantage in promoting successful prey catching. (Reciprocally, the ability of the prey animal itself to engage in such covert orienting, thus not drawing attention to itself, may be equally effective in the avoidance of predation.) A priming paradigm analogous to that used by Ingle (1975) to demonstrate covert orienting in frogs was devised for studying selective attention in humans by Posner *et al.* (1980) and variations of the 'Posner paradigm' have been used in a large number of studies of visual spatial attention over the past 20 years. The usual form of the task is to precede a target stimulus, which can appear on either the left or the right side of the screen, by either a 'valid' cue, presented at the target location, or by an 'invalid' cue, at an equivalent location on the other side. The valid prime causes the subject to make a more efficient (that is, rapid) target detection response than the invalid prime, which may indeed slow responding by comparison with a neutral cueing condition. Thus, the costs and benefits of selective attention can be readily measured in this paradigm. Recently, the technique has also been successfully applied in research with monkeys (Petersen *et al.* 1987; Bowman *et al.* 1993). In humans, the Posner paradigm or variations of it have been used with neurological populations (Posner *et al.* 1982; Morrow and Ratcliff 1988*b*) as well as in many investigations of normal subjects. It has been shown, for example, that invalid cueing of a target presented in the contralesional visual hemifield causes severe detection difficulties in patients with dorsal lesions of the parietal lobe, particularly at short cue–target intervals (Posner *et al.* 1984). As Posner *et al.* (1984) point out, this deficit resembles the 'visual extinction' observed in these same patients when presented with two stimuli simultaneously in clinical testing. This phenomenon will be considered in a later section.

None of these human experiments has addressed the relationship between attention and consciousness directly, though a necessary association is often implicitly assumed by many of the investigators (for example, Posner and Rothbart 1992). But as we have already seen in the frog, such an association is not an essential ingredient in the concept of selective attention. Indeed, the assumption as applied to humans is directly challenged by a simple neuropsychological example. Hemianopic patients who exhibit blindsight are by definition unaware of the targets to which they are able to point efficiently. Yet the efficiency of their behaviour strongly suggests that they are attending to the target. Although priming experiments have not to our knowledge yet been done to confirm this supposition directly, there is indirect evidence for such attentional processes in the 'blind' field. In particular, it has been found that a distracting visual stimulus in the hemianopic field of such a patient can appreciably lengthen the saccadic reaction time to stimuli in the 'good' hemifield (Rafal *et al.* 1990). Interestingly, it was found that key-press reaction times were unaffected in these experiments, prompting the authors to argue that the saccadic effect is mediated by the superior colliculus. Thus, like the intact frog, human patients may be relying largely upon tectal mechanisms in the midbrain when directing selective visual attention to target stimuli in their 'unaware' visual hemifield.

If this argument is correct, then what makes visual attention in a scotoma different from the more usual case, where as James (1890) put it, 'my experience is what I attend to'? That is, why should it be that some forms of attention are not associated with awareness? We would suggest that the answer to this question lies in the idea that there is more than one substrate supporting selective visual attention and that only one of these substrates is linked with conscious experience. In particular, we would propose that attentional mechanisms associated with the ventral stream are critical in determining visual awareness of objects and events in the world. Yet at the same time, we believe that there are also selective attentional mechanisms in the dorsal stream (and its associated subcortical structures such as the superior colliculus) that are not obligatorily linked to awareness. In the blindsight example, the argument would be that when the patient points to a target in his blind field, that target must have been 'selected' by attentional mechanisms in the dorsal stream (and/or associated subcortical structures) so that the appropriate visuomotor transformations could be facilitated. But since in most blindsight patients the target stimulus would have no access to mechanisms in the ventral stream, perceptual or attentional, no visual awareness of the target would be possible.

Of course, sometimes the brain damage causing hemianopia is so well-limited to area V1 that early dorsal-stream areas such as MT could remain intact and convey information received from the visual midbrain to an equally intact ventral stream, thus allowing some preserved visual awareness. This is illustrated in the report by Barbur *et al.* (1993), who found that under some test conditions not only did their patient G. Y. retain conscious motion perception, but also that moving stimuli activated his area MT much as normal (see Chapter 3). These observations seem to show that visual awareness does not depend critically on area V1, a conclusion reached on different grounds by Crick and Koch (1995). We assume that a selective visual activation of the ventral stream is possible in patients like G.Y., and that under attentive conditions this activation will be associated with awareness within that same restricted visual domain.

As we discuss later, a polysensory area located in the human inferior parietal region, outside the ventral and dorsal streams as defined in the monkey, may also be linked to visual awareness. We proposed in Chapter 4 that this region may have a supramodal role in spatial processing, in large part through an intimate association with the ventral stream; if this is correct, then an association of this area with visual awareness may well arise through prior ventral processing. First, however, we will review some electrophysiological evidence that supports the existence of multiple separate attentional systems.

7.2.2 **Physiological studies of visual attention**

7.2.2.1 The dorsal stream

The first physiological experiments to explore the neuronal basis of attention had to await the development of techniques for recording from single neurones in awake animals. It was by the use of such techniques that it was discovered over 20 years ago that neurones in the monkey superior colliculus are susceptible to attentional effects. Goldberg and Wurtz (1972) showed that although a typical cell in the superficial layers of this structure would respond to a visual stimulus flashed in its receptive field, the responses were greatly enhanced when the stimulus was relevant to the animal (Fig. 7.1). In the task used, the monkeys had been trained to switch their gaze to any new spot of light and the enhancement of the cell's activity was observed prior to the onset of the saccade. If the monkey looked elsewhere than at the relevant stimulus, however, no enhancement occurred. Since those early experiments, similar effects have been discovered in the frontal eye fields, the posterior parietal cortex, and the pulvinar nucleus (see Wurtz et al. 1980a), but not in many other visual areas such as the primary visual cortex.

The same group of investigators went on to see whether a covert switch of attention (that is, without any saccadic eye movement, as in the Posner paradigm), might be reflected in a similar enhancement effect in visual neurones. In these experiments, the monkey's task was to respond to the receptive-field stimulus only by touching it or by pressing a key, while keeping the gaze fixed centrally. No enhancement was observed in superior collicular or frontal eye-field neurones under these circumstances (Wurtz and Mohler 1976; Goldberg and Bushnell 1981). Cells were found in the posterior parietal cortex (Bushnell et al. 1981) and subsequently in part of the pulvinar (area Pdm: Petersen et al. 1985), however, that did show enhancement during such 'covert' visual orienting. Thus, it was inferred that the superior colliculus and frontal eye fields may be specifically associated with switches of attention associated with gaze shifts, while posterior parietal (area 7a) neurones also appear to be implicated in shifts of attention occurring independently of gaze. There is additional evidence that some visual cells in area 7a (Mountcastle et al. 1981), as well as in the superior colliculus (Munoz and Wurtz 1993), show augmented responses during attentive fixation. Thus, there is evidence for facilitatory effects in the posterior parietal cortex associated with selective visual attention in relation to reaching behaviour, saccadic behaviour, and ocular fixation. These results may parallel the range of other evidence we noted in Chapters 2 and 4, that implicates the posterior parietal cortex in the visuomotor control of all of these behaviours.

Fig. 7.1 Enhancement of visual responses in cortical neurones. In each of these experiments, neuronal activity was recorded during the performance by the monkey of three different tasks, on each of which it had been prevously trained. In the fixation task, a spot of light was presented within the receptive field of the neurone on each test trial while the monkey maintained its gaze on a central fixation light. In the saccade task, a spot of light again appeared in the receptive field of the cell on each trial, but this time the monkey responded to its appearance by making an eye movement to the peripheral stimulus. In the 'peripheral attention' task, the monkey maintained central fixation, but on half the trials would be required to respond to the peripheral light by releasing a response key. The displays on the left illustrate that the visual responses of posterior parietal neurones are typically enhanced prior to either a saccade or a manual response, relative to the fixation condition. In contrast, cells in the frontal eye field show enhancement only prior to a saccade to the receptive-field stimulus. The raster displays show neuronal responses on 16 consecutive trials in each case, time locked to the onset of the peripheral stimulus. Reproduced from Goldberg and Colby (1989).

On the basis of this and other physiological and neurobehavioural evidence, Rizzolatti *et al.* (1985, 1994) have proposed a 'premotor' theory of selective spatial attention. According to this account the mechanisms responsible for attention are intrinsic to the spatial coding associated with particular visuomotor systems. In other words, visual attention to a particular part of space is nothing more nor less than the facilitation of particular subsets of neurones involved in the preparation of particular visually guided actions directed at that part of space. Thus, different attentional phenomena will be associated with the activation of visuomotor circuits including the superior colliculus and the various parietofrontal circuits which we described in Chapter 2. Supportive evidence for these ideas comes from a series of experiments from Rizzolatti's laboratory. For example, it has been found that neurones in separate parts of the premotor cortex in the monkey code for near and far egocentric space and are linked, respectively, with ocular and manual movements. Lesions of these areas have been found to produce specific attentional deficits as inferred from failures to make movements to visual stimuli in near and far space, respectively.

Supportive evidence also comes from experiments with human subjects. For example, Sheliga *et al.* (1994) have shown that when a subject is cued to attend to one visual stimulus while making a saccadic eye movement to another, the trajectory of the saccade is curved away from the attended stimulus (Fig. 7.2). This result strongly supports the idea that by the very act of directing spatial attention, one is activating circuits preparatory to executing a saccade in that direction, thus influencing the dynamics of saccades made in other directions. Since the subject is instructed not to look at the attended stimulus, this activation has to be accompanied by a suppression of the incipient eye movement towards it, thus causing the observed curvature of the saccadic eye movement.

Because the fovea and foveation are so important in human and non-human primate behaviour, such partial activation of eye movement systems may play the major role in mediating selective spatial attention (Rizzolatti *et al.* 1994). Nevertheless, there is also evidence for specific attentional effects in relation to arm movements. Thus, Tipper *et al.* (1992) have shown that the effect of a distracting visual stimulus on the performance of a pointing movement is dependent on the location of that stimulus with respect to the starting position of the hand. Moreover, when subjects were using their right hand, stimuli to the right of that hand were more distracting than stimuli to the left; the opposite pattern was seen when subjects used their left hand. Taken together, these two behavioural experiments on human subjects provide strong support for Rizzolatti *et al.*'s (1985, 1994) proposal that selective attention mechanisms are intimately associated with particular effector systems.

Evidence that would appear to contradict this idea of action-specific attention, however, comes from the observations by Bushnell *et al.* (1981) mentioned earlier; they found single cells in the posterior parietal cortex whose activity was enhanced prior both to saccades and to hand movements. One could interpret this finding as supporting the hypothesis that many cells in the dorsal stream participate in a superordinate attentional process—one which is not specific to any particular effector system. According to this interpretation, when one region of the visual field is selected, it is selected for all potential response systems equally. But this is not the only possible interpretation of the

Fig. 7.2 Saccadic eye movements made from a central starting point to a square at the top or bottom of a display screen, when the subject's attention was simultaneously called to a stimulus appearing at the left or right side of the screen. A central cue (small line) instructs the subject to attend to one of the three horizontal locations (left, central, or right); an 'imperative' stimulus then occurs either visually at the cued location (calling for an upward saccade) or in the form of a non-lateralized auditory tone (calling for a downward saccade). (A) When the imperative stimulus appears on the left (top panel) the saccades are curved toward the right; when it appears on the right the saccades curve to the left (bottom panel). The difference between these mean saccadic trajectories and the central control condition (shown in the middle panel) is depicted in the small graphs to the right. (B) Comparable results on the auditory trials when the subject was cued but the stimulus did not occur at one side. The curvature effects remain, though they are smaller. Calibration marks indicate 1° of visual angle. Reproduced from Sheliga *et al.* (1994).

finding. As the experiment of Sheliga *et al.* (1994) described above demonstrates, saccade-related mechanisms are active, though suppressed, during 'covert' shifts of spatial attention in humans. Similarly, therefore, when a monkey in Bushnell *et al.*'s (1981) experiment attended to a particular location in space, there would presumably have been enhanced activity in the saccade neurones in area 7a geared to that location, even though superordinate control mechanisms (perhaps in the frontal lobe) prevented the saccade from occurring.

In other words, Bushnell *et al.* could have been recording from purely saccade-related cells and observing enhancement in them irrespective of the task performed by the monkey. The fact that neurones in the superior colliculus and frontal eye field do not show enhanced responses during the 'covert' condition does not contradict this argument. It may simply indicate that these structures are closer to the final motor output pathway, that is, are associated more closely with actual saccadic responses and not merely with the 'intention' to move the eyes.

Alternatively, it is possible that the cells showing enhanced responses during both manual and saccadic response conditions in Bushnell *et al.*'s (1981) experiments were visuomotor cells tied to orienting movements of the head and/or trunk; such movements would form a normal part of an animal's response to a peripheral visual stimulus. However, because the head was kept fixed, as in most physiological experiments of this kind, no such movements could be made. Indeed, Fogassi *et al.* (1992) observed in a comparable experimental situation that when a monkey turned its eyes to a stimulus on one side while the head was fixed, there was a tonic increase in the activity of neck muscles on that same side. Furthermore, stimulation of premotor area F4 (associated with visually guided reaching; see Chapter 4) causes neck movements but not eye movements (Gentilucci *et al.* 1988) and this area is anatomically linked to areas VIP and 7b in the parietal lobe. Thus, enhanced activity in many of the posterior parietal cells studied by Bushnell *et al.* (1981) could have been, under normal circumstances, preparatory to movements of the monkey's head and trunk. We would certainly predict, on the basis of the role we have proposed for the posterior parietal cortex, that cells related to visually elicited movements of the head and trunk will be found to exist there.

We argued in Chapter 4 that the comparable part of the human parietal cortex to the posterior parietal cortex in the monkey lies superiorly, in the region of the intraparietal sulcus. As we saw, damage in this superior parietal region causes various visuomotor disorders, including optic ataxia. It is therefore interesting that attentional modulation effects can be observed in approximately the same region in human subjects. Corbetta *et al.* (1993) have shown in a PET study that cerebral blood flow selectively increases in this location in association with selective visuospatial attention; thus their findings are directly parallel to those in the physiological recording study of Bushnell *et al.* (1981) using monkeys. Moreover, as we discuss later in this chapter, Posner *et al.* (1984) found that the parietal-lesioned patients who showed the greatest disruption in shifting attention to the contralateral visual field in a covert orienting task had most damage to this same superior region. In summary, then, in both monkeys and humans, a single parietal region appears to be intimately involved in both the visual control of action and in 'covert' attentional shifts to detect simple visual stimuli. In other words, this superior parietal region in humans may be taken as the homologue of area 7a in the monkey not only in relation to visuomotor function, but also in its participation in mediating spatial attention.

7.2.2.2 The ventral stream

However, areas within the monkey's dorsal stream or associated with it are not the only ones to show attentional modulation of neuronal activity. Cells in the ventral stream also show such effects. Fischer and Boch (1981), for example, found cells in area V4 which showed saccadic enhancement, and evidence for attentional effects in both areas V4 and IT has been reported in the context of discrimination learning and matching tasks (for example, Moran and Desimone 1985; Chelazzi *et al.* 1993). For example, Moran and Desimone (1985) monitored cells which had previously been found to be selective for shape and/or colour. The response magnitude of many cells to the preferred stimulus depended on whether the monkey was attending to it or not, even though this stimulus was present within the receptive field in either case. That is, if the discrimination task required the monkey to attend to the place in the receptive field where the cell's preferred stimulus was presented, the response of the cell was greater than when the animal had to attend elsewhere within the receptive field. Like the enhancement effects in the posterior parietal cortex, this attentional modulation in the ventral stream is spatial in nature. The major difference seems to be that an inferotemporal cell is selective for a particular stimulus in the attended place, whereas a posterior parietal cell is typically selective for a response to the attended place.

The neuronal gating discovered by Moran and Desimone (1985) seems to involve an active inhibition of unattended locations rather than a facilitation of attended ones (see also Desimone and Moran 1985). Similar suppressive effects on the activity in inferotemporal neurones, in this case produced by a neutral stimulus which was presented while the monkey attended to a discriminative stimulus, have been reported by Sato (1988). It seems likely that these gating effects in the ventral stream operate upon highly processed visual information. This would allow the learned significance of a stimulus to play a role in the selection process and would also open the way for spatial attention to select among different parts of an object whole.

More recently, effects similar to those of Moran and Desimone (1985) have been reported by Motter (1993) in V1 and V2, as well as in V4; again the effects were dependent upon the presence of competing 'distractor' stimuli. These then are all examples of the 'filtering' of irrelevant stimuli (what James (1890) called 'withdrawal from some things in order to deal effectively with others') rather than the facilitated processing of relevant ones, as seen in enhancement. But probably both positive and negative effects will ultimately be found to operate within any brain system where selective processing is required. Certainly inhibitory effects on the activity of superior colliculus neurones can be observed when stimuli are presented outside the receptive field, in both cats (Rizzolatti et al. 1974) and monkeys (Wurtz et al. 1980b), complementary to the facilitatory phenomena of enhancement described in such cells in the monkey (Goldberg and Wurtz 1972). Likewise, such inhibitory effects are also seen in the equivalent of the dorsal visual stream in the cat's cortex (Rizzolatti and Camarda 1977). These complementary processes may be needed for 'sharpening' the activities of visual processing networks throughout the brain.

7.2.2.3 Summary

We have seen then that networks of cells in both ventral and dorsal systems appear to participate in spatial attention. Indeed, it is likely that attentional processes are at work in many different brain regions. Within the dorsal stream and associated premotor and collicular structures, Rizzolatti and his co-workers (1985, 1994) have argued that a multiplicity of spatial attention mechanisms exist, each associated with an independent representation of egocentric space. We agree with this formulation of spatial attention for the visuomotor domain. We believe, however, that there are also mechanisms of selective attention operating in the ventral stream to facilitate perceptual analysis of objects in the visual array, working alongside those in the dorsal stream which facilitate particular actions directed at those objects. In both streams, there will be a need to segregate and intensify the visual processing of particular objects, though this spatial attention will operate to achieve different ends (cf. Allport 1993).

How then does damage to one or the other stream affect visual attention? There is no clear-cut answer to this question. There are, however, two well-known deficits which are commonly thought to reflect disorders of spatial attention: hemispatial neglect (or unilateral spatial neglect) and extinction. We will now briefly describe these disorders and consider how they might relate to the attentional systems we have postulated.

7.3 The 'neglect syndrome'

7.3.1 Hemispatial neglect

Hemispatial neglect is not an uncommon disorder following damage to areas around the human inferior parietal lobe and parietotemporal border, especially in the right hemisphere (Vallar and Perani 1986; Vallar 1993; see Chapter 4, in particular Section 4.3.1). A patient with this disorder may deny awareness of stimuli on the left side of space even when able to look at them and indeed even sometimes when tracing through them with a finger (Bisiach and Rusconi 1990). Neglect patients also typically fail to find leftwardly located target items in a search task and in real life may ignore potentially important stimuli in the left half of their environment.

Hemispatial neglect is a complex topic on which we cannot dwell at length here and readers interested in more detailed treatments of the subject must be referred elsewhere (Jeannerod 1987; Robertson and Marshall 1993). Some discussion is necessary, however, because it has been frequently assumed that the role of the posterior parietal cortex in spatial attention in the monkey (inferred mainly from electrophysiological studies) can be directly related to the occurrence of neglect following parietal damage in man. That is, several authors have started from the plausible assumption that human hemispatial neglect following posterior hemispheric lesions is a disorder of attention and have drawn the conclusion that neglect must be a consequence of damage to the parietal end-points of the dorsal visual stream. Clearly these views have to be reexamined in the light of the likely existence of multiple mechanisms of visual attention as outlined above.

A number of authors have argued that a spatial imbalance of attention is present in most cases of neglect (for example, De Renzi 1982; Kinsbourne 1987; De Renzi *et al.* 1989) and there is no doubt that the majority of neglect patients have lesions which include parts of the parietal lobe. There are, however, very good reasons for doubting that it is through a disruption of the dorsal visual stream that these lesions cause neglect. Not the least of these reasons is the fact that it has proved extremely difficult to mimic hemispatial neglect convincingly in monkeys by making unilateral posterior parietal lesions (see Milner 1987). This species difference cannot be dismissed purely as due to the fact that the monkey brain lacks the functional asymmetry seen in the human; although most human cases of neglect have right hemisphere damage, an appreciable minority of cases have left hemisphere damage (for example, Halligan *et al.* 1991). Indeed it has been argued that the frequency of neglect may be underestimated following comparable left-hemisphere damage because such damage typically causes severe aphasia and the patients are therefore difficult to test. In contrast to the difficulty in demonstrating neglect in monkeys with unilateral parietal lesions, it is relatively easy to produce milder disorders such as extinction, in which one of two stimuli (the one located further towards the contralesional side) tends to be ignored by the animal (for example, Rizzolatti and Camarda 1987). We shall consider the distinction between extinction and neglect in more detail below.

A second major reason for doubting the association of neglect with damage to the dorsal stream is the observation alluded to earlier that a range of evidence converges on the conclusion that the human dorsal stream terminates in the superior parietal lobe, not in the inferior part. In particular, monkey evidence associates the visual guidance of reaching, grasping, and eye movements with the dorsal stream, all of these being impaired by lesions of the monkey's posterior parietal lobule. In humans, it is lesions of superior parietal areas that are associated with optic ataxia and disorders of visually guided eye movements (see Chapter 4), strongly suggesting that such damage disrupts the human homologues of monkey dorsal stream mechanisms. In marked contrast to this, the majority of neglect patients have brain damage whose common area of overlap lies in the inferior parietal or parietotemporal region.

A third reason for questioning the identification of neglect with damage to the dorsal stream is provided by recent neuropsychological research on hemispatial neglect patients. Some years ago, Gainotti *et al.* (1986) observed that when asked to copy a picture, some patients with neglect would draw only the rightward parts of the scene, but others would instead draw only the rightward parts of each component object (trees, houses, etc.). That is, patients with hemispatial neglect not only ignore objects on the left side of egocentric space, but may also ignore left-sided parts of objects in other parts of space, at least under certain test conditions. There have been several studies of 'object-based' neglect in recent years (see Robertson and Marshall 1993; Behrmann and Tipper 1994). (Of course, neglect phenomena can never be 'object-centred' in Marr's (1982) sense, because they always relate to left/right as defined with respect to the observer's viewpoint. An object-centred description cannot by definition have a left or a right in this sense. In other words, hemispatial neglect always retains viewer-centred coordinates, even when it relates to an object-based framework.)

We use the term 'object-based' neglect rather loosely here to refer to neglect which does not operate purely in the patient's wider extrapersonal visual space, that is, it cannot be understood except with reference to some prior degree of shape or object processing. Three examples will convey what we mean. The first example is patient number 2 of Marshall and Halligan (1993), who was asked to copy first a drawing of two flowers emerging from a single stem and then two similar flowers side by side, but each with a separate stem (see Fig. 7.3) This patient copied only the right flower in the first case, but drew the right side of both flowers in the second. Evidently this patient's neglect operated differentially according to how he perceptually segmented the picture into separate 'objects'.

Secondly, Driver and Halligan (1991) have shown that a neglect patient may fail to attend to features on the left side of a figure with a clear principal axis, even when that axis is tilted to the right or left, thus in these conditions the patient might now neglect features which fall on the right side of egocentric space.

Finally, a rather different kind of object-based neglect is apparent in the patient K.L. of Young *et al.* (1990), who was selectively impaired at describing, copying, or drawing from memory the left side of a face. This left-sided neglect was mild or absent in relation to other kinds of stimulus patterns and yet was present for faces wherever in the visual field they were presented.

These and many other examples make the point that neglect need not operate within the broad coordinates of egocentric space, but in some cases operates within the internal coordinates of objects or figures (sometimes of a specific type, such as faces) themselves. It need hardly be spelled out that a spatial coding system (in the parietal cortex or anywhere else) that was independent of object identity processing could not be biased in

Fig. 7.3 Drawings produced by a patient with visual hemispatial neglect. (A) The models that the patient was asked to copy. (B) The patient's copies: they show that he omitted left-sided parts of both flowers when they were seen as separate objects, but the whole left-side flower when both were seen as forming a single whole plant. Reproduced from Marshall and Halligan (1993).

any way that would produce object-based neglect. On the contrary, we would suggest that the ventral system must be crucially involved in providing visual representations in these patients and that their symptoms reflect a failure at a higher level where the brain operates upon such representations. The elegant pioneering studies of Bisiach *et al.* (1979, 1981) also pointed to the same conclusion, by showing that the left sides of visual images, whether constructed from short- or long-term memory, may be inadequately processed in neglect patients, just like the left sides of external scenes or objects. It is hard to see how the dorsal stream could provide the raw material for detailed visual imagery and, therefore, lead to imaginal neglect phenomena when disrupted.

Bisiach and his colleagues have repeatedly argued that a representational disorder underlies perceptual neglect (Bisiach and Vallar 1988; Bisiach 1993) and a related theory has been put forward by Rizzolatti and Berti (1990). In essence, these writers propose that what is lost in neglect patients is part of the machinery needed to construct spatially extended representations of the outside world. Of course, they are not claiming that there is a discrete 'scotoma' on the leftward side of the percepts or images of neglect patients but rather that there is a relative lack of neural elements that can represent such leftward regions. As we discussed in Chapter 4, mechanisms may have evolved in the inferior parietal or parietotemporal region of humans for dealing with abstract spatial processing that are simply not available for this purpose in monkeys. These mechanisms may depend on object-based input from the ventral stream and since that stream seems to be better developed in the right hemisphere of most humans (see Chapter 5), these representational systems may themselves be better developed on the right. We suggested in Chapter 4 that this recently evolved system may have as its non-human antecedent such polysensory areas as STP, which lies in the depths of the superior temporal sulcus of the monkey. Cells there have very large receptive fields, most of them including parts of the ipsilateral visual field as well as large parts of the contralateral field (Gross *et al.* 1981). Consequently, unilateral damage would tend to have a graded effect on the ability of such networks to represent spatial arrays; the contralesional side of space would be most affected, but there would be a gradation affecting all parts of the field.

We would suggest that it is through rich interconnections with the ventral stream that activity in these representational networks acquires the associated quality of visual awareness. We would go further and suggest that object-based neglect may be a special case of this representational disorder, perhaps where there is damage which extends beyond the putative suprasensory representational systems in the inferior parietal cortex into the ventral stream itself. In such cases, it may be that damage can affect the representations of objects as well as the representation of their wider spatial distribution. It appears from the work of Desimone and colleagues (Moran and Desimone 1985; Chelazzi *et al.* 1993; see Section 7.2.2.2 above) that spatially selective gating operates in the ventral stream upon highly processed visual information. This gating may allow for selection not only between objects, but also between parts of a single object (seen from a particular egocentric viewpoint). It would only be in the ventral stream, in our view, that attention could interact with identified objects in such a way. The spatial selection that occurs in the ventral stream may serve to enable the observer to attend to identifiable parts of a configuration like a face or a flower, as well as to attend to discrete whole objects within a scene, such as the face or the flower itself. Disruption which has the effect of biasing these selective mechanisms could therefore cause neglect to become 'object-based' as well as 'space-based'.

One consequence of the loss of neurones from a representational network of the kind envisaged here might be that spatial extent or stimulus size on the contralesional side is no longer correctly computed by the brain. This might help to explain the observation that many neglect patients underestimate the length of horizontal lines in their left hemispace by comparison with the right side of space (Gainotti and Tiacci 1971; Milner *et al.* 1993; Milner and Harvey 1995). This misperception of size provides an explanation of the tendency of most patients with hemispatial neglect to bisect a horizontal line to the right of centre. Apparently the subjective midpoint for these patients lies to the right as a result of the leftward segment's being underestimated. As Harvey *et al.* (1995) have shown, however, not all neglect patients show this misperception: bisection errors can in some patients be due instead to a misdirection of the hand (see Section 7.3.3 below).

There has been much controversy as to whether neglect should be regarded as a 'representational' or an 'attentional' disorder. Bisiach (1991*a*, 1993), however, has suggested that these two interpretations are not incompatible with each other and can be regarded as operating at different levels of explanation. In other words, it may be a 'category mistake' (Ryle 1949) to regard the two accounts as being in opposition to each other. After all, at the level of neurophysiology, 'selective attention' probably amounts to no more than one way of describing an uneven distribution of neural activity within a network of cells. In other words, whichever terminology is used, neglect may amount to a biased distribution of neural activity within a representational system.

7.3.2 **Visual extinction**

Many patients with hemispatial neglect also show 'extinction' in one or more sensory modalities. That is, they will report the presence of only one of two stimuli presented simultaneously, 'ignoring' the one on the contralesional side of space. Indeed this symptom often outlasts the more obvious obvious symptoms of hemispatial neglect during the course of a patient's recovery from a stroke. There has therefore been some controversy over whether a qualitative distinction should be maintained between extinction and neglect (for example, De Renzi 1982) or whether extinction should be regarded merely as a mild form of neglect (Rizzolatti and Berti 1990; Bisiach 1991*b*). In other words, although extinction is frequently listed as a component of the 'neglect syndrome' (for example, by Heilman *et al.* 1985*b*), there is disagreement as to whether it has a separate existence within that 'syndrome'.

There have traditionally been two main arguments in favour of regarding extinction as a separate disorder from hemispatial neglect. First, patients have been described who present a double dissociation between the two, that is, as well as extinction occurring without neglect, neglect can occur without extinction (for example, De Renzi *et al.* 1984; Barbieri and De Renzi 1989; Liu *et al.* 1992). This latter is difficult to understand if extinction is merely a mild form of neglect. Second, there is an approximately equal incidence of extinction after left and right brain lesions, while neglect is preponderantly (though not universally) associated with right-hemisphere damage (De Renzi 1982).

While these seem to us to be persuasive arguments, there is now also preliminary anatomical evidence from CT imaging that visual extinction should be treated as a separate entity. As Vallar (1993) has noted, the experimental observations of Posner *et al.* (1984) on visual extinction-like effects in humans were associated with lesions in the superior parts of the posterior parietal lobe, rather than inferior regions. Thus, brain damage in this superior part of the parietal lobe has been found to be associated with both visual extinction and optic ataxia (Perenin and Vighetto 1988), but not with neglect (Vallar and Perani 1986). We would argue that this superior region in man is homologous with the posterior parietal area in the monkey and that damage here in both species, while not producing hemispatial neglect, does produce attentional deficits in the form of extinction, as well as visuomotor deficits. Extinction in sensory modalities other than vision, it should be noted, can occur after damage in a range of other brain regions, many of them concerned with sensorimotor control of different kinds.

We noted earlier that extinction phenomena in both vision and touch have been described by several experimenters following unilateral lesions of the posterior parietal cortex in monkeys (Milner 1987; Lynch and McLaren 1989).

That is, although such monkeys do not show full-blown neglect, they do tend to ignore the contralesional member of a simultaneously presented stimulus pair. Similar phenomena are also seen following lesions made in premotor areas of the frontal lobe in monkeys. Interestingly, there is a dissociation between the types of extinction seen following such premotor lesions. On the one hand, a monkey with a lesion of the frontal eye field (area 8), which receives projections from area LIP, will show extinction in 'extrapersonal' space (for example, Latto and Cowey 1971). On the other hand, following a lesion of area 7b or its frontal target in inferior area 6, extinction is only seen in personal-peripersonal space (Rizzolatti 1983; Rizzolatti *et al.* 1985). Both these parietofrontal circuits form part of the dorsal stream, supporting the idea that attentional phenomena, as well as visuomotor control, have a modular organization within this stream.

We conclude that visual extinction may follow damage to the dorsal system in either man or monkey, even though we have argued that hemispatial neglect itself does not. We therefore agree with De Renzi and his colleagues that extinction should be clearly distinguished from the other phenomena of hemispatial neglect (De Renzi *et al.* 1984; Barbieri and De Renzi 1989). Unlike neglect, extinction seems to us to be more clearly seen as an attentional than a representational disorder. While the cognitive complexity of neglect phenomena makes them difficult to understand in terms of currently known neurophysiology, extinction may be understandable more readily as an imbalance in the activity of dorsal-stream neurones in their known roles in orienting and action-related attention.

In short, extinction could be seen primarily as a failure to orient. Similar failures in orienting can be seen following unilateral lesions of the superior colliculus, in which phenomena apparently identical to extinction can be seen. In fact in many ways the dorsal stream could be seen as a cortical elaboration of the more ancient collicular circuitry. It hardly needs to be emphasized, in contrast, that the known properties of dorsal-stream neurones could not conceivably account for the common failure in neglect patients to report the left-side details of a remembered scene (Bisiach and Luzzatti 1978; Bisiach *et al.* 1981). Nor could they account for a neglect patient's failure to match shapes differing in their left halves when these shapes have never been seen *in toto*, but only piecemeal, moving behind a vertical viewing slit (Bisiach *et al.* 1979).

7.3.3 Directional hypokinesia

Another component of the 'neglect syndrome' that can be dissociated from 'perceptual' or 'representational' forms of hemispatial neglect is so-called 'directional hypokinesia', in which patients appear reluctant to make movements into contralesional space (Heilman *et al.* 1985*a*). This motor reluctance is not due to hemiparesis and, indeed, can be seen when patients use either arm. An important development in the recent literature on neglect has been the demonstration that a motor bias of this kind contributes in varying degrees to the neglect phenomena seen in an appreciable minority of patients (Bisiach *et al.* 1990; Tegnér and Levander 1991; Làdavas *et al.* 1993; Harvey *et al.* 1995). Thus, while most neglect patients may have predominantly representational neglect, others have predominantly motor-related neglect and yet others have a mixture of the two. There is a strong hint that motor-related neglect may be associated with lesions that include frontal and/or subcortical (striatal) damage, while representational neglect is associated with inferior parietal damage (see Vallar 1993). Indeed in one unusual patient with right frontal damage, extreme neglect was manifest in search tasks requiring a cancellation response, but was virtually absent when the patient was simply asked to give verbal judgements about the target stimuli throughout the stimulus array (Bottini *et al.* 1992). There are clear animal analogues of directional hypokinesia after unilateral lesions of various cortical and subcortical areas in monkeys (see Milner 1987). In more refined studies in rats, the medial corpus striatum (Brown and Robbins 1989) and parts of the frontal lobe have been specifically implicated (Brown *et al.* 1991).

In humans, directional hypokinesia is typically the result of right-hemisphere lesions and it can cause motor asymmetries not only in arm movements (Heilman *et al.* 1985*a*; Harvey *et al.* 1994), but also in the initiation of saccadic eye movements (De Renzi *et al.* 1982; Girotti *et al.* 1983). Both the non-modality specific nature of directional hypokinesia and its right-hemisphere association suggest that it is not closely tied to the dorsal stream; instead it seems most likely that it is associated with modulatory systems on the 'output side' of the brain rather than at the visuomotor interface.

7.3.4 Is there a neglect 'syndrome'?

The evidence we have reviewed above suggests that efforts to reduce the complex phenomena of neglect to the disruption of a unitary parietal mechanism of spatial attention are misguided. It is becoming clear that there are a number of separable disorders, only some of which may have direct analogues in animals and which may be amenable to explanation in current physiological terms. As we have argued, hemispatial neglect may be more related to the disruption of mechanisms associated with a polysensory (or suprasensory) representational system in the parietotemporal cortex, an area little developed in non-human primates and whose workings are presently mysterious. In contrast, extinction and directional hypokinesia may follow the disruption of quite different systems, respectively related to the dorsal stream and to motor and premotor areas in the brain.

Many neglect patients, of course, show a combination of the deficits that are dissociable in a minority of patients. The main reason for this is that their lesions are often large, encompassing several brain systems in the posterior cerebral hemisphere and beyond. Indeed, in some cases, neglect patients have lesions extending right through from occipitoparietal to frontal regions. Nevertheless, in cases of more restricted damage, we would make certain predictions. For example, the response modality used in testing for extinction might be expected to determine the detection accuracy. In particular, if the lesion was restricted to superior parietal regions (which we believe are fed by the dorsal-stream pathway), we would expect extinction to be more apparent in the patient's motor output than in perceptual reports. Exactly this result has been found by Bisiach *et al.* (1989): right brain-damaged patients reported the occurrence of a brief contralesional light stimulus significantly less often when they used a manual response than when they responded verbally.

A second expectation, given the intimate association of dorsal-stream structures with motor control, would be that this kind of superior parietal damage should occasionally lead to differential degrees of visual extinction depending on which hand is used to respond to the stimulus. According to this counterintuitive prediction, the extinction should be exhibited more clearly when the contralesional hand is responding than when the ipsilateral hand is used. A phenomenon similar to this has recently been reported by Duhamel and Brouchon (1990), in a reaction-time study on a patient whose lesion included the right superior parietal lobule and who showed severe visual extinction. This patient could initiate a response to a single stimulus light equally quickly in the two hemifields when using the right hand, but showed a significant slowing in the left hemifield when using the left hand. Finally, we would predict a strong statistical association of visual extinction with symptoms of visuomotor impairment in a large sample of right-hemisphere patients. The modularity of the dorsal stream may ensure that extinction is not invariably present in cases of optic ataxia (for example, Levine *et al.* 1978), but still we would expect optic ataxia to be more frequently associated with extinction than with hemispatial neglect.

The essential characteristic of hemispatial neglect is a selective failure of perceptual awareness of incoming stimuli. Therefore, our proposal that the visual aspects of hemispatial neglect may be caused by damage to networks closely related to the ventral stream requires that we specifically address the issue of how that stream might subserve processes of conscious attention and visual awareness.

7.4 **Consciousness and attention**

In developing our account of the functional distinctions between the dorsal and ventral streams in this book, we have invoked from time to time ideas of visual awareness and phenomenology without exploring the implications of using these terms. It is our view that there is a multiplicity of separate or quasi-separate visual processing systems in the human brain, few of which can ever be monitored consciously or reported on verbally. The dissociations between apparently conscious and unconscious visual processes that have been discovered (for example, in blindsight and in visual agnosia), while striking illustrations of this multiplicity, are not in themselves any more important than dissociations between different unconscious visual processes would be. But of course the 'marker' of visual awareness (or reportability) allows one to demonstrate dissociations particularly easily and persuasively (Milner 1992). Furthermore, it has been traditional to vest processes leading to visual phenomenology with special significance and, indeed, to regard them as the final common pathway for the visual system, except perhaps for a few more primitive reflexive mechanisms. In contrast to this traditional view, we have argued at length for an alternative account in which there is no final common pathway for vision. Visual phenomenology, in our view, can arise only from processing in the ventral stream, processing that we have linked with recognition and perception. We have assumed in contrast that visual-processing modules in the dorsal stream, despite the complex computations demanded by their role in the control of action, are not normally available to awareness. Attentional modulation of ventral-stream processing leads to conscious perception; attentional modulation in the dorsal stream leads to action (Milner 1995).

The plausibility of associating awareness with ventral-stream processing derives in large part from observations that patients with blindsight or visual form agnosia cannot offer verbal reports about visual stimuli to which they are nevertheless able to respond non-verbally. But this is not simply due to a disconnection of visual processing from verbal report. In the case of visual form agnosia, for example, there is independent evidence that visual recognition of shape, size, and orientation is lost, whether that recognition is tested using verbal report or whether the patient is asked to make a choice non-verbally. That is, as well as reporting the loss of subjective feelings of familiarity with common shapes, for example, the patient is unable to demonstrate any recognition of different shapes no matter what form of perceptual report is required, including forced-choice responding.

Although D.F. in particular seems to have lost conscious perception of shape, it is perhaps debatable whether or not the dissociation between what she can and cannot do is best captured as 'conscious' versus 'unconscious'. It could be argued that the best available characterization of the dissociations we have observed is one between perceptual report (by whatever means) and visuomotor guidance. In a strict philosophical sense, we are doubtless treading on thin ice in proposing that stimulus processing in the ventral stream is a necessary condition for visual awareness, though we are comfortable with defending the proposal that such processing is a necessary condition for visual perception and recognition. Likewise, while we suspect that the visual processing that goes on in the dorsal stream operates in the absence of awareness, all we can really defend is the contention that one is normally unable to report verbally on the contents of that processing and that it proceeds largely independently of processes of perception and recognition.

Despite these caveats, however, there are reasons why we feel that an association between visual awareness and the operation of the ventral stream is defensible. It is very striking that D.F. makes a strong distinction between what she confidently 'sees' and what she 'guesses' is out there. When her visual responses are successful, they are generally either guided by perceptually experienced object qualities such as colour or fine texture or they are expressed through the medium of visually guided action. We conclude from this pattern of spared abilities and deficits that recognition is rather closely associated with conscious perception, for example D.F. has both recognition and awareness in relation to colour, but she has neither recognition nor awareness in relation to shape. While this argument must necessarily remain tentative, it may be that with the accumulation of other neurological cases where there is a selective loss of different visual qualities, our conjecture that awareness and recognition are closely tied in the functioning of the ventral stream will become progressively strengthened. It is also possible, of course, that such further evidence may only serve to disprove our hypothesis.

As we argued at the end of Chapter 2, the evidence on the visual cortex of rodents suggests that it is dominated by the kinds of visuomotor functions that we have argued to characterize the dorsal stream in primates. It may be that not only did ventral-stream mechanisms for perceptual processing arrive on the scene rather late in mammalian evolution, but also that *ipso facto* so did visual awareness. But for this new departure to be successful, it would need to have remained insulated from interference from the viewer-centred coding elaborated in the dorsal stream. That is, the perceptual constancies intrinsic to many operations within the ventral system would need to be protected from intrusions that could disrupt the continuity of object identities across changing viewpoints and illumination conditions (Goodale and Milner 1992).

7.5 The integrated action of perceptual and visuomotor systems

We saw good evidence in the previous chapter for this quasi-independence of the two visual streams, in a series of demonstrations of contradictory visual processing for perception and action. Yet clearly both systems have to be able to influence behaviour and to do so in a harmonious, non-competitive way. Indeed, efficiently programmed and coordinated behaviour requires that neither the ventral nor the dorsal stream should work in isolation: they should cooperate. It is therefore to be expected that there will be reciprocal cross-connections between areas in the two streams and there is extensive anatomical evidence that this is so (Felleman and Van Essen 1991). Indeed it is even a matter of some debate as to whether certain areas, such as V3A and MT, belong in one stream or the other.

Good examples of the need for cooperative action are in the selection of targets for prehension and in the use of stored object information in the programming of the act of prehension itself. Grasping an object is the end result of a complex interaction of many different brain systems ranging from motivation to praxis. An early part of this process probably involves the transfer of high-level visual information between the two streams. Understanding these interactions would take us some way towards answering what is one of the central questions in modern neuroscience: how is sensory information transformed into purposeful acts?

We have argued that the dorsal stream carries out the necessary computations for efficient on-line control of a grasping movement directed at a goal object. However, a necessary first prerequisite to the execution of that action is the selection of the goal object that is to be addressed, a computational problem that was identified as such by P. M. Milner (1974) some years before the two cortical visual pathways were distinguished anatomically or otherwise. It is unlikely that the dorsal stream plays the major role in mediating this initial selection process, since object recognition and 'semantic knowledge' may have to be taken into account. Instead, it seems more likely that during processing by the ventral stream, the goal object is 'marked' or 'flagged' in some way, perhaps by the kind of enhanced activity we call 'attentional'. Then this indexing must somehow be conveyed to the appropriate networks in the dorsal stream, perhaps there too in the form of an attentional modulation. Of course, what the 'appropriate networks' in the dorsal stream would be could not be determined by the ventral or dorsal streams by themselves, but if the attentional modulation occurs at an early stage in the stream of processing, it could be carried forward to all of the spatiomotor subsystems. (Conversely, of course, it is plausible to suppose that when action-related visual attention shifts, the 'spotlight' of awareness in the ventral stream will tend to shift with it.)

Having flagged the object (presumably spatially), the second prerequisite is to convey whatever 'top-down' knowledge about the object is needed to supplement the 'bottom-up' sensory information used routinely by the visuomotor networks involved in prehension. For example, one could grip a fork efficiently using sensory information only, that is, without knowing the fork's function, but one's grip would not necessarily be appropriate for the use to which one would put the fork. We propose that a higher-level praxic system needs to have access to the products of the ventral stream's processing, so that it can then 'instruct' the relevant visuomotor systems. Only in this superordinate fashion, however, could the visuomotor systems be said to be governed by object-centred information. Evidence from apraxia in humans indicates that such a praxic system may be partially based in the left parietal lobe (Kimura 1993). In the monkey there are anatomical connections from the inferotemporal cortex which could transmit highly processed visual information to inform parietofrontal areas concerned in praxis (Seltzer and Pandya 1980; Cavada and Goldman-Rakic 1989b; Andersen *et al.* 1990a; Harries and Perrett 1991).

There is no direct evidence for this postulated role of temporoparietal connections in transmitting information about familiar objects to the praxic and visuomotor systems. It is, however, interesting that a patient has recently been described who behaves as if her praxic system selectively lacks these object-identity inputs (Sirigu *et al.* 1995). The patient's two cortical visual systems seem to be essentially intact, as indicated by her ability to organize her hand to grasp an object efficiently and to recognize familiar objects, that is, she suffers from neither optic ataxia nor visual agnosia. But when the patient is shown a familiar object and asked to pick it up, she will often do so using a grasp that, while efficient, is placed inappropriately for the use of the object. Thus, although the two systems appear to be functioning adequately in isolation, they may be disconnected from each other.

We have recently tested the apperceptive agnosic patient D.F. with everyday objects in the same way. When there is enough textural or other local information to allow her to identify an object, she then grasps it (and mimes its use) correctly. But when she fails to identify an object, she behaves like Sirigu *et al.*'s (1995) patient and is liable to grasp it efficiently but inappropriately. Presumably in these instances object-identity information is unavailable to

D.F.'s praxic and visuomotor systems, just as in Sirigu *et al.*'s (1995) patient. But since D.F. does grasp identified objects appropriately (identified, for example, through colour or visual texture or through other sense modalities), we infer that representations of object identity, when successfully activated, must be able to inform her praxic and visuomotor systems through intact links.

Although there is a very long way to go, these new scraps of evidence suggest that the complex interactions that precede the execution of acts of prehension may be penetrable to some degree by a careful and systematic examination of how such behaviour can be disrupted by brain damage. It is our belief, indeed, that neuropsychological and behavioural research of this kind is essential for understanding how different subsystems in the brain operate and interact. As recent history has shown, a substantial body of physiological and anatomical evidence can be compatible with more than one different functional interpretation. It has been through the interleaving of detailed behavioural analysis with such neurobiological data that the particular interpretations we have put forward in this book gain their strength and plausibility. While we do not expect all our readers to agree with our proposals, we hope that our arguments taken as a whole serve to make the point forcibly that behavioural analysis is an indispensable element in making theoretical advances in visual neuroscience.

Chapter 8

Epilogue: twelve years on

In this book, our aim was to set out a new way of looking at the organization of the visual brain. According to our scheme, the ventral stream of visual processing in the cerebral cortex constructs the representations that underlie our perceptual experience of the world whereas the dorsal stream provides the moment-to-moment visual control of our actions. In proposing this division of labour, we emphasized the different transformations of the visual input that are required to achieve these very different functional endpoints. In the years since we first put forward these ideas, visual neuroscience has advanced rapidly on several fronts. In this chapter, we re-evaluate the perception–action model in the light of these developments.

The fact that much has happened since 1994 means that the story has become more complex, but we believe that the idea of a fundamental distinction between perceptual representation and visuomotor control is still essential for understanding the organization of the visual system. Indeed, new findings, particularly from functional MRI (fMRI), have strengthened the evidence base for this two-stream model of visual processing. At the time we wrote the first edition of the book, the bulk of our evidence came from behavioural and neuropsychological studies of brain-damaged humans and monkeys, from nonhuman primate neuroanatomy and neurophysiology, and from a limited range of research on visuomotor control in healthy human subjects. There were very few relevant positron emission tomography (PET) studies of the human visual system, and fMRI was still in its infancy. The organization of the visual brain beyond area V1 had thus barely begun to be explored in humans.

In the present chapter, we review this new literature and at the same time offer some refinements and clarifications of our original account in the light of recent findings. As will become clear, the findings from a broad range of fMRI studies, both with D.F. and with neurologically intact subjects, have provided strong convergent support for the conclusions of our earlier neuropsychological investigations. But in addition, fMRI has revealed a great deal more about the functional complexities of the dorsal and ventral streams— providing new insights into the organization of the 'streams within streams' we speculated on in Chapter 7. At the same time, there has been a renaissance in monkey neurophysiological research, which has generated a vast array of new information about the organization of the two streams and their mutual inter-actions, as well as their interactions with higher-order cognitive and motor areas. Both neurophysiological work in monkeys and neuroimaging studies in humans have shed new light on the role of the two streams in the perception of actions in others—and the relationship between neural activity in the two streams and visual awareness. Researchers have also begun to employ other methodologies, such as transcranial magnetic stimulation (TMS), to work out not only the locations of critical brain regions for perception and action but also the timing of the underlying computations. The past decade has also seen an amazing growth in the number of 'psychophysical' studies of the visual control of action, particularly on the topic of whether or not actions such as grasping are immune to perceptual illusions. Much of the research in this area has been contentious—and a number of alternative accounts of the percep-tion/action distinction have been put forward to explain the different findings. But as we point out in our discussion, these accounts have tended to focus on a rather limited set of data (mostly derived internally from illusion studies them-selves) and cannot deal with the broad range of evidence that is continuing to emerge from human neuroimaging and neuropsychological studies, and mon-key neurophysiology. These and a number of other issues, including the role of the dorsal stream and other structures in the acquisition of new motor skills, are explored in this chapter. A less detailed, but more accessible, account of much of the updated material discussed here can be found in our recent book, *Sight Unseen* (Goodale and Milner 2004).

8.1 New insights into the ventral and dorsal streams

8.1.1 The functional organization of the ventral stream

The broad functional organization and connectivity of ventral-stream areas in the monkey were already well understood when we wrote the book in 1994. One reason for this was the fact that visual neurones in ventral-stream areas are not modulated by the motor activity of the monkey—and thus can be studied in passive or even anaesthetized preparations. Indeed, as we reviewed in Chapter 2, work on the visual properties of neurones in the ventral stream has been going on since the late 1960s, whereas work on the dorsal stream, which requires the use of alert behaving monkeys, did not begin until the mid-1970s. One major recent development in the study of ventral-stream processing in the monkey has been the exploration of more medial areas in the temporal lobe, including entorhinal, perirhinal, and parahippocampal cortex. These areas, which have been implicated in recognition memory, appear to provide the interface between visual processing in the ventral stream and mnemonic systems in medial temporal and prefrontal cortex (Brown and Aggleton 2001; Holscher and Rolls 2002). In fact, the boundary between perception and memory is rather blurred (Murray and Richmond 2001), particularly with respect to the status of visual working memory, which in many ways resembles perception itself.

The putative human homologues of these areas, however, were not accessible to investigation at that time, and we could only guess at their organization from comparisons with the monkey. Thanks to the development and the now-widespread use of fMRI, of course, this state of affairs has changed dramatically. Indeed the past 10 years have witnessed a virtual explosion of information about the organization of the visual cortical areas in humans. The first steps were taken by Tootell and colleagues, who mapped out a series of retinotopic areas beyond V1 (including V2, V3, V3A, V4, MT, and an area specialized for colour processing that they call V8) in human extrastriate cortex (Tootell *et al.* 1996; Hadjikhani *et al.* 1998). This work revealed a good correspondence between the layout of these early areas in monkeys and humans and provided clear evidence in the human cortex for a separation into dorsal and ventral pathways (Van Essen *et al.* 2001; Tootell *et al.* 2003). A recent summary of the visual areas so far mapped in the human brain is shown in Plate 1 (top) in comparison with the known layout in the macaque monkey.

Subsequent work has built on these foundations and extended the explorations deep into the ventral stream. Areas selectively responsive to different categories of visual stimuli have been identified, starting with the discovery by Malach and colleagues (1995) of an area on the ventrolateral convexity of the occipital lobe that is specialized for the processing of objects. As Plate 1 (bottom) illustrates, this area, which Malach called the lateral occipital area (or area LO), shows more activation for intact drawings or photographs of objects as compared with scrambled or fragmented versions of the same images. Since this pioneering work, there have been many studies of area LO, confirming and clarifying the role of this area in object perception. It has been shown, for example, that LO is activated by the presentation of objects irrespective of whether these objects are defined by differences in motion, texture, or luminance contrast (Grill-Spector *et al.* 1998). This result fits nicely with data reported for the inferotemporal cortex of the monkey, in which single neurones sensitive to shape showed a similar generalization across different defining cues (Sáry *et al.* 1993; see Section 2.6.1 in Chapter 2).

Kourtzi and Kanwisher (2001) explored whether activity in area LO was related to the shape of the object or simply to the local contours defining that object. To do this, they took advantage of fMR adaptation, in which the haemodynamic response to pairs of successively presented stimuli is typically lower when the stimuli (or some features of the stimuli) are identical than when they are different. They found that adaptation occurred in area LO when the perceived shape of successively presented objects was identical but the defining contours differed, but not when the contours were identical but the perceived shape changed. This strongly suggests that area LO represents higher-level shape information, such as form, rather than simple image features, such as edges or contours. Although there is evidence that area LO shows some sensitivity to changes in object viewpoint, recent work using fMR adaptation has shown that at least part of area LO is insensitive to such changes and appears to treat different views of the same object as equivalent (James *et al.* 2002; Valyear *et al.* 2005).

More recently still, McKyton and Zohary (2006) have shown that the coding of object location in area LO is independent of eye position. Thus, they found adaptation in area LO when the object's position on the viewing screen remained fixed, regardless of changes in the object's retinal position caused by eye movements. No adaptation was observed when the object's position on the display screen was changed while eyes remained fixed. These results show first that object location is coded in area LO, and second that this coding is non-retinotopic but is instead represented within some sort of head, body, or even scene-based coordinate system. This kind of coding would be useful for maintaining information about object location across eye movements, a prerequisite for perceptual stability. McKyton and Zohary's findings provide compelling evidence for our original contention that 'where' an object is in a scene as well as 'what' it is are both coded in the ventral stream. By this means information can be combined to provide a detailed perceptual representation of the whole spatial array.

Just as there are ensembles of ventral-stream neurones specialized for faces in the monkey (see Section 2.6.1), there appear to be regions in the human ventral stream that are similarly specialized. The existence of an area in the fusiform gyrus that is activated selectively by images of faces was demonstrated simultaneously in two separate laboratories (Kanwisher *et al.* 1997; McCarthy *et al.* 1997). This area, which is often referred to as the fusiform face area (FFA: see Plate 2, top), is much less responsive to non-face objects—and is also less responsive to inverted faces. Despite the now-extensive literature on area FFA, however, there is still a lively debate as to whether the area is truly face-specific (Grill-Spector *et al.* 2004), or whether it is an area specialized for fine within-category discriminations (Tarr and Gauthier 2000). Support for the latter view comes from the observation that some prosopagnosic patients are severely impaired on difficult discriminations between members of the same class of objects (such as 'greebles', a class of abstract 3-dimensional objects devised by Gauthier and Tarr 1997). On the other hand, however, support for the face-specialization view comes from a recent paper on the interesting patient C.K., first described by Moscovitch et al. (1997). In direct contrast to prosopagnosic patients, C.K. has severe object agnosia, but remarkably intact face perception: yet when tested with greebles, he showed a severe impairment. It appears that whatever underlies C.K.'s good face perception is not capable of handling this kind of fine within-class object discrimination task (Gauthier et al. 2004). In addition to the FFA, other areas that are apparently specialized for faces have been identified, including an area in the superior temporal sulcus (STS) (Puce et al. 1998) and another region adjacent to area LO on the lateral occipital surface, which has been called the occipital face area (OFA: Halgren et al. 1999; Haxby et al. 1999). It seems likely that these three ventral-stream areas, together with other areas such as the amygdala, form a network for dealing with different aspects of facial processing, including the recognition of identity, emotional expression, and lip movements (Haxby et al. 2002; Ganel et al. 2005).

The FFA, which (by definition) is activated by faces, is much less interested in other body parts such as the hands (Kanwisher et al. 1997). In direct contrast, another area has been discovered in the ventral stream that is responsive to static images of human body parts but not to faces (Downing et al. 2001; Grossman and Blake 2002). This area, which is located close to areas LO and MT, has been named the extrastriate body area (EBA). Recently, a possible functional significance of this area has been revealed in a study by Urgesi et al. (2004). These investigators found that disruption of the EBA by TMS caused a slowing of reaction times in a body-part discrimination task, but not in a task where subjects were required to discriminate parts of faces or of motorcycles. There is also evidence that, in addition to being sensitive to images of other people's body parts, the EBA is modulated by limb movements performed by the observer (Astafiev et al. 2004). The EBA in the right hemisphere (but not the left) appears to prefer images presented in an orientation that is consistent with looking at someone else's limbs rather than one's own (Saxe et al. 2006). In addition to the EBA, another body-selective area in the fusiform gyrus (the FBA) immediately adjacent to the FFA has recently been identified (Peelen and Downing 2005; Schwarzlose et al. 2005: see Plate 2, bottom). While both the EBA and the FBA seem to be concerned with static views of the body, a posterior part of the STS (Grossman et al. 2000) contains a region that is sensitive to moving bodies, including point-light displays. This area (STSp) seems likely to be homologous with a similarly located region in monkey STS containing neurones tuned for biological motion (area STP: Puce and Perrett 2003; see Chapter 2, Section 2.6.1). Thus, the perception of bodies, like the perception of faces, appears to be mediated by a network of different areas in the ventral stream (although, as we discuss later, the perception of body movements performed by others may also depend on processing in the premotor and parietal regions).

Finally, fMRI studies have identified a region in the parahippocampal gyrus which is activated by buildings (Aguirre *et al.* 1998) and scenes (Epstein and Kanwisher 1998), a finding that dovetails neatly with the locations of lesions that cause topographical agnosia discussed earlier in the book (see Section 5.4.2). In other words, there is good functional evidence that this area may play a critical role in enabling us to find our way around the world by recognizing familiar landmarks such as buildings (Aguirre and D'Esposito 1999). The fact that this area (generally called the parahippocampal place area or PPA; see Plate 2, top) is located in the medial temporal lobe close to the hippocampus again speaks to the idea mentioned earlier that there is a close relationship between perceptual and mnemonic processing. The available evidence suggests that PPA may be involved in encoding new perceptual information about the appearance and layout of scenes (Epstein *et al.* 1999).

As more and more fMRI studies of visual perception accumulate, it is becoming increasingly clear that the organization of the visual areas within the human ventral stream is exceedingly complex. Is the ventral stream really compartmentalized into a number of discrete functional modules, each processing just one category of stimuli to the exclusion of all others? Or are there distributed systems with some 'nodes' of higher activation that might correspond to what are thought to be specialized modules? There is much discussion and debate about this issue. One thing that is clear is that all these ventral-stream areas are responsive to some degree to all these categories of stimuli; the differences are in degree, not in kind. Indeed Haxby *et al.* (2001) have shown that even without taking into account the activity in a putative 'specialized' area (for example, FFA), the nature of the stimulus can be deduced reliably from the pattern of remaining activations in other ventral stream regions. This notion of a partially distributed system rather than discrete and localized functional areas applies equally well to monkey inferotemporal cortex. Although there is evidence from single-unit recording studies for a columnar organization for object features and combinations of features in this region (see Tanaka 2003), those studies provide only limited evidence for subregions specialized for different classes of objects. Recent fMRI studies in monkeys, however, have revealed the existence of several discrete patches of cortex that are selectively activated by images of faces or bodies, embedded within the large swathe of occipito-temporal cortex (TE and TEO) that is activated by objects (Tsao *et al.* 2003). The use of functional MRI with monkeys in several laboratories around the world is now opening up exciting new possibilities for establishing direct homologies with human brain areas (Sereno *et al.* 2002; Tootell *et al.* 2003; Denys *et al.* 2004). Monkey neuroimaging will also help guide neurophysiological experiments and is sure to provide new insights into the relationship between single-neurone activity and population encoding in different perceptual and visuomotor networks.

There is still a lot to learn about the detailed organization of the ventral stream in both monkey and human brains. One possible organizing principle might be derived from the basic retinotopic nature of the visual system. Malach and colleagues have suggested that the anatomical segregation of areas specialized for different object categories such as objects, faces, and scenes may reflect the typical retinotopic locus in which these stimuli are encountered (Hasson *et al.* 2002, 2003). Faces, for example, are typically viewed centrally whereas the processing of scenes requires integration across a much broader expanse of the visual field. Their proposal, then, is that the large-scale organization of the different specialized areas emerged (phylogenetically and/or ontogenetically) from what they call a single 'proto-representation' of the visual array which is laid out retinotopically on the surface of the cortex. Of course, at present this idea remains little more than speculation and in some ways does not fit easily (at least at first blush) with the observation mentioned earlier that activity in area LO is independent of eye position (McKyton and Zohary 2006). Another complication is the recent demonstration that different regions of the ventral stream appear to be specialized for the processing of different features of objects and scenes, with more posterolateral regions (including area LO) specialized for the processing of object form and more anteromedial regions (overlapping parts of the FFA and PPA) specialized for the processing of surface properties, such as visual texture (Cant and Goodale 2006). These observations, coupled with the demonstration of a quasi-retinotopic organization in the ventral stream, are consistent with the suggestion (Haxby *et al.* 2001) that the local activations associated with particular categories of visual stimuli (for example, faces, animate objects, tools, and places) are points in a distributed network where the stimulus dimensions important for identifying exemplars from those categories intersect within the appropriate retinal locations. There is no doubt that future imaging experiments will uncover even more complexities within these networks.

The various lines of research using fMRI with healthy subjects have already shed a great deal of interesting light on the functional organization of the human ventral stream. But even though fMRI can establish the involvement of different brain areas in perception, a full understanding of their role also requires knowing what happens when those areas are damaged. Earlier in the book, we described in detail our case study of patient D.F., who has severe visual form agnosia. Our interpretation of her pattern of impaired form perception but spared visuomotor control was to assume that her brain damage (as a consequence of hypoxia) interrupted the normal flow of shape and contour information into her ventral stream without affecting the processing of shape and contour information by her dorsal stream. The only anatomical evidence we had to go on was a low-resolution structural MRI carried out just over a year after her accident (Milner *et al.* 1991). Nevertheless, the pattern of damage evident in this early scan combined with what was known about the visual areas in the monkey brain led us to argue that the pathway mediating form vision in D.F.'s ventral stream had been compromised. At the same time, we proposed that visual input to the dorsal stream remained largely intact.

All of this was essentially conjecture, because at the time almost nothing was known about the organization of the visual areas beyond area V1 in the human brain, and we also had no direct evidence of how a damaged brain like D.F.'s might deal with incoming visual information. More recently, however, we carried out both a high-resolution structural MRI investigation and an fMRI study of object recognition and object-directed grasping in D.F. (James *et al.* 2003). The new structural MRI revealed that the lateral occipital area (LO) is essentially destroyed bilaterally (see Plate 3, top, A). The lesions, however, did not extend medially into the fusiform object areas or into the parahippocampal gyri (see Plate 3, top, B). The fMRI study showed no differential activation for line drawings of common objects (versus scrambled versions) anywhere in D.F.'s remaining ventral stream (Plate 3, top, C). Healthy subjects, of course, showed robust activation of area LO in this task. The lack of activation with line drawings mirrored D.F.'s poor performance in identifying the objects depicted in the drawings. In fact, these results strongly suggest that area LO is essential for form perception, generating the geometrical structure of objects by combining information about edges and surfaces that has already been extracted from the visual array by low-level visual feature detectors (see also Cant and Goodale 2006).

When D.F. was presented with coloured and grey-scale images in the magnet—stimuli that she was able to identify more often than line drawings—she showed some ventral-stream activation outside of area LO, particularly in the fusiform and parahippocampal gyri. This activation, however, was more widely distributed than that seen in control subjects. The presence of such activation in the more medial regions of D.F.'s ventral stream suggests that these areas play a significant role in the processing of surface features such as colour and visual texture, allowing her to make inferences as to the material properties of objects (see also Cant and Goodale 2006).

D.F. has also been tested in the scanner with pictures of landscapes and man-made scenes, such as cities and markets, all of which she has some success at categorizing, particularly if the scenes are shown in their correct colours (Steeves *et al.* 2004). She showed robust activation in the parahippocampal gyri in an area corresponding to the PPA in healthy subjects (see Plate 3, bottom). This finding fits well with evidence showing that scene 'gist' can be rapidly extracted from patches of texture and colour information without any prior processing of the objects comprising the scene (Oliva and Schyns 1997; Schyns and Oliva 1997). Most recently, D.F. was tested with faces, both behaviourally and in the scanner (Steeves *et al.* 2006). Despite her dense prosopagnosia, D.F. is able to distinguish faces from objects. She also shows activation in an area that appears to be FFA, which presumably underlies that ability. But if FFA is intact, why does she have no ability to recognize individual faces or facial expressions? The answer may be that her lesion of area LO extends to include the OFA, which in the normal brain lies just posterior to area LO (see Plate 3, bottom). These data suggest that the OFA may be an essential component in the network of face-responsive areas that normally mediate the recognition of faces and facial expression.

In summary, research in both human neuroimaging and monkey neurophysiology has provided a huge amount of new information about the organization of the ventral stream, but the findings fit remarkably well with our broad view of what the system is doing. Indeed, all of the new work serves to reinforce the idea that processing in the ventral stream provides the basis for visual perception: including not just the perception of objects, but also the perception of the spatial layout of the visual world in which they are embedded. With the advent of research tools such as fMR adaptation and TMS, increased attention can now be turned to the more difficult question of exactly how the processing that takes place in the ventral stream leads to perception.

8.1.2 The functional organization of the dorsal stream

As we discussed in Chapter 2, there is good evidence from monkey neurophysiology that neurones in the posterior parietal cortex are concerned with transforming visual information into the appropriate coordinates for motor acts. There was already clear evidence when we wrote that chapter that the visuomotor transformations for different effector systems tend to reside in separate specialized areas, and these findings have been broadly confirmed in later research (see Andersen and Buneo (2003) and Sakata (2003) for reviews). Thus, an area in the lateral bank of the intraparietal sulcus (area LIP) appears to play a primary role in the visual control of voluntary saccadic eye movements, whereas a quite separate area, located more anteriorly within the intraparietal sulcus (area AIP), is involved in the visual control of object-directed grasping movements (see Plate 4, top). At the time, however, it was not clear where in the monkey's parietal cortex the visuomotor transformations required for reaching movements were carried out. Subsequent research (Galletti *et al.* 1997; Snyder *et al.* 1997) has discovered a concentration of reach-related neurones in the medial bank of the intraparietal sulcus (area MIP) and in the parieto-occipital sulcus (area V6A), areas that are referred to collectively as the parietal reach region (PRR) by Andersen and his colleagues (Plate 4, top). There is recent evidence from Galletti's laboratory that neurones in V6A may also be involved in the control of visually guided grasping movements (Fattori *et al.* 2004).

Neuronal activity in the intraparietal sulcus, particularly in area LIP, has also been linked to shifts of visual attention and the updating of spatial location (Colby and Goldberg 1999). Nevertheless, a seminal study from Andersen's laboratory has demonstrated that activity in these areas is at the same time related to the specific motor act the animal intends to perform with respect to a visual stimulus, and not just to a shift of general spatial attention to that stimulus (Snyder *et al.* 1997). In their experiments, monkeys were trained to respond to the same visual stimulus with either a saccadic eye movement or an aiming movement with the hand, conditional on a colour cue presented at fixation. Neurones in area LIP were selectively activated during the eye movement but not the arm movement, whereas neurones in the PRR showed the opposite pattern of activity. In other words, even though the monkeys were attending to the stimulus location in both tasks, the neurones in area LIP and the PRR were differentially recruited according to the response requirements of the task the animal was performing at the time. These results provide support for our contention that the modular organization of the dorsal stream reflects the output requirements of the system rather than a general spatial coding of visual stimuli. As we will argue later, however, this fact need not exclude an important role of area LIP (in particular) in the control of visual attention switching across spatial locations.

The advent of fMRI—in particular, event-related fMRI—has revealed the presence of homologous visuomotor areas to the monkey's LIP, AIP, VIP, and PRR in the human parietal cortex (Culham and Kanwisher 2001; see Plate 5, top). Of particular interest has been the demonstration of an area in the human brain that appears to correspond to AIP in the monkey (Binkofski *et al.* 1999; Culham *et al.* 2003). To study grasping movements in the MRI environment, Culham and her colleagues devised a hydraulically driven apparatus that could present real 3-D graspable objects within the bore of a high-field magnet. Using this device, which was dubbed the 'grasparatus', they were able to compare reach-to-grasp movements with simple reaching movements directed at target objects that varied in orientation and size (Culham *et al.* 2003). They found that reaching out and grasping objects consistently activated AIP more than simply reaching towards them did (see Plate 4, bottom, top-left graph). Although ventral-stream area LO too was activated during both reaching and grasping tasks, there was no difference in the amount of activation between the two conditions (Plate 4, bottom, bottom-left graph). In contrast, when subjects were presented with intact versus scrambled 2-D grey-scale drawings of objects, which produced a robust differential activation for intact objects in area LO (bottom-right graph), neither stimulus produced any activation in AIP (top-right graph).

It could be argued, of course, that this failure to see activation associated with object drawings in AIP was related not so much to the task demands but rather to the fact that the images were presented in 2-D, rather than in 3-D as they had been in the grasping task. In a more recent study, however, Culham and her colleagues have shown that when subjects are asked to discriminate between 3-D objects that vary in size, the amount of AIP activation is much less than that associated with grasping the same objects. Furthermore, the level of AIP activation in the size discrimination task did not differ from that of two other conditions in which subjects were required to either reach out and touch one of the objects or to discriminate between differences in visual texture on the surface of the objects. Finally, there was no difference in the amount of activation in area LO associated with the grasping, reaching, or size discrimination tasks, although all three of these conditions resulted in more LO activation than the texture discrimination task (Culham *et al.* 2004). Taken together, these results show that AIP becomes maximally engaged only when subjects are required to *grasp* the visual target. This confirms our original hypothesis that AIP processes object features such as size for pre-shaping the hand, but not for purposes of perception. Furthermore, the inference from these normal studies that area AIP does this without assistance from area LO is considerably strengthened by a study in which patient D.F. was scanned during grasping and reaching tasks using the same procedures and apparatus (James *et al.* 2003). Despite the fact that D.F. has no area LO, she showed robust differential activation in area AIP for grasping (compared with reaching), as shown in Plate 5 (bottom).

We have emphasized throughout the book that the activity of most visually sensitive neurones in the dorsal stream is modulated by the current motor demands faced by the animal. It is important to note, however, that even in their initial reports Mountcastle and his colleagues (1975) also described what appeared to be 'purely visual' neurones, that is, neurones whose visual responses were unaffected by what the animal was doing. Of course, as we pointed out in Chapter 2, this is exactly what one would expect to see in a network of neurones devoted to converting visual information into the required coordinates for action. More recently, a particularly large concentration of such apparently 'purely visual' neurones has been localized in the monkey brain, at the most caudal part of the intraparietal sulcus (cIPS, Shikata *et al.* 1996). These intriguing neurones appear to be implicated in the analysis of the 3-D structure of objects: responding selectively, for example, to surfaces tilted in depth. It has been proposed that this region provides critical information about the size, orientation, and shape of goal objects for onward transmission to area AIP for the control of grasping movements (Sakata *et al.* 1997).

An area in the caudal part of the human intraparietal sulcus that may be homologous with monkey cIPS has been found to be regularly activated during both passive and active viewing of 3-D objects (for example, Faillenot *et al.* 1997; Kraut *et al.* 1997). Recent studies (James *et al.* 2002; Valyear *et al.* 2005) used fMR adaptation to examine the nature of the activation in this 'human cIPS' area, which appears to extend from the caudal part of IPS into immediately adjacent parieto-occipital cortex. Responses in this region showed adaptation to subsequent images of the same object, but only if the object was viewed again from the identical vantage point. Depth-rotated images of an object were treated by this human version of cIPS as if they were pictures of a completely new object. As already noted (Section 8.1.1), quite different results were found when responses in area LO were examined. Here, clear fMR adaptation effects emerged when the identity of the object remained the same, even if the orientation had changed. This difference in the pattern of fMR adaptation in these dorsal and ventral areas neatly reflects the need for viewer-centred coding in the control of object-directed action in the former but a more generalized representation for the recognition of objects in the latter.

Before ending this discussion of dorsal-stream function, it is perhaps important to emphasize (as we already did in Chapter 2) that area MT has a special status with respect to the two streams. Despite the fact that this motion-sensitive area has traditionally been regarded by anatomists as part of the dorsal rather than the ventral stream, it has strong functional relationships with both visual streams. Like area V1, from which it receives strong direct projections, MT projects heavily to areas in both the dorsal and the ventral stream (Felleman and Van Essen 1991). And as we pointed out in Chapter 2, it probably plays a role not just in the guidance of movements such as visual pursuit, but also in the recognition both of moving objects and of the actions being performed by another animal (see Sections 2.5.3 and 2.6.1). In agreement with this, we now know that damage to area MT in humans (sometimes called 'V5') results in both perceptual and visuomotor deficits. For example, patient L.M., the famous 'motion-blind' patient (Zihl *et al.* 1983), whose lesions included MT in both hemispheres, showed a profound impairment in motion perception and at the same time was unable to intercept moving objects using her hand (Schenk *et al.* 2000). These neuropsychological findings have been mimicked using TMS to temporarily interfere with the function of area MT in healthy subjects. Thus, delivering TMS to area MT not only interferes with motion perception (Walsh *et al.* 1998) but also disrupts performance on the same interception task that was used to test L.M. (Schenk *et al.* 2005*a*). It may be the case that the computational requirements for accurate and rapid motion processing for both perception and action led to the evolution of a single dedicated module for this purpose. Such rapid processing would be useful both in situations where an animal needs to recognize a moving predator (or prey object) and where it needs to react to it, for example, by grasping a moving prey object. In other words, it might make most sense to treat MT as an 'early' visual area, one that has the same relationship with the two streams as primary visual cortex, but which is specialized for motion processing.

8.1.3 Mirror neurones: an interaction between the two streams

While we were writing the first edition of this book, an important discovery was made by Rizzolatti and his colleagues that cuts across what had previously seemed a clear distinction between 'visuomotor' and 'perceptual' coding in individual neurones. The Rizzolatti laboratory identified a class of neurones in ventral premotor cortex (area F5) that fired not only when the monkey grasped an object, but also when the monkey observed another individual (monkey or human) doing the same thing (see Plate 6, top). Because they appeared to have both visuomotor and perceptual properties, these cells were dubbed 'mirror neurones' (Di Pellegrino *et al.* 1992; Gallese *et al.* 1996). The fact that these cells have visuomotor properties is not surprising, in that they are located in a region that is part of a larger parieto-frontal 'grasp' circuit involving area AIP (see Section 2.5.4). Their 'perceptual' properties, however, could not arise from these dorsal-stream links, but instead must involve interconnections with ventral stream areas. In fact, area F5 has extensive reciprocal connections with area PF (7b) in the inferior parietal lobule (IPL), which in turn receives substantial projections from visual area STP (Cavada and Goldman-Rakic 1989*a*; Rozzi *et al.* 2005). As we noted earlier, this latter ventral stream region, which gets inputs from both

MT and the inferotemporal cortex (Seltzer and Pandya 1994), contains a population of neurones that respond when the monkey views the actions of others (Perrett *et al.* 1989). Completing this circuit, neurones have more recently been discovered in the monkey's IPL as well. Interestingly, these neurones have been found to be sensitive to the behavioural context within which a given act (for example, grasping) is embedded, both on the part of the monkey and the observed actor (Fogassi *et al.* 2005). In other words, the discharge rate of an IPL mirror neurone appears to depend on what is eventually done with the object grasped by the monkey or by the actor the monkey is observing. Some IPL neurones, for example, fire best if the monkey or the actor eats the object that is grasped; others fire best if the monkey or actor places the grasped object into a container. Moreover, it is the goal of the action, not its precise kinematics, that determines the tuning of the mirror neurones. This suggests that these neurones receive inputs relating to the overall planning of an action, that is, about the purpose for which an object is being grasped.

This research on mirror neurones by Rizzolatti and his colleagues provides a compelling example of a convergence between the two visual streams. The functional role of the mirror system, however, remains uncertain. Rizzolatti, Gallese, and colleagues have suggested that it may play an important role in action recognition, thereby forming part of a network underlying both imitation and action understanding, but this interpretation is far from being fully established.

Earlier in the book (Section 4.3.2), we mentioned the idea, first put forward by Boussaoud *et al.* (1990), that the projections from MT to areas in the superior temporal sulcus, including STP, could constitute a third 'stream' of visual processing. This idea has recently been extended to include the inferior parietal region by Rizzolatti and Matelli (2003), who see this 'third stream' as a distinct branch of the dorsal stream (the 'v-d stream') whose role is to process visual information for action understanding and spatial perception. Rizzolatti and Matelli's terminology, however, would imply that this STP/IPL system is anatomically separate and distinct from the ventral stream, as well as from the dorsal stream as usually understood. Yet the visual functions of the IPL—which may well include action understanding as well as high-level spatial processing, particularly in the human brain—appear to depend on direct inputs from the ventral stream (via STP; Saleem *et al.* 2000), as well as on indirect inputs from the dorsal stream (via the premotor cortex). Therefore proposals to describe this system as a separate *stream*, either within or outside of the dorsal stream, remain, in our view, premature. In fact we suspect that the system may turn out to function principally as an elaboration of the ventral stream, by providing perceptual representations of the actions of others as well as the perception of spatial relations among elements in a scene (Milner 1997).

8.2 From consciousness to action

8.2.1 The roles of the dorsal and ventral streams in visual awareness

The crux of our position has been that the ventral and dorsal streams serve different but equally important and complementary roles in the service of behaviour. In Chapter 1, we took an explicit evolutionary approach to understanding vision, emphasizing the adaptive advantages of having two separate visual systems, which both have a role in governing behaviour, but which do so in very different ways. According to our scheme, the perceptual representations constructed by the ventral stream merely exert their visual control over behaviour in a much more indirect way than that exercised by the dorsal stream. Unfortunately, perhaps, by using the shorthand terms of 'perception' versus 'action' in referring to this distinction, we have led some readers to disregard our argument that both systems have the same ultimate *raison d'être*. Yet as we pointed out in our very first chapter (Section 1.3.2), unless percepts can somehow be translated into action, they will have no consequences for the individual possessing them. Nor indeed would the brain systems that generate them ever have evolved. In other words, perception *per se* is not what the ventral stream is there for: perception is not an end in itself, in biological terms, but rather a means to an end. It is worth reiterating once more that ultimately both visual streams exist to serve action—the difference between them is that the dorsal stream provides direct, moment-to-moment, control of our movements, whereas the ventral stream exerts its control in a much more indirect fashion.

One reason why these misunderstandings arose may be related to our proposal that the contents of visual consciousness depend upon activity in the ventral stream. As described below, there are now even better reasons for believing that there is a close relationship between consciousness and ventral-stream processing than we were able to adduce when we wrote the first edition of the book. Nonetheless it does not follow from this idea that the construction of a conscious percept is somehow an end in itself. On the contrary, our argument would be that consciousness must endow something upon the products of ventral stream processing that renders them particularly effective in the control of behaviour. In other words, we would claim that visual phenomenology must confer some kind of evolutionary advantage: that the capacity for conscious perception must give an organism an edge in natural selection. Setting aside the philosophical issue of qualia, on which we have nothing new to say, we propose that only those representations that reach consciousness can enter working memory, and potentially thereby become part of our long-term visual knowledge. Working memory enables visual information to be used 'off-line' and thus makes possible the flexibility in control of behaviour that characterizes the higher primates. In particular, when an animal is aware of what it sees, it can use this information to decide between different actions (including making no action), to plan future actions, and to communicate what it sees (or has seen) to its conspecifics.

We propose that only the ventral stream can provide the contents of our visual experience in this way. But it should be noted that this does not imply that the workings of the dorsal stream play no role at all in the determining our awareness. Indeed, as we argued already in Section 7.2 and discuss further below, at least one area within the dorsal stream (LIP) seems to play a role in both the control of eye movements and selective attention, thus causing changes in the content of visual awareness by switching between different sources of environmental information. Nor of course do we claim that one is unaware of the actions that are guided by the dorsal stream. People are usually aware of the actions they perform, although there are interesting instances in normal as well as pathological behaviour where this may not be the case (Daprati *et al.* 1997; Blakemore *et al.* 2002; Johnson *et al.* 2002). Furthermore, we do not wish to deny the obvious fact that when carrying out a visuomotor act a person is typically visually aware of the stimulus to which their action is directed, and of the limb that is making that action. It is our claim, however, that all of this *visual* awareness will be mediated by processing in the ventral stream and that this processing will typically unfold independently of, and in parallel with, the visual control of the action itself. This does not contradict our claim that the visual information *used* by the dorsal stream to specify and control the constituent movements of a goal-directed action (including an eye movement) is inaccessible to consciousness. The compelling nature of visual consciousness makes it difficult to resist the intuition that it is one's perception of the goal object that is guiding the action. But sometimes the truth can be counterintuitive (for a philosophical examination of this issue, see Clark 2002).

The original evidence on which we based our proposal that visual processing in the ventral stream is necessary for visual awareness came from neuropsychological studies of blindsight and of our patient D.F with visual form agnosia. There is now more direct evidence for the role of the ventral stream in giving rise to visual awareness, deriving from single-unit and lesion studies in the monkey and fMRI studies in humans. Of course, to study awareness in a monkey is not easy, and no purchase on the problem had been achieved when we were writing the first edition of the book. Although human subjects can readily report verbally on what they see, monkeys have to make their reports in other ways, having first been trained to do so. Cowey and Stoerig (1995) were the first investigators to succeed in such a training endeavour. They devised an elegant technique through which a monkey was trained to press a touch screen to indicate whether or not a stimulus had been present somewhere on the screen. Cowey and Stoerig found that even though monkeys that had undergone unilateral removal of area V1 could point towards a stimulus presented in their blind field, they categorized the same stimulus as a blank (stimulus-absent) when they confronted it in the detection task. In other words, the monkeys exhibited blindsight (see Chapter 3). This result provides a compelling confirmation of the reality of blindsight, showing that visuomotor control can remain virtually intact despite the absence of visual awareness. Such a profound dissociation supports our original contention that visual awareness depends on inputs to the ventral stream from area V1.

But perhaps the most convincing evidence for the relationship between awareness of a visual stimulus and activity in the ventral stream has come from studies using the phenomenon of binocular rivalry. Logothetis and his collaborators have applied this technique to monkeys by training them to make a manual response to signal a switch between seeing stimulus A (say a cloudburst pattern) and stimulus B (say a face). When the two stimuli are then presented simultaneously, one to the left eye and the other to the right, the monkey reports fluctuations in what it sees, in much the same manner as a human observer facing the same rivalrous images. This in itself was an important result, in that it showed how a monkey could be trained to report on the actual content of its inner visual experience. But more important for present purposes was that Sheinberg and Logothetis (1997) were able to show that the activity of single neurones in inferior temporal cortex that responded selectively (say to the face stimulus) exhibited correlated fluctuations in their responses according to what the monkey reported seeing (see Fig. 8.1). A cell in this region fired more when the monkey reported seeing the preferred stimulus for that cell and less when it reported a switch to seeing the other stimulus. This correlation was much less clear at a lower level of the ventral stream (V4) and was quite absent in V1. Presumably V1 neurones received the visual stimuli from both eyes, with both stimuli receiving equal processing weight. These striking results showed for the first time that there is a direct link between the activity of particular neurones in the ventral stream and what the organism perceives.

Fig. 8.1 Distribution of perception-related neuronal activity in different regions of the ventral visual stream (and area MT) of the monkey during the presentation of rivalrous visual images to the two eyes. The neurones that are affected by suppression are almost all exclusively binocular. The histograms show the proportion of these binocular neurones that are driven only when the preferred stimulus is perceived (that is, what the monkey reports seeing: shown in grey), as opposed to those that respond only when the preferred stimulus is suppressed (white). The neurones tend to be increasingly selective for the perceived stimulus alone as one moves to higher processing stages of the visual system. In fact, the firing of neurones in inferotemporal cortex reflects only what the monkey perceives: if the driving stimulus is perceptually suppressed, then the neurones do not fire. Adapted with permission from Logothetis (1998).

Of course, one could make the case that a monkey's visual awareness may not resemble ours or that even if it does it may not be determined by the same factors. Recent research with human subjects, however, argues strongly against this view. It has now become possible to record from single neurones in the human brain, typically in patients with epilepsy who have had electrodes implanted in their brains to localize the seizure onset focus. A recent study using a variant of the binocular rivalry paradigm (flash suppression) demonstrated that visual neurones in the medial temporal lobe responded only to the perceived stimulus, never responding to the suppressed stimulus presented to the other eye (Kreiman *et al.* 2002).

Functional neuroimaging studies have also provided convergent results on the role of the human ventral stream in perceptual awareness. Tong *et al.* (1998)

used a paradigm similar to that of Sheinberg and Logothetis, in which observers were presented with rivalrous images of a face and a building. They studied activation in two areas of the human ventral stream known to be involved in the processing of such stimuli: the fusiform face area and the parahippocampal place area, respectively (see Section 8.1.1 above). Tong and his colleagues found that activation in the FFA and PPA fluctuated in a reciprocal fashion with their subjects' visual awareness of the face or building (see Plate 6, bottom). Evidently whatever switching processes determined the changes in awareness did so by modulating the relative activity levels in these two parts of the ventral stream. Of course, such studies do not demonstrate that the differential fMRI activation associated with conscious versus unconscious processing is *restricted* to the ventral stream: after all, pictures of objects can activate areas in the intraparietal sulcus as well (James *et al.* 2002; Valyear *et al.* 2005). Recently, however, Fang and He (2005) have shown that such activation in the dorsal stream is not modulated by awareness. Even when observers were quite unaware of pictures of objects presented to one eye due to interocular suppression, the pictures still elicited substantial fMRI activation in the dorsal stream, and indeed this activation was just as great as when the image was consciously perceived. As we would expect from previous data, however, Fang and He found large differences in activation in area LO between these 'aware' and 'unaware' conditions.

In other studies, asking subjects simply to view perceptually ambiguous stimuli such as the well-known Rubin face/vase figure has yielded comparable results. For example, it was found that FFA responded more strongly when subjects reported seeing the faces rather than the vase, despite the fact that an identical physical stimulus gave rise to the two different percepts (Hasson *et al.* 2001; Andrews *et al.* 2002). Such changes were not seen in the PPA or area LO. These results allow us to generalize well beyond the paradigms of interocular rivalry and suppression, which may seem somewhat contrived and distant from everyday visual life. Indeed, we suggest that all of these phenomena of perceptual switching are special cases of what happens all the time as one's visual attention jumps continually from one place or object in the environment to another. There is now some evidence for a parietofrontal control system which is active in synchrony with the perceptual switches seen in both binocular rivalry (Lumer *et al.* 1998) and when ambiguous figures are viewed (Kleinschmidt *et al.* 1998). We shall argue later that this network is part of the brain's general control system for switching visual attention.

Shifts of attention do not need to be between spatially separated objects, but can occur between different parts of the same object or even between two superimposed images. In one striking study, O'Craven *et al.* (1999) presented subjects with stimuli consisting of a face transparently superimposed on a house, with one moving and the other stationary. In different conditions, subjects attended to the face, the house, or the motion, and fMRI was used to examine the activation of the corresponding cortical areas (FFA, PPA and MT/MST). They found that whichever attribute of an object was attended to (such as the motion of a moving face) caused enhanced neural activation not only in its corresponding cortical area (MT/MST) but also in the area related to the other attribute of the same object (in this instance, FFA), compared with attributes of the other object (that is, the house). Results like these have led to the regular use of differential attentional engagement as a general investigative paradigm for deciding whether or not a visual area is involved in processing particular classes of features or objects.

A rather different, but complementary, approach was taken by Ferber *et al.* (2003). They used a structure-from-motion display, in which an object shape could be seen only by the relative movement of its constituent elements relative to background elements. After the motion stops in these displays, the percept of the shape typically persists for a few seconds before fading away completely. The investigators found that although the moving display activated both areas MT and LO, only area LO maintained its activity after the motion stopped, with the activity slowly declining as the percept faded away. In other words, the activity in the ventral stream was correlated with the time-course of perception, quite independently of any changes in the physical stimulus. In a converse study, Andrews and Schluppeck (2004) used 'Mooney' faces, which at first sight often appear to be simply a random collection of black blobs on a white background, but on cueing or more prolonged inspection can be seen as facial images in which the shades of grey of a photograph have been converted to sharp black and white boundaries. They reported that the neural response in the FFA was greater when subjects reported seeing a face than when they perceived the image as a collection of blobs (see Fig. 8.2). No such differential response associated with face versus no-face percepts was seen in area LO.

But while all of these studies (and many others that are appearing all the time) provide good evidence that visual consciousness is closely correlated with activity in the ventral stream, this does not of course mean that *all* activity in the ventral stream generates visual consciousness. If we were conscious of everything our ventral stream processed, we would be overwhelmed with information, and consciousness could serve no function. In any event, the primate studies of Logothetis described above refute any simple-minded notion that everything reaching the ventral stream is represented in visual consciousness. Even when stimulus A is suppressed during rivalry, it still results in some

Fig. 8.2 The difference in integrated fMRI activity between 'face perceived' and 'face not perceived' trials with Mooney faces in the fusiform face area (FFA), superior temporal sulcus (STS), parahippocampal place area (PPA), and the lateral occipital area (LO). The data are averaged across subjects. Error bars represent ±1 SE. Adapted with permission from Andrews and Schluppeck (2004).

activation of inferior temporal neurones that prefer this stimulus, though much less than when stimulus B is suppressed instead. Similarly the fMRI effects observed in the experiments by Tong and colleagues (1998) and by Andrews and colleagues (2002, 2004) were not absolute: when the studied areas were suppressed during perceptual fluctuations, they nonetheless still responded above control levels. Presumably an active inhibitory process operates within the ventral stream to damp down (but not abolish) the activity elicited by a suppressed or unattended stimulus, causing it to fall below some threshold required for awareness to supervene.

This evidence on healthy subjects is complemented nicely by fMRI data gathered from brain-damaged patients with hemispatial neglect and/or visual extinction (see Section 7.3 in the previous chapter of this book). Awareness of visual stimuli in such patients can be compromised much more globally than in the above studies of perceptual fluctuations in normal subjects, even though their visual pathways may remain essentially intact. In one study, Rees *et al.* (2000) tested a patient suffering from visual extinction, in which they presented images of faces or houses bilaterally. On the majority of the trials, the stimulus present in the patient's contralesional visual field was extinguished; that is, it was absent from the patient's visual experience: yet it still resulted in substantial (if somewhat reduced) activation in striate cortex and in the appropriate ventral stream areas (see Plate 7, top). Similar results were found in a study of a patient with combined hemispatial neglect and extinction (Vuilleumier *et al.* 2001). Clearly, therefore, here too we must conclude that ventral-stream activity *per se* does not provide a sufficient condition for visual awareness.

Our contention, however, is that ventral-stream activity plays a *necessary* role in generating such awareness. Needless to say of course, such necessary participation of the ventral stream does not imply that the ventral stream is itself the seat of visual consciousness. After all, the eyes are necessary for visual consciousness, yet we do not suppose that they *embody* those conscious experiences. A more likely hypothesis for the embodiment of our visual experience is suggested by the studies above by Rees and colleagues (2000) and Vuilleumier and colleagues (2001). Both of their patients had right inferior parietal damage, which is typically associated with neglect and/or extinction, and we may assume that this damage resulted in the loss of visual experience in their contralesional visual field. One possible hypothesis is that in the intact human brain, the right inferior parietal lobule (IPL) provides a flexible high-level representational medium within which the contents of visual consciousness are constructed (Milner 1997, 1998; Driver and Mattingley 1998). As we noted earlier, the IPL in the monkey is already known to receive strong projections from area STP in the ventral stream. According to the hypothesis, this system could combine the products of several separate processing areas within the ventral stream (FFA, EBA, LO, PPA, etc.) into a dynamic spatial representation that would correlate closely with one's visual experience (including the contents of one's visual working memory) at any instant. The reason why such a system would tend to be asymmetrically distributed between the two hemispheres is not hard to see, given our assumption that the system must depend critically upon highly processed inputs from the ventral stream. The fact is that the human ventral stream is itself heavily asymmetrical, with the right cerebral hemisphere playing the major role. Evidence for this comes first from disorders such as topographical agnosia and prosopagnosia, which are associated much more with right occipito-temporal lesions than with left (see Grüsser and Landis 1991, for review). But functional MRI also regularly reveals corresponding asymmetries (for example in the FFA and PPA); indeed, sometimes area FFA is not detectable in the left hemisphere at all. It would therefore not be surprising that a system for representing objects and their spatial relationships would also be heavily concentrated in the right hemisphere. Indeed the very existence of this putative representational system in the inferior parietal lobule may have been a product of developments in hominid evolution that proceeded in parallel with the evolution of the highly asymmetrical human brain.

8.2.2 Knowledge and action

A full understanding of the visual control of action has been limited by the fact that most experiments on visually guided grasping have used a limited range of simple geometrical solids such as cylinders and blocks, all made of the same material. Everyday life, however, poses a range of problems for the brain that go well beyond picking up such meaningless objects. After all, people typically pick something up for a reason, to eat it, for example, or to use it as a tool. In fact, the very way one grasps an object such as a screwdriver or a banana reflects what one intends to do with it. For this to be possible, there needs to be top-down modulation of actions by previously acquired knowledge: one needs to know which part of the screwdriver, for example, is the handle, and which is the business end. The dorsal stream would not be able to do this in isolation because it has no direct access to semantic knowledge. It works only with what is available on the retina, that is, it is largely a bottom-up system. The ventral stream, in contrast, has intimate links with structures concerned with memory and knowledge (see Section 2.6.2 and Suzuki and Amaral (1994)). To put it another way, the dorsal system by itself can ensure that the screwdriver is grasped in a metrically accurate manner, but only the ventral stream can ensure that it is picked up at the right end. D.F.'s behaviour is instructive here. When confronted with a screwdriver, she is as likely as not to pick it up at the wrong end, although her grasp is beautifully calibrated with respect to its size and orientation (Carey *et al.* 1996). Interestingly, even a healthy person will behave like D.F., making 'functional' but not 'metric' visuomotor errors, under conditions of cognitive overload from a concurrent verbal memory task (Creem and Proffitt 2001). Given the close association of apraxia with left-hemisphere lesions (Kimura 1993), it may be significant that a concurrent visuospatial task did not interfere with grip selection in this experiment (Creem and Proffitt 2001), perhaps because, like praxis, the semantics of tool use is a left-hemisphere specialization (Johnson-Frey *et al.* 2005).

Although the dorsal stream can compute the size, orientation, location, and overall shape of a goal object from bottom-up retinal input, there are other basic attributes of the object that the dorsal stream cannot work out by itself—attributes such as the object's weight, fragility, surface friction, and compliance (Goodale and Haffenden 2003). When one reaches out to pick up an object, expectations about these properties determine the grip and lift forces that are applied during initial contact with the object's surface. These expectations are presumably prompted by perceptual processing carried out in the ventral stream. Some of the evidence for this comes from studies using pictorial illusions of size, which have been shown to have no effect on the scaling of grip aperture in flight (see Section 6.4, and Section 8.4.2 below). Such illusions nevertheless show a clear effect on the calibration of grip forces used to pick up the target object, presumably because the ventral stream 'sees' the objects as having different sizes and therefore different weights (Brenner and Smeets 1996; Jackson and Shaw 2000).

Curiously, however, the visual calibration of grip force can be dissociated from the visual processing underlying the well-known perceptual size–weight illusion, in which a small object feels heavier than a larger one of the same weight. Even though subjects can rapidly learn to apply the same grip forces to both objects, they continue to believe that the small one is heavier (Flanagan and Beltzner 2000; Mon-Williams and Murray 2000). This finding (illustrated in Fig. 8.3) contradicts a long-standing explanation of the size-weight illusion

Fig. 8.3 Changes in handgrip force during testing for the size-weight illusion. A: A small and large cube of identical weight each lifted by gripping a force sensor fixed to the top. B: Grip force data showing that after many practice trials subjects learn to apply the same force to both objects. C: Choice data showing that the smaller object continues to feel heavier than a larger one even after such training. Adapted with permission from Flanagan and Beltzner (2000).

(for example, Claparède 1901), which we ourselves endorsed in this book (Section 6.6): that the illusion is a secondary consequence of applying inappropriate lift forces to the different sized objects, leading to unexpected proprioceptive feedback. Instead, it appears that the calibration of grip force and high-level conscious beliefs about weight are independent, though both are informed by ventral-stream processes. Our evidence that the influence of visual size on judgements of weight depends on the ventral stream comes from D.F. and a second patient with similar ventral-stream lesions, S.B. (Lê *et al.* 2002). Both patients failed to show a significant visual size–weight illusion, although in a separate test they both experienced a strong kinesthetic size–weight illusion, in which they simply felt the size and shape of the objects while blindfolded (Dijkerman *et al.* 2004). Even though the ventral-stream processing contributes to both the (visual) size–weight illusion and the calibration of the required grip and lift forces, it has been proposed by Grandy and Westwood (2006) that quite different computations are involved. According to their proposal, the perception of heaviness is driven in part by density information, which signals important differences between classes of objects, whereas action systems, which need information only about the weight of the current goal object, focus on its absolute mass.

8.2.3 The role of attention in integrating the two streams in adaptive behaviour

Perhaps the biggest single problem that remains unsolved is how the two visual streams work together to provide us with a seamless visual life. In trying to understand how this might unfold, we have drawn a parallel with the problems faced by robotic engineers (Goodale and Humphrey 1998; Goodale and Milner 2004). In particular, we have suggested that there is a close analogy between the interaction of the two visual streams and 'tele-assistance', one of the most efficient schemes that has been devised for the remote control of robots working in hostile environments. Consider the case of a human operator on earth communicating with a semi-autonomous robot operating on the surface of the moon. In the tele-assistance mode, the human operator can identify potential goal objects, such as an interesting rock, by viewing the moon's surface via a video camera mounted on the robot—and then send an instruction to the robot to pick up the rock. A robot working with tele-assistance in this way is much more flexible than a completely autonomous robot, which could not cope with events that its programmers have not anticipated. The only way to ensure that the robot performs appropriately in unforeseen circumstances, at least in the present state of robotics, is to have a human operator somewhere in the loop. Nonetheless, tele-assistance has to be distinguished from 'tele-operation', in which the human operator exerts direct control by sending instructions that are simply reproduced in a one-to-one fashion by the robot, as for example in a nuclear research facility where a joystick might directly control the movements of a robot arm in a radioactive laboratory. This method of control cannot cope well with sudden changes in scale on the video monitor or with a significant delay between the communicated action and feedback from that action. In tele-assistance, however, the human operator simply identifies or 'flags' a target object and specifies what kind of action is to be performed, in general terms, to achieve the desired goal. Once this information is communicated to the semi-autonomous robot, the robot can use its on-board rangefinders and other sensing devices to program and control the required movements for achieving the specified goal. Thus tele-assistance combines the flexibility of tele-operation with the precision of autonomous robotic control.

Our current conception of how the two visual streams interact in the animal or human brain corresponds nicely to this engineering principle. The perceptual systems in the ventral stream, in association with memory and other cognitive systems in the brain, perform the role of the human operator in recognizing a potentially important target. They identify different objects in the scene, using a representational system that is rich and detailed but not metrically precise. When a particular goal object has been flagged, dedicated visuomotor networks in the dorsal stream, in conjunction with output systems elsewhere in the brain (located in other brain structures including the premotor cortex, basal ganglia, and brainstem), are activated to perform the desired motor act. In other words, dorsal stream networks, with their precise egocentric coding of the location, size, orientation, and shape of the goal object, are like the robotic component of tele-assistance. Both systems have to work together in the production of purposive behaviour—one system to select the goal object from the visual array, the other to carry out the required metrical computations for the goal-directed action. Yet there remain several missing links, of course. We need to explain how once a target object has been identified using ventral stream processing, it is selected for action, and how this selection is then communicated to the visuomotor systems in the dorsal stream.

The ventral stream alone does not constitute an intelligent operator that can make such assessments and plans. In fact the ventral and dorsal streams are merely two players in a highly complex and recursive system. There has to be some sort of top-down executive control—probably vested in prefrontal mechanisms—that can initiate the operation of attentional search and thus set the whole process in motion (Desimone and Duncan 1995; Miller and Cohen 2001; Goodale and Haffenden 2003). Two-way parieto-frontal networks may then play a critical role in recruiting specialized systems located in dorsal-stream areas, such as the lateral intraparietal area, LIP, which seem to control both exogenous and endogenous shifts of spatial attention in monkeys and humans (Corbetta *et al.* 2002; Bisley and Goldberg 2003). In fact we would like to suggest a direct analogy between the 'flagging' of a target object in the tele-assistance case and the brain's shifting of the focus of visual attention from one place to another within a visual scene. In some sense, area LIP can be seen as acting like the video camera scanning the visual scene in tele-assistance, and thereby providing new inputs that the ventral stream can process and pass back to frontal systems that can assess their potential importance. (Of course in practice the video camera (or LIP) system will not scan the environment randomly: it will be constrained to a greater or lesser degree by top-down information about the nature of the potential targets and where those targets might be located, information that reflects the priorities of the operator/organism that are presumably elaborated in prefrontal systems.) When such a positive evaluation has been made, a recurrent message transmitted back along fronto-parietal pathways to high-level representational systems in the IPL (especially in the right hemisphere in humans) might then reactivate the target location in readiness for subsequent actions to be performed.

But before instructions can be transmitted to the dorsal visuomotor control systems (the semi-autonomous robot) to act upon, the nature of the action required needs to be determined. As we already noted in the last section of Chapter 7, 'a high-level praxic system needs to have access to the products of the ventral stream's processing, so that it can then "instruct" the relevant visuomotor systems'. To enable this step to occur, information presumably has to be exchanged between right IPL and left IPL, where, as we have noted elsewhere, brain damage is liable to cause apraxia. Then, finally, the dorsal stream has to be informed as to the task it has to perform and the locus of the target on which to perform it. One way that this ventral–dorsal transmission could happen is via recurrent projections from the spatial foci of activity in the ventral stream and IPL back downstream to area V1 and other adjacent visual areas. Once a target has been 'highlighted' on these retinotopic maps, its location could then finally be forwarded to the dorsal stream for action (Lamme and Roelfsema 2000). There is evidence from neurophysiological studies that when a monkey pays attention to a visual stimulus in a particular location, the activity of neurones corresponding to that location is enhanced in many visual areas (Moore 2006), including primary visual cortex (Supèr *et al.* 2001). This 'highlighting' may correspond to the subjective experience of enhanced perception that is associated with our visual attention to one object rather than another (James 1890: his famous description of 'what attention is' is quoted in Chapter 7, Section 7.2.1).

It is relevant here to revisit our discussion in Chapter 7 of the book (Section 7.2.1), in which we argued that the brain's basic visuospatial attention-switching mechanisms may be quite ancient in origin and indeed operate at a visually unconscious level even in humans. There is now direct evidence that this is so, from an elegant series of experiments in which Kentridge and his colleagues (1999, 2004) have tested patients with blindsight (see Chapter 3) using variations of the Posner cueing paradigm. They have shown that these patients can switch their visual attention between stimuli that are not consciously perceived, and can do so even in response to cues that are themselves not consciously perceived. As Kentridge and colleagues point out, these demonstrations of 'attention without awareness' imply that although attention may well be a necessary condition, it is not a *sufficient* condition for conscious perception (Kentridge *et al.* 2004). According to our model, the ability of blindsight patients to shift their visual attention would be mediated by structures such as LIP (perhaps in conjunction with the superior colliculus: Kustov and Robinson 1996) acting under instructions implemented by the prefrontal cortex, and does not in itself require ventral stream activation. If the ventral stream can receive visual information, of course, then such switches of attention would be expected to have conscious effects: but ventral stream activation would be the *sine qua non* for this. The blindsight patient would accordingly not experience William James's 'taking possession by the mind, in clear and vivid form, of one out of what seem several simultaneously possible objects or trains of thought', since some parts of the circuitry that we suggest above would provide that this experience have been compromised. Thus William James's 'focalization and concentration' may well still be present in blindsight, but if so they are unaccompanied by the vividness of consciousness that would normally go with them. The fact that different aspects of attention can thus be dissociated from one another reinforces the constant need to be beware of using everyday experience to guide theorizing in cognitive neuroscience.

Although the above sketch of the systems involved in the orchestration of planned acts is clearly no more than speculative, it is eminently clear that whatever complex interactions are required cannot be mediated by any simple serial processing system. There must be multiple iterative processing, achieved through the constant interplay among different control systems at different levels of processing.

Plate 1

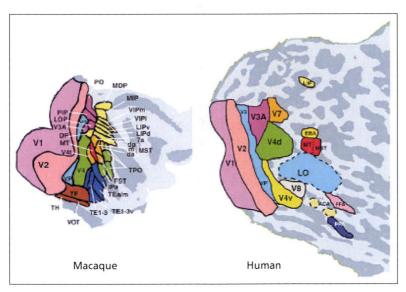

Macaque   Human

A comparison of the layout of visual areas in macaque monkey and human brain, presented as flattened representations of the cortical surface. Areas believed to be homologous in the two species share the same colour. Adapted with permission from Tootell *et al.* (2003).

The lateral occipital area (LO). Functional MRI has revealed the existence of a human cortical area that responds selectively to pictures of objects. This area shows a higher activation to intact pictures of objects than to pictures of non-objects such as faces or random shapes, or to fragmented versions of pictures of objects (as illustrated here). The diagram on the right illustrates the typical subtraction pattern resulting from responses to intact objects minus those to fragmented objects.

Plate 2

The relative locations of the lateral occipital area LO (shown in blue), fusiform face area FFA (shown in red), and parahippocampal place area PPA (shown in green), represented on a ventral surface view of the human cerebral hemispheres.

High-resolution images of the fusiform face area (FFA: defined by faces > objects) and the fusiform body area (FBA: defined by bodies > objects) (A) FFA (blue) and FBA (red) activation as well as the overlap (white) between the two regions are shown on functional images from three subjects. The slices are horizontal and left–right reversed, with posterior regions shown at the bottom of each image and the cerebellum at the top. (B) The same regions in the same three subjects mapped onto the inflated ventral surface of the right temporo-occipital cortex, with the occipital pole at the bottom. Note the considerable variation in the sizes and relative locations of these areas. Adapted with permission from Schwarzlose *et al*. (2005).

Plate 3

D.F.'s lesions. (A) A right lateral view of D.F.'s brain, showing a lesion marked in blue that encompasses area LO. (B) A ventral view of D.F.'s cerebral hemispheres, showing that the lesions of area LO are bilateral. (C) fMRI activation for line drawings (versus scrambled drawings) plotted on a horizontal section through D.F.'s brain at the level of the red line on panel A. D.F. shows no selective activation for line drawings either in area LO or in neighbouring areas. In contrast, a control subject shows robust activation to the same drawings. The activation in the control subject's brain, which has been mathematically morphed to fit onto D.F.'s brain, coincides well with her LO lesions.

Top: The pattern of activation in D. F.'s PPA and FFA when D.F. was shown images of scenes (versus scrambled scenes) and faces (versus scrambled faces) respectively. Her lesions, which include area LO bilaterally, are shown in blue. Bottom: The approximate location of area OFA, which, unlike area FFA, was probably destroyed bilaterally in D.F.'s brain. This may explain why she can no longer recognize individual faces.

Plate 4

Diagram of the approximate locations of the parietal reach region (PRR), the lateral intra-parietal sulcus area (area LIP), and the anterior intraparietal sulcus area (area AIP) in the monkey. These have been mapped using single-neurone recording techniques, in conjunction with various anatomical criteria. Reproduced with permission from Cohen and Andersen (2002).

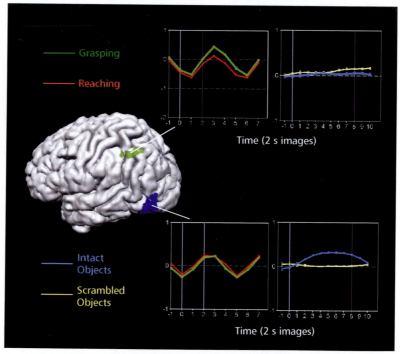

fMRI correlates of grasping and object recognition in healthy subjects. The activation (% BOLD signal change) for a single subject is shown on a 3-D rendered brain. Activation in AIP (grasping versus reaching) is shown in green and activation for area LO (intact versus scrambled objects) is shown in blue. The time-courses on the right-hand side of the figure illustrate that area LO shows no differential activation for object-directed grasping and AIP shows no differential activation for viewing objects. This shows that the object analysis required for grasping does not involve area LO and that AIP is not driven by 2-D images of objects (when grasping is not required). Data from Culham et al. (2003).

Plate 5

The locations of the homologues of areas PRR, LIP, and AIP in humans. These are
defined by use of fMRI to locate the regions specifically activated during visually
guided reaching, saccadic eye movements, and grasping, respectively.

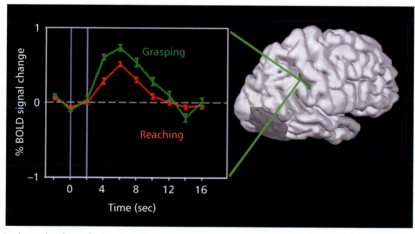

Brain activations during reaching and grasping in patient D.F. Right: The activation
corresponding to grasping vs. reaching is shown in green in the right hemisphere for
D.F. Left: The averaged event-related time-course of activations for grasping and
reaching trials in AIP. Note that these time-courses are very similar to those of
healthy subjects shown in Plate 4 (bottom).

Plate 6

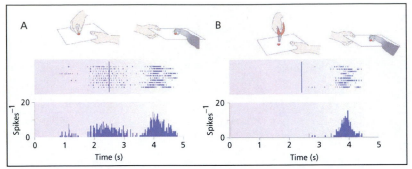

Example of a mirror neurone. The activity of a neurone recorded in the monkey premotor cortex area F5 is illustrated here. (A) The raster trace in the top part of the figure shows the cell's responses during a protocol in which the monkey first observes a grasping movement made by the experimenter and then performs a similar grasping movement itself. The vertical line shows the time at which the observed grasp is completed. (B) Here the object is first grasped with tweezers by the experimenter and then by the monkey. The neurone shows a visual response only when the monkey observes a manual grasp. Adapted with permission from Rizzolatti et al. (2001).

Relationship between brain activation in the FFA and the PPA of the human brain in response to rivalrous visual images of a face and of a house as measured by fMRI. The level of activation switches between the two brain areas in step with reports of rivalry (top) in just the same way as those measured when the two pictures are physically presented and removed (bottom) in a manner mimicking the alternations of rivalry. Reproduced with permission from Tong et al. (1998).

Plate 7

fMRI activation in a patient with a profound left-sided extinction following right parietal damage, shown in parasagittal slices through the brain. Even though the patient failed to perceive images of faces or houses presented in his left visual field on extinction trials, he continued to show activation in both primary visual cortex and ventral stream areas (left column) in the same locations within the right hemisphere as the activation seen on trials when he perceived these stimuli (right column). The activation on the bilateral extinction trials, however, was less robust than that seen on left unilateral trials. Adapted with permission from Rees *et al.* (2000).

(A) The pattern of brain activation during reaching to a visual target after making a saccade to it. (B) The pattern of activation during reaching to a visual target without making a saccade to it. The activation patterns are shown on superior (left) and posterior (right) views of a rendered three-dimensional brain of one of the participants. The dorsal stream is activated in the medial intraparietal (mIPS) region in both tasks, but also in the region of the parieto-occipital junction (POJ) in the case where the target remains in the peripheral visual field of the subject. Adapted with permission from Prado *et al.* (2005).

Plate 8

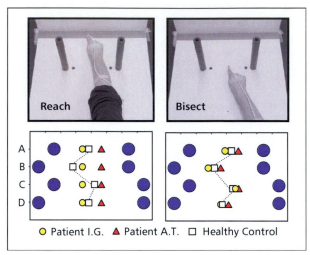

Reaching between potential obstacles. Patients were faced with a board on which two cylinders were placed, one to the left and one to the right of centre, each cylinder varying from trial to trial between two possible locations. The patients were asked either to reach between the two objects to touch a grey strip at the back of the board (top left) or to point to the midpoint between the two cylinders (top right). In both tasks, control subjects varied their action trajectories lawfully depending on the four different cylinder configurations A–D. The optic ataxia patients A.T. and I.G. did so in the bisection task (bottom right), but were unaffected by the obstacles in the reaching task (bottom left). Adapted with permission from Schindler *et al.* (2004).

Apparatus for testing perceptual judgements and visuomotor control with the hollow-face illusion. (A) Two small magnets (marked in red) were placed on the cheek and forehead of either the normal face or the hollow mask.(B) The fast flicking movement made towards normal face. (C) The same movement made towards the illusory (actually hollow) face. Inset shows a photograph of bottom-lit hollow face, creating the illusion of a normal convex face.

8.3 **Operating principles of the dorsal stream: new insights**

8.3.1 **Does the dorsal stream care about non-target objects?**

In presenting our original conception of dorsal-stream function, we may have given the impression that the action system processes the target object and nothing else. This is due to the fact that almost all visuomotor research on the dorsal stream has used tasks in which a single target is presented in an otherwise empty field. But in the real world there are often other objects in the scene, some of which might be obstacles for a target-directed movement. New data indicate that the dorsal stream not only directs the reaching hand towards the target object, but it also modulates the reach trajectory with respect to *non*-target objects. Patients with bilateral dorsal-stream lesions have been found not to modify the path of their hand from trial to trial as they reach between two potential obstacles whose locations vary, behaving as if the obstacle configuration was not changing at all (Schindler *et al.* 2004). Yet remarkably, when asked to point midway between the same two objects, again varying in position from trial to trial, the patients do just as well as healthy control subjects. Presumably they do better here because the bisection task, which requires a perceptual judgement, is readily handled by the ventral stream—which is intact in these patients—with little or no help from the dorsal stream.

In complete contrast, patients with visual form agnosia (D.F. and S.B.) perform within the normal range on this reaching task, adjusting their hand path as the obstacles change position from trial to trial (Rice *et al.* 2006). Yet they take little account of the locations of the two objects when trying to indicate the midpoint between them. This suggests that the ventral stream is not an essential part of the circuitry that underlies the automatic adjustments we make to non-target objects while making rapid reaches. Nor, it seems, are the right parieto-temporal areas typically damaged in patients with hemispatial neglect. In a study by McIntosh *et al.* (2004*a*), 10 out of 12 such patients behaved completely normally in the reaching task, whereas all 12 of them showed a predictable asymmetry in the extent to which they took the left object into account during the bisection task. Taken together, these new data offer a glimpse into the workings of the dorsal stream during everyday reaching behaviour in a cluttered environment. But of course, this is not to say that the ventral stream is never involved in obstacle avoidance. For example when reaching around fragile or noxious obstacles (such as a wine glass or a cactus), we make slower and more deliberate movements, presumably with the help of ventral-stream processing. Parenthetically, these experiments provide a graphic illustration of the fact that different visuospatial systems come into play for different visuospatial tasks. In other words, the dorsal stream is not a general-purpose spatial processor, as was originally proposed by Ungerleider and Mishkin (1982). Instead, both streams appear to process spatial information, doing so in different ways and for different purposes.

We may infer from these data that automatic obstacle avoidance behaviour is critically dependent on the integrity of the dorsal stream, while depending little or not at all on ventral stream processing. This conclusion prompts an important prediction. We argued in Section 8.2.1 above that ventral-stream activity plays a *necessary* role in generating visual awareness. One inevitable prediction that must follow from this claim is that visuomotor skills that depend exclusively on dorsal stream processing should proceed on the basis of 'unconscious' visual information, that is without the need for concomitant visual awareness of the stimuli controlling the behaviour. In a recent experiment we have gathered data on obstacle avoidance that support this prediction (McIntosh et al. 2004*b*). We tested a patient, V.E., who exhibited visual (and tactile) extinction for left-sided stimuli following a right temporo-parietal infarct. The reaching behaviour of this patient followed identical (and normal) trajectories between two potential obstacles, irrespective of whether he reported the presence of the left-side object or not. Moreover, his reaches showed a marked shift towards the left on other trials when there truly was no left object present. It thus appears that although V.E.'s damaged ventral/IPL system was unable to provide any conscious experience of the left object on many trials, his dorsal stream was still able to take full account of the object.

It should be noted that the obstacle-avoidance impairment that Schindler *et al.* (2004) observed in bilateral optic ataxia was obtained in a task where the non-target stimuli appeared in peripheral vision. The specificity of the impairment is strikingly illustrated in a patient (M.H.) with unilateral optic ataxia due to a left parietal lesion, who showed a selective disorder of pointing with his right hand only, and only to targets presented in his right visual hemifield (M.G. Edwards and G.W. Humphreys, unpublished observations). When tested on Schindler *et al.*'s (2004) reaching task, M.H. took full account of both potential obstacles when using his left hand to reach, but took account only of the object on the left when using his right hand (Rice *et al.* 2005). In other words, M.H. showed a selective failure to respond to non-target objects on the right when making right-hand reaches, but showed no such failure when using his left hand. These striking data confirm the visuomotor (rather than purely visuospatial) nature of the dorsal stream's role in guiding the reaching arm around obstacles and suggest that non-target stimuli activate specific nodes in the same visuomotor network (presumably the PRR) that governs the visuomotor processing of the target itself, thereby biasing the programming of the reaching movement to the target.

Our use of a central fixation point in these studies of optic ataxic patients arose from the frequent observation that when the eyes are permitted to move to the target, pointing accuracy is typically much less impaired. This improvement is apparent in A.T. (Jeannerod *et al.* 1994; Milner *et al.* 1999) and I.G. (Milner *et al.* 2003), and also in M.H. (M.G. Edwards and G.W. Humphreys, unpublished observations). (It should be noted, however, that inaccuracy (in the form of variable error) still remains to some degree when the target is located centrally (Milner *et al.* 1999; Pisella *et al.* 2000; Rossetti *et al.* 2005).) Rossetti and colleagues (2003) have argued that this relative preservation of reaching accuracy to central targets implies a highly restricted visuomotor role for the dorsal stream, that is, one limited to peripheral targets. This conclusion, if correct, would it make it impossible to sustain our proposal that the dorsal stream is the major player in visuomotor control considered as a whole. Recent evidence using event-related fMRI in healthy subjects, however, suggests an alternative interpretation. Prado and colleagues (2005) have demonstrated two quite distinct patterns of dorsal-stream activation according to whether their subjects reached toward central or peripheral visual targets. The areas activated during central pointing included the medial intraparietal sulcus, while those activated during reaching in peripheral vision also included the parieto-occipital junction (POJ). These overlapping patterns are illustrated in Plate 7 (bottom) in a representative subject. It is notable that the two distinct systems extend also into the dorsal premotor cortex (PMd): central pointing activated the caudal part of PMd, whereas peripheral pointing also activated a more rostral part of PMd. Prado and colleagues relate their findings to the recent report of a subtractive anatomical study by Karnath and Perenin (2005), which indicates that the POJ is the most frequent site of lesions that cause optic ataxia. One implication of their argument would be that less typical more extensive parietal lesions, invading more anterior regions of the intraparietal sulcus, would lead to reaching impairments in central as well as peripheral vision.

8.3.2 The dorsal stream as an 'automatic pilot'

In our original proposal, we assumed that the dorsal stream plays a critical role both in the initial programming of reaching movements and in the automatic online corrections of those movements once they are underway. More recently, however, it has been suggested that although the online control of reaching is indeed a dorsal stream function, the initial programming of the movement may be governed by visual information processed in a different system, such as the ventral stream (Rossetti *et al.* 2003; Glover 2004). There is certainly now very good evidence for an essential role of the dorsal stream in the online control of reaches in response to unpredictable shifts of target position (see Section 6.2). For example, TMS administered over the medial intra-parietal sulcus has been found to cause a selective impairment in making such online adjustments (Desmurget *et al.* 1999) and it is severely impaired in patients with bilateral optic ataxia (Pisella *et al.* 2000; Gréa *et al.* 2002). But this is not the only problem that patients with optic ataxia have in guiding their reaching movements: the very same patients head off in the wrong direction right from the start of their reaching movements (Milner *et al.* 2003). Similarly, they exhibit an initial directional failure in the programming of movement trajectories in the obstacle avoidance experiments described above. Because these experiments were run in visual open loop, the patients had to plan their movements right from the start (Schindler *et al.* 2004). The weight of current evidence therefore confirms that the dorsal stream is implicated in both the programming *and* the online control of reaching. Of course, it is still possible that the initial programming of heading and later online control depend on separate subsystems in the dorsal stream. In fact, if this were true, it could explain why Desmurget *et al.*'s TMS study showed a deficit only in online control. Most patients with optic ataxia are likely to have damage to both subsystems, but it is entirely possible that other patients could have damage to one system and not the other.

As well as operating without the necessary intervention of an 'intention' to shift one's trajectory, such automatic self-corrections seem also to occur without the need for visual awareness of the location of one's hand during the course of the reach. Our evidence for this comes from a study carried out with the extinction patient V.E., whom we introduced in Section 8.3.1 above. Schenk and colleagues (2005*b*) used a paradigm in which an LED was attached to the left (reaching) hand of the subject in an otherwise darkened room. While V.E. made reaching movements to a target LED placed 5 cm to the right or left of the body midline, the hand LED flashed briefly on a proportion of the trials, thus providing feedback information on the hand's precise location during the reach. As expected, since the hand LED was always seen to the left of the target, V.E. 'extinguished' it on many of these feedback trials—that is, he failed to report it. Yet despite this, V.E. reached significantly more accurately on trials when the hand LED was flashed, and this improvement with feedback occurred whether or not he was aware of the flash.

8.4 Spatial and temporal constraints on perception and visuomotor control

8.4.1 Metrics and frames of reference

As we argued at the beginning of Chapter 6, successful grasping of an object requires that the brain compute the actual (absolute) size of the object and its orientation and position. Moreover, the information about the orientation and position of the object must be computed in egocentric frames of reference—in other words, in frames of reference that take into account the orientation and position of the object with respect to the effector that is to be used to perform the action. Equally critical is the time at which these computations are performed. Observers and goal objects rarely stay in a static relationship with one another and, as a consequence, the egocentric coordinates of a target object can often change dramatically from moment to moment. It makes sense, therefore, that the required coordinates for action be computed immediately before the movements are initiated and it would be of little value for these ephemeral coordinates (or the resulting motor programs) to be stored in memory.

The situation is quite different for perception, both in terms of the frames of reference used to construct the percept and the time period over which that percept (or some version of it) can be accessed. Perceptual processing appears not to rely on computations about the absolute size of objects or their egocentric locations—a fact that explains why we have no difficulty watching television, a medium in which there are no absolute metrics at all. Instead, the perceptual system computes the size, location, shape, and orientation of an object primarily in relation to other objects and surfaces in the scene. In other words, the metrics of perception are inherently relative and the frames of reference are largely scene-based. Encoding an object in a scene-based frame of reference (what we earlier in the book called an allocentric frame of reference—see Chapter 4) permits a perceptual representation of the object that preserves the relations between the object parts and its surroundings without requiring precise information about the absolute size of the object or its exact position with respect to the observer. Furthermore, detailed visual information at any one moment is limited to what is present within a few degrees of the fovea. Indeed, if our perceptual machinery attempted to deliver the real size and distance of all the objects in the visual array, the computational load on the system would be astronomical. (For a more detailed discussion of these issues, see Goodale and Humphrey (1998).) But perception also operates over a much longer time scale than that used in the visual control of action. We can recognize objects we have seen minutes, hours, days, or even years before.

When objects are coded in scene-based frames of reference, it is much easier to preserve their identity over relatively long periods of time. In other words, we can recognize objects that we have seen before, even though the position of those objects with respect to our body might have changed considerably since the last time we saw them. But of course, this stored information is not only available for mediating recognition of previously encountered objects, but also potentially for contributing to the control of our movements, particularly when we are working in off-line mode.

In the next two sections we will discuss recent research that bears upon both the spatial and the temporal aspects of perceptual and visuomotor function.

8.4.2 Action and illusion

In Section 6.3, we presented evidence showing that real-time actions were very often insensitive to familiar illusions of spatial position. Thus, in an early experiment, Wong and Mack (1981) demonstrated that when a large frame surrounding a single stationary dot changed position, the dot was perceived to shift in the direction opposite to the frame. Yet despite this illusion of location, a saccadic eye movement was directed to the true not the apparent position of the dot. In a related study, Bridgeman *et al.* (1997) used a modified form of the Roelofs illusion. In this experiment, a stationary dot presented within a stationary frame offset from the observer's midline appeared to be shifted in location in a direction opposite to the direction of the offset of the frame. Rapid pointing or jabbing movements directed towards the dot, however, were quite accurate. Bridgeman and colleagues interpreted this result as evidence for separate 'cognitive and sensorimotor maps' of visual space, a position quite consistent with the two-visual-systems model set out in this book.

One plausible account for the Roelofs illusion is that it is mediated by a change in the 'perceived straight ahead' (PSA), and indeed there is clear evidence that the PSA becomes shifted towards the centre of the offset frame. Thus, if the PSA is shifted away from the midline, then the perceived position of the dot would be shifted in the opposite direction. We would argue that even though the perceived position of the dot is influenced by the shift in the PSA, the visuomotor system should continue to operate within an egocentric frame of reference quite independently of the PSA. Alternatively, however, Dassonville *et al.* (2004) have shown that one can explain the apparently correct pointing (and saccadic eye movements) without assuming (as we would) that the visuomotor networks are immune to the shift in PSA. They point out that if the visuomotor system uses the same (shifted) frame of reference as the perceptual system, then the programming of the hand or eye movement will be made with reference to the shifted PSA and as a consequence will still end up on the target. Dassonville *et al.* (2004) tried to disentangle our account against this 'biased-midline' explanation with the use of complex 'anti-responding' experiments. As we have previously argued, however, anti-responding (looking or pointing to a location on the opposite side of the midline that mirrors the perceived position of the stimulus) is fundamentally different from target-directed responding (Dijkerman *et al.* 1997). Anti-responding is, by its very nature, a cognitively driven activity and as a consequence will engage ventral-stream mechanisms. Thus, in our account, anti-responding movements will be reflected across the *perceived* straight ahead, whereas target-directed responding will continue to use egocentric frames of reference.

Dassonville *et al.* (2004) do, in fact, acknowledge in their discussion that our two-visual-systems model can still account for their data. It is true that, considered solely in the context of the Roelofs experiments, their assumption of a single visual representation governing both perception and action provides a more parsimonious account than does our two-visual-systems model. But our model does not stand or fall solely as an account of Roelofs data. As we argue throughout this book, it also accounts for a wide range of other data as well, extending across many different empirical domains. Logic requires that rejecting our model within the Roelofs context would *ipso facto* imply a rejection all of that broader explanatory power as well. Appealing to parsimony is a useful guiding principle in scientific thinking, but only if it includes all of the available data, not just those from a single experimental paradigm.

Not only are actions often insensitive to illusions of position, they can also be resistant to illusions of size. In what has become a widely cited study, Aglioti *et al.* (1995) found that the powerful Titchener Circles (or Ebbinghaus) illusion had no effect on visually guided grasping (see Section 6.4 of this book). In their experiment, pairs of discs were presented within annular arrays of (respectively) smaller or larger circles, generating a strong perceptual size illusion: yet the illusion did not affect the maximal opening of the hand when subjects reached out to pick up one of the discs. We argued that this dissociation reflects the different metrics and frames of reference used by perception and action. Since 1995, many studies have produced similar dissociations to those of Aglioti *et al.* using a whole range of different illusions. Nevertheless, it must be acknowledged that some studies have found significant effects (albeit generally weak ones) of perceptual illusions on action (for reviews, see Bruno 2001; Carey 2001; Franz 2001).

It is important to note, however, that being able to demonstrate that action is resistant to visual illusions under any circumstances is a powerful argument for separate visual processing for perception and action. Nevertheless, the studies that have apparently challenged the idea that the control of action is immune to perceptual illusions are of interest in their own right. These challenges fall into several categories, including non-replication (Franz et al. 2000), the contention that early studies did not adequately match action and perception tasks for various input, attention, and output demands (Vishton et al. 1999; Bruno 2001; Smeets and Brenner 2001), and the idea that action tasks involve multiple stages of processing from purely perceptual to more 'automatic' visuomotor control (Glover and Dixon 2001; Glover 2002). Most of these challenges can readily be accommodated within the basic framework of the perception–action hypothesis, yet each provides important new insights into the nature of the processing mechanisms underlying perception versus action.

The fact that grasping is sometimes sensitive to illusory displays (for example, Franz et al. 2000), is not by itself, of course, a refutation of the idea of two visual systems. Indeed, one should not be surprised that perception affects our motor behaviour; after all, as we have repeatedly argued, ultimately perception has to affect our actions or it would never have evolved. As mentioned above, the real surprise is that we can sometimes demonstrate, even in normal observers, instances where visually guided action is apparently unaffected by perception. The optimal task for finding such a dissociation is one in which the required action is rapid and 'automatic' — the kind of behaviour that would be expected to be dominated by the dorsal stream. The more deliberate and unpractised the movement, the more likely it is that ventral-stream 'perceptual' effects will intrude. In the case of the Ebbinghaus experiments, it is important to note that there are other, non-illusory, aspects of the display that can influence the grasp. An apparent effect of the illusion on grip aperture sometimes arises from the fact that the surrounding annulus, under some circumstances, is treated unwittingly as a potential obstacle by the visuomotor system (Haffenden and Goodale 2000). As we saw in Section 8.3.1, there is plenty of evidence to suggest that reaching and grasping network in the dorsal stream are sensitive to the location of potential obstacles. Moreover, manipulations of the position of the circles making up the annulus in the Ebbinghaus display have been shown to exert a powerful effect on the scaling of grasp quite independently of any illusion (Haffenden et al. 2001; de Grave et al. 2005). Finally, a recent study by Gonzalez et al. (2006) showed that sensitivity to the apparent size of the targets in both the Ebbinghaus and the Ponzo illusions depends on which hand is doing the grasping. They found that the scaling of grip aperture in the left hand was sensitive to the illusions, even though, as many have shown before, the right hand was not (see Fig. 8.4). Although it is not yet fully understood whether this difference between the hands reflects hemispheric

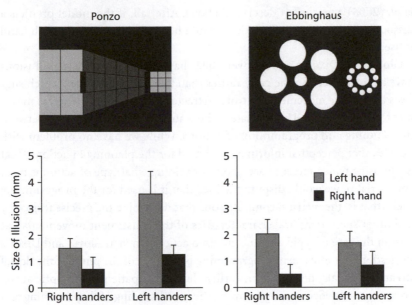

Fig. 8.4 The effects of geometric visual illusions on grasping with the right and left hand. In both the Ponzo (left) and Ebbinghaus (right) illusions, right-handed subjects showed no significant effect of the illusion on their handgrip size when using the right hand (black bars), yet showed a strong and significant effect when using the left hand (grey bars). Left-handed subjects also showed a similar effect of larger illusion magnitude when using the left hand. Adapted with permission from Gonzalez *et al.* (2006).

asymmetries in visuomotor control or differences in skill (or both), it is clear that the findings cannot be accommodated within any model of visual behaviour that argues for a single representation of the world—because that same representation would have to control grasps made by either hand.

Although not denying that illusions often fail to affect grasping, Smeets and co-workers (Smeets and Brenner 2001; Smeets *et al.* 2002) have argued that the reason the grasp is unaffected is because the final positions of the finger and thumb are computed separately—and there is thus no need for the grasp to take into account target size *per se*. The only thing that is required is the computation of two separate spatial locations. According to this view, dissociations between judgement and action occur because pictorial size illusions affect the perception of extent but not location (c.f., Mack *et al.* 1985). Although this idea sounds reasonable, it has been challenged not only by other theoretical accounts (Mon-Williams and McIntosh 2000; Mon-Williams and Tresilian 2001), but also by the results of the Gonzalez *et al.* (2006) experiment described above. After all, if the model predicts a dissociation, then this dissociation should be present no matter which hand is used.

Glover and Dixon (2001; Glover 2002) have reported that visual illusions have a larger effect on the early rather than late stages of action, which suggests that online movement control is refractory to perception, whereas movement planning is not. Unfortunately, these authors fail to distinguish between the planning and programming of actions. While we have no problem with the idea that perceptual information is used for the planning of actions (that is, choosing which target to act upon or deciding what type of action is most appropriate), we would dispute the idea that it is used for the programming itself (that is, the metrical computations that determine the precise trajectory and other spatiotemporal characteristics of the constituent movements), at least in the case of rapid and automatized actions. In fact, Glover and Dixon's suggestion that movement programming is not part of the remit of the dorsal stream is partially derived from earlier claims that patients with optic ataxia do not show a deficit in programming the initial heading of their reaching and grasping movements. But as we have already noted above, patients with dorsal-stream damage show deficits in both the initial programming of their reaching movements as well as in online control—suggesting that the visual transformations used by both of these aspects of motor control are mediated by the dorsal stream. Finally, Glover and Dixon's claims that the effects of illusions can be seen early in the movement have not been replicated by others using the Ebbinghaus illusion (Danckert *et al.* 2002).

Two recent lines of evidence have helped to clarify the relation between object perception and object-directed action in the context of visual illusions. First, one important reason why a perceptual illusion may influence a visually guided action relates to *where in the brain the illusion originates*. It is likely that 'contextual' illusions such as the Ebbinghaus originate in higher-order areas within the ventral stream. But other illusions may arise in primary visual cortex or in one of the other retinotopic cortical areas, which feed not only into the ventral stream but also into the dorsal stream. Dyde and Milner (2002) have shown that the orientation of the grasping hand is sensitive to a simultaneous tilt illusion (STI)—similar to that used by Glover and Dixon (2001)—but not a rod-and-frame illusion (RFI), even though the two visual displays have equivalent effects on judgements of target orientation. Dyde and Milner argue that the STI arises from 'early' (area V1 or area V2) stages of visual processing and thereby misleads both the dorsal and ventral visual pathways. The RFI in contrast is thought to arise during later stages of processing (that is, in inferotemporal cortex) and should consequently not affect action, because the encapsulated visuomotor systems within the dorsal stream do not have direct access to this processing.

The second line of evidence comes from another class of illusions that often (but not always) show similar effects on perception and action, namely illusions of movement (Yamagishi *et al.* 2001; Whitney *et al.* 2003). Many of these illusions are thought to arise in MT, the major motion processing area, which as we noted earlier in this chapter (Section 8.1.2) is actually an early visual module that receives direct connections from area V1 and projects to both the ventral and the dorsal streams (Felleman and Van Essen 1991; Van Essen *et al.* 2001). Similar accounts have been put forward to explain the fact that there are reliable directional anisotropies in the perception of the direction of motion even though such anisotropies are not present in smooth pursuit eye movements (Churchland *et al.* 2003) and the observation that fast reaching movements are sensitive to target mislocalization errors induced by distant visual motion signals (Whitney *et al.* 2003).

Although the discussion so far has been an examination of why dissociations between perception and action in normal observers are sometimes difficult to demonstrate, there have been many new and instructive examples of dissociations in the context of visual illusions. One striking dissociation was described recently by Króliczak *et al.* (2006) using the well-known hollow-face illusion. This illusion is a knowledge-based, top-down effect, where extensive and powerful (though implicit) knowledge of convex faces rejects the correct hollow perception in favour of reversed depth (Gregory 1997). The hollow-face illusion presumably arises entirely within the ventral stream—unusually among the illusions that have been used in this context—and should therefore not affect the visuomotor computations in the dorsal stream. In the Króliczak *et al.* experiment, subjects estimated the positions of small targets placed on the actually hollow but apparently normal face and used their fingers to 'flick' the targets off (see Plate 8, bottom). Despite the presence of a compelling illusion of a normal face, the flicking movements were directed at the real not the illusory locations of the targets (see Fig. 8.5). This demonstrates that the visuomotor system can use bottom-up sensory inputs (for example, vergence) to guide movements to the veridical locations of targets in the real world, even when the perceived positions of the targets are influenced, or even reversed, by top-down processing.

8.4.3 Reaching into the past

As we discussed earlier, not only do the two streams use different frames of reference but they also have different temporal characteristics. The dorsal stream may enable us to reach out and grasp objects with exquisite ease, but it

Fig. 8.5 Dissociation between perception and action with the hollow-face illusion. Perceptual task: Subjects marked (with reference to a line on a piece of paper) the perceived positions of the target on the foreheads and cheeks of the faces. The mean distances of the pencil marks from the line indicating the reference plate (see Plate 8 bottom) are shown on the abscissa. The illusory face (which was actually hollow) appeared to be a normal convex face; the hollow face (lower set of bars) was revealed for what it was by increasing the overhead illumination in the room. Error bars indicate standard errors of the mean. Flicking task: the mean distance of the hand at the moment the subject attempted to flick the target off the cheek or forehead of the illusory (actually hollow), normal, or hollow face. In the case of the illusory face, the end points of the flicking movements corresponded to the actual distances of the targets, not to consciously seen distances. Error bars indicate standard errors of the mean. Adapted with permission from Króliczak et al. (2006).

appears to be trapped in the present. Acting alone, the system can deal only with objects that are visible when the action is being programmed (Hu and Goodale 2000; Rossetti et al. 2000; Goodale et al. 2004). The ventral stream, in contrast, allows us to escape the present, and bring to bear visual information from the past. As described in earlier chapters of the book (Sections 5.4.3.1 and 6.5), we can study this 'offline' control of action in the laboratory by using delayed reaching and grasping tasks. For example, instead of reaching out to grasp a visible object, a subject can be required to wait and then carry out the action a few seconds later, when the object has been removed from view (Goodale et al. 1994a). While the first reach-and-grasp response is truly goal-directed, the second is a simulated or 'pantomimed' act. The former, we argue, engages only the dorsal stream, while the latter has to also make use of a stored representation initially derived from ventral-stream processing.

When we wrote the first edition of the book, we assumed that when a delay was imposed before a response could be made, a visuomotor program that was initially formed somehow 'decayed' during that delay, to be replaced by a perceptual representation stored in working memory. In a recent experiment, however, Westwood and Goodale (2003) challenged this view and provided evidence that the response is not programmed until the very moment the decision to act is made. In this experiment, subjects were presented with two objects, one of which was marked as the target. The companion object was either larger or smaller than the target object, or of the same size—leading to a size-contrast illusion in which the target object was perceived on some trials to be larger or smaller than it really was. Subjects were shown the two objects for 500 ms and then were given an instructional cue to reach out and pick up the target object. On half the trials, the objects remained visible until the hand began to move, allowing subjects to use visual information while programming their grasp; on the other trials, the objects vanished from view as soon as the cue to move was given, forcing the subjects to program the action in the absence of any visual information. These two kinds of trials were randomly interleaved. Despite the fact that there was no delay between seeing the object and the instruction to move on the vision-absent trials, the scaling of the grip aperture was influenced by the size-contrast illusion in exactly the same way as had been demonstrated after 5 s delays in an earlier experiment by Hu and Goodale (2000). In contrast, on the vision-present trials, subjects scaled their grip to the real, not the relative, size of the target just as had been previously reported by Hu and Goodale. Taken together, these results suggest that the dorsal stream uses 'just-in-time' computations and carries out the requisite transformations on retinal information only at the moment the movement is about to be performed. This proposal is similar in spirit to a 'conversion-on-demand' model put forward by Henriques et al. (1998), in which they argue that the selected target is transformed into the required head, body, and limb coordinates only at the moment a movement is executed. When a grasping movement is carried out in the absence of visual information, stored perceptual representations must always be used—even when the delay between last seeing the target and initiating the movement is extremely short.

As we noted in Chapter 5, Patient D.F. has real problems with delay tasks. Thus, even though she is able to perform a real-time grasping task with exquisite precision, she fails dramatically when asked to pantomime a grasp to an object seen only 2 s earlier (Goodale et al. 1994a). We argued that the damage to D.F.'s ventral stream means that she cannot construct a representation of the object's form when it is first presented to her and thus has no useful information to store for later calibration of the delayed pantomimed act. The same of course would be true of any act that depended on ventral stream processing—for example one carried out several days after an object had been seen.

This interpretation of D.F.'s failure to perform pantomimed grasping has been strengthened by more recent research on patients with optic ataxia following damage to the dorsal stream. As discovered in the 1980s by the Lyon group (Jeannerod 1986; Perenin and Vighetto 1988), this misreaching is only one component of a broader visuomotor spectrum that includes a failure to pre-shape the hand during grasping. Recent work has shown that such patients show a paradoxical improvement of reaching accuracy (Milner *et al.* 1999) when action is delayed, and a similar improvement is found in hand pre-shaping in the delayed pantomime paradigm (Milner *et al.* 2001). This pattern of data provides a mirror-image of D.F.'s data, allowing us to argue that patients with dorsal-stream damage can still use visual information to guide their behaviour, by using the ventral stream as their route to action. We would further argue that this indirect route to action is not just a fallback, for use when the dorsal system is damaged—but rather a good example of how the ventral stream contributes to the control of action by bringing the past into the present (Rossetti and Pisella 2003; Goodale *et al.* 2004; Rossetti *et al.* 2005).

8.4.4 Learning new skills

In discussing the role of the ventral and dorsal streams in the planning and control of actions such as grasping, we have focused almost entirely on the performance of actions that are automatic and overlearned. But humans typically acquire many visuomotor skills in their lifetime, from learning to catch a ball to driving a car. It is therefore relevant to ask how these skills are initially acquired, and more specifically what the relative contributions of the dorsal and ventral streams are at different stages in the learning of such skills.

When an unfamiliar action is first performed, the movements are typically performed in a deliberate and cognitively controlled fashion. After the action has been performed a number of times, however, and one has become quick and adept at achieving the desired goal, these slow cognitive control processes seem to get short-circuited. In the early stages of acquiring proficiency in a skilled activity, it seems likely that the ventral stream must play a significant role in the visual control of the movements, just as it does when people are asked to pantomime skilled movements such as grasping (see Section 8.4.3). Conscious perceptual monitoring is coupled with close attentional control over both the overall action itself and the specific limb movements made with respect to the goal object. But as the movements become more and more practised, we would suggest, their visual control becomes encapsulated within the visuomotor modules of the dorsal stream, which together with networks in the pons and cerebellum (Glickstein and May 1982; Glickstein 2003) allow the movements to be executed in an automated fashion. At present, little is known about how this putative shift from ventral to dorsal processing occurs, in part because the acquisition of these kinds of skilled visuomotor acts has not yet been the subject of neurophysiological or neuroimaging research. Instead, the focus has been almost entirely on the learning of arbitrary stimulus-response mappings, which are much easier to study within an experimental setting. In a typical experiment, for example, humans (or monkeys) might be required to make arbitrary finger movements in response to the presentation of different visual patterns. The acquisition of skills such as prehension, of course, cannot be studied in adult humans or monkeys since the subjects are already experts by the time they are brought into the laboratory. Although some individuals are not yet experts at prehension—namely young children and infant monkeys—they have seldom been studied in neurophysiological or neuroimaging experiments.

One influential account of the role of the dorsal and ventral streams in the learning of arbitrary stimulus–response associations has been put forward by Passingham and Toni (2001). On the basis of a series of neuroimaging experiments in humans and lesion studies in monkeys, these authors have argued that the selection of a particular movement on the basis of its association with an arbitrary visual stimulus recruits networks involving both the dorsal and ventral streams, with the prefrontal cortex acting as an integrator for the information from the two streams. According to their proposal, prefrontal cortex plays a pivotal role in integrating information about the external context, the targets of action, and the success of the response. Mechanisms in the dorsal stream certainly participate in specifying the coordinates of potential actions, but the processing in prefrontal cortex acts in a top-down fashion to modulate activity in the parietal cortex and premotor cortex, in those situations where the subjects have learned to associate particular actions with arbitrary object features. The identification of the relevant object features (and the context in which they occur) depends on an interaction between mechanisms in the ventral stream and prefrontal cortical areas.

But learning arbitrary associations between visual cues and motor output, such as sight-reading when playing the piano and pressing the accelerator when a traffic light turns green, is quite different from learning skills such as skiing, fencing, and catching a ball, where the relationship between the controlling visual information and the required motor output is, by its very nature, non-arbitrary. In these cases, the actions are constrained by the physics of the world. For example, to catch a ball one must ensure that one's hands are in the right place at the right time. There is nothing arbitrary about the stimulus–response mapping. This is not the case for playing the piano or pressing the accelerator of the car, where the relationships between the controlling stimuli and the required responses are based entirely on arbitrary conventions. This distinction between arbitrary and non-arbitrary visuomotor acts is reflected in the fact that different brain regions have been found to underlie their performance. Using PET, for example, Toni *et al.* (2001) directly contrasted human brain activity during the performance of a grasping task, in which the movement reflected the physical features of the goal objects, with activity during the performance of a quite different task in which a hand movement was arbitrarily associated with the same objects used to elicit the grasping movements. For the grasping movement, activation was observed in the parietal cortex and premotor cortex, whereas for the arbitrary task, activation was seen in the ventral prefrontal cortex, the striatum, and more dorsal areas of the precentral gyrus. Toni and colleagues concluded that in the arbitrary association tasks reciprocal fronto-striatal loops play a critical role in specifying what action should be performed in a particular context. This idea is similar to a proposal put forward by Wise and his colleagues (1996; Murray *et al.* 2000) that a distributed network involving regions of the premotor and prefrontal cortex, the basal ganglia, and (in the initial stages) the hippocampus compute these arbitrary object-to-action mappings. Indeed, the notion that networks in the prefrontal cortex (and the striatum) permit humans and other primates to learn context-dependent associations between particular stimuli and particular actions is an idea that has been put forward (in various forms) by many authors (for reviews, see Wise *et al.* 1996; Miller and Cohen 2001).

Even though it is clear that arbitrary stimulus–response mappings invoke different brain circuits from those mediating the one-to-one mappings that characterize actions such as grasping, it is not yet known whether or not, in the early stages of acquiring skills such as grasping (or other familiar goal-directed actions), prefrontal networks are also engaged. In other words, perhaps if one were to study brain activity during the acquisition of familiar skills in children (such as reaching and grasping) or even less familiar ones in adults (such as fencing or tennis), one might also see evidence of activity in prefrontal-striatal pathways, which would dissipate as the skills become more automatic and control is passed to premotor–parietal–cerebellar circuits. In other words, it could be the case that there are no fundamental differences between the neural networks mediating the so-called arbitrary and non-arbitrary visuomotor behaviours. This idea receives some support from single-unit studies in the monkey in which it has been demonstrated that the learning of arbitrary associations between certain stimuli and saccadic eye movements can eventually affect the visual tuning of neurones in dorsal-stream structures such as LIP (Sereno and Maunsell 1998; Toth and Assad 2002). Alternatively, it is possible that quite different networks are involved in the coding of acquired skills. After all, actions such as grasping are universal in humans (and our primate cousins) and the specific circuits supporting them have undoubtedly been shaped directly by natural selection. The same is not true, however, for more arbitrary actions such as playing a piano and driving a car. Although the neural networks mediating the acquisition and performance of these actions too must have been shaped by natural selection, there has been no direct selection for specialized 'piano-playing' or 'driving' circuits. Instead, a general capacity for learning new skills has emerged. In fact, even in the case of universal actions such as reaching and grasping, these actions are typically not performed whenever a goal object comes into view. Real-world behaviour is more complicated than that. A major function of the prefrontal-striatal circuits may be the acquisition and implementation of the contextual information used to guide behaviour, even 'automatic' behaviour. Such a system would permit a more flexible mapping between objects and actions—and would allow humans and other primates to resist the impulsive demands of their sensory world. Understanding how this system operates—and how it develops in early life—remains one of the great challenges of cognitive neuroscience.

8.5 The future

The material reviewed in this chapter, although representative rather than exhaustive, illustrates well the immense excitement and activity that characterizes current research in the cognitive neuroscience of visual perception and visuomotor control. The area is not only alive and well, but has also become so intensively studied as to be almost impossible for individual researchers to keep up with. Considerable progress in the field has been made since the initial publication of this book in 1995, and although our particular theoretical approach has not been universally shared by other researchers, it has certainly had heuristic value in generating and shaping a number of the questions that have been addressed over the past 12 years, thereby realizing the hope that we expressed in the original Preface to our book.

We have tried in this new chapter to clarify our position, which has evolved steadily over the intervening years though without departing radically from what it was in 1995. In doing this we feel that it is as important to clarify what the theory does not say, as well as what it does. It is first and foremost a theory about the function of the two main incoming streams of visual processing in the primate cortex. It certainly does not claim to be a theory of consciousness (or even visual consciousness), let alone of brain function in general (or even visual function in general). For example, we do not claim to have much to say about how intended courses of action are chosen in the first place, before the ventral and dorsal streams and their associated networks can be purposively engaged. The theory sheds no light on how is it that humans can decide to do something well before any goal objects are in sight. As will be clear from our earlier discussion (Section 8.2.3), our assumption is that this kind of long-range planning and executive control probably depends in large part on mechanisms that reside in prefrontal cortex. Once such mechanisms have generated an intended course of action, they would provide a top-down constraint on the nature of the search process to be engaged, and the whole process of achieving the desired intention could thus be set in motion. We do not, however, dwell on these ideas here, because this would go beyond the scope of this book, and more importantly our theory simply does not speak directly to these issues. Nonetheless teasing out how these interactions operate is now the focus of an intense research effort in laboratories around the world, and the picture will undoubtedly become clearer over the next few years.

References

Adams, J.H., Brierley, J.B., Connor, R.C.R., and Treip, C.S. (1966). The effects of systemic hypotension upon the human brain. Clinical and neuropathological observations in 11 cases. *Brain*, **89**, 235–68.

Adler, A. (1944). Disintegration and restoration of optic recognition in visual agnosia. *Arch. Neurol. Psychiatr.*, **51**, 243–59.

Adler, A. (1950). Course and outcome of visual agnosia. *J. Nerv. Ment. Dis.*, **111**, 41–51.

Aglioti, S., Goodale, M.A., and DeSouza, J.F.X. (1995). Size-contrast illusions deceive the eye but not the hand. *Curr. Biol.*, **5**, 679–85.

Aguirre, G.K. and D'Esposito, M. (1999). Topographical disorientation: a synthesis and taxonomy. *Brain*, **122**, 1613–28.

Aguirre, G.K., Zarahn, E., and D'Esposito, M. (1998). An area within human ventral cortex sensitive to 'building' stimuli: evidence and implications. *Neuron*, **21**, 373–83.

Alexander, M.P. and Albert, M.L. (1983). The anatomical basis of visual agnosia. In *Localization in neuropsychology*, ed. A. Kertesz, pp. 393–415, Academic Press, New York.

Allport, A. (1993). Attention and control: have we been asking the wrong questions? A critical review of twenty-five years. In *Attention and performance XIV: synergies in experimental psychology, artificial intelligence, and cognitive neuroscience*, (ed. D.E. Meyer and S. Kornblum), pp. 183–218, MIT Press, Cambridge, MA.

Andersen, R.A. (1987). Inferior parietal lobule function in spatial perception and visuomotor integration. In *Handbook of physiology section 1: the nervous system, Volume V: higher functions of the brain, part 2*, (ed. F. Plum, V.B. Mountcastle, and S.R. Geiger), pp. 483–518. Amer. Physiological Society, Bethesda, MD.

Andersen, R.A. and Buneo, C.A. (2003). Sensorimotor integration in posterior parietal cortex. *Adv. Neurol.*, **93**, 159–77.

Andersen, R.A., Essick, G.K., and Siegel, R.M. (1985). Encoding of spatial location by posterior parietal neurons. *Science*, **230**, 456–8.

Andersen, R.A., Asanuma, C., Essick, G., and Siegel, R.M. (1990a). Corticocortical connections of anatomically and physiologically defined subdivisions within the inferior parietal lobule. *J. Comp. Neurol.*, **296**, 65–113.

Andersen, R.A., Bracewell, R.M., Barash, S., Gnadt, J.W., and Fogassi, L. (1990b). Eye position effects on visual, memory, and saccade-related activity in areas LIP and 7A of macaque. *J. Neurosci.*, **10**, 1176–96.

Andersen, R.A., Brotchie, P.R., and Mazzoni, P. (1992). Evidence for the lateral intraparietal area as the parietal eye field. *Curr. Opin. Neurobiol.*, **2**, 840–6.

Andrews, T.J. and Schluppeck, D. (2004). Neural responses to Mooney images reveal a modular representation of faces in human visual cortex. *Neuroimage*, **21**, 91–8.

Andrews, T.J., Schluppeck, D., Homfray, D., Matthews, P., and Blakemore, C. (2002). Activity in the fusiform gyrus predicts conscious perception of Rubin's vase-face illusion. *Neuroimage*, **17**, 890–901.

Asanuma, C., Andersen, R.A., and Cowan, W.M. (1985). The thalamic relations of the caudal inferior parietal lobule and the lateral prefrontal cortex in monkeys: divergent cortical projections from cell clusters in the medial pulvinar nucleus. *J. Comp. Neurol.*, 241, 357–81.

Astafiev, S.V., Stanley, C.M., Gordon L Shulman, G.L., and Corbetta, M. (2004). Extrastriate body area in human occipital cortex responds to the performance of motor actions. *Nat. Neurosci.*, 7, 542–8.

Baizer, J.S., Ungerleider, L.G., and Desimone, R. (1991). Organization of visual inputs to the inferior temporal and posterior parietal cortex in macaques. *J. Neurosci.*, 11, 168–90.

Baizer, J.S., Desimone, R., and Ungerleider, L.G. (1993). Comparison of subcortical connections of inferior temporal and posterior parietal cortex in monkeys. *Vis. Neurosci.*, 10, 59–72.

Baleydier, C. and Morel, A. (1992). Segregated thalamocortical pathways to inferior parietal and inferotemporal cortex in macaque monkey. *Vis. Neurosci.*, 8, 391–405.

Bálint, R. (1909). Seelenlähmung des 'Schauens', optische Ataxie, räumliche Störung der Aufmerksamkeit. *Monatsschr. Psychiatr. Neurol.*, 25, 51–81. English translation: Harvey (1995).

Baloh, R.W., Yee, R.D., and Honrubia, V. (1980). Optokinetic nystagmus and parietal lobe lesions. *Ann. Neurol.*, 7, 269–76.

Barbas, H. (1988). Anatomic organization of basoventral and mediodorsal visual recipient prefrontal regions in the rhesus monkey. *J. Comp. Neurol.*, 276, 313–42.

Barbieri, C. and De Renzi, E. (1989). Patterns of neglect dissociation. *Behav. Neurol.*, 2, 13–24.

Barbur, J.L., Watson, J.D.G., Frackowiak, R.S.J., and Zeki, S.M. (1993). Conscious visual perception without V1. *Brain*, 116, 1293–302.

Barton, R.A. and Dean, P. (1993). Comparative evidence indicating neural specialization for predatory behaviour in mammals. *Proc. R. Soc. Lond.*, B254, 63–8.

Bates, J.A.V. and Ettlinger, G. (1960). Posterior parietal ablations in the monkey. *AMA Arch. Neurol.*, 3, 177–92.

Bechterev, W. (1884). Über die Funktion der Vierhügel. *Pflügers Arch. gesamte Physiol. Menschen und Tiere*, 33, 413–39.

Becker, W., and Fuchs, A.F. (1969). Further properties of the human saccadic system: eye movements and correction saccades with and without visual fixation points. *Vision Res.*, 9, 1247–58.

Behrmann, M. and Tipper, S.P. (1994). Object-based visual attention: evidence from unilateral neglect. In *Attention and performance XV. Conscious and nonconscious information processing*, (ed. C. Umiltà and M. Moscovitch), pp. 351–75. MIT Press, Cambridge, MA.

Bender, D.B. (1973). Visual sensitivity following inferotemporal and foveal prestriate lesions in the rhesus monkey. *J. Comp. Physiol. Psychol.*, 84, 613–21.

Bender, D.B. (1982). Receptive-field properties of neurons in the macaque inferior pulvinar. *J. Neurophysiol.*, 48, 1–17.

Bender, D.B. (1983). Visual activation of neurons in the primate pulvinar depends on cortex but not colliculus. *Brain Res.*, 279, 258–61.

Benevento, L.A. and Fallon, J.H. (1975). The ascending projections of the superior colliculus in the rhesus monkey (*Macaca mulatta*). *J. Comp. Neurol.*, 160, 339–62.

Benevento, L.A. and Standage, G.P. (1983). The organization of projections of the retinore-
cipient and nonretinorecipient nuclei of the pretectal complex and layers of the superior colliculus to the lateral pulvinar and medial pulvinar in the macaque monkey.
J. Comp. Neurol., **217**, 307–36.

Benevento, L.A. and Yoshida, K. (1981). The afferent and efferent organization of the lateral
geniculo-prestriate pathways in the macaque monkey. *J. Comp. Neurol.*, **203**, 455–74.

Benson, D.F. (1989). Disorders of visual gnosis. In *Neuropsychology of visual perception*,
(ed. J.W. Brown), pp. 59–78. Erlbaum, Hillsdale, NJ.

Benson, D.F. and Greenberg, J.P. (1969). Visual form agnosia: a specific deficit in visual
discrimination. *Arch. Neurol.*, **20**, 82–9.

Biguer, B., Jeannerod, M., and Prablanc, C. (1982). The coordination of eye, head, and arm
movements during reaching at a single visual target. *Exp. Brain Res.*, **46**, 301–4.

Binkofski, F., Buccino, G., Stephan, K.M., Rizzolatti, G., Seitz, R.J., and Freund, H.-J.
(1999). A parieto-premotor network for object manipulation: evidence from
neuroimaging. *Exp. Brain Res.*, **128**, 210–13.

Bisiach, E. (1991*a*). The nature of spatial neglect in man. *Paper at the EBBS Annual
Meeting*, Cambridge.

Bisiach, E. (1991*b*). Extinction and neglect: same or different? In *Brain and space*,
(ed. J. Paillard), pp. 251–7. Oxford University Press, Oxford.

Bisiach, E. (1993). Mental representation in unilateral neglect and related disorders: the
twentieth Bartlett Memorial Lecture. *Q. J. Exp. Psychol.*, **46A**, 435–61.

Bisiach, E. and Luzzatti, C. (1978). Unilateral neglect of representational space. *Cortex*,
14, 129–33.

Bisiach, E. and Rusconi, M.L. (1990). Break-down of perceptual awareness in unilateral
neglect. *Cortex*, **26**, 643–49.

Bisiach, E. and Vallar, G. (1988). Hemineglect in humans. In *Handbook of neuropsychology*,
Vol. 1, (ed. F. Boller and J. Grafman), pp. 195–222. Elsevier, Amsterdam.

Bisiach, E., Luzzatti, C., and Perani, D. (1979). Unilateral neglect, representational schema
and consciousness. *Brain*, **102**, 609–18.

Bisiach, E., Capitani, E., Luzzatti, C., and Perani, D. (1981). Brain and conscious representation of outside reality. *Neuropsychologia*, **19**, 543–51.

Bisiach, E., Vallar, G., and Geminiani, G. (1989). Influence of response modality on perceptual awareness of contralesional visual stimuli. *Brain*, **112**, 1627–36.

Bisiach, E., Geminiani, G., Berti, A., and Rusconi, M.L. (1990). Perceptual and premotor
factors in unilateral neglect. *Neurology*, **40**, 1278–81.

Bisley, J.W. and Goldberg, M.E. (2003). Neuronal activity in the lateral intraparietal area
and spatial attention. *Science*, **299**, 81–6.

Blakemore, S.J., Wolpert, D.M., and Frith, C.D. (2002). Abnormalities in the awareness of
action. *Trends Cogn. Sci.* **6**, 237–42.

Blythe, I.M., Bromley, J.M., Kennard, C., and Ruddock, K.H. (1986). Visual discrimination
of target displacement remains intact after damage to the striate cortex in humans.
Nature, **320**, 619–21.

Blythe, I.M., Kennard, C., and Ruddock, K.H. (1987). Residual vision in patients with
retrogeniculate lesions of the visual pathways. *Brain*, **110**, 887–905.

Bottini, G., Sterzi, R., and Vallar, G. (1992). Directional hypokinesia in spatial hemineglect: a case study. *J. Neurol. Neurosurg. Psychiat.*, **55**, 562–65.

Boussaoud, D., Ungerleider, L.G. and Desimone, R. (1990). Pathways for motion analysis: cortical connections of the medial superior temporal and fundus of the superior temporal visual areas in the macaque. *J. Comp. Neurol.*, **296**, 462–95.

Boussaoud, D., Desimone, R. and Ungerleider, L.G. (1992). Subcortical connections of visual areas MST and FST in macaques. *Vis. Neurosci.*, **9**, 291–302.

Bowman, E.M., Brown, V.J., Kertzman, C., Schwartz, U., and Robinson, D.L. (1993). Covert orienting of attention in macaques I. Effects of behavioral context. *J. Neurophysiol.*, **70**, 431–43.

Brain, W.R. (1941). Visual disorientation with special reference to lesions of the right cerebral hemisphere. *Brain*, **64**, 244–72.

Braun, D., Weber, H., Mergner, T., and Schulte-Mönting, J. (1992). Saccadic reaction times in patients with frontal and parietal lesions. *Brain*, **115**, 1359–86.

Brenner, E. and Smeets, J.B.J. (1996). Size illusion influences how we lift but not how we grasp an object. *Exp. Brain Res.*, **111**, 473–6.

Bridgeman, B. (1983). Mechanisms of space constancy. In *Spatially oriented behavior*, (ed. A. Hein and M. Jeannerod), pp. 263–79. Springer-Verlag, New York.

Bridgeman, B. and Staggs, D. (1982). Plasticity in human blindsight. *Vision Res.*, **22**, 1199–203.

Bridgeman, B., Lewis, S., Heit, G., and Nagle, M. (1979). Relation between cognitive and motor-oriented systems of visual position perception. *J. Exp. Psychol. (Hum. Percept.)*, **5**, 692–700.

Bridgeman, B., Kirch, M., and Sperling, A. (1981). Segregation of cognitive and motor aspects of visual function using induced motion. *Percept. Psychophys.*, **29**, 336–42.

Bridgeman, B., Peery, S., and Anand, S. (1997). Interaction of cognitive and sensorimotor maps of visual space. *Percept. Psychophys.*, **59**, 456–69.

Brierley, J.B. and Excell, B.J. (1966). The effect of profound systemic hypotension upon the brain of *M-rhesus*: physiological and pathological observations. *Brain*, **89**, 269–99.

Broadbent, D.B. (1958). *Perception and communication*. Pergamon Press, London.

Brothers, L. and Ring, B. (1993). Mesial temporal neurons in the macaque monkey with responses selective for aspects of social stimuli. *Behav. Brain Res.*, **57**, 53–61.

Brown, M.W. and Aggleton, J.P. (2001). Recognition memory: what are the roles of the perirhinal cortex and hippocampus? *Nat. Rev. Neurosci.*, **2**, 51–61.

Brown, S. and Schäfer, E.A. (1888). An investigation into the functions of the occipital and temporal lobes of the monkey's brain. *Phil. Trans. R. Soc. Lond.*, **179**, 303–27.

Brown, V.J. and Robbins, T.W. (1989). Elementary processes of response selection mediated by distinct regions of the striatum. *J. Neurosci.*, **9**, 3760–65.

Brown, V.J., Bowman, E.M., and Robbins, T.W. (1991). Response-related deficits following unilateral lesions of the medial agranular cortex in the rat. *Behav. Neurosci.*, **105**, 567–78.

Bruce, C.J. (1990). Integration of sensory and motor signals in primate frontal eye fields. In *Local and global order in perceptual maps*, (ed. G.M. Edelman, W.E. Gall, and W.M. Cowan), pp. 261–314. Wiley-Liss, New York.

Bruce, C.J. and Goldberg, M.E. (1984). Physiology of the frontal eye fields. *Trends Neurosci.*, **7**, 436–41.

Bruno, N. (2001). When does action resist visual illusions? *Trends Cogn. Sci.*, **5**, 379–82.

Buchbinder, S.B., Dixon, Y.W., Wang, H., May, J.G., and Glickstein, M. (1980). The effects of cortical lesions on visual guidance of the hand. *Soc. Neurosci. Abstr.*, **6**, 675.

Bushnell, M.C., Goldberg, M.E., and Robinson, D.L. (1981). Behavioral enhancement of visual responses in monkey cerebral cortex. I. Modulation in posterior parietal cortex related to selective visual attention. *J. Neurophysiol.*, **46**, 755–72.

Bülthoff, H.H. and Edelman, S. (1992). Psychophysical support for a two-dimensional view interpolation theory of object recognition. *Proc. Natl Acad. Sci. USA*, **89**, 60–4.

Butter, C.M., Mishkin, M., and Rosvold, H.E. (1965). Stimulus generalization in monkeys with inferotemporal and lateral occipital lesions. In *Stimulus generalization*, (ed. D.I. Mostofsky), pp. 119–33. Stanford University Press, Stanford, CA.

Butters, N., Barton, M., and Brody, B.A. (1970). Role of the right parietal lobe in the mediation of cross-modal associations and reversible operations in space. *Cortex*, **6**, 174–90.

Byrne, R.W. (1979). Memory for urban geography. *Q. J. Exp. Psychol.*, **31**, 147–54.

Byrne, R.W. (1982). Geographical knowledge and orientation. In *Normality and pathology in cognitive functions*, (ed. A.W. Ellis), pp. 239–264. Academic Press, London.

Caminiti, R., Johnson, P.B., Galli, C., Ferraina, S., and Burnod, Y. (1991). Making arm movements within different parts of space: the premotor and motor cortical representation of a coordinate system for reaching to visual targets. *J. Neurosci.*, **11**, 1182–97.

Campion, J. (1987). Apperceptive agnosia: the specification and description of constructs. In *Visual object processing: a cognitive neuropsychological approach*, (ed. G.W. Humphreys and M.J. Riddoch), pp. 197–232. Erlbaum, London.

Campion, J. and Latto, R. (1985). Apperceptive agnosia due to carbon monoxide poisoning. An interpretation based on critical band masking from disseminated lesions. *Behav. Brain Res.*, **15**, 227–40.

Campion, J., Latto, R., and Smith, Y.M. (1983). Is blindsight an effect of scattered light, spared cortex, and near-threshold vision? *Behav. Brain Sci.*, **6**, 423–86.

Campos-Ortega, J.A., Hayhow, W.R., and Clüver, P.F.D. (1970). A note on the problem of retinal projections to the inferior pulvinar nucleus of primates. *Brain Res.*, **22**, 126–30.

Cant, J.S. and Goodale, M.A. (2006). Attention to form or surface properties modulates different regions of human occipitotemporal cortex. *Cerebral Cortex*, published online 28 April 2006.

Carey, D.P. (2001). Do action systems resist visual illusions? *Trends Cogn. Sci.*, **5**, 109–13.

Carey, D.P., Harvey, M., and Milner, A.D. (1996). Visuomotor sensitivity for shape and orientation in a patient with visual form agnosia. *Neuropsychologia*, **34**, 329–38.

Casagrande, V.A. (1994). A third parallel visual pathway to primate area V1. *Trends Neurosci.*, **17**, 305–10.

Castiello, U., Paulignan, Y., and Jeannerod, M. (1991). Temporal dissociation of motor responses and subjective awareness. *Brain*, **114**, 2639–55.

Cavada, C. and Goldman-Rakic, P.S. (1989a). Posterior parietal cortex in rhesus monkey: I. Parcellation of areas based on distinctive limbic and sensory corticocortical connections. *J. Comp. Neurol.*, **287**, 393–421.

Cavada, C. and Goldman-Rakic, P.S. (1989b). Posterior parietal cortex in rhesus monkey: II. Evidence for segregated corticocortical networks linking sensory and limbic areas with the frontal lobe. *J. Comp. Neurol.*, **287**, 422–45.

Cavada, C. and Goldman-Rakic, P.S. (1991). Topographic segregation of corticostriatal projections from posterior parietal subdivisions in the macaque monkey. *Neuroscience*, **42**, 683–96.

Cavada, C. and Goldman-Rakic, P.S. (1993). Multiple visual areas in the posterior cortex of primates. In *Progress in brain research*, Vol. 95, (ed. T.P. Hicks, S. Molotchnikoff, and T. Ono), pp. 123–37. Elsevier, Amsterdam.

Chelazzi, L., Miller, E.K., Duncan, J., and Desimone, R. (1993). A neural basis for visual search in inferior temporal cortex. *Nature*, **363**, 345–7.

Chow, K.L. (1950). A retrograde cell degeneration study of the cortical projection field of the pulvinar in the monkey. *J. Comp. Neurol.*, **93**, 313–40.

Churchland, A.K., Gardner, J.L., Chou, I., Priebe, N.J., and Lisberger, S.G. (2003). Directional anisotropies reveal a functional segregation of visual motion processing for perception and action. *Neuron*, **37**, 1001–11.

Claparède, E. (1901). Expériences sur la vitesse du soulèvement des poids de volumes différents. *Arch. Psychol. Suisse Romande*, **1**, 69–94.

Clark, A. (2002). Is seeing all it seems? Action, reason and the grand illusion. *J. Conscious. Studies*, **9**, 181–202.

Clarke, S. (1993). Callosal connections and functional subdivision of the human occipital cortex. In *Functional organisation of the human visual cortex*, (ed. B. Gulyás, D. Ottoson, and P.E. Roland), pp. 137–49. Pergamon Press, Oxford.

Cogan, D.G. (1965). Ophthalmic manifestations of bilateral non-occipital cerebral lesions. *Br. J. Ophthalmol.*, **49**, 281–97.

Cohen, Y.E. and Andersen, R.A. (2002). A common reference frame for movement plans in the posterior parietal cortex. *Nat. Rev. Neurosci.*, **3**, 553–62.

Colby, C.L. and Duhamel, J.-R. (1991). Heterogeneity of extrastriate visual areas and multiple parietal areas in the macaque monkey. *Neuropsychologia*, **29**, 517–37.

Colby, C.L. and Goldberg, M.E. (1999). Space and attention in parietal cortex. *Annu. Rev. Neurosci.*, **22**, 319–49.

Colby, C.L., Gattas, R., Olson, C.R., and Gross, C.G. (1988). Topographic organization of cortical afferents to extrastriate visual area PO in the macaque: a dual tracer study. *J. Comp. Neurol.*, **269**, 392–413.

Cole, M.C., Schutta, H.S., and Warrington, E.K. (1962). Visual disorientation in homonymous half-fields. *Neurology*, **12**, 257–63.

Corballis, M.C. (1982). Mental rotation: anatomy of a paradigm. In *Spatial abilities. Development and physiological foundations*, (ed. M. Potegal), pp. 173–98. Academic Press, New York.

Corbetta, M., Miezin, F.M., Shulman, G.L., and Petersen, S.E. (1993). A PET study of visuospatial attention. *J. Neurosci.*, **13**, 1202–26.

Corbetta, M., Kincade, M.J., and Shulman, G.L. (2002). Two neural systems for visual orienting and the pathophysiology of unilateral spatial neglect. In *The cognitive and neural bases of spatial neglect* (ed. H.-O. Karnath, A. D. Milner, and G. Vallar) pp. 259–73. Oxford University Press, Oxford.

Corkin, S. (1965). Tactually-guided maze learning in man: effects of unilateral cortical lesions and bilateral hippocampal lesions. *Neuropsychologia*, **3**, 339–51.

Cowey, A. (1968). Discrimination. In *The analysis of behavioral change*, (ed.L. Weiskrantz), pp. 189–238. Harper and Row, New York.

Cowey, A. (1982). Sensory and non-sensory visual disorders in man and monkey. *Phil. Trans. R. Soc. Lond.* **B298**, 3–13.

Cowey, A. and Gross, C.G. (1970). Effects of foveal prestriate and inferotemporal lesions on visual discrimination by rhesus monkeys. *Exp. Brain Res.*, **11**, 128–44.

Cowey, A. and Stoerig, P. (1989). Projection patterns of surviving neurons in the dorsal lateral geniculate nucleus following discrete lesions of striate cortex: implications for residual vision. *Exp. Brain Res.*, **75**, 631–8.

Cowey, A. and Stoerig, P. (1992). Reflections on blindsight. In *The neuropsychology of consciousness*, (ed. A.D. Milner and M.D. Rugg), pp. 11–38. Academic Press, London.

Cowey, A. and Stoerig, P. (1995). Blindsight in monkeys. *Nature*, **373**, 247–9.

Cowey, A. and Weiskrantz, L. (1963). A perimetric study of visual field defects in monkeys. *Q. J. Exp. Psychol.*, **15**, 91–115.

Cowey, A. and Weiskrantz, L. (1967). A comparison of the effects of inferotemporal and striate cortex lesions on the visual behaviour of rhesus monkeys. *Q. J. Exp. Psychol.*, **19**, 246–53.

Creem, S.H. and Proffitt, D.R. (2001). Grasping objects by their handles: a necessary interaction between cognition and action. *J. Exp. Psychol. (Hum. Percept. Perform.)*, **27**, 218–28.

Creutzfeldt, O. (1981). Diversification and synthesis of sensory systems across the cortical link. In *Brain mechanisms of perceptual awareness and purposeful behaviour*, (ed. O. Pompeiano and C. Ajmone-Marsan), pp. 153–65. Raven Press, New York.

Creutzfeldt, O. (1985). Multiple visual areas: multiple sensori-motor links. In *Models of the visual cortex*, (ed. D. Rose and V.G. Dobson), pp. 54–61. Wiley, New York.

Crick, F. and Koch, C. (1995). Are we aware of neural activity in primary visual cortex? *Nature*, **375**, 121–3.

Culham, J.C. and Kanwisher, N.G. (2001). Neuroimaging of cognitive functions in human parietal cortex, *Curr, Opin Neurobiol.*, **11**, 157–63.

Culham, J.C., Danckert, S.L., DeSouza, J.F.X., Gati, J.S., Menon, R.S., and Goodale, M.A. (2003). Visually-guided grasping produces fMRI activation in dorsal but not ventral stream brain areas. *Exp. Brain Res.*, **153**, 180–9.

Culham, J.C., Pratesi, C.C., and Goodale, M.A. (2004). Object size matters for grasping but not perception in the human anterior intraparietal area. *Soc. Neurosci. Abstr.*, **30**, 487.5.

Damasio, A.R. and Benton, A.L. (1979). Impairment of hand movements under visual guidance. *Neurology*, **29**, 170–8.

Damasio, A.R. and Damasio, H. (1983). The anatomic basis of pure alexia and color 'agnosia'. *Neurology*, **33**, 1573–83.

Danckert, J.A., Sharif, N., Haffenden, A.M., Schiff, K.C., and Goodale, M.A. (2002). A temporal analysis of grasping in the Ebbinghaus illusion: planning versus online control. *Exp. Brain Res.*, **144**, 275–80.

Daprati, E., Franck, N., Georgieff, N., Proust, J., Pacherie, E., Dalery, J., and Jeannerod, M. (1997). Looking for the agent: an investigation into consciousness of action and self-consciousness in schizophrenic patients. *Cognition*, **65**, 71–86.

Dassonville, P., Bridgeman, B., Kaur Bala, J., Thiem, P., and Sampanes, A. (2004). The induced Roelofs effect: two visual systems or the shift of a single reference frame? *Vis. Res.*, **44**, 603–11.

Davis, R.T., Lampert, A., and Rumelhart, D.E. (1964). Perception by monkeys II. Use of cues at a distance by young and old monkeys. *Psychon. Sci.*, **1**, 107–8.

de Grave, D.D., Biegstraaten, M., Smeets, J.B.J., and Brenner, E. (2005). Effects of the Ebbinghaus figure on grasping are not only due to misjudged size. *Exp. Brain Res.*, **163**, 58–64.

De Renzi, E. (1982). *Disorders of space exploration and cognition*. Wiley, Chichester, UK.

De Renzi, E. (1985). Disorders of spatial orientation. In Handbook of clinical neurology Vol. 1(45): *Clinical Neuropsychology*, (ed. J.A.M. Frederiks), pp. 405–22. Elsevier, Amsterdam.

De Renzi, E. (1986). Current issues on prosopagnosia. In *Aspects of face processing*, (ed. H. Ellis, M.A. Jeeves, F. Newcombe, and A. Young), pp. 243–52. Martinus Nijhoff, Dordrecht

De Renzi, E. (1989). Apraxia. In *Handbook of neuropsychology*, Vol. 2, (ed. F. Boller and J. Grafman), pp. 245–63. Elsevier, Amsterdam.

De Renzi, E. and Nichelli, P. (1975). Verbal and non-verbal short-term memory impairment following hemispheric damage. *Cortex*, **11**, 341–54.

De Renzi, E., Scotti, G., and Spinnler, H. (1969). Perceptual and associative disorders of visual recognition. Relationship to the side of the cerebral lesion. *Neurology*, **19**, 634–42.

De Renzi, E., Faglioni, P. and Villa, P. (1977). Topographical amnesia. *J. Neurol. Neurosurg. Psychiat.*, **40**, 498–505.

De Renzi, E., Colombo, A., Faglioni, P., and Gibertoni, M. (1982). Conjugate gaze paresis in stroke patients with unilateral damage. An unexpected instance of hemispheric asymmetry. *Arch. Neurol.*, **39**, 482–6.

De Renzi, E., Gentilini, P., and Pattacini, F. (1984). Auditory extinction following hemispheric damage. *Neuropsychologia*, **22**, 733–44.

De Renzi, E., Zambolin, A., and Crisi, G. (1987). The pattern of neuropsychological impairment associated with left posterior cerebralartery infarcts. *Brain*, **110**, 1099–116.

De Renzi, E., Gentilini, P., Faglioni, P., and Barbieri, C. (1989). Attentional shift towards the rightmost stimuli in patients with left visual neglect. *Cortex*, **25**, 231–7.

De Yoe, E.A. and Van Essen, D.C. (1985). Segregation of efferent connections and receptive field properties in visual area V2 of the macaque. *Nature*, **317**, 58–61.

De Yoe, E.A. and Van Essen, D.C. (1988). Concurrent processing streams in monkey visual cortex. *Trends Neurosci.*, **11**, 219–26.

Dean, P. (1976). Effects of inferotemporal lesions on the behaviour of monkeys. *Psychol. Bull.*, **83**, 41–71.

Dean, P. (1978). Visual cortex ablation and thresholds for successively presented stimuli in rhesus monkeys. I. Orientation. *Exp. Brain Res.*, **32**, 445–58.

Dean, P. (1982). Visual behavior in monkeys with inferotemporal lesions. In *Analysis of visual behavior*, (ed. D.J. Ingle, M.A. Goodale, and R.J.W. Mansfield), pp. 587–628. MIT Press, Cambridge, MA.

Dean, P. (1990). Sensory cortex: visual perceptual functions. In *The cerebral cortex of the rat*, (ed. B. Kolb and R.C. Tees), pp. 275–307. MIT Press, Cambridge, MA.

Dean, P., Redgrave, P., and Westby, G.W.M. (1989). Event or emergency? Two response systems in the mammalian superior colliculus. *Trends Neurosci.*, **12**, 137–47.

Denys, K.A., Vanduffel, W., Fize, D., Nelissen, K., Peuskens, H., Van Essen, D.C., and Orban, G.A. (2004). The processing of visual shape in the cerebral cortex of human and nonhuman primates: a functional magnetic resonance imaging study. *J. Neurosci.*, **24**, 2551–65.

Desimone, R. (1991). Face-selective cells in the temporal cortex of monkeys. *J. Cogn. Neurosci.*, **3**, 1–8.

Desimone, R. and Duncan, J. (1995). Neural mechanisms of selective visual attention. *Annu. Rev. Neurosci.*, **18**, 193–222.

Desimone, R. and Moran, J. (1985). Mechanisms for selective attention in area V4 and inferior temporal cortex of the macaque. *Soc. Neurosci. Abstr.*, **11**, 1245.

Desimone, R. and Schein, S.J. (1987). Visual properties of neurons in area V4 of the macaque—sensitivity to stimulus form. *J. Neurophysiol.*, **57**, 835–68.

Desimone, R. and Ungerleider, L.G. (1989). Neural mechanisms of visual processing in monkeys. In *Handbook of neuropsychology*, Vol.2, (ed. F. Boller and J. Grafman), pp. 267–299. Elsevier, Amsterdam.

Desmurget, M., Epstein, C.M., Turner, R.S., Prablanc, C., Alexander, G.E., and Grafton, S.T. (1999). Role of the posterior parietal cortex in updating reaching movements to a visual target. *Nat. Neurosci.*, **2**, 563–7.

Di Pellegrino, G., Fadiga, L., Fogassi, L., Gallese, V., and Rizzolatti, G. (1992). Understanding motor events: a neurophysiological study. *Exp. Brain Res.*, **91**, 176–80.

Dijkerman, H.C., Milner, A.D., and Carey, D.P. (1997). Impaired delayed and anti-saccades in a visual form agnosic. *Exp. Brain Res. Suppl.*, **117**, S66.

Dijkerman, H.C., Lê, S., Démonet, J.-F., and Milner, A.D. (2004). Visuomotor performance in a patient with visual agnosia due to an early lesion. *Cogn. Brain Res.*, **20**, 12–25.

Distler, C., Boussaoud, D., Desimone, R., and Ungerleider, L.G. (1993). Cortical connections of inferior temporal area TEO in macaque monkeys. *J. Comp. Neurol.*, **334**, 125–50.

Doma, H. and Hallett, P.E. (1988). Rod-cone dependence of saccadic eye-movement latency in a foveating task. *Vision Res.*, **28**, 899–913.

Downing, P.E., Jiang, Y., Shuman, M., and Kanwisher, N. (2001). A cortical area selective for visual processing of the human body. *Science*, **293**, 2470–3.

Dreher, B., Fukada, Y., and Rodieck, R.W. (1976). Identification, classification and anatomical segregation of cells with X-like and Y-like properties in the lateral geniculate nucleus of old-world primates. *J. Physiol. (Lond.)*, **258**, 433–52.

Dreher, B., Potts, R.A., Ni, S.Y.K., and Bennett, M.R. (1984). The development of heterogeneities in distribution and soma sizes of rat ganglion cells. In *Development of visual pathways in mammals*, (ed. J. Stone, B. Dreher, and D.H. Rapaport), pp. 39–58. Liss, New York.

Driver, J. and Halligan, P.W. (1991). Can visual neglect operate in object-centred coordinates? An affirmative single case study. *Cogn. Neuropsychol.*, 8, 475–496.

Driver, J. and Mattingley, J.B. (1998). Parietal neglect and visual awareness. *Nat. Neurosci.*, 1, 17–22.

Duffy, C.J. and Wurtz, R.H. (1991). Sensitivity of MST neurons to optic flow stimuli. I. A continuum of response selectivity to large field stimuli. *J. Neurophysiol.*, **65**, 1329–45.

Duhamel, J.-R. and Brouchon, M. (1990). Sensorimotor aspects of unilateral neglect: a single case analysis. *Cogn. Neuropsychol.*, **7**, 57–74.

Duhamel, J.-R., Colby, C.L., and Goldberg, M.E. (1991). Congruent representations of visual and somatosensory space in single neurons of monkey ventral intra-parietal cortex (area VIP). In *Brain and space*, (ed. J. Paillard), pp. 223–36. Oxford University Press, Oxford.

Duhamel, J.-R., Colby, C.L., and Goldberg, M.E. (1992). The updating of the representation of visual space in parietal cortex by intended eye movements. *Science*, **255**, 90–2.

Dürsteler, M.R. and Wurtz, R.H. (1988). Pursuit and optokinetic deficits following chemical lesions of cortical areas MT and MST. *J. Neurophysiol.*, **60**, 940–65.

Dürsteler, M.R., Wurtz, R.H., and Newsome, W.T. (1987). Directional pursuit deficits following lesions of the foveal representation within the superior temporal sulcus of the macaque monkey. *J. Neurophysiol.*, **57**, 1262–87.

Dyde, R.T. and Milner, A.D. (2002). Two illusions of perceived orientation: one fools all of the people some of the time, but the other fools all of the people all of the time. *Exp. Brain Res.*, **144**, 518–27.

Efron, R. (1969). What is perception? *Boston Studies Phil. Sci.*, **4**, 137–73.

Ellard, C.G. and Goodale, M.A. (1986). The role of the predorsal bundle in head and body movements elicited by electrical stimulation of the superior colliculus in the Mongolian gerbil. *Exp. Brain Res.*, **64**, 421–33.

Ellard, C.G. and Goodale, M.A. (1988). A functional analysis of the collicular output pathways: a dissociation of deficits following lesions of the dorsal tegmental decussation and the ipsilateral collicular efferent bundle in the Mongolian gerbil. *Exp. Brain Res.*, **71**, 307–19.

Elliott, D. and Madalena, J. (1987). The influence of premovement visual information on manual aiming. *Q. J. Exp. Psychol.*, **39A**, 541–59.

Enroth-Cugell, C. and Robson, J.G. (1966). The contrast sensitivity of retinal ganglion cells of the cat. *J. Physiol. (Lond.)*, **187**, 517–52.

Epstein, R. and Kanwisher, N. (1998). A cortical representation of the local visual environment. *Nature*, **392**, 598–601.

Epstein, R., Harris, A., Stanley, D., and Kanwisher, N. (1999). The parahippocampal place area: recognition, navigation, or encoding? *Neuron*, **23**, 115–25.

Eskandar, E.N., Optican, L.M., and Richmond, B.J. (1992a). Role of inferior temporal neurons in visual memory. 2. Multiplying temporal wave-forms related to vision and memory. *J. Neurophysiol.*, **68**, 1296–306.

Eskandar, E.N., Richmond, B.J., and Optican, L.M. (1992b). Role of inferior temporal neurons in visual monkey. 1. Temporal encoding of information about visual images, recalled images, and behavioral context. *J. Neurophysiol.*, **69**, 1277–95.

Ettlinger, G. (1959). Visual discrimination following successive temporal ablations in monkeys. *Brain*, **82**, 232–50.

Ettlinger, G. (1977). Parietal cortex in visual orientation. In *Physiological aspects of clinical neurology*, (ed. F.C. Rose), pp. 93–100. Blackwell, Oxford.

Ettlinger, G. (1990). 'Object vision' and 'spatial vision': the neuropsychological evidence for the distinction. *Cortex*, **26**, 319–41.

Ettlinger, G. and Kalsbeck, J.E. (1962). Changes in tactile discrimination and in visual reaching after successive and simultaneous bilateral posterior parietal ablations in the monkey. *J. Neurol. Neurosurg. Psychiat.*, **25**, 256–68.

Ettlinger, G. and Wegener, J. (1958). Somaesthetic alternation, discrimination and orientation after frontal and parietal lesions in monkeys. *Q.J. Exp. Psychol.*, **10**, 177–86.

Ettlinger, G., Warrington, E.K., and Zangwill, O.L. (1957). A further study of visual-spatial agnosia. *Brain*, **80**, 335–61.

Ewert, J.-P. (1987). Neuroethology of releasing mechanisms: prey-catching in toads. *Behav. Brain Sci.*, **10**, 337–405.

Fahy, F.L., Riches, I.P., and Brown, M.W. (1993). Neuronal activity related to visual recognition memory: long-term memory and the encoding of recency and familiarity information in the primate anterior and medial inferior temporal and rhinal cortex. *Exp. Brain Res.*, **96**, 457–72.

Faillenot, I., Toni, I., Decety, J., Grégoire, M.-C., and Jeannerod, M. (1997). Visual pathways for object-oriented action and object recognition: functional anatomy with PET. *Cerebral Cortex*, **7**, 77–85.

Fang, F. and He, S. (2005). Cortical responses to invisible objects in the human dorsal and ventral pathways. *Nat. Neurosci.*, **8**, 1380–5.

Farah, M.J. (1990). *Visual agnosia. Disorders of object recognition and what they tell us about normal vision*. MIT Press, Cambridge, MA.

Farah, M.J. (1991.) Patterns of co-occurrence among the associative agnosias: implications for visual object recognition. *Cogn. Neuropsychol.*, **8**, 1–19.

Fattori, P., Breveglieri, R., Amoroso, K., and Galletti, C. (2004). Evidence for both reaching and grasping activity in the medial parieto-occipital cortex of the macaque. *Eur. J. Neurosci.*, **20**, 2457–66.

Faugier-Grimaud, S., Frenois, C., and Stein, D.G. (1978). Effects of posterior parietal lesions on visually guided behavior in monkeys. *Neuropsychologia*, **16**, 151–68.

Feigenbaum, J.D. and Rolls, E.T. (1991). Allocentric and egocentric spatial information processing in the hippocampal formation of the behaving primate. *Psychobiology*, **19**, 21–40.

Feldman, J.A. (1985). Four frames suffice: a provisional model of vision and space. *Behav. Brain Sci.*, **8**, 265–89.

Felleman, D.J. and Van Essen, D.C. (1991). Distributed hierarchical processing in the primate cerebral cortex. *Cerebral Cortex*, **1**, 1–47.

Ferber, S., Humphrey, G.K., and Vilis, T. (2003). The lateral occipital complex subserves the perceptual persistence of motion-defined groupings. *Cerebral Cortex*, **13**, 716–21.

Ferrera, V.P., Nealey, T.A., and Maunsell, J.H.R. (1992). Mixed parvocellular and magnocellular geniculate signals in visual area V4. *Nature*, **358**, 756–8.

Ferrera, V.P., Nealey, T.A., and Maunsell, J.H.R. (1994). Responses in macaque visual area V4 following inactivation of the parvocellular and magnocellular LGN pathways. *J. Neurosci.*, **14**, 2080–8.

Ferrier, D. (1875). Experiments on the brain of monkeys—No. I. *Proc. R. Soc. Lond.*, **23**, 409–30.

Ferrier, D. (1886). *The functions of the brain*. Smith, Elder, London.

Ferrier, D. (1890). *Cerebral localisation (the Croonian lectures)*. Smith, Elder, London.

Ferrier, D. and Yeo, G.F. (1884). A record of experiments on the effects of lesion of different regions of the cerebral hemispheres. *Phil. Trans. R. Soc.*, **175**, 479–564.

Fischer, B. and Boch, R. (1981). Enhanced activation of neurons in prelunate cortex before visually guided saccades of trained rhesus monkeys. *Exp. Brain Res.*, **44**, 129–37.

Fitzpatrick, D., Lund, J.S. and Blasdel, G.G. (1985). Intrinsic connections of macaque striate cortex: Afferent and efferent connections of lamina 4C. *J. Neurosci.*, **5**, 3324–49.

Flanagan, J.R. and Beltzner, M.A. (2000). Independence of perceptual and sensorimotor predictions in the size–weight illusion. *Nat. Neurosci.*, **3**, 737–41.

Flanders, M., Tillery, S.I.H., and Soechting, J.F. (1992). Early stages in a sensorimotor transformation. *Behav. Brain Sci.*, **15**, 309–20.

Fogassi, L., Gallese, V., Di Pellegrino, G., Fadiga, L., Gentilucci, M., Pedotti, A. and Rizzolatti, G. (1992). Space coding by premotor cortex. *Exp. Brain Res.*, **89**, 686–90.

Fogassi, L., Ferrari, P.F., Gesierich, B., Rozzi, S., Chersi, F., and Rizzolatti, G. (2005). Parietal lobe: from action organization to intention understanding. *Science*, **308**, 662–7.

Franz, V.H. (2001). Action does not resist visual illusions. *Trends Cogn. Sci.*, **5**, 457–9.

Franz, V.H., Gegenfurtner, K.R., Bülthoff, H.H., and Fahle, M. (2000). Grasping visual illusions: no evidence for a dissociation between perception and action. *Psychol. Sci.*, **11**, 20–5.

Fries, W. (1981). The projection from the lateral geniculate nucleus to the prestriate cortex of the macaque monkey. *Proc. R. Soc. Lond.*, **B213**, 73–80.

Fujita, I., Tanaka, K., Ito, M., and Cheng, K. (1992). Columns for visual features of objects in monkey inferotemporal cortex. *Nature*, **360**, 343–6.

Funahashi, S., Bruce, C.J., and Goldman-Rakic, P.S. (1989). Mnemonic coding of visual space in the monkey's dorsolateral prefrontal cortex. *J. Neurophysiol.*, **61**, 331–49.

Fuster, J.M. (1989). *The prefrontal cortex*. Raven Press, New York.

Gaffan, D., Harrison, S., and Gaffan, E.A. (1986). Visual identification following inferotemporal ablation in the monkey. *Q. J. Exp. Psychol.*, **38B**, 5–30.

Gaffan, E.A., Gaffan, D., and Harrison, S. (1988). Disconnection of the amygdala from visual association cortex impairs visual reward-association learning in monkeys. *J. Neurosci.*, **8**, 3144–59.

Gainotti, G. and Tiacci, C. (1971). The relationship between disorders of visual perception and unilateral spatial neglect. *Neuropsychologia*, **9**, 451–8.

Gainotti, G., D'Erme, P., Monteleone, D., and Silveri, M.C. (1986). Mechanisms of unilateral spatial neglect in relation to laterality of cerebral lesions. *Brain*, **109**, 599–612.

Gallese, V., Fadiga, L., Fogassi, L., and Rizzolatti, G. (1996). Action recognition in the premotor cortex. *Brain*, **119**, 593–609.

Galletti, C. and Battaglini, P.P. (1989). Gaze-dependent visual neurons in area V3A of monkey prestriate cortex. *J. Neurosci.*, **9**, 1112–25.

Galletti, C., Battaglini, P.P., and Fattori, P. (1991). Functional properties of neurons in the anterior bank of the parieto-occipital sulcus of the macaque monkey. *Eur. J. Neurosci.*, **3**, 452–61.

Galletti, C., Battaglini, P.P., and Fattori, P. (1993). Parietal neurons encoding spatial locations in craniotopic coordinates. *Exp. Brain Res.*, **96**, 221–9.

Galletti, C., Fattori, P., Kutz, D.F., and Battaglini, P.P. (1997). Arm movement-related neurons in the visual area V6A of macaque superior parietal lobule. *Eur. J. Neurosci.*, **9**, 410–14.

Ganel, T., Valyear, K.F., Goshen-Gottstein, Y., and Goodale, M.A. (2005). The involvement of the 'fusiform face area' in processing facial expression. *Neuropsychologia*, **43**, 1645–54.

Gaska, J.P., Jacobson, L.D., and Pollen, D.A. (1988). Spatial and temporal frequency selectivity of neurons in visual cortical area V3A of the macaque monkey. *Vision Res.*, **28**, 1179–91.

Gattass, R., Sousa, A.P.B., and Covey, E. (1985). Cortical visual areas of the macaque: possible substrates for pattern recognition mechanisms. In *Pattern recognition mechanisms*, (ed. C. Chagas, R. Gattass, and C. Gross), pp. 1–20. Springer–Verlag, Berlin.

Gauthier, I. and Tarr, M.J. (1997). Becoming a 'Greeble' expert: exploring mechanisms for face recognition. *Vis. Res.*, **37**, 1673–82.

Gauthier, I., Behrmann, M., and Tarr, M.J. (2004). Are Greebles like faces? Using the neuropsychological exception to test the rule. *Neuropsychologia*, **42**, 1961–70.

Gentilucci, M., Scandolara, C., Pigarev, I.N., and Rizzolatti, G. (1983). Visual responses in the postarcuate cortex (area 6) of the monkey that are independent of eye position. *Exp. Brain Res.*, **50**, 464–8.

Gentilucci, M., Fogassi, L., Luppino, G., Matelli, M., Camarda, R., and Rizzolatti, G. (1988). Functional organization of inferior area 6 in the macaque monkey. I. Somatotopy and the control of proximal movements. *Exp. Brain Res.*, **71**, 475–90.

Gibson, J.J. (1950). *The perception of the visual world*. Houghton Mifflin, Boston.

Gibson, J.J. (1966). *The senses considered as perceptual systems*. Houghton Mifflin, Boston.

Gibson, J.J. (1977). On the analysis of change in the optic array in contemporary research in visual space and motion perception. *Scand. J. Psychol.*, **18**, 161–3.

Girard, P. and Bullier, J. (1989). Visual activity in area V2 during reversible inactivation of area 17 in the macaque monkey. *J. Neurophysiol.*, **62**, 1287–302.

Girard, P., Salin, P.A., and Bullier, J. (1991*a*). Visual activity in areas V3A and V3 during reversible inactivation of area V1 in the macaque monkey. *J. Neurophysiol.*, **66**, 1493–503.

Girard, P., Salin, P.A. and Bullier, J. (1991*b*). Visual activity in macaque area V4 depends on area 17 input. *NeuroReport*, **2**, 81–4.

Girard, P., Salin, P.A., and Bullier, J. (1992). Response selectivity of neurons in area MT of the macaque monkey during reversible inactivation of area V1. *J. Neurophysiol.*, **67**, 1437–46.

Girotti, F., Casazza, M., Musicco, M., and Avanzini, G. (1983). Oculomotor disorders in cortical lesions in man: the role of unilateral neglect. *Neuropsychologia*, **21**, 543–53.

Glickstein, M. (2003). Subcortical projections of the parietal lobes. *Adv. Neurol.*, **93**, 43–55.

Glickstein, M. and May, J.G. (1982). Visual control of movement: the circuits which link visual to motor areas of the brain with special reference to the visual input to the pons and cerebellum. In *Contributions to sensory physiology*, Vol. 7, (ed. W.D. Neff), pp. 103–45. Academic Press, New York.

Glickstein, M., Cohen, J.L., Dixon, B., Gibson, A., Hollins, M., LaBossiere, E., and Robinson, F. (1980). Corticopontine visual projections in macaque monkeys. *J. Comp. Neurol.*, **190**, 209–29.

Glickstein, M., May, J.G., and Mercier, B.E. (1985). Corticopontine projection in the macaque: the distribution of labelled cortical cells after large injections of horseradish peroxidase in the pontine nuclei. *J. Comp. Neurol.*, **235**, 343–59.

Glickstein, M., Buchbinder, S., and May, J.L. (1998). Visual control of the arm, the wrist and the fingers: pathways through the brain. *Neuropsychologia*, **36**, 981–1001.

Glover, S. (2002). Visual illusions affect planning but not control. *Trends Cogn. Sci.*, **6**, 288–92.

Glover, S. (2004). Separate visual representations in the planning and control of action. *Behav. Brain Sci.*, **27**, 3–78.

Glover, S.R. and Dixon, P. (2001). Dynamic illusion effects in a reaching task: evidence for separate visual representations in the planning and control of reaching. *J. Exp. Psychol.: Hum. Percept. Perform.*, **27**, 560–72.

Gnadt, J.W., Bracewell, R.M., and Andersen, R.A. (1991). Sensorimotor transformation during eye movements to remembered visual targets. *Vision Res.*, **31**, 693–715.

Godschalk, M., Lemon, R.N., Kuypers, H.G.J.M., and Ronday, H.K. (1984). Cortical afferents and efferents of monkey postarcuate area: an anatomical and electrophysiological study. *Exp. Brain Res.*, **56**, 410–24.

Godwin-Austen, R.B. (1965). A case of visual disorientation. *J. Neurol. Neurosurg. Psychiat.*, **28**, 453–8.

Goldberg, M.E. and Bushnell, M.C. (1981). Behavioral enhancement of visual responses in monkey cerebral cortex. II. Modulation in frontal eye fields specifically related to saccades. *J. Neurophysiol.*, **46**, 773–87.

Goldberg, M.E. and Colby, C.L. (1989). The neurophysiology of spatial vision. In *Handbook of neuropsychology*, Vol. 2, (ed. F. Boller and J. Grafman), pp. 301–15. Elsevier, Amsterdam.

Goldberg, M.E. and Wurtz, R.H. (1972). Activity of superior colliculus in behaving monkey. I. Visual receptive fields of single neurons. *J. Neurophysiol.*, **35**, 542–59.

Goldstein, K. and Gelb, A. (1918). Psychologische Grundlagen hirnpathologischer Fälle auf Grund von Untersuchungen Hirnverletzter. *Z. Neurol. Psychiat.*, **41**, 1–142.

Gonzalez, C.L.R., Ganel, T., and Goodale, M.A. (2006). Hemispheric specialization for the visual control of action is independent of handedness. *J. Neurophysiol.*, **95**, 3496–3501.

Goodale, M.A. (1983a). Vision as a sensorimotor system. In *Behavioral approaches to brain research*, (ed. T.E. Robinson), pp. 41–61. Oxford University Press, New York.

Goodale, M.A. (1983b). Neural mechanisms of visual orientation in rodents: target versus places. In *Spatially oriented behaviour*, (ed. A. Hein and M. Jeannerod), pp. 35–61. Springer-Verlag, New York.

Goodale, M.A. (1988). Modularity in visuomotor control: from input to output. In *Computational processes in human vision: an interdisciplinary perspective*, (ed. Z.W. Pylyshyn), pp. 262–285. Ablex, Norwood, NJ.

Goodale, M.A. (1990). Brain asymmetries in the control of reaching. In *Vision and action: the control of grasping*, (ed. M.A. Goodale), pp. 14–32. Ablex, Norwood, NJ.

Goodale, M.A. (1998). Visuomotor control: where does vision end and action begin? *Curr. Biol.*, **8**, R489–91.

Goodale, M.A. and Carey, D.P. (1990). The role of cerebral cortex in visuomotor control. In *The cerebral cortex of the rat*, (ed. B. Kolb and R.C. Tees), pp. 309–340. MIT Press, Cambridge, MA.

Goodale, M.A. and Graves, J.A. (1982). Retinal locus as a factor in interocular transfer in the pigeon. In *Analysis of visual behavior*, (ed. D.J. Ingle, M.A. Goodale, and R.J.W. Mansfield), pp. 211–240. MIT Press, Cambridge, MA.

Goodale, M.A. and Haffenden, A.M. (1998). Frames of reference for perception and action in the human visual system. *Neurosci. Biobehav. Rev.*, **22**, 161–72.

Goodale, M.A. and Haffenden, A.M. (2003). Interactions between dorsal and ventral streams of visual processing. In *Advances in neurology (Vol. 93): The Parietal Lobe* (ed. A. Siegel, R.A. Andersen, H.-J. Freund, and D. Spencer) Lippincott-Raven, Philadelphia.

Goodale, M.A. and Humphrey, G.K. (1998). The objects of action and perception. *Cognition*, **67**, 181–207.

Goodale, M.A. and Milner, A.D. (1982). Fractionating orienting behavior in rodents. In *Analysis of visual behavior*, (ed. D.J. Ingle, M.A. Goodale, and R.J.W. Mansfield, pp. 267–99. MIT Press, Cambridge, MA.

Goodale, M.A. and Milner, A.D. (1992). Separate visual pathways for perception and action. *Trends Neurosci.*, **15**, 20–5.

Goodale, M.A. and Milner, A.D. (2004). *Sight unseen: an exploration of conscious and unconscious vision*. Oxford University Press, Oxford.

Goodale, M.A. and Murison, R.C.C. (1975). The effects of lesions of the superior colliculus on locomotor orientation and the orienting reflex. *Brain Res.*, **88**, 241–61.

Goodale, M.A. and Servos, P. (1996). The visual control of prehension. In *Advances in motor learning and control*, (ed. H. Zelaznik), Human Kinetics Publishers, Champaign, IL.

Goodale, M.A., Pélisson, D., and Prablanc, C. (1986). Large adjustments in visually guided reaching do not depend on vision of the hand or perception of target displacement. *Nature*, **320**, 748–50.

Goodale, M.A., Milner, A.D., Jakobson, L.S., and Carey, D.P. (1991). A neurological dissociation between perceiving objects and grasping them. *Nature*, **349**, 154–6.

Goodale, M.A., Murphy, K.J., Meenan, J.-P., Racicot, C.I., and Nicholle, D.A. (1993). Spared object perception but poor object-calibrated grasping in a patient with optic ataxia. *Soc. Neurosci. Abstr.*, **19**, 775.

Goodale, M.A., Jakobson, L.S. and Keillor, J.M. (1994a). Differences in the visual control of pantomimed and natural grasping movements. *Neuropsychologia*, **32**, 1159–78.

Goodale, M.A., Jakobson, L.S., Milner, A.D., Perrett, D.I., Benson, P.J. and Hietanen, J.K. (1994b). The nature and limits of orientation and pattern processing supporting visuo-motor control in a visual form agnosic. *J. Cogn. Neurosci*, **6**, 46–56.

Goodale, M.A., Meenan, J.P., Bülthoff, H.H., Nicolle, D.A., Murphy, K.J. and Racicot, C.I. (1994c). Separate neural pathways for the visual analysis of object shape in perception and prehension. *Curr. Biol.*, **4**, 604–10.

Goodale, M.A., Westwood, D.A., and Milner, A.D. (2004). Two distinct modes of control for object-directed action. *Prog. Brain Res.*, **144**, 131–44.

Gordon, A.M., Forssberg, H., Johansson, R.S., and Westling, G. (1991a). Visual size cues in the programming of manipulative forces during precision grip. *Exp. Brain Res.*, **83**, 477–82.

Gordon, A.M., Forssberg, H., Johansson, R.S., and Westling, G. (1991b). The integration of haptically acquired size information in the programming of precision grip. *Exp. Brain Res.*, **83**, 483–88.

Grafton, S.T., Mazziotta, J.C., Woods, R.P., and Phelps, M.E. (1992). Human functional anatomy of visually guided finger movements. *Brain*, **115**, 565–87.

Grandy M.S. and Westwood, D.A. (2006). Opposite perceptual and sensorimotor responses to a size–weight illusion. *J. Neurophysiol.*, **95**, 3887–92.

Grasse, K.L. and Cynader, M. (1991). The accessory optic system in frontal-eyed animals. In *Vision and visual dysfunction, volume 4: the neural basis of visual function*, (ed. A.G. Leventhal), pp. 111–39. Macmillan, London.

Graziano, M.S.A. and Gross, C.G. (1993). A bimodal map of space: somatosensory receptive fields in the macaque putamen with corresponding visual receptive fields. *Exp. Brain Res.*, **97**, 96–109.

Gréa, H., Pisella, L., Rossetti, Y., Desmurget, M., Tilikete, C., Grafton, S., Prablanc, C., and Vighetto, A. (2002). A lesion of the posterior parietal cortex disrupts on-line adjustments during aiming movements. *Neuropsychologia*, **40**, 2471–80.

Gregory, R.L. (1997). Knowledge in perception and illusion. *Phil. Trans. R. Soc. Lond., B: Biol. Sci.*, **352**, 1121–7.

Grill-Spector, K., Knouf, N., and Kanwisher, N. (2004). The fusiform face area subserves face perception, not generic within-category identification. *Nat. Neurosci.*, **7**, 555–62.

Grill-Spector, K., Kushnir, T., Edelman, S., Itzchak, Y., and Malach, R. (1998). Cue-invariant activation in object-related areas of the human occipital lobe. *Neuron*, **21**, 191–202.

Gross, C.G. (1973). Visual functions of inferotemporal cortex. In *Handbook of sensory physiology, volume VII/3. Central processing of visual information, part B: visual centers in the brain*, (ed. R. Jung), pp. 451–82. Springer-Verlag, Berlin.

Gross, C.G. (1978). Inferior temporal lesions do not impair discrimination of rotated patterns in monkeys. *J. Comp. Physiol. Psychol.*, **92**, 1095–109.

Gross, C.G. (1991). Contribution of striate cortex and the superior colliculus to visual function in area MT, the superior temporal polysensory area and inferior temporal cortex. *Neuropsychologia*, **29**, 497–515.

Gross, C.G. (1992). Representation of visual stimuli in inferior temporal cortex. *Phil. Trans. R. Soc. Lond.*, **B335**, 3–10.

Gross, C.G., Rocha-Miranda, C.E., and Bender, D.B. (1972). Visual properties of neurons in the inferotemporal cortex of the macaque. *J. Neurophysiol.*, **35**, 96–111.

Gross, C.G., Bender, D.B., and Mishkin, M. (1977). Contributions of the corpus callosum and the anterior commissure to visual activation of inferior temporal neurons. *Brain Res.*, **131**, 227–39.

Gross, C.G., Bruce, C.J., Desimone, R., Fleming, J., and Gattass, R. (1981). Cortical visual areas of the temporal lobe. Three areas in the macaque. In *Cortical sensory organization. Vol. 2: multiple visual areas*, (ed. C.N. Woolsey), pp. 187–216. Humana Press, Clifton, NJ.

Gross, C.G., Desimone, R., Albright, T.D., and Schwartz, E.L. (1985). Inferior temporal cortex and pattern recognition. In *Pattern recognition mechanisms*, (ed. C. Chagas, R. Gattass, and C. Gross), pp. 179–201. Springer-Verlag, Berlin.

Grossman, E., Donnelly, M., Price, R., Pickens, D., Morgan, V., Neighbor, G., and Blake, R. (2000). Brain areas involved in perception of biological motion. *J. Cogn. Neurosci.*, **12**, 711–20.

Grossman, E.D. and Blake, R. (2002). Brain areas active during visual perception of biological motion. *Neuron*, **35**, 1167–75.

Grüsser, O.-J. and Landis, T. (1991). *Vision and visual dysfunction, volume 12: Visual agnosias and other disturbances of visual perception and cognition*. Macmillan, London.

Guitton, D., Buchtel, H.A., and Douglas, R.M. (1985). Frontal lobe lesions in man cause difficulties in suppressing reflexive glances and in generating goal-directed saccades. *Exp. Brain Res.*, **58**, 455–72.

Haaxma, R. and Kuypers, H.G.J.M. (1975). Intrahemispheric cortical connexions and visual guidance of hand and finger movements in the rhesus monkey. *Brain*, **98**, 239–60.

Habib, M. and Sirigu, A. (1987). Pure topographic disorientation: a definition and anatomical basis. *Cortex*, **23**, 73–85.

Hadjikhani, N., Liu, A.K., Dale, A.M., Cavanagh, P., and Tootell, R.B.H. (1998). Retinotopy and color sensitivity in human cortical area V8. *Nat. Neurosci.*, **1**, 235–41.

Haenny, P. and Schiller, P.H. (1988). State dependent activity in monkey visual cortex. I. Single unit activity in V1 and V4 on visual tasks. *Exp. Brain Res.*, **69**, 225–44.

Haffenden, A.M. and Goodale, M.A. (2000). Independent effects of pictorial displays on perception and action. *Vis. Res.*, **40**, 1597–607.

Haffenden, A.M., Schiff, K.C., and Goodale, M.A. (2001). The dissociation between perception and action in the Ebbinghaus illusion: non-illusory effects of pictorial cues on grasp. *Curr. Biol.*, **11**, 177–81.

Halgren, E., Dale, A.M., Sereno, M.I., Tootell, R.B., Marinkovic, K., and Rosen, B.R. (1999). Location of human face-selective cortex with respect to retinotopic areas. *Hum. Brain Map.*, 7, 29–37.

Halligan, P.W., Cockburn, J. and Wilson, B.A. (1991). The behavioural assessment of visual neglect. *Neuropsychol Rehab.*, 1, 5–32.

Hansen, R.M. and Skavenski, A.A. (1985). Accuracy of spatial localization near the time of a saccadic eye movement. *Vision Res.*, 25, 1077–82.

Hari, R., Salmelin, R., Tissari, S.O., Kajola, M., and Virsu, V. (1994). Visual stability during eyeblinks. *Nature*, 367, 121–2.

Harries, M.H. and Perrett, D.I. (1991). Visual processing of faces in temporal cortex: physiological evidence for a modular organization and possible anatomical correlates. *J. Cogn. Neurosci.*, 3, 9–24.

Hartje, W. and Ettlinger, G. (1974). Reaching in the light and dark after unilateral posterior parietal ablations in the monkey. *Cortex*, 9, 346–54.

Hartline, H.K. (1938). The responses of single optic nerve fibers of the vertebrate eye to illumination of the retina. *Am. J. Physiol.*, 121, 400–15.

Harvey, M. (1995). Translation of 'Psychic paralysis of gaze, optic ataxia, and spatial disorder of attention' by Rudolph Bálint. *Cognitive Neuropsychology*, 12, 261–82.

Harvey, M., Milner, A.D., and Roberts, R.C. (1994). Spatial bias in visually-guided reaching and bisection following right cerebral stroke. *Cortex*, 30, 343–50.

Harvey, M., Milner, A.D., and Roberts, R.C. (1995). An investigation of hemispatial neglect using the landmark task. *Brain Cogn.*, 27, 59–78.

Hasselmo, M.E., Rolls, E.T., Baylis, G.C., and Nalwa, V. (1989). Object-centered encoding by face-selective neurons in the cortex in the superior temporal sulcus of the monkey. *Exp. Brain Res.*, 75, 417–29.

Hasson, U., Hendler, T., Ben Bashat, D., and Malach, R. (2001). Vase or face? A neural correlate of shape-selective grouping processes in the human brain. *J. Cogn. Neurosci.*, 13, 744–53.

Hasson, U., Levy, I., Behrmann, M., Hendler, T., and Malach, R. (2002). Eccentricity bias as an organizing principle for human high-order object areas. *Neuron*, 34, 479–90.

Hasson, U., Harel, M., Levy, I., and Malach, R. (2003). Large-scale mirror-symmetry organization of human occipito-temporal object areas. *Neuron*, 37, 1027–41.

Haxby, J.V., Grady, C.L., Horwitz, B., Ungerleider, L.G., Mishkin, M., Carson, R.E. *et al.* (1991). Dissociation of object and spatial visual processing pathways in human extrastriate cortex. *Neurobiology*, 88, 1621–5.

Haxby, J.V., Grady, C.L., Horwitz, B., Salerno, J., Ungerleider, L.G., Mishkin, M. *et al.* (1993). Dissociation of object and spatial visual processing pathways in human extrastriate cortex. In *Functional organisation of the human visual cortex*, (ed. B. Gulyás, D. Ottoson, and P.E. Roland), pp. 329–340. Pergamon Press, Oxford.

Haxby, J.V., Ungerleider, L.G., Clark, V.P., Schouten, J.L., Hoffman, E.A., and Martin, A. (1999). The effect of face inversion on activity in human neural systems for face and object perception. *Neuron*, 22, 189–99.

Haxby, J.V., Gobbini, M.I., Furey, M.L., Ishai, A., Schouten, J.L., and Pietrini, P. (2001). Distributed and overlapping representations of faces and objects in ventral temporal cortex. *Science*, 293, 2425–30.

Haxby, J.V., Hoffman, E.A., and Gobbini, M.I. (2002). Human neural systems for face recognition and social communication. *Biol. Psychiat.*, 51, 59–67.

Hecaen, H. and Ajuriaguerra, J. (1954). Balint's syndrome (psychic paralysis of visual fixation) and its minor forms. *Brain*, 77, 373–400.

Heilman, K.M., Watson, R.T., Valenstein, E., and Damasio, A.R. (1983). Localization of lesions in neglect. In *Localization in neuropsychology*, (ed. A. Kertesz), pp. 471–492. Academic Press, New York.

Heilman, K.M., Bowers, D., Coslett, H.D., Whelan, H., and Watson, R.T. (1985a). Directional hypokinesia: prolonged reaction time for leftward movements in patients with right hemisphere lesions and neglect. *Neurology*, 35, 855–9.

Heilman, K.M., Valenstein, E., and Watson, R.T. (1985b). The neglect syndrome. In *Handbook of clinical neurology vol. 1(45): clinical neuropsychology*, (ed. J.A.M. Frederiks), pp. 153–83. Elsevier, Amsterdam.

Hendrickson, A.E. (1985). Dots, stripes and columns in monkey visual cortex. *Trends Neurosci.*, 8, 406–10.

Hendry, S.H.C. and Yoshioka, T. (1994). A neurochemically distinct third channel in the macaque dorsal lateral geniculate nucleus. *Science*, 264, 575–7.

Henriques, D.Y., Klier, E.M., Smith, M.A., Lowy, D., and Crawford, J.D. (1998). Gaze-centered remapping of remembered visual space in an open-loop pointing task. *J. Neurosci.*, 18, 1583–94.

Hess, W.R., Bürgi, S., and Bucher, V. (1946). Motorische Funktion des Tektal- und Segmentalgebietes. *Monatsschr. Psychiatr. Neurol.*, 112, 1–52.

Hietanen, J.K. and Perrett, D.I. (1993). Motion sensitive cells in the macaque superior temporal polysensory area. I. Lack of response to the sight of the animal's own limb movement. *Exp. Brain Res.*, 93, 117–28.

Hietanen, J.K., Perrett, D.I., Oram, M.W., Benson, P.J., and Dittrich, W.H. (1992). The effects of lighting conditions on responses of cells selective for face views in the macaque temporal cortex. *Exp. Brain Res.*, 89, 157–71.

Hoffmann, K.-P. and Distler, C. (1989). Quantitative-analysis of visual receptive-fields of neurons in nucleus of the optic tract and dorsal terminal nucleus of the accessory optic tract in macaque monkey. *J. Neurophysiol.*, 62, 416–28.

Hoffmann, K.-P., Distler, C., and Erickson, R. (1991). Functional projections from striate cortex and superior temporal sulcus to the nucleus of the optic tract (NOT) and dorsal terminal nucleus of the accessory optic tract (DTN) of macaque monkeys. *J. Comp. Neurol.*, 313, 707–24.

Hoffmann, K.-P., Distler, C., and Ilg, U. (1992). Callosal and superior temporal sulcus contributions to receptive field properties in the macaque monkey's nucleus of the optic tract and dorsal terminal nucleus of the accessory optic tract. *J. Comp. Neurol.*, 321, 150–62.

Holding, D.H. (1968). Accuracy of delayed aiming responses. *Psychon. Sci.*, 12, 125–6.

Holmes, E.J. and Gross, C.G. (1984). Effects of inferior temporal lesions on discrimination of stimuli differing in orientation. *J. Neurosci.*, 4, 3063–8.

Holmes, G. (1918). Disturbances of visual orientation. *Brit. J. Ophthalmol.*, 2, 449–68; 506–16.

Holmes, G. (1919). Disturbances of visual space perception. *Brit. Med. J.*, 2, 230–3.

Holscher, C. and Rolls, E.T. (2002). Perirhinal cortex neuronal activity is actively related to working memory in the macaque. *Neural Plasticity*, 9, 41–51.

Horton, J.C. and Hubel, D.H. (1981). Regular patchy distribution of cytochrome oxidase staining in primary visual cortex of macaque monkey. *Nature*, 292, 762–4.

Howard, R., Trend, P., and Russell, R.W.R. (1987). Clinical features of ischemia in cerebral arterial border zones after periods of reduced cerebral blood flow. *Arch. Neurol.*, **44**, 934–40.

Hoyt, W.F. and Walsh, F.B. (1958). Cortical blindness with partial recovery following acute cerebral anoxia from cardiac arrest. *Arch. Ophthalmol.*, **60**, 1061–9.

Hu, Y. and Goodale, M.A. (2000). Grasping after a delay shifts size-scaling from absolute to relative metrics. *J. Cogn. Neurosci.*, **12**, 856–68.

Hubel, D.H. and Livingstone, M.S. (1987). Segregation of form, color, and stereopsis in primate area 18. *J. Neurosci.*, **7**, 3378–415.

Hubel, D.H. and Wiesel, T.N. (1959). Receptive fields of single neurones in the cat's striate cortex. *J. Physiol. (Lond.)*, **148**, 574–91.

Hubel, D.H. and Wiesel, T.N. (1962). Receptive fields, binocular interaction and functional architecture in the cat's visual cortex. *J. Physiol.* (Lond.) **160**, 106–54.

Hubel, D.H. and Wiesel, T.N. (1968). Receptive fields and functional architecture of monkey striate cortex. *J. Physiol. (Lond.)*, **195**, 215–43.

Hubel, D.H. and Wiesel, T.N. (1970). Cells sensitive to binocular depth in area 18 of the macaque monkey cortex. *Nature*, **225**, 41–2.

Humphrey, G.K. (1996). The McCollough effect: misperception and reality. In *Visual constancies: why things look as they do*, (ed. V. Walsh and J. Kulikowski), Cambridge University Press, Cambridge. (In press.)

Humphrey, G.K., Goodale, M.A. and Gurnsey, R. (1991). Orientation discrimination in a visual form agnosic: evidence from the McCollough effect. *Psychol. Sci.*, **2**, 331–5.

Humphrey, G.K., Goodale, M.A., Jakobson, L.S. and Servos, P. (1994). The role of surface information in object recognition: studies of a visual form agnosic and normal subjects. *Perception*, **23**, 1457–81.

Humphrey, N.K. and Weiskrantz, L. (1969). Size constancy in monkeys with inferotemporal lesions. *Q.J. Exp. Psychol.*, **21**, 225–38.

Humphreys, G.W. and Riddoch, M.J. (1987). The fractionation of visual agnosia. In *Visual object processing: a cognitive neuropsychological approach*, (ed. G.W. Humphreys and M.J. Riddoch), pp. 281–306. Erlbaum, London.

Hyvärinen, J. and Poranen, A. (1974). Function of the parietal associative area 7 as revealed from cellular discharges in alert monkeys. *Brain*, **97**, 673–92.

Ingle, D. (1973). Two visual systems in the frog. *Science*, **181**, 1053–5.

Ingle, D.J. (1975). Selective visual attention in frogs. *Science*, **188**, 1033–5.

Ingle, D.J. (1980). Some effects of pretectum lesions on the frog's detection of stationary objects. *Behav. Brain Res.*, **1**, 139–63.

Ingle, D.J. (1982). Organization of visuomotor behaviors in vertebrates. In *Analysis of visual behavior*, (ed. D.J. Ingle, M.A. Goodale, and R.J.W. Mansfield), pp. 67–109. MIT Press, Cambridge, MA.

Ingle, D.J. (1991). Functions of subcortical visual systems in vertebrates and the evolution of higher visual mechanisms. In *Vision and visual dysfunction, volume 2: evolution of the eye and visual system*, (ed. R.L. Gregory and J. Cronly-Dillon), pp. 152–64. Macmillan, London.

Itaya, S.K. and Van Hoesen, G.W. (1983). Retinal projections to the inferior and medial pulvinar nuclei in the old-world monkey. *Brain Res.*, **269**, 223–30.

Iwai, E. and Mishkin, M. (1969). Further evidence of the locus of the visual area in the temporal lobe of monkeys. *Exp. Neurol.*, **25**, 585–94.

Iwai, E. and Yukie, M. (1987). Amygdalofugal and amygdalopetal connections with modality-specific visual cortical areas in the macaques (*Macaca fuscata, M. mulatta, M. fascicularis*). *J. Comp. Neurol.*, **261**, 362–87.

Jackson, J.H. (1876). Case of large cerebral tumour without optic neuritis and with left hemiplegia and imperception. *R. Lond. Ophthalmol. Hosp. Rep.*, **8**, 434–44.

Jackson, S.R. and Shaw, A. (2000). The Ponzo illusion affects grip-force but not grip-aperture scaling during prehension movements. *J. Exp. Psychol.: Hum. Percept. Perform.*, **26**, 418–23.

Jakobson, L.S. and Goodale, M.A. (1989). Trajectories of reaches to prismatically-displaced targets: evidence for "automatic" visuomotor recalibration. *Exp. Brain Res.*, **78**, 575–87.

Jakobson, L.S. and Goodale, M.A. (1991). Factors affecting higher-order movement planning: a kinematic analysis of human prehension. *Exp. Brain Res.*, **86**, 199–208.

Jakobson, L.S., Archibald, Y.M., Carey, D.P., and Goodale, M.A. (1991). A kinematic analysis of reaching and grasping movements in a patient recovering from optic ataxia. *Neuropsychologia*, **29**, 803–9.

James, W. (1890). *Principles of psychology*. Macmillan, London.

James, T.W., Humphrey, G.K., Gati, J.S., Menon, R.S., and Goodale, M.A. (2002). Differential effects of viewpoint on object-driven activation in dorsal and ventral streams. *Neuron*, **35**, 793–801.

James, T.W., Culham, J., Humphrey, G.K., Milner, A.D., and Goodale, M.A. (2003). Ventral occipital lesions impair object recognition but not object-directed grasping: a fMRI study. *Brain*, **126**, 2463–75.

Jeannerod, M. (1986). The formation of finger grip during prehension: a cortically mediated visuomotor pattern. *Behav. Brain Res.*, **19**, 99–116.

Jeannerod, M. (1987). *Neurophysiological and neuropsychological aspects of spatial neglect*. Elsevier, Amsterdam.

Jeannerod, M. (1988). *The neural and behavioural organization of goal-directed movements*. Oxford University Press, Oxford.

Jeannerod, M. and Biguer, B. (1982). Visuomotor mechanisms in reaching within extrapersonal space. In *Analysis of visual behavior*, (ed. D.J. Ingle, M.A. Goodale, and R.J.W. Mansfield), pp. 387–409. MIT Press, Cambridge, MA.

Jeannerod, M., Decety, J., and Michel, F. (1994). Impairment of grasping movements following bilateral posterior parietal lesion. *Neuropsychologia*, **32**, 369–80.

Jeeves, M.A. (1984). The historical roots and recurring issues of neurobiological studies of face perception. *Human Neurobiol.*, **3**, 191–6.

Johansson, G. (1973). Visual perception of biological motion and a model for its analysis. *Percept. Psychophys.*, **14**, 201–11.

Johansson, R.S. (1991). How is grasping modified by somatosensory input? In *Motor control: concepts and issues. Dahlem Konferenzen*, (ed. D.R. Humphrey and H.-J. Freund), pp. 331–355. Wiley, Chichester, UK.

Johnson, H., Van Beers, R.J., and Haggard, P. (2002). Action and awareness in pointing tasks. *Exp. Brain Res.*, **146**, 451–9.

Johnson-Frey, S.H., Newman-Norlund, R., and Grafton, S.T. (2005). A distributed left hemisphere network active during planning of everyday tool use skills. *Cerebral Cortex*, **15**, 681–95.

Jones, E.G. and Powell, T.P.S. (1970). An anatomical study of converging sensory pathways within the cerebral cortex of the monkey. *Brain*, **93**, 793–820.

Kaas, J.H. and Huerta, M.F. (1988). The subcortical visual system of primates. In *Comparative primate biology, volume 4: neurosciences*, (ed. H.D. Steklis and J. Erwin), pp. 327–91. Wiley-Liss, New York

Kadoya, S., Wolin, L.R., and Massopust, L.C. (1971). Collicular unit responses to mono-chromatic stimulation in squirrel monkey. *Brain Res.*, **32**, 251–4.

Kanwisher, N., McDermott, J., and Chun, M.M. (1997). The fusiform face area: a module in human extrastriate cortex specialized for face perception. *J. Neurosci.* **17**, 4302–11.

Karnath, H.O. and Perenin, M.T. (2005). Cortical control of visually guided reaching: evidence from patients with optic ataxia. *Cerebral Cortex*, **15**, 1561–9.

Keating, E.G. (1979). Rudimentary color vision in the monkey after removal of striate and preoccipital cortex. *Brain Res.*, **179**, 379–84.

Keay, K.A., Redgrave, P. and Dean, P. (1988). Cardiovascular and respiratory changes elicited by stimulation of rat superior colliculus. *Brain Res. Bull.*, **20**, 13–26.

Kentridge, R.W., Heywood, C.A., and Weiskrantz, L. (1999). Attention without awareness in blindsight. *Proc. R. Soc. Lond. B: Biol. Sci.*, **266**, 1805–11.

Kentridge, R.W., Heywood, C.A., and Weiskrantz, L. (2004). Spatial attention speeds dis-crimination without awareness in blindsight. *Neuropsychologia*, **42**, 831–5.

Kilpatrick, I.C., Collingridge, G.L., and Starr, M.S. (1982). Evidence for the participation of nigrotectal gamma-aminobutyrate-containing neurons in striatal and nigral-derived circling in the rat. *Neuroscience*, **7**, 207–22.

Kimura, D. (1982). Left-hemisphere control of oral and brachial movements and their rela-tion to communication. *Phil. Trans. R. Soc. Lond.*, **B298**, 135–49.

Kimura, D. (1993). *Neuromotor mechanisms in human communication*. Oxford University Press, New York.

Kinsbourne, M. (1987). Mechanisms of unilateral neglect. In *Neurophysiological and neuro-psychological aspects of spatial neglect*, (ed. M. Jeannerod), pp. 69–86. Elsevier, Amsterdam.

Kisvárday, Z.F., Cowey, A., Stoerig, P., and Somogyi, P. (1991). Direct and indirect retinal input into degenerated dorsal lateral geniculate nucleus after striate cortical removal in monkey: implications for residual vision. *Exp. Brain Res.*, **86**, 271–92.

Kleinschmidt, A., Buchel, C., Zeki, S., and Frackowiak, R.S. (1998). Human brain activity during spontaneously reversing perception of ambiguous figures. *Proc. R. Soc. Lond. B: Biol. Sci.*, **265**, 2427–33.

Kling, A. and Brothers, L. (1992). The amygdala and social behavior. In *The amygdala: neu-robiological aspects of emotion, memory, and mental dysfunction*, (ed. J. Aggleton), pp. 353–77. Wiley-Liss, New York.

Klüver, H. and Bucy, P.C. (1937). 'Psychic blindness' and other symptoms following bilat-eral temporal lobectomy in rhesus monkeys. *Am. J. Physiol.*, **119**, 352–3.

Klüver, H. and Bucy, P.C. (1938). An analysis of certain effects of bilateral temporal lobectomy in the rhesus monkey, with special reference to "psychic blindness". *J. Psychol.*, **5**, 33–54.

Klüver, H. and Bucy, P.C. (1939). Preliminary analysis of functions of the temporal lobes in monkeys. *Arch. Neurol. Psychiat.*, **42**, 979–1000.

Kobatake, E. and Tanaka, K. (1994). Neuronal selectivities to complex object features in the ventral visual pathway of the macaque cerebral cortex. *J. Neurophysiol.*, **71**, 856–67.

Koenderink, J.J. (1986). Optic flow. *Vision Res.*, **26**, 161–80.

Koerner, F. and Teuber, H.-L. (1973). Visual field defects after missile injuries to the geniculo-striate pathway in man. *Exp. Brain Res.*, **18**, 88–112.

Komatsu, H. and Wurtz, R.H. (1988). Relation of cortical areas MT and MST to pursuit eye movements. I. Localization and visual properties of neurons. *J. Neurophysiol.*, **60**, 580–603.

Komatsu, H., Ideura, Y., Kaji, S., and Yamane, S. (1992). Color selectivity of neurons in the inferior temporal cortex of the awake macaque monkey. *J. Neurosci.*, **12**, 408–24.

Kosslyn, S.M. (1987). Seeing and imaging in the cerebral hemispheres: a computational approach. *Psychol. Rev.*, **94**, 148–75.

Kourtzi, Z. and Kanwisher, N. (2001). Representation of perceived object shape by the human lateral occipital complex. *Science*, **293**, 1506–9.

Kraut, M., Hart, J., Soher, B.J., and Gordon, B. (1997). Object shape processing in the visual system evaluated using functional MRI. *Neurology*, **48**, 1416–20.

Kreiman, G., Fried, I., and Koch, C. (2002). Single-neuron correlates of subjective vision in the human medial temporal lobe. *Proc. Natl Acad. Sci., USA*, **99**, 8378–83.

Króliczak, G., Heard, P., Goodale, M.A., and Gregory, R.L. (2006). Dissociation of perception and action unmasked by the hollow-face illusion. *Brain Res.*, **1080**, 9–16.

Kuffler, S.W. (1953). Discharge patterns and functional organization of the mammalian retina. *J. Neurophysiol.*, **16**, 37–68.

Kurtz, D. and Butter, C.M. (1980). Impairments in visual discrimination performance and gaze shifts in monkeys with superior colliculus lesions. *Brain Res.*, **196**, 109–24.

Kurylo, D.D. and Skavenski, A.A. (1991). Eye movements elicited by electrical stimulation of area PG in the monkey. *J. Neurophysiol.*, **65**, 1243–53.

Kustov, A.A. and Robinson, D.L. (1996). Shared neural control of attentional shifts and eye movements. *Nature*, **384**, 74–7.

Lachica, E.A., Beck, P.D. and Casagrande, V.A. (1992). Parallel pathways in macaque striate cortex: anatomically defined columns in layer III. *Proc. Natl. Acad. Sci., USA*, **89**, 3566–70.

Làdavas, E., Umiltà, C., Ziani, P., Brogi, A., and Minarini, M. (1993). The role of right side objects in left side neglect: a dissociation between perceptual and directional motor neglect. *Neuropsychologia*, **31**, 761–73.

Lamme, V.A.F. and Roelfsema, P.R. (2000). The distinct modes of vision offered by feedforward and recurrent processing. *Trends Neurosci.*, **23**, 571–9.

Lamotte, R.H. and Acuña, C. (1978). Deficits in accuracy of reaching after removal of posterior parietal cortex in monkeys. *Brain Res.*, **139**, 309–26.

Landis, T., Graves, R., Benson, D.F. and Hebben, N. (1982). Visual recognition through kinaesthetic mediation. *Psychol. Med.*, **12**, 515–31.

Landis, T., Cummings, J.L., Benson, D.F., and Palmer, E.P. (1986). Loss of topographic familiarity. An environmental agnosia. *Arch. Neurol.*, **43**, 132–6.

Latto, R. (1986). The role of inferior parietal cortex and the frontal eye-fields in visuospatial discriminations in the macaque monkey. *Behav. Brain Res.*, **22**, 41–52.

Latto, R. and Cowey, A. (1971). Visual field defects after frontal eye-field lesions in monkeys. *Brain Res.*, **30**, 1–24.

Lawler, K.A. and Cowey, A. (1987). On the role of posterior parietal and prefrontal cortex in visuo-spatial perception and attention. *Exp. Brain Res.*, **65**, 695–8.

Lê, S., Cardebat, D., Boulanouar, K., Hénaff, M.-A., Michel, F., Milner, A.D., Dijkerman, H.C., Puel, M., and Démonet, J.-F. (2002). Seeing, since childhood, without ventral stream: a behavioural study. *Brain*, **125**, 58–74.

Lee, D.N. (1976). A theory of visual control of braking based on information about time to collision. *Perception*, **5**, 437–57.

Lee, D.N. and Lishman, J.R. (1975). Visual proprioceptive control of stance. *J. Human Movement Studies*, **1**, 87–95.

Lee, D.N. and Thomson, J.A. (1982). Vision in action: the control of locomotion. In *Analysis of visual behavior*, (ed. D.J. Ingle, M.A. Goodale, and R.J.W. Mansfield), pp. 411–433. MIT Press, Cambridge, MA.

Lennie, P. (1980). Parallel visual pathways: a review. *Vision Res.*, **20**, 561–94.

Lennie, P., Krauskopf, J., and Sclar, G. (1990). Chromatic mechanisms in striate cortex of macaque. *J. Neurosci.*, **10**, 649–69.

Lettvin, J.Y., Maturana, H.R., McCulloch, W.S., and Pitts, W.H. (1959). What the frog's eye tells the frog's brain. *Proc. I.R.E.*, **47**, 1940–51.

Leventhal, A.G., Rodieck, R.W., and Dreher, B. (1981). Retinal ganglion cell classes in the Old World monkey: morphology and central projections. *Science*, **213**, 1139–42.

Levine, D.N., Kaufman, K.J., and Mohr, J.P. (1978). Inaccurate reaching associated with a superior parietal lobe tumor. *Neurology*, **28**, 556–61.

Li, L., Miller, E.K. and Desimone, R. (1993). The representation of stimulus familiarity in anterior inferior temporal cortex. *J. Neurophysiol.*, **69**, 1918–29.

Lissauer, H. (1890). Ein Fall von Seelenblindheit nebst einem Beitrag zur Theorie derselben. *Arch. Psychiat.*, **21**, 222–70.

Liu, G.T., Bolton, A.K., Price, B.H., and Weintraub, S. (1992). Dissociated perceptual-sensory and exploratory-motor neglect. *J. Neurol. Neurosurg. Psychiatr.*, **55**, 701–6.

Livingstone, M. and Hubel, D. (1988). Segregation of form, color, movement, and depth: anatomy, physiology, and perception. *Science*, **240**, 740–9.

Livingstone, M.S. and Hubel, D.H. (1984). Anatomy and physiology of a color system in the primate visual cortex. *J. Neurosci.*, **4**, 309–56.

Logothetis, N.K. (1998). Single units and conscious vision. *Phil. Trans. R. Soc. Lond. B: Biol. Sci.*, **353**, 1801–18.

Loomis, J.M., Da Silva, J.A., Fujita, N. and Fukusima, S.S. (1992). Visual space perception and visually directed action. *J. Exp. Psychol. (Human Percept. Perform.)* **18**, 906–21.

Lumer, E.D., Friston, K.J., and Rees, G. (1998) Neural correlates of perceptual rivalry in the human brain. *Science*, **280**, 1930–4.

Lund, J.S., Lund, R.D., Hendrickson, A.E., Bunt, A.H., and Fuchs, A.F. (1975). The origin of efferent pathways from the primary visual cortex, area 17, of the macaque monkey. *J. Comp. Neurol.*, **164**, 287–304.

Lynch, J.C. (1980). The functional organization of posterior parietal association cortex. *Behav. Brain Sci.*, **3**, 485–534.

Lynch, J.C. and McLaren, J.W. (1982). The contribution of parieto-occipital association cortex to the control of slow eye movements. In *Functional basis of ocular mobility disorders*, (ed. G. Lennerstrand, D.S. Lee, and E.L. Keller), pp. 501–10. Pergamon Press, Oxford.

Lynch, J.C. and McLaren, J.W. (1983). Optokinetic nystagmus deficits following parieto-occipital cortex lesions in monkey. *Exp. Brain Res.*, **49**, 125–30.

Lynch, J.C. and McLaren, J.W. (1989). Deficits of visual attention and saccadic eye movements after lesions of parietooccipital cortex in monkeys. *J. Neurophysiol.*, **61**, 74–90.

Lynch, J.C., Graybiel, A.M., and Lobeck, L.J. (1985). The differential projection of two cytoarchitectural subregions of the inferior parietal lobule of macaque upon the deep layers of the superior colliculus. *J. Comp. Neurol.*, **235**, 241–54.

McCarthy, G., Puce, A., Gore, J.C., and Allison, T. (1997). Face-specific processing in the human fusiform gyrus. *J. Cogn. Neurosci.*, **9**, 605–10.

McCarthy, R. (1993). Assembling routines and addressing representations: an alternative conceptualization of 'what' and 'where' in the human brain. In *Spatial representation*, (ed. N. Eilan, R. McCarthy, and B. Brewer), pp. 373–99. Blackwell, Oxford.

McCarthy, R.A. and Warrington, E.K. (1986). Visual associative agnosia: a clinico-anatomical study of a single case. *J. Neurol. Neurosurg. Psychiat.*, **49**, 1233–40.

McCarthy, R.A. and Warrington, E.K. (1990). *Cognitive neuropsychology*. Academic Press, New York.

McCollough, C. (1965). Color adaptation of edge-detectors in the human visual system. *Science*, **149**, 1115–16.

McFie, J., Piercy, M.F., and Zangwill, O.L. (1950). Visual-spatial agnosia associated with lesions of the right cerebral hemisphere. *Brain*, **73**, 167–90.

McFie, J. and Zangwill, O.L. (1960). Visual-constructive disabilities associated with lesions of the left cerebral hemisphere. *Brain*, **83**, 243–60.

McIntosh, R.D., McClements, K.I., Dijkerman, H.C., Birchall, D., and Milner, A.D. (2004*a*). Preserved obstacle avoidance during reaching in patients with left visual neglect. *Neuropsychologia*, **42**, 1107–17.

McIntosh, R.D., McClements, K.I., Schindler, I., Cassidy, T.P., Birchall, D., and Milner, A.D. (2004*b*). Avoidance of obstacles in the absence of visual awareness. *Proc. R. Soc. Lond. B: Biol. Sci.*, **271**, 15–20.

MacKay, W.A. (1992). Properties of reach-related neuronal activity in cortical area 7A. *J. Neurophysiol.*, **67**, 1335–45.

McKyton, A. and Zohary, E. (2006). Beyond retinotopic mapping: the spatial representation of objects in the human lateral occipital complex. *Cerebral Cortex.*, published online, 3 July 2006.

McNeil, J.E. and Warrington, E.K. (1991). Prosopagnosia: a reclassification. *Q. J. Exp. Psychol.*, **43A**, 267–87.

Mack, A., Heuer, F., Villardi, K. and Chambers, D. (1985). The dissociation of position and extent in Müller-Lyer figures. *Percept. Psychophys.*, **37**, 335–344.

Malach, R., Reppas, J.B., Benson, R.B., Kwong, K.K., Jiang, H., Kennedy, W.A., Ledden, P.J., Brady, T.J., Rosen, B.R., and Tootell, R.B.H. (1995). Object-related activity revealed by functional magnetic resonance imaging in human occipital cortex. *Proc. Nat. Acad. Sci., USA*, **92**, 8135–8.

Malpeli, J.G., Schiller, P.H., and Colby, C.L. (1981). Response properties of single cells in monkey striate cortex during reversible inactivation of individual lateral geniculate laminae. *J. Neurophysiol.*, **46**, 1102–19.

Marcar, V.L. and Cowey, A. (1992). The effect of removing superior temporal cortical motion areas in the macaque monkey: II. Motion discrimination using random dot displays. *Eur. J. Neurosci.*, **4**, 1228–38.

Marcel, A.J. (1983). Conscious and unconscious perception: an approach to the relations between phenomenal experience and perceptual processes. *Cogn. Psychol.*, **15**, 238–300.

Marcel, A.J. (1993). Slippage in the unity of consciousness. In *Experimental and theoretical studies of consciousness*, (ed. G.R. Bock and J. Marsh), pp. 168–180. Wiley, Chichester, UK.

Marr, D. (1982). *Vision*. Freeman, San Francisco.

Marshall, J.C. and Halligan, P.W. (1993). Visuo-spatial neglect: a new copying test to assess perceptual parsing. *J. Neurol.*, **240**, 37–40.

Matelli, M., Camarda, R., Glickstein, M. and Rizzolatti, G. (1986). Afferent and efferent projections of the inferior area 6 in the macaque monkey. *J. Comp. Neurol.*, **251**, 281–98.

Maunsell, J.H.R. (1987). Physiological evidence for two visual subsystems. In *Matters of intelligence*, (ed. L.M. Vaina), pp. 59–87. Reidel, Dordrecht.

Maunsell, J.H.R. and Ferrera, V.P. (1993). Extraretinal representations in visual areas of macaque cerebral cortex. In *Brain mechanisms of perception and memory: From neuron to behavior*, (ed. T. Ono, L. R. Squire, M. E. Raichle, D. I. Perrett, and M. Fukuda), pp. 104–18. Oxford University Press, New York.

Maunsell, J.H.R. and Newsome, W.T. (1987). Visual processing in monkey extrastriate cortex. *Ann. Rev. Neurosci.*, **10**, 363–401.

Maunsell, J.H.R. and Van Essen, D.C. (1983a). Functional properties of neurons in middle temporal visual area of the macaque monkey. I. Selectivity for stimulus direction, speed, and orientation. *J. Neurophysiol.*, **49**, 1127–47.

Maunsell, J.H.R. and Van Essen, D.C. (1983b). The connections of the middle temporal visual area (MT) and their relationship to a cortical hierarchy in the macaque monkey. *J. Neurosci.*, **3**, 2563–86.

Maunsell, J.H.R., Nealey, T.A. and DePriest, D.D. (1990). Magnocellular and parvocellular contributions to responses in the middle temporal visual area (MT) of the macaque monkey. *J. Neurosci.*, **10**, 3323–34.

Maunsell, J.H.R., Sclar, G., Nealey, T.A. and DePriest, D.D. (1991). Extraretinal representations in area V4 in the macaque monkey. *Vis. Neurosci.*, **7**, 561–73.

May, J.G. and Andersen, R.A. (1986). Different patterns of corticopontine projections from separate cortical fields within the inferior parietal lobule and dorsal prelunate gyrus of the macaque. *Exp. Brain Res.*, **63**, 265–78.

Mazzoni, P., Andersen, R.A. and Jordan, M.I. (1991). A more biologically plausible learning rule for neural networks. *Proc. Natl Acad. Sci. USA*, **88**, 4433–7.

Mendoza, J.E. and Thomas, R.K. (1975). Effects of posterior parietal and frontal neocortical lesions in the squirrel monkey. *J. Comp. Physiol. Psychol.*, **89**, 170–82.

Merigan, W.H. and Maunsell, J.H.R. (1993). How parallel are the primate visual pathways? *Ann. Rev. Neurosci.*, **16**, 369–402.

Merigan, W.H., Byrne, C., and Maunsell, J.H.R. (1991a). Does primate motion perception depend on the magnocellular pathway? *J. Neurosci.*, **11**, 3422–9.

Merigan, W.H., Katz, L.M. and Maunsell, J.H.R. (1991b). The effects of parvocellular lateral geniculate lesions on the acuity and contrast sensitivity of macaque monkeys. *J. Neurosci.*, **11**, 994–1001.

Mestre, D.R., Brouchon, M., Ceccaldi, M., and Poncet, M. (1992). Perception of optical flow in cortical blindness: a case report. *Neuropsychologia*, **30**, 783–95.

Michel, M., Poncet, M., and Signoret, J.L. (1989). Les lésions responsables de la prosopagnosie sont-elles toujours bilatérales? *Rev. Neurol. (Paris)*, **146**, 764–70.

Miller, E.K. and Cohen, J.D. (2001). An integrative theory of prefrontal cortex function. *Annu. Rev. Neurosci.*, **24**, 167–202.

Milner, A.D. (1987). Animal models for the syndrome of spatial neglect. In *Neurophysiological and neuropsychological aspects of spatial neglect*, (ed. M. Jeannerod), pp. 259–88. Elsevier, Amsterdam.

Milner, A.D. (1992). Disorders of perceptual awareness—commentary. In *The neuropsychology of consciousness*, (ed. A.D. Milner and M.D. Rugg), pp. 139–58. Academic Press, London.

Milner, A.D. (1995). Cerebral correlates of visual awareness. *Neuropsychologia*, **33**, 1117–30.

Milner, A.D. (1997). Neglect, extinction, and the cortical streams of visual processing. In *Parietal lobe contributions to orientation in 3D space* (ed. P. Thier and H.-O. Karnath), pp. 3–22. Springer-Verlag, Heidelberg.

Milner, A.D. (1998). Streams and consciousness: visual awareness and the brain. *Trends Cogn. Sci.*, **2**, 25–30.

Milner, A.D. and Goodale, M.A. (1993). Visual pathways to perception and action. In *Progress in brain research*, Vol. 95, (ed. T.P. Hicks, S. Molotchnikoff, and T. Ono), pp. 317–37. Elsevier, Amsterdam.

Milner, A.D. and Harvey, M. (1995). Distortion of size perception in visuospatial neglect. *Curr. Biol.*, **5**, 85–9.

Milner, A.D. and Heywood, C.A. (1989). A disorder of lightness discrimination in a case of visual form agnosia. *Cortex*, **25**, 489–94.

Milner, A.D., Ockleford, E.M., and Dewar, W. (1977). Visuo-spatial performance following posterior parietal and lateral frontal lesions in stumptail macaques. *Cortex*, **13**, 350–60.

Milner, A.D., Perrett, D.I., Johnston, R.S., Benson, P.J., Jordan, T.R., Heeley, D. W. *et al.* (1991). Perception and action in "visual form agnosia". *Brain*, **114**, 405–28.

Milner, A.D., Harvey, M., Roberts, R.C. and Forster, S.V. (1993). Line bisection errors in visual neglect: misguided action or size distortion? *Neuropsychologia*, **31**, 39–49.

Milner, A.D., Paulignan, Y., Dijkerman, H.C., Michel, F., and Jeannerod, M. (1999). A paradoxical improvement of optic ataxia with delay: new evidence for two separate neural systems for visual localization. *Proc. R. Soc. Lond. B: Biol. Sci.*, **266**, 2225–30.

Milner, A.D., Dijkerman, H.C., Pisella, L., McIntosh, R.D., Tilikete, C., Vighetto, A., and Rossetti, Y. (2001). Grasping the past: delay can improve visuomotor performance. *Curr. Biol.*, **11**, 1896–901.

Milner, A.D., Dijkerman, H.C., McIntosh, R.D., Rossetti, Y., and Pisella, L. (2003). Delayed reaching and grasping in patients with optic ataxia. *Prog. Brain Res.*, **142**, 225–42.

Milner, B. (1965). Visually-guided maze learning in man: effects of bilateral hippocampal, bilateral frontal, and unilateral cerebral lesions. *Neuropsychologia*, **3**, 317–38.

Milner, P.M. (1974). A model for visual shape recognition. *Psychol. Rev.*, **81**, 521–35.

Mishkin, M. (1954). Visual discrimination performance following partial ablations of the temporal lobe. II. Ventral surface vs. hippocampus. *J. Comp. Physiol. Psychol.*, **47**, 187–93.

Mishkin, M. (1966). Visual mechanisms beyond the striate cortex. In *Frontiers of physiological psychology*, (ed. R. Russell) pp. 93–119. Academic Press, New York.

Mishkin, M. and Murray, E.A. (1994). Stimulus recognition. *Curr. Opin. Neurobiol.*, 4, 200–6.

Mishkin, M. and Pribram, K.H. (1954). Visual discrimination performance following partial ablations of the temporal lobe: I. Ventral vs. lateral. *J. Comp. Physiol. Psychol.*, 47, 14–20.

Mishkin, M. and Ungerleider, L.G. (1982). Contribution of striate inputs to the visuospatial functions of parieto-preoccipital cortex in monkeys. *Behav. Brain Res.*, 6, 57–77.

Mishkin, M., Lewis, M.E., and Ungerleider, L.G. (1982). Equivalence of parieto-preoccipital subareas for visuospatial ability in monkeys. *Behav. Brain Res.*, 6, 41–55.

Mishkin, M., Ungerleider, L.G. and Macko, K.A. (1983). Object vision and spatial vision: two cortical pathways. *Trends Neurosci.*, 6, 414–17.

Mistlin, A.J. and Perrett, D.I. (1990). Visual and somatosensory processing in the macaque temporal cortex: the role of 'expectation'. *Exp. Brain Res.*, 82, 437–50.

Mohler, C.W. and Wurtz, R.H. (1977). Role of striate cortex and superior colliculus in visual guidance of saccadic eye movements in monkeys. *J. Neurophysiol.*, 40, 74–94.

Mon-Williams, M. and McIntosh, R.D. (2000). A test between two hypotheses and a possible third way for the control of prehension. *Exp. Brain Res.*, 134, 268–73.

Mon-Williams, M. and Murray, A.H. (2000). The size of the visual size cue used for programming manipulative forces during precision grip. *Exp. Brain Res.*, 135, 405–10.

Mon-Williams, M. and Tresilian, J.R. (2001). A simple rule of thumb for elegant prehension. *Curr. Biol.*, 11, 1058–61.

Moore, T. (2006). The neurobiology of visual attention: finding sources. *Curr. Opin. Neurobiol.*, 16, 159–165.

Moran, J. and Desimone, R. (1985). Selective attention gates visual processing in the extrastriate cortex. *Science*, 229, 782–4.

Morel, A. and Bullier, J. (1990). Anatomical segregation of two cortical visual pathways in the macaque monkey. *Vis. Neurosci.*, 4, 555–78.

Morris, R.G.M., Hagan, J.J. and Rawlins, J.N.P. (1986). Allocentric spatial learning by hippocampectomised rats: a further test of the 'spatial mapping' and 'working memory' theories of hippocampal function. *Q. J. Exp. Psychol.*, 38B, 365–95.

Morrow, L. and Ratcliff, G. (1988a). The neuropsychology of spatial cognition. In *Spatial cognition. Brain bases and development*, (ed. J. Stiles-Davis, M. Kritchevsky, and U. Bellugi), pp. 5–32. Erlbaum, Hillsdale, NJ.

Morrow, L.A. and Ratcliff, G. (1988b). The disengagement of covert attention and the neglect syndrome. *Psychobiology*, 3, 261–9.

Morrow, M.J. and Sharpe, J.A. (1993). Retinotopic and directional deficits of smooth pursuit initiation after posterior cerebral hemispheric lesions. *Neurology*, 43, 595–603.

Moscovitch, M., Winocur, G., and Bermann, M. (1997). What is special about face recognition? Nineteen experiments on a person with visual object agnosia and dyslexia but normal face recognition. *J. Cogn. Neurosci.*, 9, 555–604.

Motter, B.C. (1991). Beyond extrastriate cortex: the parietal visual system. In *Vision and visual dysfunction, volume 4: the neural basis of visual function*, (ed. A.G. Leventhal), pp. 371–387. Macmillan, London.

Motter, B.C. (1993). Focal attention produces spatially selective processing in visual cortical areas V1, V2, and V4 in the presence of competing stimuli. *J. Neurophysiol.*, **70**, 909–19.

Motter, B.C. and Mountcastle, V.B. (1981). The functional properties of the light-sensitive neurons of the posterior parietal cortex studied in waking monkeys: foveal sparing and opponent vector organization. *J. Neurosci.*, **1**, 3–26.

Mountcastle, V.B., Lynch, J.C., Georgopoulos, A., Sakata, H., and Acuña, C. (1975). Posterior parietal association cortex of the monkey: command functions for operations within extrapersonal space. *J. Neurophysiol.*, **38**, 871–908.

Mountcastle, V.B., Andersen, R.A. and Motter, B.C. (1981). The influence of attentive fixation upon the excitability of the light-sensitive neurons of the posterior parietal cortex. *J. Neurosci.*, **1**, 1218–35.

Movshon, J.A., Adelson, E.H., Gizzi, M.S., and Newsome, W.T. (1985). The analysis of moving visual patterns. In *Pattern recognition mechanisms*, (ed. C. Chagas, R. Gattass, and C. Gross), pp. 117–51. Springer-Verlag, Berlin.

Munoz, D.P. and Wurtz, R.H. (1993). Fixation cells in monkey superior colliculus. I. Characteristics of cell discharge. *J. Neurophysiol.*, **70**, 559–75.

Murphy, K.J., Racicot, C.I. and Goodale, M.A. (1993). The use of visuomotor cues as a strategy for making perceptual judgements in a visual form agnosic. In *Canadian Society for Brain, Behaviour, and Cognitive Science, Third Annual Meeting*, Toronto, p. 28.

Murray, E.A. and Richmond, B.J. (2001). Role of perirhinal cortex in object perception, memory, and associations. *Curr. Opin. Neurobiol.*, **11**, 188–93.

Murray, E.A., Bussey, T.J., and Wise, S.P. (2000). Role of prefrontal cortex in a network for arbitrary visuomotor mapping. *Exp. Brain Res.*, **133**, 114–29.

Nagel-Leiby, S., Buchtel, H.A., and Welch, K.M.A. (1990). Cerebral control of directed visual attention and orienting saccades. *Brain*, **113**, 237–76.

Nakagawa, S. and Tanaka, S. (1984). Retinal projections to the pulvinar nucleus of the macaque monkey: a re-investigation using autoradiography. *Exp. Brain Res.*, **57**, 151–7.

Nakamura, H., Gattass, R., Desimone, R., and Ungerleider, L.G. (1993). The modular organization of projections from areas V1 and V2 to areas V4 and TEO in macaques. *J. Neurosci.*, **13**, 3681–91.

Nealey, T.A. and Maunsell, J.H.R. (1994). Magnocellular and parvocellular contributions to the responses of neurons in macaque striate cortex. *J. Neurosci.*, **14**, 2069–79.

Newcombe, F. and Ratcliff, G. (1989). Disorders of visuospatial analysis. In *Handbook of neuropsychology*, Vol. 2, (ed. F. Boller and J. Grafman), pp. 333–56. Elsevier, Amsterdam.

Newcombe, F. and Russell, W.R. (1969). Dissociated visual perceptual and spatial deficits in focal lesions of the right hemisphere. *J. Neurol. Neurosurg. Psychiat.*, **32**, 73–81.

Newcombe, F, Ratcliff, G., and Damasio, H. (1987). Dissociable visual and spatial impairments following right posterior cerebral lesions: clinical, neuropsychological and anatomical evidence. *Neuropsychologia*, **25**, 149–161.

Newsome, W.T. and Paré, E.B. (1988). A selective impairment of motion perception following lesions of the middle temporal visual area (MT). *J. Neurosci.*, **8**, 2201–11.

Newsome, W.T., Wurtz, R.H., Dürsteler, M.R., and Mikami, A. (1985). Deficits in visual motion processing following ibotenic acid lesions of the middle temporal visual area of the macaque monkey. *J. Neurosci.*, **5**, 825–40.

Newsome, W.T., Wurtz, R.H. and Komatsu, H. (1988). Relation of cortical areas MT and MST to pursuit eye movements. II. Differentiation of retinal from extraretinal inputs. *J. Neurophysiol.*, **60**, 604–20.

Niki, H. and Watanabe, M. (1976). Prefrontal unit activity and delayed response: relation to cue location *versus* direction of response. *Brain Res.*, **105**, 79–88.

Nishijo, H., Ono, T., Tamura, R., and Nakamura, K. (1993). Amygdalar and hippocampal neuron responses related to recognition and memory in monkey. *Prog. Brain. Res.*, **95**, 339–57.

O'Craven, K.M., Downing, P.E., and Kanwisher, N. (1999). fMRI evidence for objects as the units of attentional selection. *Nature*, **401**, 584–7.

O'Keefe, J. and Nadel, L. (1978). *The hippocampus as a cognitive map*. Clarendon Press, Oxford.

O'Mara, S.M., Rolls, E.T., Berthoz, A., and Kesner, R.P. (1994). Neurons responding to whole-body motion in the primate hippocampus. *J. Neurosci.*, **14**, 6511–23.

Oliva, A. and Schyns, P.G. (1997). Coarse blobs or fine edges? Evidence that information diagnosticity changes the perception of complex visual stimuli. *Cognit. Psychol.* **34**, 72–107.

Oram, M.W. and Perrett, D.I. (1994). Responses of anterior superior temporal polysensory (STPa) neurons to "biological motion" stimuli. *J. Cogn. Neurosci.*, **6**, 99–116.

Pallis, C.A. (1955). Impaired identification of faces and places with agnosia for colours. *J. Neurol. Neurosurg. Psychiat.*, **18**, 218–24.

Palmer, S., Rosch, E. and Chase, P. (1981). Canonical perspective and the perception of objects. In *Attention and performance IX*, (ed. J. Long and A. Baddeley), pp. 135–51. Erlbaum, Hillsdale, NJ.

Pandya, D.N., Seltzer, B., and Barbas, H. (1988). Input–output organization of the primate cerebral cortex. In *Comparative primate biology, volume 4: neurosciences*, (ed. H.D. Steklis and J. Erwin), pp. 39–80. Wiley-Liss, New York.

Parkinson, J.K., Murray, E.A., and Mishkin, M. (1988). A selective mnemonic role for the hippocampus in monkeys: memory for the location of objects. *J. Neurosci.*, **8**, 4159–67.

Pasik, P. and Pasik, T. (1964). Oculomotor function in monkeys with lesions of the cerebrum and the superior colliculi. In *The oculomotor system*, (ed. M.B. Bender), pp. 40–80. Hoeber, New York.

Passingham, R.E. and Toni, I. (2001). Contrasting the dorsal and ventral visual systems: guidance of movement versus decision making. *Neuroimage*, **14**, S125–31.

Paterson, A. and Zangwill, O.L. (1944). Disorders of visual space perception associated with lesions of the right cerebral hemisphere. *Brain*, **67**, 331–58.

Paterson, A. and Zangwill, O.L. (1945). A case of topographical disorientation associated with a unilateral cerebral lesion. *Brain*, **68**, 188–212.

Peelen, M.V. and Downing, P.E. (2005). Selectivity for the human body in the fusiform gyrus. *J. Neurophysiol.*, **93**, 603–8.

Perenin, M.T. (1978). Visual function within the hemianopic field following early cerebral hemidecortication in man. II. Pattern discrimination. *Neuropsychologia*, **16**, 697–708.

Perenin, M.-T. (1991). Discrimination of motion direction in perimetrically blind fields. *NeuroReport*, **2**, 397–400.

Perenin, M.T. and Jeannerod, M. (1975). Residual vision in cortically blind hemifields. *Neuropsychologia*, **13**, 1–7.

Perenin, M.T. and Jeannerod, M. (1978). Visual function within the hemianopic field following early cerebral hemidecortication in man: I. Spatial localization. *Neuropsychologia*, **16**, 1–13.

Perenin, M.T. and Rossetti, Y. (1993). Residual grasping in a hemianopic field. In *25th Annual Meeting of European Brain and behaviour Society*, abstract no. 716.

Perenin, M.T. and Vighetto, A. (1983). Optic ataxia: a specific disorder in visuomotor coordination. In *Spatially oriented behavior*, (ed. A. Hein and M. Jeannerod), pp. 305–26. Springer-Verlag, New York.

Perenin, M.-T. and Vighetto, A. (1988). Optic ataxia: a specific disruption in visuomotor mechanisms. I. Different aspects of the deficit in reaching for objects. *Brain*, **111**, 643–74.

Perenin, M.T., Vighetto, A., Maugiere, F., and Fischer, C. (1979). L'ataxie optique et son intérêt dans l'étude de la coordination oeil-main. *Lyon Médical*, **242**, 349–58.

Perrett, D.I., Rolls, E.T., and Caan, W. (1982). Visual neurones responsive to faces in the monkey temporal cortex. *Exp. Brain Res.*, **47**, 329–42.

Perrett, D.I., Smith, P.A.J., Potter, D.D., Mistlin, A.J., Head, A.S., Milner, A.D., and Jeeves, M.A. (1984). Neurones responsive to faces in the temporal cortex: studies of functional organization, sensitivity to identity and relation to perception. *Human Neurobiol.*, **3**, 197–208.

Perrett, D.I., Mistlin, A.J., and Chitty, A.J. (1987). Visual neurones responsive to faces. *Trends Neurosci.*, **10**, 358–64.

Perrett, D.I., Harries, M.H., Bevan, R., Thomas, S., Benson, P.J., Mistlin, A.J. *et al.* (1989). Frameworks of analysis for the neural representation of animate objects and actions. *J. Exp. Biol.*, **146**, 87–113.

Perrett, D.I., Harries, M.H., Benson, P.J., Chitty, A.J. and Mistlin, A.J. (1990). Retrieval of structure from rigid and biological motion: an analysis of the visual responses of neurones in the macaque temporal cortex. In *AI and the eye*, (ed. A. Blake and T. Troscianko), pp. 181–99. Wiley, London.

Perrett, D.I., Oram, M.W., Harries, M.H., Bevan, R., Hietanen, J.K., Benson, P.J., and Thomas, S. (1991). Viewer-centred and object-centred coding of heads in the macaque temporal cortex. *Exp. Brain Res.*, **86**, 159–73.

Perry, V.H. and Cowey, A. (1984). Retinal ganglion cells that project to the superior colliculus and pretectum in the macaque monkey. *Neuroscience*, **12**, 1125–37.

Petersen, S.E., Robinson, D.L., and Keys, W. (1985). Pulvinar nuclei of the behaving rhesus monkey: visual responses and their modulation. *J. Neurophysiol.*, **54**, 867–86.

Petersen, S.E., Robinson, D.L., and Morris, J.D. (1987). Contributions of the pulvinar to visual spatial attention. *Neuropsychologia*, **25**, 97–105.

Petrides, M. and Iversen, S. (1979). Restricted posterior parietal lesions in the rhesus monkey and performance on visuospatial tasks. *Brain Res.*, **161**, 63–77.

Petrides, M. and Pandya, D.N. (1984). Projections to the frontal cortex from the posterior parietal region in the rhesus monkey. *J. Comp. Neurol.*, **228**, 105–16.

Pierrot-Deseilligny, C., Gray, F., and Brunet, P. (1986). Infarcts of both inferior parietal lobules with impairment of visually guided eye movements, peripheral visual inattention and optic ataxia. *Brain*, **109**, 81–97.

Pierrot-Deseilligny, C., Rivaud, S., Penet, C., and Rigolet, M.-H. (1987). Latencies of visually guided saccades in unilateral hemispheric cerebral lesions. *Ann. Neurol.*, **21**, 138–48.

Pierrot-Deseilligny, C., Gautier, J.-C., and Loron, P. (1988). Acquired ocular motor apraxia due to bilateral frontoparietal infarcts. *Ann. Neurol.*, **23**, 199–202.

Pierrot-Deseilligny, C., Rivaud, S., Gaymard, B., and Agid, Y. (1991). Cortical control of reflexive visually-guided saccades. *Brain*, **114**, 1473–85.

Pigott, S. and Milner, B. (1993). Memory for different aspects of complex visual scenes after unilateral temporal- or frontal-lobe resection. *Neuropsychologia*, **31**, 1–15.

Pisella, L., Gréa, H., Tilikete, C., Vighetto, A., Desmurget, M., Rode, G., Boisson, D., and Rossetti, Y. (2000). An 'automatic pilot' for the hand in human posterior parietal cortex: toward reinterpreting optic ataxia. *Nat. Neurosci.* **3**, 729–36.

Plum, F., Posner, J.B. and Hain, R.F. (1962). Delayed neural deterioration after anoxia. *Arch. Intern. Med.*, **110**, 56–63.

Pohl, W. (1973). Dissociation of spatial discrimination deficits following frontal and parietal lesions in monkeys. *J. Comp. Physiol. Psychol.*, **82**, 227–39.

Pöppel, E., Held, R., and Frost, D. (1973). Residual visual function after brain wounds involving the central visual pathways in man. *Nature*, **243**, 295–6.

Posner, M.I. (1980). Orienting of attention. *Q.J. Exp. Psychol.*, **32**, 3–25.

Posner, M.I. and Rothbart, M.K. (1992). Attentional mechanisms and conscious experience. In *The neuropsychology of consciousness*, (ed. A.D. Milner and M.D. Rugg), pp. 91–111. Academic Press, London.

Posner, M.I., Snyder, C.R.R. and Davidson, B.J. (1980). Attention and the detection of signals. *J. Exp. Psychol. (Gen.)*, **109**, 160–74.

Posner, M.I., Cohen, Y. and Rafal, R.D. (1982). Neural systems control of spatial orienting. *Phil. Trans. R. Soc. Lond.*, **B298**, 187–98.

Posner, M.I., Walker, J.A., Friedrich, F.J., and Rafal, R.D. (1984). Effects of parietal lobe injury on covert orienting of attention. *J. Neurosci.*, **4**, 1863–74.

Prado, J., Clavagnier, S., Otzenberger, H., Scheiber, C., Kennedy, H., and Perenin, M. T. (2005). Two cortical systems for reaching in central and peripheral vision. *Neuron*, **48**, 849–58.

Pribram, K.H. (1967). Memory and the organization of attention. In *Brain function*. Vol IV. *UCLA Forum in Medical Sciences 6*, (ed. D.B. Lindsley and A.A. Lumsdaine), pp. 79–112. University of California Press, Berkeley.

Ptito, A., Lassonde, M., Lepore, F. and Ptito, M. (1987). Visual discrimination in hemispherectomized patients. *Neuropsychologia*, **25**, 869–79.

Ptito, A., Lepore, F., Ptito, M. and Lassonde, M. (1991). Target detection and movement discrimination in the blind field of hemispherectomized patients. *Brain*, **114**, 497–512.

Puce, A. and Perrett, D. (2003). Electrophysiology and brain imaging of biological motion. *Phil. Trans. R. Soc. of Lond. B: Biol. Sci.*, **358**, 435–45.

Puce, A., Allison, T., Bentin, S., Gore, J.C., and McCarthy, G. (1998). Temporal cortex activation in humans viewing eye and mouth movements. *J. Neurosci.*, **18**, 2188–99.

Rafal, R.D., Smith, J., Krantz, J., Cohen, J., and Brennan, C. (1990). Extrageniculate vision in hemianopic humans: saccade inhibition by signals in the blind field. *Science*, **250**, 118–21.

Ratcliff, G. (1979). Spatial thought, mental rotation and the right cerebral hemisphere. *Neuropsychologia*, **17**, 49–54.

Ratcliff, G. (1982). Disturbances of spatial orientation associated with cerebral lesions. In *Spatial abilities. Development and physiological foundations*, (ed. M. Potegal), pp. 301–331. Academic Press, New York.

Ratcliff, G. and Davies-Jones, G.A.B. (1972). Defective visual localization in focal brain wounds. *Brain*, **95**, 49–60.

Ratcliff, G. and Newcombe, F. (1973). Spatial orientation in man: effects of left, right and bilateral posterior cerebral lesions. *J. Neurol. Neurosurg. Psychiatry*, **36**, 448–54.

Ratcliff, G. and Newcombe, F. (1982). Object recognition: some deductions from the clinical evidence. In *Normality and pathology in cognitive functions*, (ed. A.W. Ellis), pp. 147–171. Academic Press, London.

Rees, G., Wojciulik, E., Clarke, K., Husain, M., Frith, C., and Driver, J. (2000). Unconscious activation of visual cortex in the damaged right hemisphere of a parietal patient with extinction. *Brain*, **123**, 1624–33.

Rice, N.J., McIntosh, R.D., Schindler, I., Démonet, J.-F., and Milner, A.D. (2006). Automatic avoidance of obstacles in patients with visual form agnosia. *Exp. Brain Res.*, published online 6 May 2006.

Rice N.J., Schindler, I., McIntosh, R.D., Rossetti, Y., Edwards, M., Humphreys, G.W., and Milner, A.D. (2005). Obstacle avoidance: insights from patients with damage to the dorsal or ventral stream. *J. Cogn. Neurosci. Suppl.*, abstract A229, p. 40.

Richardson, J.C., Chambers, R.A. and Heywood, P.M. (1959). Encephalopathies of anoxia and hypoglycemia. *AMA Arch. Neurol.*, **1**, 178–190.

Richmond, B.J. and Sato, T. (1987). Enhancement of inferior temporal neurons during visual discrimination. *J. Neurophysiol.*, **58**, 1292–306.

Riddoch, G. (1917). Dissociation of visual perceptions due to occipital injuries, with especial reference to appreciation of movement. *Brain*, **40**, 15–57.

Riddoch, G. (1935). Visual disorientation in homonymous half-fields. *Brain*, **58**, 376–82.

Riddoch, M.J. and Humphreys, G.W. (1987). A case of integrated visual agnosia. *Brain*, **110**, 1431–62.

Ridley, R.M. and Ettlinger, G. (1975). Tactile and visuo-spatial discrimination performance in the monkey: the effects of total and partial posterior parietal removals. *Neuropsychologia*, **13**, 191–206.

Rizzolatti, G. (1983). Mechanisms of selective attention in mammals. In *Advances in vertebrate neuroethology*, (ed. J.-P. Ewert, R.R. Capranica, and D.J. Ingle), pp. 261–97. Plenum Press, London.

Rizzolatti, G. and Berti, A. (1990). Neglect as a neural representation deficit. *Rev. Neurol. (Paris)*, **146**, 626–34.

Rizzolatti, G. and Camarda, R. (1977). Influence of the presentation of remote visual stimuli on visual responses of cat area 17 and lateral suprasylvian area. *Exp. Brain Res.*, **29**, 107–22.

Rizzolatti, G. and Camarda, R. (1987). Neural circuits for spatial attention and unilateral neglect. In Neurophysiological and neuropsychological aspects of spatial neglect, (ed. M. Jeannerod), pp. 289–313. Elsevier, Amsterdam.

Rizzolatti, G. and Gentilucci, M. (1988). Motor and visual-motor functions of the premotor cortex. In *Neurobiology of neocortex*, (ed. P. Rakic and W. Singer), pp. 269–284. Wiley, Chichester, UK.

Rizzolatti, G. and Matelli, M. (2003). Two different streams form the dorsal visual system: anatomy and function. *Exp. Brain Res.*, **153**, 146–57.

Rizzolatti, G., Camarda, R., Grupp, L.A., and Pisa, M. (1974). Inhibitory effect of remote visual stimuli on the visual responses of the cat superior colliculus: spatial and temporal factors. *J. Neurophysiol.*, **37**, 1262–75.

Rizzolatti, G., Gentilucci, M. and Matelli, M. (1985). Selective spatial attention: one center, one circuit, or many circuits? In *Attention and performance XI*, (ed. M.I. Posner and O.S.M. Marin), pp. 251–65. Erlbaum, Hillsdale, NJ.

Rizzolatti, G., Camarda, R., Fogassi, L., Gentilucci, M., Luppino, G., and Matelli, M. (1988). Functional organization of inferior area 6 in the macaque monkey. II. Area F5 and the control of distal movements. *Exp. Brain Res.*, **71**, 491–507.

Rizzolatti, G., Riggio, L. and Sheliga, B.M. (1994). Space and selective attention. In *Attention and performance XV. Conscious and nonconscious information processing*, (ed. C. Umiltà and M. Moscovitch), pp. 231–265. MIT Press, Cambridge, MA.

Robertson, I.H. and Marshall, J.C. (1993). *Unilateral neglect: clinical and experimental studies*. Erlbaum, Hove, UK.

Robinson, D.L. and McClurkin, J.W. (1989). The visual superior colliculus and pulvinar. In *The neurobiology of saccadic eye movements*, (ed. R.H. Wurtz and M.E. Goldberg), pp. 337–60. Elsevier, Amsterdam.

Robinson, D.L., Goldberg, M.E. and Stanton, G.B. (1978). Parietal association cortex in the primate: sensory mechanisms and behavioral modulations. *J. Neurophysiol.*, **41**, 910–32.

Rocha-Miranda, C.E., Bender, D.B., Gross, C.G., and Mishkin, M. (1975). Visual activation of neurons in inferotemporal cortex depends on striate cortex and forebrain commissures. *J. Neurophysiol.*, **38**, 475–91.

Rodieck, R.W. (1979). Visual pathways. *Ann. Rev. Neurosci.*, **2**, 193–225.

Rodman, H.R., Gross, C.G. and Albright, T.D. (1989). Afferent basis of visual response properties in area MT of the macaque. I. Effects of striate cortex removal. *J. Neurosci.*, **9**, 2033–50.

Rodman, H.R., Gross, C.G. and Albright, T.D. (1990). Afferent basis of visual response properties in area MT of the macaque: II. Effects of superior colliculus removal. *J. Neurosci.*, **10**, 1154–64.

Rolls, E.T. (1991). Functions of the primate hippocampus in spatial processing and memory. In *Brain and space*, (ed. J. Paillard), pp. 353–376. Oxford University Press, Oxford.

Rolls, E.T. and O'Mara, S. (1993). Neurophysiological and theoretical analysis of how the primate hippocampus functions in memory. In *Brain mechanisms of perception and memory: from neuron to behavior*, (ed. T. Ono, L.R. Squire, M.E. Raichle, D.I. Perrett, and M. Fukuda), pp. 276–300. Oxford University Press. New York.

Rolls, E.T., Perrett, D.I., Thorpe, S.J., Puerto, A., Roper-Hall, A., and Maddison, S. (1979). Responses of neurons in area 7 of the parietal cortex to objects of different significance. *Brain Res.*, **169**, 194–8.

Rondot, P. (1989). Visuomotor ataxia. In: *Neuropsychology of visual perception*, (ed. J.W. Brown), pp. 105–9. Erlbaum, Hillsdale, NJ.

Rondot, P., De Recondo, J., and Ribadeau Dumas, J.L. (1977). Visuomotor ataxia. *Brain*, **100**, 355–76.

Rossetti, Y. and Pisella, L. (2003). Mediate responses as direct evidence for intention: neuropsychology of Not to-, Not now- and Not there- tasks. In *Taking action: cognitive neuroscience perspectives on intentional acts*, (ed. S.H. Johnson-Frey) pp. 67–105. MIT Press, Cambridge, MA.

Rossetti, Y., Pisella, L., and Pélisson, D. (2000). New insights on eye blindness and hand sight: temporal constraints of visuo-motor networks. *Vis. Cogn.*, 7, 785–809.

Rossetti, Y., Pisella, L., and Vighetto, A. (2003). Optic ataxia revisited: visually guided action versus immediate visuomotor control. *Exp. Brain Res.*, 153, 171–9.

Rossetti, Y., McIntosh, R.D., Revol, P., Pisella, L., Rode, G., Danckert, J., Tilikete, C., Dijkerman, H.C., Boisson, D., Vighetto, A., Michel, F., and Milner, A.D. (2005). Visually guided reaching: bilateral posterior parietal lesions cause a switch from fast visuomotor to slow cognitive control. *Neuropsychologia*, 43, 162–77.

Ross-Russell, R.W. and Bharucha, N. (1978). The recognition and prevention of border zone cerebral ischaemia during cardiac surgery. *Q. J. Med. New Ser.*, 47, 303–32.

Ross-Russell, R.W. and Bharucha, N. (1984). Visual localisation in patients with occipital infarction. *J. Neurol. Neurosurg. Psychiatr.*, 47, 153–8.

Roy, J.-P., Komatsu, H., and Wurtz, R.H. (1992). Disparity sensitivity of neurons in monkey extrastriate area MST. *J. Neurosci.*, 12, 2478–92.

Rozzi, S., Calzavara, R., Belmalih, A., Borra, E., Gregoriou, G.G., Matelli, M., and Luppino, G. (2005). Cortical connections of the inferior parietal cortical convexity of the macaque monkey. *Cerebral Cortex*, published online 23 November 2005.

Ryle, G. (1949). *The concept of mind*. Hutchinson, London.

Saito, H., Yukie, M., Tanaka, K., Hikosaka, K., Fukada, Y., and Iwai, E. (1986). Integration of direction signals of image motion in the superior temporal sulcus of the macaque monkey. *J. Neurosci.*, 6, 145–57.

Sakata, H. (2003). The role of the parietal cortex in grasping. *Adv. Neurol.* 93, 121–39.

Sakata, H., Taira, M., Mine, S., and Murata, A. (1992). Hand-movement-related neurons of the posterior parietal cortex of the monkey: their role in the visual guidance of hand movements. In *Control of arm movement in space*, (ed. R. Caminiti, P.B. Johnson, and Y. Burnod), pp. 185–98. Springer-Verlag, Berlin.

Sakata, H., Taira, M., Kusunoki, M., Murata, A., and Tanaka, Y. (1997). The parietal association cortex in depth perception and visual control of hand action. *Trends Neurosci.*, 20, 350–7.

Saleem, K.S., Suzuki, W., Tanaka, K., and Hashikawa, T. (2000). Connections between anterior inferotemporal cortex and superior temporal sulcus regions in the macaque monkey. *J. Neurosci.*, 20, 5083–101.

Sanders, M.D., Warrington, E.K., Marshall, J., and Weiskrantz, L. (1974). 'Blindsight': vision in a field defect. *Lancet*, 20, 707–8.

Sáry, G., Vogels, R. and Orban, G.A. (1993). Cue-invariant shape selectivity of macaque inferior temporal neurons. *Science*, 260, 995–7.

Sato, T. (1988). Effects of attention and stimulus interaction on visual responses of inferior temporal neurons in macaque. *J. Neurophysiol.*, 60, 344–64.

Savelsbergh, G.J.P., Whiting, H.T.A. and Bootsma, R.J. (1991). Grasping tau. *J. Exp. Psychol. (Human Percept.)* 17, 315–22.

Saxe, R., Jamal, N., and Powell, L. (2006). My body or yours? The effect of visual perspective on cortical body representations. *Cerebral Cortex*, 16, 178–82.

Sayner, R.B. and Davis, R.T. (1972). Significance of sign in an S-R separation problem. *Percept. Mot. Skills*, **34**, 671–6.

Schenk, T., Mai, N., Ditterich, J., and Zihl, J. (2000). Can a motion-blind patient reach for moving objects? *Eur. J. Neurosci.*, **12**, 3351–60.

Schenk, T., Ellison, A., Rice, N.J., and Milner, A.D. (2005a). The role of V5/MT+ in the control of catching movements: an rTMS study. *Neuropsychologia*, **43**, 189–98.

Schenk, T., Schindler, I., McIntosh, R.D., and Milner, A.D. (2005b). The use of visual feedback is independent of visual awareness: evidence from visual extinction. *Exp. Brain Res.*, **167**, 95–102.

Schilder, P., Pasik, P., and Pasik, T. (1972). Extrageniculate vision in the monkey. III. Circle vs. triangle and 'red vs. green' discrimination. *Exp. Brain Res.*, **14**, 436–48.

Schiller, P.H. (1986). The central visual system. *Vision Res.*, **26**, 1351–86.

Schiller, P.H. (1993). The effects of V4 and middle temporal (MT) area lesions on visual performance in the rhesus monkey. *Vis. Neurosci.*, **10**, 717–46.

Schiller, P.H. and Logothetis, N.K. (1990). The color-opponent and broad-band channels of the primate visual system. *Trends Neurosci.*, **13**, 392–8.

Schiller, P.H., Malpeli, J.G., and Schein, S.J. (1979). Composition of geniculostriate input to superior colliculus of the rhesus monkey. *J. Neurophysiol.*, **42**, 1124–33.

Schiller, P.H., Logothetis, N.K., and Charles, E.R. (1990). Role of the color-opponent and broad-band channels in vision. *Vis. Neurosci.*, **5**, 321–46.

Schindler, I., Rice, N.J., McIntosh, R.D., Rossetti, Y., Vighetto, A., and Milner, A.D. (2004). Automatic avoidance of obstacles is a dorsal stream function: evidence from optic ataxia. *Nat. Neurosci.*, **7**, 779–84.

Schmahmann, J.D. and Pandya, D.N. (1990). Anatomical investigation of projections from thalamus to posterior parietal cortex in the rhesus monkey: a WGA-HRP and fluorescent tracer study. *J. Comp. Neurol.*, **295**, 299–326.

Schmahmann, J.D. and Pandya, D.N. (1993). Prelunate, occipitotemporal, and parahippocampal projections to the basis pontis in rhesus monkey. *J. Comp. Neurol.*, **337**, 94–112.

Schneider, G.E. (1969). Two visual systems: brain mechanisms for localization and discrimination are dissociated by tectal and cortical lesions. *Science*, **163**, 895–902.

Schone, H. (1962). Optisch gesteuerte Lageänderungen (Versuche an Dytiscidenlarven zur Vertikalorientierung). *Z. Verg. Physiol.*, **45**, 590–604.

Schyns, P.G. and Oliva, A. (1997). Flexible, diagnosticity-driven, rather than fixed, perceptually determined scale selection in scene and face recognition. *Perception*, **26**, 1027–38.

Schwarzlose, R.F., Baker, C.I., and Kanwisher, N. (2005). Separate face and body selectivity on the fusiform gyrus. *J. Neurosci.*, **25**, 11055–9.

Segraves, M.A., Goldberg, M.E., Deng, S.-Y., Bruce, C.J., Ungerleider, L.G., and Mishkin, M. (1987). The role of striate cortex in the guidance of eye movements in the monkey. *J. Neurosci.*, **7**, 3040–58.

Seltzer, B. and Pandya, D.N. (1978). Afferent cortical connections and architectonics of the superior temporal sulcus and surrounding cortex in the rhesus monkey. *Brain Res.*, **149**, 1–24.

Seltzer, B. and Pandya, D.N. (1980). Converging visual and somatic sensory cortical input to the intraparietal sulcus of the rhesus monkey. *Brain Res.*, **192**, 339–51.

Seltzer, B. and Pandya, D.N. (1989). Frontal lobe connections of the superior temporal sulcus in the rhesus monkey. *J. Comp. Neurol.*, **281**, 97–113.

Seltzer, B. and Pandya, D.N. (1994). Parietal, temporal, and occipital projections to cortex of the superior temporal sulcus in the rhesus monkey: a retrograde tracer study. *J. Comp. Neurol.*, **343**, 445–63.

Semmes, J., Weinstein, S., Ghent, L., and Teuber, H.-L. (1955). Spatial orientation in man after cerebral injury: I. Analyses by locus of lesion. *J. Psychol.*, **39**, 227–44.

Sengelaub, D.R., Windrem, M.S., and Finlay, B.L. (1983). Increased cell number in the adult hamster retinal ganglion cell layer after early removal of one eye. *Exp. Brain Res.*, **52**, 269–76.

Sereno, A.B. and Maunsell, J.H. (1998). Shape selectivity in primate lateral intraparietal cortex. *Nature*, **395**, 500–3.

Sereno, M.E., Trinath, T., Augath, M., and Logothetis, N.K. (2002). Three-dimensional shape representation in monkey cortex. *Neuron*, **33**, 635–52.

Sheinberg, D.L. and Logothetis, N.K. (1997). The role of temporal cortical areas in perceptual organization. *Proc. Natl Acad. Sci., USA*, **94**, 3408–13.

Sheliga, B.M., Riggio, L., and Rizzolatti, G. (1994). Orienting of attention and eye movements. *Exp. Brain Res.*, **98**, 507–22.

Sherman, S.M., Wilson, J.R., Kass, J.H., and Webb, S.V. (1976). X-and Y-cells in the dorsal lateral geniculate nucleus of the owl monkey (*Aotus trivirgatus*). *Science*, **192**, 474–7.

Shibutani, H., Sakata, H., and Hyvärinen, J. (1984). Saccade and blinking evoked by microstimulation of the posterior parietal association cortex of the monkey. *Exp. Brain Res.*, **55**, 1–8.

Shikata, E., Tanaka, Y., Nakamura, H., Taira, M., and Sakata, H. (1996). Selectivity of the parietal visual neurones in 3D orientation of surface of stereoscopic stimuli. *Neuroreport*, **7**, 2389–94.

Shipp, S. and Zeki, S.M. (1985). Segregation of pathways leading from area V2 to areas V4 and V5 of macaque monkey visual cortex. *Nature*, **315**, 322–5.

Simpson, J.I. (1984). The accessory optic system. *Ann. Rev. Neurosci.*, **7**, 13–41.

Simpson, J.I., Leonard, C.S. and Soodak, R.E. (1988). The accessory optic system of rabbit. II. Spatial organization of direction selectivity. *J. Neurophysiol.*, **60**, 2055–72.

Sirigu, A., Cohen, L., Duhamel, J.-R., Pillon, B., Dubois, B. and Agid, Y. (1995). A selective impairment of hand posture for object utilization in apraxia, *Cortex*, **31**, 41–55.

Skinner, B. F. (1938). *The Behavior of Organisms*. Appleton-Century-Crofts, New York.

Smeets, J.B.J. and Brenner, E. (2001). Independent movements of the digits in grasping. *Exp. Brain Res.*, **139**, 92–100.

Smeets, J.B.J., Brenner, E., de Grave, D.D., and Cuijpers, R.H. (2002). Illusions in action: consequences of inconsistent processing of spatial attributes. *Exp. Brain Res.*, **147**, 135–44.

Smit, A.C., Van Gisbergen, J.A.M. and Cools, A.R. (1987). A parametric analysis of human saccades in different experimental paradigms. *Vision Res.*, **27**, 1745–62.

Smith, M.L. and Milner, B. (1981). The role of the right hippocampus in the recall of spatial location. *Neuropsychologia*, **19**, 781–93.

Snyder, L.H., Batista, A.P., and Andersen, R.A. (1997). Coding of intention in the posterior parietal cortex. *Nature*, **386**, 167–70.

Sokolov, E.N. (1960). Neuronal models and the orienting reflex. In *The central nervous system and behavior: transactions of third conference*, (ed. M.A.B. Brazier), pp. 187–276. Macy Foundation, New York.

Solomon, S.J., Pasik, T., and Pasik, P. (1981). Extrastriate vision in the monkey. VIII. Critical structures for spatial localization. *Exp. Brain Res.*, **44**, 259–70.

Sparks, D.L. (1986). Translation of sensory signals into commands for control of saccadic eye movements: role of primate superior colliculus. *Physiol. Rev.*, **66**, 118–71.

Sparks, D.L. and Hartwich-Young, R. (1989). The deep layers of the superior colliculus. In *The neurobiology of saccadic eye movements*, (ed. R.H. Wurtz and M.E. Goldberg), pp. 213–255. Elsevier, Amsterdam.

Sparks, D.L. and May, L.E. (1990). Signal transformations required for the generation of saccadic eye movements. *Ann. Rev. Neurosci.*, **13**, 309–36.

Sparr, S.A., Jay, M., Drislane, F.W. and Venna, N. (1991). A historic case of visual agnosia revisited after 40 years. *Brain*, **114**, 789–800.

Spiegler, B.J. and Mishkin, M. (1981). Evidence for the sequential participation of inferior temporal cortex and amygdala in the acquisition of stimulus-reward associations. *Behav. Brain Res.*, **3**, 303–17.

Steeves, J.K.E., Humphrey, G.K., Culham, J.C., Menon, R.S., Milner, A.D., and Goodale, M.A. (2004). Behavioral and neuroimaging evidence for a contribution of color and texture information to scene classification in a patient with visual form agnosia. *J. Cogn. Neurosci.*, **16**, 955–65.

Steeves, J.K.E., Culham, J.C., Duchaine, B.C., Cavina Pratesi, C., Valyear, K.F., Schindler, I., Humphrey, G.K., Milner, A.D., and Goodale, M.A. (2006). The fusiform face area is not sufficient for face recognition: evidence from a patient with dense prosopagnosia and no occipital face area. *Neuropsychologia*, **44**, 594–609.

Stein, J. (1978). Effects of parietal lobe cooling on manipulative behavior in the monkey. In *Active touch*, (ed. G. Gordon), pp. 79–90. Pergamon Press, Oxford.

Stein, J.F. (1991). Space and the parietal association areas. In *Brain and space*, (ed. J. Paillard), pp. 185–222. Oxford University Press, Oxford.

Stein, J.F. (1992). The representation of egocentric space in the posterior parietal cortex. *Behav. Brain Sci.*, **15**, 691–700.

Stein, J.F. and Glickstein, M. (1992). Role of the cerebellum in visual guidance of movement. *Physiol. Rev.*, **72**, 967–1017.

Stoerig, P. (1987). Chromaticity and achromaticity: evidence for a functional differentiation in visual field defects. *Brain*, **110**, 869–86.

Stoerig, P. and Cowey, A. (1989). Wavelength sensitivity in blindsight. *Nature*, **342**, 916–18.

Stoerig, P. and Cowey, A. (1992). Wavelength discrimination in blindsight. *Brain*, **115**, 425–44.

Stone, J. and Hoffmann, K.-P. (1972). Very slow-conducting ganglion cells in the cat's retina: a major, new functional type? *Brain Res.*, **43**, 610–16.

Sugishita, M., Ettlinger, G. and Ridley, R.M. (1978). Disturbance of cage-finding in the monkey. *Cortex*, **14**, 431–8.

Sundqvist, A. (1979). Saccadic reaction-time in parietal-lobe dysfunction. *Lancet*, **1**, 870.

Supèr, H., Spekreijse, H., and Lamme, V.A.F. (2001). Two distinct modes of sensory processing observed in monkey primary visual cortex (V1). *Nat. Neurosci.*, **4**, 304–10.

Suzuki, W.A. and Amaral, D.G. (1994). Perirhinal and parahippocampal cortices of the macaque monkey: cortical afferents. *J. Comp. Neurol.*, **350**, 497–533.

Symmes, D. (1965). Flicker discrimination by brain-damaged monkeys. *J. Comp. Physiol. Psychol.*, **60**, 470–3.

Taira, M., Mine, S., Georgopoulos, A.P., Mutara, A., and Sakata, H. (1990). Parietal cortex neurons of the monkey related to the visual guidance of hand movements. *Exp. Brain Res.*, **83**, 29–36.

Tamura, R., Ono, T., Fukuda, M., and Nakamura, K. (1990). Recognition of egocentric and allocentric visual and auditory space by neurons in the hippocampus of monkeys. *Neurosci. Lett.*, **109**, 293–8.

Tanaka, K. (1993). Neuronal mechanisms of object recognition. *Science*, **262**, 685–8.

Tanaka, K. (2003). Columns for complex visual object features in the inferotemporal cortex: clustering of cells with similar but slightly different stimulus selectivities. *Cerebral Cortex*, **13**, 90–9.

Tanaka, K. and Saito, H. (1989). Analysis of motion of the visual field by direction, expansion/contraction, and rotation cells clustered in the dorsal part of the medial superior temporal area of the macaque monkey. *J. Neurophysiol.*, **62**, 626–41.

Tanaka, K., Hikosaka, K., Saito, H., Yukie, M., Fukada, Y., and Iwai, E. (1986). Analysis of local and wide-field movements in the superior temporal visual areas of the macaque monkey. *J. Neurosci.*, **6**, 134–44.

Tanaka, K., Saito, H.-A., Fukada, Y., and Moriya, M. (1991). Coding visual images of objects in the inferotemporal cortex of the macaque monkey. *J. Neurophysiol.*, **66**, 170–89.

Tarr, M.J. and Gauthier, I. (2000). FFA: a flexible fusiform area for subordinate-level visual processing automatized by expertise. *Nat. Neurosci.*, **3**, 764–9.

Tarr, M.J. and Pinker, S. (1989). Mental rotation and orientation dependence in shape recognition. *Cogn. Psychol.*, **21**, 233–82.

Tegnér, R. and Levander, M. (1991). Through a looking glass. A new technique to demonstrate directional hypokinesia in unilateral neglect. *Brain*, **114**, 1943–51.

Ter Braak, J.W.G., Schenk, V.W.D. and van Vliet, A.G.M. (1971). Visual reactions in a case of long-lasting cortical blindness. *J. Neurol. Neurosurg. Psychiat.*, **34**, 140–7.

Thier, P. and Erickson, R. (1992). Responses of visual-tracking neurons from cortical area MST-l to visual, eye and head motion. *Eur. J. Neurosci.*, **4**, 539–53.

Tipper, S.P., Lortie, C., and Baylis, G.C. (1992). Selective reaching: evidence for action-centered attention. *J. Exp. Psychol. (Human Percept. Perform.)* **18**, 891–905.

Toth, L.J. and Assad, J.A. (2002). Dynamic coding of behaviourally relevant stimuli in parietal cortex. *Nature*, **415**, 165–8.

Tong, F., Nakayama, K., Vaughan, J.T., and Kanwisher, N. (1998). Binocular rivalry and visual awareness in human extrastriate cortex. *Neuron*, **21**, 753–9.

Toni, I., Rushworth, M.F.S., and Passingham, R.E. (2001). Neural correlates of visuomotor associations. Spatial rules compared with arbitrary rules. *Exp. Brain Res.*, **141**, 359–69.

Tootell, R.B.H., Dale, A.M., Sereno, M.I., and Malach, R. (1996). New images from human visual cortex. *Trends Neurosci.*, **19**, 481–9.

Tootell, R.B.H., Tsao, D., and Vanduffel, W. (2003). Neuroimaging weighs in: humans meet macaques in "primate" visual cortex. *J. Neurosci.* **23**, 3981–9.

Toye, R.C. (1986). The effect of viewing position on the perceived layout of space. *Percept. Psychophys.*, **40**, 85–92.

Traverse, J. and Latto, R. (1986). Impairments in route negotiation through a maze after dorsolateral frontal, inferior parietal or premotor lesions in cynomolgus monkeys. *Behav. Brain Res.*, **20**, 203–15.

Trevarthen, C.B. (1968). Two mechanisms of vision in primates. *Psychol. Forschung*, **31**, 299–337.

Troost, B.T. and Abel, L.A. (1982). Pursuit disorders. In *Functional basis of ocular motility disorders*, (ed. G. Lennerstrand, D.S. Zee, and E.L. Keller) pp. 511–15. Pergamon Press, Oxford.

Tsao, D.Y., Freiwald, W.A., Knutsen, T.A., Mandeville, J.B. and Tootell, R.B.H. (2003). Faces and objects in macaque cerebral cortex. *Nat. Neurosci.*, **6**, 989–95.

Tyler, H.R. (1968). Abnormalities of perception with defective eye movements (Balint's syndrome). *Cortex*, **4**, 154–71.

Tzavaras, A. and Masure, M.C. (1976). Aspects différents de l'ataxie optique selon la latéralisation hémisphérique de la lésion. *Lyon Médical*, **236**, 673–83.

Ungerleider, L.G. (1985). The corticocortical pathways for object recognition and spatial perception. In *Pattern recognition mechanisms*, (ed. C. Chagas, R. Gattass, and C. Gross), pp. 21–37. Springer-Verlag, Berlin.

Ungerleider, L.G. and Brody, B.A. (1977). Extrapersonal spatial orientation: the role of posterior parietal, anterior frontal, and inferotemporal cortex. *Exp. Neurol.*, **56**, 265–80.

Ungerleider, L.G. and Desimone, R. (1986). Cortical connections of visual area MT in the macaque. *J. Comp. Neurol.*, **248**, 190–222.

Ungerleider, L.G. and Mishkin, M. (1982). Two cortical visual systems. In *Analysis of visual behavior*, (ed. D.J. Ingle, M.A. Goodale, and R.J.W. Mansfield), pp. 549–586. MIT Press, Cambridge, MA.

Ungerleider, L.G., Ganz, L., and Pribram, K.H. (1977). Size constancy in rhesus monkeys: effects of pulvinar, prestriate, and inferotemporal lesions. *Exp. Brain Res.*, **27**, 251–69.

Ungerleider, L.G., Desimone, R., Galkin, T.W., and Mishkin, M. (1984). Subcortical projections of area MT in the macaque. *J. Comp. Neurol.*, **223**, 368–86.

Urgesi, C., Berlucchi, G., and Aglioti, S.M. (2004). Magnetic stimulation of extrastriate body area impairs visual processing of nonfacial body parts. *Curr. Biol.*, **14**, 2130–4.

Vaina, L.M. (1990). 'What' and 'where' in the human visual system: two hierarchies of visual modules. *Synthese*, **83**, 49–91.

Vallar, G. (1993). The anatomical basis of spatial hemineglect in humans. In *Unilateral neglect: clinical and experimental studies*, (ed. I.H. Robertson and J.C. Marshall), pp. 27–59. Erlbaum, Hove, UK.

Vallar, G. and Perani, D. (1986). The anatomy of unilateral neglect after right-hemisphere stroke lesions. A clinical / CT-scan correlation study in man. *Neuropsychologia*, **24**, 609–22.

Valyear, K.F., Culham, J.C., Sharif, N., Westwood, D.A., and Goodale, M.A. (2006). A double dissociation between sensitivity to changes in object identity and object orientation in the ventral and dorsal visual streams: a human fMRI study. *Neuropsychologia*, **44**, 218–28.

Van Essen, D.C., Lewis, J.W., Drury, H.A., Hadjikhani, N., Tootell, R.B., Bakircioglu, M., and Miller, M.I. (2001). Mapping visual cortex in monkeys and humans using surface-based atlases. *Vis. Res.*, **41**, 1359–78.

Vishton, P.M., Rea, J.G., Cutting, J.E., and Nunez, L.N. (1999). Comparing effects of the horizontal–vertical illusion on grip scaling and judgment: relative versus absolute, not perception versus action. *J. Exp. Psychol.: Hum. Percept. Perform.*, **25**, 1659–72.

Volkmann, F.C., Schick, A.M.L., and Riggs, L.A. (1968). Time course of visual inhibition during voluntary saccades. *J. Opt. Soc. Am.*, **58**, 562–69.

Von Cramon, D.Y. and Kerkhoff, G. (1993). On the cerebral organization of elementary visuo-spatial perception. In *Functional organisation of the human visual cortex*, (ed. B. Gulyás, D. Ottoson, and P.E. Roland), pp. 211–231. Pergamon Press, Oxford.

Vuilleumier, P., Sagiv, N., Hazeltine, E., Poldrack, R.A., Swick, D., Rafal, R.D., and Gabrieli, J.D. (2001). Neural fate of seen and unseen faces in visuospatial neglect: combined event-related functional MRI and event-related potential study. *Proc. Natl Acad. Sci., USA*, **98**, 3495–500.

Wagner, M. (1985). The metric of visual space. *Percept. Psychophys.*, **38**, 483–95.

Walsh, V., Ellison, A., Battelli, L., and Cowey, A. (1998). Task-specific impairments and enhancements induced by magnetic stimulation of human visual area V5. *Phil. Trans. R. Soc. Lond. B: Biol. Sci.*, **265**, 537–43.

Wang, Y.-C. and Frost, B.J. (1992). "Time to collision" is signalled by neurons in the nucleus rotundus of pigeon. *Nature*, **356**, 236–8.

Warrington, E.K. (1982). Neuropsychological studies of object recognition. *Phil. Trans. R. Soc. Lond.*, **B298**, 15–33.

Warrington, E.K. (1985a). Agnosia: the impairment of object recognition. In *Handbook of clinical neurology, vol. 1 (45): clinical neuropsychology*, (ed. J.A.M. Frederiks), pp. 333–49. Elsevier, Amsterdam.

Warrington, E.K. (1985b). Visual deficits associated with occipital lobe lesions in man. In *Pattern recognition mechanisms*, (ed. C. Chagas, R. Gattass, and C. Gross), pp. 247–261. Springer-Verlag, Berlin

Warrington, E.K. and James, M. (1988). Visual apperceptive agnosia: a clinico-anatomical study of three cases. *Cortex*, **24**, 13–32.

Warrington, E.K. and Taylor, A.M. (1973). The contribution of the right parietal lobe to object recognition. *Cortex*, **9**, 152–64.

Webster, M.J., Ungerleider, L.G., and Bachevalier, J. (1991). Connections of inferior temporal areas TE and TEO with medial temporal-lobe structures in infant and adult monkeys. *J. Neurosci.*, **11**, 1095–116.

Webster, M.J., Bachevalier, J., and Ungerleider, L.G. (1993). Subcortical connections of inferior temporal areas TE and TEO in macaque monkeys. *J. Comp. Neurol.*, **335**, 73–91.

Wechsler, I.S. (1933). Partial cortical blindness with preservation of color vision. Report following asphyxia (carbon monoxide poisoning?); a consideration of the question of color vision and its cortical localization. *AMA. Arch. Ophthalmol.*, **9**, 957–65.

Weiskrantz, L. (1986). *Blindsight: a case study and implications.* Oxford University Press, Oxford.

Weiskrantz, L. (1987). Residual vision in a scotoma. A follow-up study of 'form' discrimination. *Brain*, **110**, 77–92.

Weiskrantz, L. (1990). Outlooks for blindsight: explicit methodologies for implicit processes. *Proc. R. Soc. Lond.*, **B239**, 247–278.

Weiskrantz, L. and Cowey, A. (1963). Striate cortex lesions and visual acuity of the rhesus monkey. *J. Comp. Physiol. Psychol.*, **56**, 225–32.

Weiskrantz, L. and Saunders, R.C. (1984). Impairments of visual object transforms in monkeys. *Brain*, **107**, 1033–72.

Weiskrantz, L., Warrington, E.K., Sanders, M.D., and Marshall, J. (1974). Visual capacity in the hemianopic field following a restricted occipital ablation. *Brain*, **97**, 709–28.

Werner, W. (1993). Neurons in the primate superior colliculus are active before and during arm movements to visual targets. *Eur. J. Neurosci.*, **5**, 335–40.

Westby, G.W.M., Keay, K.A., Redgrave, P., Dean, P., and Bannister, M. (1990). Output pathways from the rat superior colliculus mediating approach and avoidance have different sensory properties. Exp. *Brain Res.*, **81**, 626–38.

Westwood, D.A. and Goodale, M.A. (2003). Perceptual illusion and the real-time control of action. *Spatial Vision*, **16**, 243–54.

Whiteley, A.M. and Warrington, E.K. (1977). Prosopagnosia: a clinical, psychological and anatomical study of three patients. *J. Neurol. Neurosurg. Psychiat.*, **40**, 395–430.

Whitlock, D.G. and Nauta, W.J. (1956). Subcortical projections from the temporal neocortex in Macaca Mulatta. *J. Comp. Neurol.*, **106**, 183–212.

Whitney, D., Westwood, D.A., and Goodale, M.A. (2003). The influence of visual motion on fast reaching movements to a stationary object. *Nature*, **423**, 869–73.

Wise, S.P., Murray, E.A., and Gerfen, C.R. (1996). The frontal cortex–basal ganglia system in primates. *Crit. Rev. Neurobiol.*, **10**, 317–56.

Wong, E. and Mack, A. (1981). Saccadic programming and perceived location. *Acta Psychol.*, **48**, 123–31.

Wong-Riley, M.T.T., Hevner, R.F., Cutlan, R., Earnest, M., Egan, R., Frost, J. and Nguyen, T. (1993). Cytochrome oxidase in the human visual cortex: distribution in the developing and the adult brain. *Vis. Neurosci.*, **10**, 41–58.

Wurtz, R.H. and Hikosaka, O. (1986). Role of the basal ganglia in the initiation of saccadic eye movements. In *Progress in brain research*, Vol. 64, (ed. H.-J. Freund, U. Buttner, B. Cohen, and J. North), pp. 175–90. Elsevier, Amsterdam.

Wurtz, R.H. and Mohler, C.W. (1976). Organization of monkey superior colliculus: enhanced visual response of superficial layer cells. *J. Neurophysiol.*, **39**, 745–65.

Wurtz, R.H., Goldberg, M.E., and Robinson, D.L. (1980*a*). Behavioral modulation of visual responses in the monkey: stimulus selection for attention and movement. In: *Progress in psychobiology and physiological psychology*, Vol. 9, (ed. J.M. Sprague and A.N. Epstein), pp. 43–83. Academic Press, New York.

Wurtz, R.H., Richmond, B.J. and Judge, S.J. (1980*b*). Vision during saccadic eye movements III: visual interactions in monkey superior colliculus. *J. Neurophysiol.*, **43**, 1168–81.

Wurtz, R.H., Richmond, B.J. and Newsome, W.T. (1984). Modulation of cortical visual processing by attention, perception and movement. In *Dynamic aspects of neocortical function*, (ed. G.M. Edelman, W.E. Gall, and W.M. Cowan), pp. 195–217. Wiley, New York.

Yamagishi, N., Anderson, S.J., and Ashida, H. (2001). Evidence for dissociation between the perceptual and visuomotor systems in humans. *Proc. R. Soc. Lond. B: Biol. Sci.*, **268**, 973–7.

Young, A.W., De Haan, E.H.F., Newcombe, F., and Hay, D.C. (1990). Facial neglect. *Neuropsychologia*, **28**, 391–415.

Young, M.P. (1992). Objective analysis of the topological organization of the primate cortical visual system. *Nature*, **358**, 152–5.

Yukie, M. and Iwai, E. (1981). Direct projection from the dorsal lateral geniculate nucleus to the prestriate cortex in macaque monkeys. *J. Comp. Neurol.*, **201**, 81–97.

Zeki, S.M. (1969). Representation of central visual fields in prestriate cortex of monkey. *Brain Res.*, **14**, 271–91.

Zeki, S.M. (1971). Cortical projections from two prestriate areas in the monkey. *Brain Res.*, **34**, 19–35.

Zeki, S.M. (1973). Colour coding in the rhesus monkey prestriate cortex. *Brain Res.*, **53**, 422–7.

Zeki, S.M. (1980). A direct projection from area V1 to area V3 of rhesus monkey visual cortex. *Proc. R. Soc. Lond.*, **B207**, 499–506.

Zeki, S.M. (1990*a*). Functional specialization in the visual cortex: the generation of separate constructs and their multistage integration. In *Signal and sense. Local and global order in perceptual maps*, (ed. G.M. Edelman, W.E. Gall, and W.M. Cowan), pp. 85–130. Wiley-Liss, New York.

Zeki, S.M. (1990*b*). A century of cerebral achromatopsia. *Brain*, **113**, 1721–77.

Zeki, S.M. (1990*c*). The motion pathways of the visual cortex. In: *Vision: coding and efficiency*, (ed. C. Blakemore), pp. 321–45. Cambridge University Press, Cambridge.

Zeki, S.M. and Shipp, S. (1988). The functional logic of cortical connections. *Nature*, **335**, 311–17.

Zeki, S.M. and Shipp, S. (1989). Modular connections between areas V2 and V4 of macaque monkey visual cortex. *Eur. J. Neurosci.*, **1**, 494–506.

Zeki, S., Watson, J.D.G., Lueck, C.J., Friston, K.J., Kennard, C., and Frackowiak, R.S.J. (1991). A direct demonstration of functional specialization in human visual cortex. *J. Neurosci.*, **11**, 641–9.

Zihl, J. (1980). 'Blindsight': improvement of visually guided eye movements by systematic practice in patients with cerebral blindness. *Neuropsychologia*, **18**, 71–7.

Zihl, J. and Von Cramon, D. (1980). Registration of light stimuli in the cortically blind hemifield and its effect on localization. *Behav. Brain Res.*, **1.**, 287–98.

Zihl, J., Tretter, F. and Singer, W. (1980). Phasic electrodermal responses after visual stimulation in the cortically blind hemifield. *Behav. Brain Res.*, **1**, 197–203.

Zihl, J., Von Cramon, D., and Mai, N. (1983). Selective disturbance of movement vision after bilateral brain damage. *Brain*, **106**, 313–40.

Zilles, K. and Schleicher, A. (1993). Cyto- and myeloarchitecture of human visual cortex and the periodical GABAa receptor distribution. In *Functional organisation of the human visual cortex*, (ed. B. Gulyás, D. Ottoson, and P.E. Roland), pp. 111–22. Pergamon Press, Oxford.

Index